SOUND, SPEECH, MUSI
POST-SOVIET CINEMA

SOUND, SPEECH, MUSIC IN SOVIET AND POST-SOVIET CINEMA

*Edited by Lilya Kaganovsky and
Masha Salazkina*

Indiana University Press

Bloomington and Indianapolis

This book is a publication of

Indiana University Press
Office of Scholarly Publishing
Herman B Wells Library 350
1320 E. 10th Street
Bloomington, Indiana 47405-3907 USA

iupress.indiana.edu

Telephone 800-842-6796
Fax 812-855-7931

Library of Congress Cataloging-in-Publication Data

Sound, speech, music in Soviet and post-Soviet cinema / edited by
Lilya Kaganovsky and Masha Salazkina.
       pages cm
   Includes bibliographical references and index.
   ISBN 978-0-253-01104-6 (paperback) — ISBN 978-0-253-01095-7
(cloth) — ISBN 978-0-253-01110-7 (ebook)   1. Motion pictures—
Soviet Union.   2. Film soundtracks—Soviet Union.   3. Motion
picture music—Soviet Union—History and criticism.
I. Kaganovsky, Lilya, editor.   II. Salazkina, Masha, editor.
   PN1993.5.R8S67 2013
   781.5'420947084—dc23

                                           2013042567

1 2 3 4 5 19 18 17 16 15 14

Contents

Part III. Music in Film; or, The Sound Track

Acknowledgments

Tʜɪs ᴠᴏʟᴜᴍᴇ ᴄᴀᴍᴇ about as a result of our mutual frustration with the lack of English-language materials on sound in Soviet and post-Soviet cinema. In it, we have tried to bring together new work by scholars from several disciplines, providing a larger historical framework for the discussion of the "sonic turn" in Soviet film studies, as well as close readings of individual films that pay particular attention to the way sound, speech, and music operate in Soviet and post-Soviet cinema. We are grateful to Indiana University Press and in particular to our editor Raina Polivka, for her enthusiasm, advice, and support of this project. We also owe many thanks to the commitment and patience of our contributors to this project as the volume has gone through its various incarnations, as well as to the support and interest of several fellow-travelers and interlocutors, in particular Polina Barskova, Birgit Beumers, Vincent Bohlinger, Andrew Chapman, Katerina Clark, Nancy Condee, Julian Graffy, Naum Kleiman, Vera Kropf, Susan Larsen, John MacKay, Joshua Malitsky, Simon Morrison, Sergei Oushakine, Amy Sargeant, and Mark Slobin, as well as to our two external reviewers, whose attentive appraisals helped shape this book.

Likewise, we owe many thanks to our translators Andrée Lafontaine, Sergei Levchin, and Katrina Sark, and our team of editorial assistants for their work on this collection. We are particularly grateful to Dru Jeffries, whose meticulous readings helped bring this volume to completion.

Sound, Speech, Music in Soviet and Post-Soviet Cinema received generous support at both of our home institutions, as well as from national organizations, and of course, from family and friends.

Lilya Kaganovsky would like to thank the University of Illinois's Research Board; the federally funded Russian, East European, and Eurasian Center; the Department of Slavic Languages and Literatures; and the Program in Comparative and World Literature for providing research assistance, conference travel, and research travel support; and the American Council of Learned Societies, together with the National Endowment for the Arts and Social Science Research Council, for fellowship support that provided leave time for this project. She is particularly grateful to her friends and colleagues at Illinois, Cambridge, and beyond; and most importantly to R.R., S.R., H.K., A.K., and O.П.

Masha Salazkina would like to thank Concordia University's Aid to Research Related Events, Exhibition, Publication, and Dissemination Activities and the Faculty of Fine Arts for providing research and translation funds for this project, as well as her colleagues at the Mel Hoppenheim School of Cinema for their advice and support. Without Igor Salazkin's tireless search for books and Luca Caminati's unfaltering patience and unconditional support, none of this would have been possible.

* * *

Two of the chapters in the present volume were originally published in Russian in the excellent collection *Sovetskaia vlast' i media* (Soviet Power and the Media, 2006), edited by Hans Günther and Sabine Hänsgen. We are grateful to the editors, Günther and Hänsgen, and to the authors, Nikolai Izvolov and Evgeny Margolit, for their permission to translate their work here. While the volume itself is out of print, an electronic version of the text is available at http://pub.uni-bielefeld.de/publication/23050177.

Note on Transliteration

THE TRANSLITERATION SYSTEM we use in this volume aims for readability in the text and accuracy in the notes. Russian names in the text are given in their conventional English-language spelling to render them more accessible, while Library of Congress system of transliteration is followed in all other instances. In translating titles of Russian films, we have also inserted articles where English fluency requires them.

Abbreviations

Gosudarstvennyi arkhiv Rossiiskoi Federatsii (**GARF**)—State Archive of the Russian Federation

Gosudarstvennyi fond kinofil'mov Rossiiskoi Federatsii—Gosfil'mofond

Rossiiskii gosudarstvennyi arkhiv ekonomiki (**RGAE**)—Russian State Archive for Economics

Rossiiskii gosudarstvennyi arkhiv kinofotodokumentov (**RGAKFD**)—Russian State Archive of Film and Photo Documents

Rossiiskii gosudarstvennyi arkhiv literatury i iskusstva (**RGALI**)—Russian State Archive for Literature and the Arts

Rossiiskii gosudarstvennyi arkhiv sotsial'no-politicheskoi istorii (**RGASPI**)—Russian State Archive of Socio-Political History

Tsentral'nyi gosudarstvennyi arkhiv literatury i iskusstva, Sankt-Peterburg (**TSGALI SPb**)—Central State Archive for Literature and Art, St. Petersburg

SOUND, SPEECH, MUSIC IN SOVIET AND POST-SOVIET CINEMA

Introduction

Masha Salazkina

Kira Muratova, one of the most celebrated and original contemporary Russian film auteurs, was asked in a 1995 interview what she had learned from her film-school mentor Sergei Gerasimov, whose filmmaking was so distinct from hers. She answered that he taught her "to listen and to hear, awakening [in her] an interest in and an elation from listening."[1] In the same interview Muratova identified endless manipulations of accents, modes of delivery, and systems of repetition as distinguishing markers of her personal authorial style. There is little doubt that Muratova is the contemporary Russian director with the most developed sense of hearing; that she is a product of an institutional apparatus with its own complex relationship to the aural dimensions of cinema—which her comment about Gerasimov seems to imply—might well serve as a vector for reconsidering the aural in the larger tradition of the Soviet cinema.

The contributions that make up *Sound, Speech, Music in Soviet and Post-Soviet Cinema* take their cue from this elation of listening and the gift of hearing exemplified by Muratova by bringing together essays addressing different aspects of sound in the context of Soviet and post-Soviet film culture. The collection sees itself as an invitation to "deep listening": to attuning our ears to the complexity of meanings that emerge if we not only take sound as an equal partner in audiovisual representation but also engage in what Steven Feld has referred to as "acoustemology," that is, an investigation of the primacy of sound as a modality of knowing and being in the world.[2]

The Sonic Turn

In the course of the past thirty years, a number of scholars in cinema and media studies, the humanities, and the social sciences have been challenging the centrality given to "the visual" in our social and cultural lives by uncovering the often-dominant function of sound in our experience and understanding of the world. In the process, they have raised questions not only about the material culture of sound but also about the curiously muted interest traditionally shown in it, which for so long kept the audible systematically subordinate to the visual in theorizing audiovisual media. The challenge of sound studies, reproducing the dialectic that brought forth visual studies as a reaction to the previous hegemony of the text in the study of culture and history in modernity, has arisen in the face of what Jonathan Crary has labeled the "expanding visuality industry."[3] In particular, media studies have grown increasingly sensitive to the force of arguments for the sonic by producing more and more sophisticated accounts of its role in media expression and production.

The genealogy of contemporary sound studies must accord a large place to the publication of the groundbreaking 1980 issue of *Yale French Studies* (edited by Rick Altman) titled "Cinema/Sound," which brought together contemporary essays on film history, theory, and analysis. This pioneering work was followed in 1985 by the publication of a large volume, *Film Sound: Theory and Practice*, edited by Elisabeth Weis and John Belton, which included certain classic texts on sound (including those by Eisenstein and Pudovkin) as well as more contemporary scholarship. In the introduction to *Sound Theory, Sound Practice* (1992), Rick Altman, the editor of the collection, provided a canonical survey of the new field and pointed to an ongoing methodological shift from the formalist and structuralist approaches of the early 1980s to a broader understanding of the function of sound as a cultural and social practice. At around the same time, seminal texts by the French composer, writer, and director Michel Chion began to appear in English translation, affecting the whole Anglophone field.[4]

This pioneering work did not go unnoticed; by the first decade of the twenty-first century, sound studies had gained widespread recognition not only as an autonomous field but also as an integral part of the study of film and media. In the past fifteen years, there has been a flood of monographs and edited essay collections on sound, producing a counterweight to the accounts of film and media that have tended to overemphasize the visual. In a 1999 essay, Rick Altman was surely right to triumphantly proclaim that sound studies "was an idea whose time has come!"[5] and the Society for Cinema and Media Studies has recently recognized the importance of the intervention of sound scholarship in the field by forming a scholarly interest group on sound. Their "In Focus" rubric of the fall 2008 issue of *Cinema Journal* was dedicated to sound studies, reflecting an institutional and public-opinion change, a "sonic turn" much like the visual turn of the late 1970s.

The Sound of Cinema(s)

The recent flurry of sound studies, however, has tended to focus primarily on American and, to a lesser degree, certain European cinematic traditions, by and large neglecting other "world" cinemas. Correspondingly, the historical and thematic objects of sound studies have been framed by this context. This narrow focus can lead to false claims about the universality of the theoretical and historical paradigms these studies present. It is therefore crucial to shift scholarly attention toward a broader range of culturally specific sites in sound studies.

Despite the seminal importance of theoretical and artistic experimentations with sound in the Soviet Union, their accounts in the English-language literature have been limited for the most part to rehearsals of the arguments put forth by the film theorists of the 1920s. This omission may in part be because of the difficulty of locating the former Soviet Union in relation to the existing geopolitical categories (should Russia or the Soviet Union be included in collections on sound in European cinema? In "world" cinema?) and in part because of the legacy of the Cold War perception of Soviet autarky in all aesthetic spheres. But it is also symptomatic of the fact that the field of Russian studies has been slow to respond to the "sonic turn," confining the explorations of the acoustic in Russian and Soviet culture to musicology and failing to enter into the current interdisciplinary dialogue.[6] This pattern is repeated within the field of Soviet and post-Soviet cinema and media, where "sound" as a formal and thematic category still gets short shrift.

Thus, even the fundamental and well-studied historical topic of the transition to sound, which generated a wealth of theoretical and artistic experimentations by such canonical figures as Eisenstein, Pudovkin, Vertov, Shub, and Dovzhenko, has been generally treated parenthetically in studies of the Soviet film industry. Between detailed accounts of the avant-garde cinema of the 1920s and the socialist realism of the 1930s, well-respected Soviet film scholars such as Peter Kenez, Richard Taylor, Denise Youngblood, and Neya Zorkaya mention the Soviet industry's backwardness with regard to sound film and its difficult assimilation of the new technology, but they never look at the deeper implications and consequences of the transition.[7]

The effect of the sonic studies of the past two decades can be traced in several outstanding recent explorations of acoustic aesthetics and ideologies in the Soviet cinema, but these monographs tend to treat the works of isolated "sound *auteurs*."[8] The only genre and period to receive significant scholarly attention in relation to sound has been the Stalinist-era musical.[9] However, even here scholars have not gone far beyond the films directed by Grigori Alexandrov and, to a lesser degree, Ivan Pyriev.[10] Since Katerina Clark, in the pathbreaking 1995 essay "Aural Hieroglyphics? Some Reflections on the Role of Sound in Recent Russian Films and Its Historical Context," proposed readdressing the crucial role of "songs, music, and sound in general," Tatiana Egorova's survey *Soviet Film Music* still remains the only English language book devoted exclusively to this broad subject.[11]

One of the problems facing the field, even as it may expand to study certain national cinemas, is to put these culturally and historically specific areas of investigation into dialogue with the scholarship on sound studies in other national or global cinemas. At its inception, sound studies put a predominant emphasis on popular music and scoring practices, and on genres and auteurs, but as the field matures, issues concerning material culture have come to the fore, bringing larger questions concerning audio technologies, acoustic ecology, and wider media practices and reception into the discussion. This shift has yet to be reflected in the published scholarship on Soviet and post-Soviet media.[12] As a result, sound studies in Soviet and post-Soviet cinema suffer from a systematic neglect of both the theoretical and the historical dimensions of sound studies in audiovisual media.

"Cinema without Cinema"

This volume arises from a common frustration that we, as scholars and teachers of Russian and Soviet audiovisual culture, have experienced as we compare the paucity of English-language scholarship on the topic of Soviet sound to the richness of the primary sources: aesthetic, historical, and theoretical. It is our hope that this collection will both connect previously disjunct lines of research and suggest new directions for the exploration of sound in Soviet and post-Soviet audiovisual media. The editorial principle governing this collection is to articulate a diversity of sonic topics. The overall approach of the volume, then, is one that covers not only audiovisual texts but also discourses, technologies, institutions, and practices of "audio-vision" in the Soviet Union and Russia. The goal of this introduction is to foreground some of the shared themes and preoccupations that emerge from the chapters that follow, and in so doing to point to new directions and venues for further research.

The problematic status of sound in Soviet film scholarship is well illustrated by a comment made by Mikhail Yampolsky in the 1990s (discussed in detail in Peter Schmelz's contribution to this volume). Yampolsky singles out the logocentricity of Russian cinema, or as he conceptualizes it, the excessive and single-minded reliance on language and other script-based elements that have gone into making a "cinema without cinema."[13] His examples come largely from contemporary (perestroika-era) popular films, yet he certainly extends his critique to Soviet cinema at large, pointing to both the lack of state-of-the-art technology in the film industry and the continuing primacy of the literary in Russian culture. While the technological base for film production has changed drastically over the past twenty years in Russia, as elsewhere, Yampolsky's critique in many ways mirrors the concerns of our contemporary Hollywood critics about the mono-aural and overly saturated sound in blockbuster cinema and betrays a decisive preference for a rather Bazinian conception of cinematic realism, which is shared by many cinephiles and art film connoisseurs. Nevertheless, there is something culturally specific about the logocentricity of Russian cinema, whether in comparison to Hollywood, Bollywood, or other national and regional cinemas. In film scholarship, the lack of interest in the specifically cinematic qualities of Soviet or post-Soviet film sound production is symptomatic of larger forces that have structured the trajectory of Soviet and Russian cinematic institutions since the silent period. The inadequacy of the treatment of sound in cinematic education, combined with both the technological lag in developing audio equipment and the lack of any fresh conceptualizing of the sonic as a film element, was explicitly raised in the Soviet Union as early as 1962 in an open letter to the ministers of culture and education by "a group of distinguished film and music professionals." The letter drew attention to the paucity of intellectual, artistic, and institutional dialogue between music and film, and the absence of any developed conceptual framework or didactic program that could be used to prepare film directors, composers, sound editors, and film theorists alike to address the complexities of sound in cinema.[14] While the Thaw allowed renewed discussions of the Soviet avant-garde, the textbooks of the 1960s and 1970s indicate that the discourse on sound remained frozen in the terms set by the debates of the 1920s and 1930s.

It wasn't until the 1980s and 1990s that Soviet scholarship and criticism began to catch up with sonic theory and technology in other world cinemas. The revitalization was inaugurated by E. Averbakh's collection *The Emergence of the Sound Image: The Artistic Problems of Sound Recording in Screen Arts and the Radio,* and received a further impulse from Yuri Lotman and Yuri Tsivian's *Dialogue with the Screen,* which introduced a semiotic analysis of film language that included sound as one of its structural components.[15] All the same, the legacy of the early Soviet experimentations with sound in both theory and in practice continued to be the shared point of reference that shaped the debate in these volumes.

Soviet Modernity and the "Statement on Sound"

This collection, in continuity with those earlier works, contains a number of essays that reflect upon the wide interest in sound in the early years of the Soviet "talkies." The relationship among image, sound, and text become central to the discussion of film as a revolutionary medium between 1928 and 1935, leading some filmmakers to experiment with alternative modes of sound practice, while others saw the establishment of many of the patterns that would shape Soviet cinema long into the post-Stalinist period. Institutionally and technologically, cinema's transition to sound was explicitly linked to the Soviet modernization project. Thus, many of the discourses on sound were framed by the debates on the role of cinema and its aesthetic, technological, and ideological potential. In this vein, we might find models in cognate work by Jonathan Sterne, Emily Thompson, and James Lastra, who have examined listening practices, applied acoustics, and sound technology in American cultural history under the aegis of describing the parameters of a new acoustic modernity.[16] Similar work has been done on German audiovisual cultures and the modernizing project.[17] For the most part, these studies view the aural manifestations of modernity as driven primarily by capitalist commodity culture. Locating this phenomenon within a distinctly different discursive field—that of Soviet modernity—could significantly broaden the general theoretical parameters of such work. At the same time, however, we should keep in mind that dialogues with American sound cultures in particular did form an important part of the Soviet experience (as Valérie Pozner and Lilya Kaganovsky explore in different contexts in this volume). New approaches to sound in Soviet cinema pose questions concerning the limits of the framework of national cinemas as we begin to understand the transnational nature of cinematic modernity and the cultural and historical specificities of its manifestation.

The transition to sound coincided and no doubt contributed to the shift from the avant-garde to the realist aesthetic and discourse in Europe and the United States. Nowhere was this shift as dramatic as in the Soviet Union, where it corresponded to the move toward socialist realism and the integration of the revolutionary energies of cinema into the Stalinist culture at large, with its cult of personality, attacks on formalism and cosmopolitanism, and state endorsement of the aesthetic ideologies formerly eschewed by the 1920s avant-garde as extensions of the bourgeois consciousness. The late silent and early sound period in Soviet cinema witnessed complex and diverse artistic negotiations between what we traditionally call avant-garde and realist models. The inclusion of sound on the screen introduced a range of possible affective regimes and modalities, contributing to what Emma Widdis has termed the "sensory reeducation" of the Soviet citizen, which began as a larger project of revolutionizing the relationship between the human subjects and the material world around them by creating a new sensory regime for the spectator.[18] By the 1930s, sound and music in particular became battlegrounds for quickly changing ideologies, on and off the screen (see Joan Titus's and Kevin Bartig's contributions in this volume). Many of the essays in this collection present detailed examinations of this terrain, contributing to a much more nuanced understanding of the conditions and terms of this watershed cultural and historical moment.

When dealing with the early years of Soviet sound cinema, one must address the symbolic weight and the overwhelming legacy of Eisenstein, Pudovkin, and Alexandrov's famous 1928 treatise "Statement on Sound," which was for a long time the only significant piece of writing explicitly theorizing sound in cinema.[19] It was appropriate for the "Theory" section of Weis and Belton's seminal collection *Film Sound: Theory and Practice* to open with this classic essay by the Soviet directors, as it remains widely read and debated by film scholars and film students to this day.[20] "Statement on Sound" laid the foundation for the ideological and didactic use of media for political subject formation by, first, placing the invention of sound films in its political context (i.e., of the capitalist film industry in the United States and Germany), and then drawing the consequences for another political context (the Soviet Union) in which sound could be either an instrument that "destroys the formal achievements" of cinema as an art—by allowing sound to be used as an audio correlate to naturalism, perfectly lining up sound to image—or an instrument that can deepen the dialectical and organic unity of cinema by means of counterpoint (i.e., the intentional non-synchronization of sound to visual image). This theoretical approach is certainly culturally specific, as much of Soviet film theory and practice was formed in dialogue with the Russian formalist ideas of engaged spectatorship, leading to the prioritization of conflict and dissonance between the image and the soundtrack as a structuring compositional principle (see Joan Neuberger's essay for another elaboration on this in Eisenstein's work). Yet for all this theoretical foregrounding, the technical advance from the silents in Soviet cinema did not play out in terms of the formal dynamic that these early theorists advocated for. The actual sound practices, as well as their artistic inspirations, varied a great deal from the Eisenstein-Pudovkin-Alexandrov position. Many experimental strands of artistic practices at the time placed sound at their conceptual center rather than merely testing and marking its limitations; however, they could not easily fit under the explanatory category of "montage" or "counterpoint."[21] Indeed, it may be useful to consider Arseny Avraamov's experiments in noise and sound visualizations, Dziga Vertov's interest in bodily rhythm perception, or the use of silence to heighten the sensory engagement of the audience in films by Abram Room as distinct conceptual reference points, even though all of these figures shared the rejection of "easy listening" and purely illustrative functions of film sound with the authors of the "Statement." Different aspects of this dynamic are explored in the essays by Nikolai Izvolov and Emma Widdis in this collection. The "Statement on Sound" was symptomatic of early Soviet film theory's rejection of synchronized sound, and it has implicitly invited generations of scholars to undervalue the conceptual, artistic, and ideological complexities of the more "common" varieties of aural expression in cinema. Thus, the iconic status of the "Statement" may stand as an obstacle to a more historically grounded critical evaluation of a spectrum of actual sonic practices and their ideologies. While it would be irresponsible to downplay the enormous importance of the early Soviet avant-garde ethos (of which the "Statement" forms an important part, being perhaps its last collective breath), or of the formal and phenomenological complexities and ambitions of the modernist and/or art cinema, it may be that, in the words of Michel Chion, "it is time to take stock of what really happened rather than what was dreamed of. No more grumbling about sound film's outcome on the basis that people had wanted it to turn out differently, no more endless quoting of Adorno and Eisler, and the Three Russians and Vertov—all still recruited to condemn, eighty years later, the direction the cinema has taken."[22] And this direction has extended much more widely than the original montage problematic—or an emphasis on the new cinematic language—would account for. Nor, for example, was the theory of counterpoint the only current in the 1930s for thinking about sound among the theoreticians and practitioners of film music, many of whom were invested in a classical music heritage, its representation, and its affective didactic power (see Anna Nisnevich's essay in this volume). Moreover, the actual practices of early sound in Soviet film were often completely removed from any of the theoretical discussions, whether artistically progressive or conservative. Instead, they were often governed by direct political pressures, the dynamics of which are best revealed through an analysis of institutional discourses and industrial practices (as Valérie Pozner, Kevin Bartig, and Natalie Ryabchikova all show in this volume).

Logocentrism versus Polyglossia

The emphasis on the institutional discourses of music brings us back to the problem of logocentrism pointed out by Yampolsky in "Cinema without Cinema." Perhaps this overemphasis on linguistic expression in Soviet cinema is at least in part linked to the anxiety of cinema in a multi-nation—and multilingual—state, and to the challenges of and political resistances to translating this polyglossia on the screen. As Nataša Durovicová has noted, film language policies created cinema's varied acoustic representational space and a "national acoustic projection" reflecting the particularities of governing ideological configurations.[23] The introduction of sound in the 1930s made audible a voice of ideology—one issuing directly from the screen—that altered expectations about the relationship between viewer and film, between citizenship and Soviet power. The language of that ideology was, undeniably, Russian. The conventions of dubbing other languages were established in the Soviet Union under conditions not unlike those of fascist Italy, where post-synchronized dubbing created a false representation of cultural and linguistic unity through use of a generic Tuscan dialect as standard Italian (the fascist state even implemented laws prohibiting the exhibition of foreign films in the original language, as well as the use of dialects in Italian films).[24] However, as Evgeny Margolit's essay in this volume discusses, the dominance of monolingualism in Soviet cinema was a gradual phenomenon, and many of the early Soviet sound films were in fact multilingual, challenging assumptions about the function of language(s) in cinema. Moreover, the uneven levels of ideological control in the different film studios of the Soviet Union and their varying production norms and different markets created a patchwork of policies and practices of recorded sound.[25] More historically grounded work remains to be done on the language of Soviet films as a site of negotiations of national and ethnic identities in a multi-nation state.

Moreover, if we extend our understanding of the audiovisual beyond textual analysis to the context of cinematic exhibition and circulation practices, another range of uses of language and speech emerges. This includes the practice of commenting on the silent films, which was prevalent in prerevolutionary Russia, as elsewhere in the world,[26] and continued after the revolution.[27] While this form of oral commentary died out (except in the form of the lecture accompanying film exhibitions in certain local contexts, such as screenings at the local cultural centers, or *doma kul'tury*), oral translation of the cinematic text continued throughout the Soviet period in other forms. Because subtitling was not practiced and professional dubbing both was costly and required a significant investment of time, many foreign films and the majority of the television shows released in the Soviet Union were dubbed by a single person reading over a script. This practice extended to the illegal circulation of foreign films, from the videotapes with voice-over by a nasal monotone in the 1980s and 1990s (the translators pinched their noses to disguise their voices, as the legend has it) to the contemporary pirated DVD market. It has even evolved as a subgenre through, for example, the famous parodic and irreverent commentary dubbing by Dmitri Puchkov, a.k.a. "Goblin," of such blockbusters as Peter Jackson's *Lord of the Rings* trilogy (2001–3).[28] What makes this format particularly culturally compelling is that it stands in ironic relation not only to the films but also to the practice of dubbing itself, bringing the role of the interpreter-commentator to the fore. In his groundbreaking *Cinema Babel: Translating Global Cinema*, Abé Mark Nornes laid the foundation for the study of the role of dubbing and subtitling of foreign-language films as an oblique form of interpretation and cultural translation.[29] Following Nornes, Elena Razlogova's contribution to this volume explores the work of the simultaneous film translators in Moscow and the conflicting political pressures and cultural expectations that shaped such practices. These extra-cinematic uses of language are intrinsic to a certain experience of film spectatorship, especially as films cross borders (either licitly or as smuggled goods), producing layers of meaning added to the "original." Given the obvious threat to power relations (from controls on speech to controls on intellectual property) involved in such practices, this aural flow—both on and off the screen—has been subject to strict hierarchies and control. It would be a mistake, however, to assume that this power was ever total; actual sound practices demonstrate the degree to which such control is inscribed in a complex network of historically and geographically specific and often conflicting and shifting priorities. Moreover, a closer analysis of these practices points to a certain inherent indeterminacy of and/or in sound. In shifting the emphasis from the textual basis to its cinematic performance, speech inevitably acquires corporeality, positioning the body not only in diegetic space but also in historical time, where it necessarily emerges as a vocal embodiment of a particular sociocultural dynamic (as Oksana Bulgakowa demonstrates in her comparison of vocal deliveries on the screen between the 1930s and the 1960s in her contribution to this volume). As speech is vocalized and synchronized with the images on the screen, it aligns itself with other elements of the soundtrack, such as music, ambient noise, and sound effects.

Thus, soundscapes of Soviet cinema opened a rich but shifting terrain of articulations and negotiations of cultural and political categories, of what is perceived as "national," "local," "foreign," "authentic," and so on. Because the greatest level of centralized censorship in Soviet cinema was exercised upon the written word in the form of the official approval of the script, the nonverbal aspects of the oral delivery and the overall soundscape could bring out the nuances and carry the burden of coloring the "official word" with individual expression, operating on the affective level in relationship to the spectator or listener, creating—or dividing—affective communities through sound. This was particularly true of the radio with the iconic voices of Yuri Levitan or Olga Vysotskaya, but it also shaped the aural aesthetic of Soviet cinema. These practices affected the conventions of both documentary and fiction voice-overs (as Jeremy Hicks discusses in his essay),[30] as well as the styles of individual actors' vocal delivery (as Bulgakowa points out). Moreover, given the enormous power of the affective and sensory regimes of sound in the formation of given historical subjectivities, acoustic aspects of audiovisual culture register within historical traumas, such as those undergone by the Soviet Union under Stalin's purges and labor camps and the devastating Nazi invasion. Peter Schmelz theorizes the sonic dimension of this in his essay on Tengiz Abuladze's *Monanieba* (Repentance, 1984), and Jeremy Hicks employs this approach to explore the soundscapes as testimonies of the lived experiences of the Second World War and their traumatic reverberations through documentary.

Listening between the Lines

The logocentrism of Soviet cinema and its impact on the total soundtrack extend beyond the theatrical film. Indeed, two of the biggest Soviet TV film blockbusters of the Stagnation period—*Semnadtsat' mgnovenii vesny* (Seventeen Moments of Spring, dir. Lioznova, 1973) and *Mesto vstrechi izmenit' nel'zia* (The Meeting Place Cannot Be Changed, dir. Govorukhin, 1979)—owe much of their iconic status to the particularity of speech performances and the specific use of sound effects. More so than any visuals from the film, it was the colorful colloquial quality of the vocal performances of *Meeting Place*'s characters (further enhanced by Vladimir Vysotsky's iconic voice, which evoked associations with his career as a singer-songwriter) that made the series such a success. Similarly, Yefim Kopelyan's voice-over narration in *Seventeen Moments of Spring* and the official

"Nazi" language of the personal files have given the series a legendary status (not least through the oral tradition of *anekdoty*). Combined with the many other memorable uses of sound in the series (including the theme song, recognizable by its very first chords, and the extended use of silence), it was the aural quality of the voice-over that was responsible for creating a highly complex web of identification in the film. Its narration is immediately reminiscent of the legendary radio announcers of the wartime period and thus partakes in a nostalgia for an officially heroic period while also allowing for an implicit critique of the ossified language of official Soviet ideology and bureaucracy in the Stagnation era.

It would be incorrect, however, to emphasize the role of language in Soviet cinema to the exclusion of popular songs in it. Unlike Hollywood—which was largely dominated by original scores and where the inclusion of songs in a film tended to be limited to the musical genre, especially in the postwar period (although of course there are notable exceptions to this)—in Soviet sound cinema the inclusion of songs written specifically for the film—and often in conversation with the director—was a widespread practice throughout its history, regardless of whether or not the film was considered a "musical."[31] The comparably privileged status given to songs could be seen as further evidence of the enduring logocentrism of Soviet cinema, as lyrics greatly contributed to the popularity of film music.

However, this also prompts us to discuss the status of popular music in the Soviet Union, as it embodied the tensions among national, cross-cultural, and international transfers, in particular through its defining role in youth culture. Starting with jazz in the 1920s, the battle against "Western" influences in the Soviet Union (made more difficult by the West's desire to continue to exert precisely that influence) took place within the international mass culture of popular music and fashion, which gradually intensified in the postwar culture. This Cold War rhetoric is still with us on both sides of the former Iron Curtain: as a recent PBS documentary claims, it was the Beatles who brought down the wall,[32] or, as Mosfil'm director Karen Shakhnazarov recently put it in an interview with *Izvestiia*: "I am convinced that empires crumble at the level of the personal. . . . It wasn't the deployment of soldiers to Afghanistan in December [1978] that was responsible for the Soviet empire falling apart, but Beatles and Rolling Stones records."[33]

Popular songs brought out these cultural connotations, adding another level of cultural meaning to the text and texture of the films.[34] Beyond the shifts in the ideology of the musicals of the 1930s and 1940s, the "guitar poetry" (*avtorskaia pesnia*) that emerged during the Thaw featured prominently in films as different as Marlen Khutsiev's *Iul'skii dozhd'* (July Rain, 1966) and the Oscar-winning *Moskva slezam ne verit* (Moscow Does Not Believe in Tears, dir. Menshov, 1980), contributing to the generational appeal of both films. And in the 1980s, Soviet cinema witnessed a veritable sonic explosion through the introduction of rock and post-punk music and its stars. The cultural importance of such landmark films of perestroika as *ASSA* (dir. Soloviev, 1987), *Igla* (The Needle, dir. Nugmanov, 1988), *Vzlomshchik* (The Burglar, dir. Ogorodnikov, 1988), and Sergei Uchitel's documentary *Rok* (Rock, 1989) cannot be underestimated. These films' cult status and longevity (of *ASSA* and *The Needle* in particular) are largely because they were the first films to feature the stars of the "informal"—or unofficial—rock movement, producing a hollowed-out yet instantly recognizable and politically resonant version of the bohemian underground aesthetics from which this music emerged. These films came to define the era, and the song "We Are Waiting for Changes" ("Peremen"), performed by Tsoi in the final sequence of *ASSA*, became a youth-cultural anthem of perestroika.

The echoes of this cultural moment resonate in Valery Todorovsky's postmodern musical *Stilyagi* (The Hipsters, 2008), which figures at the center of Lilya Kaganovsky's essay concluding this volume. On the one hand, it is a musical, in which the songs are integrated into the narrative and performed by the characters; on the other hand, it relies on new versions of previously recorded songs, producing a series of uncanny cultural and historical displacements, akin to the kind of pastiche attempted in Baz Luhrmann's *Moulin Rouge!* (2001) or, more pointedly, in Julien Temple's *Absolute Beginners* (1996). However, it is precisely the prima facie cultural differences between *Stilyagi* and these films that point to the extraordinary weight and high ideological stakes underlying the use of popular music in Soviet and post-Soviet cinematic contexts. Through their musical pastiche, these films reflect a historical consciousness of three periods in the Soviet Union in particular—the struggle between liberalization and retrenchment in the 1960s, the Stagnation era of the 1980s, and the triumph of consumerism combined with commodified and multilayered Soviet nostalgia of the present day—in which the existential stakes of the survival of the Soviet model are played out as a generational drama. The compulsive return of these musical referents in the post-Soviet context indicates the persistent lack of closure concerning just what went wrong in the Soviet Union, encoded in the conversation about music as the space of geopolitical definitions of Soviet national cultural identity vis-à-vis "the West." From the logocentric view, there is something incomprehensible, even frivolous, in the idea that music played and continues to play this role. But as we widen our understanding of the aural as a cultural product, we may find that it is not incomprehensible at all but simply underconceptualized and distorted by our tendency to revert to tropes from a rhetoric centrally oriented to textual devices.

However, it would be wrong to think that music traveled only in one direction: from the West to the East. After all, the dominant hegemony in Europe and North America was having its own difficulties understanding the music coming from subaltern groups suddenly revolting against things "Western."[35] Moreover, it was not only "the West" that entered Soviet and post-Soviet homes via cinema and television screens: Indian cinema's popularity from the 1960s through the 1980s was due at least in part to the appeal of its musical numbers; the popularity of Latin American dance music in the 1980s also coincided with the arrival and temporary dominance of Latin American soap operas on Soviet television. In other words, if this collection is limited to a marked European (and Western) focus, it is intended to serve as an invitation to further research that would extend far beyond the areas represented here and toward a broader, transnational cultural analysis.

Nor should these histories be limited to popular music: much research remains to be done, for example, on both modernist and avant-garde or experimental (including electronic) musicians working in Soviet and post-Soviet cinema. Film work was the bread and butter of many experimental composers. The history of their collaborations is very rich, and Peter Schmelz's contribution to this volume points to the importance of this topic to the discussion of Soviet audiovisual culture. From Andrei Tarkovsky's famous collaboration with Eduard Arsenyev to the use of the ANS synthesizer in such popular films as *Siberiada* (dir. Konchalovsky, 1979) and *Zharkoe leto v Kabule* (Hot Summer in Kabul, dir. Khamrayev, 1983), not to mention Schnittke's work on Elem Klimov's and Alexander Mitta's films, these audiovisual compositions raise further questions about the relationship between high and low culture and the status of cinema therein, but they have yet to be fully explored from a cinematic perspective.[36] One other relatively unexploited avenue of analysis is exploration of the relationship between technology and the aesthetics of production, reception, and consumption of film. Furthermore, the filmic use of popular songs and the effect of the commercial success of compilation soundtracks on contemporary cinema bring the contours of convergence culture into sharp relief. From this moment, we can reconsider a full array of audiovisual phenomena in Soviet and post-Soviet cinema and media: such theoretical notions as Vertov's "cine-eye" versus "radio-eye," mass culture phenomena as the Soviet pop song and movie stardom,[37] and technological developments from the introduction of the reel-to-reel player in the 1970s to Internet fandom and video piracy. These issues bring out the larger implications of how audiovisual media is produced, distributed, and received, articulating the conditions of possibility that create and shape its emergence. While a wide area remains to be fully explored by scholars and cultural critics, the analysis of sound in Soviet and post-Soviet audiovisual media ultimately questions our involvement—sensory and affective, cultural, and social—in it. Muratova's "elation of listening" (which could be a number of things—for instance, an aesthetic appreciation of the everyday life of sound, or, in contrast, the eavesdropper's enjoyment of the "secret" revealed by sound) helps us gain a better understanding of cinema and media as both an aesthetic and a social experience, as well as a cultural product. Through this volume, we hope to suggest directions for an agenda of sound studies that turns us toward the historically and culturally grounded nature of spectatorship, whether understood as ideological subject formation or interpellation or as social and cultural reception. The contributions here are meant to provoke a conversation that may change the way we look at the history of our modernity.

Notes

1. Kira Muratova, "Iskusstvo rodilos' iz zapretov, styda i strakha," *Iskusstvo Kino* 2 (1995), reprinted in *Iskusstvo kino* (2001): 140.

2. Michael Bull and Les Back, eds., *The Auditory Culture Reader* (Oxford, UK: Berg, 2003), 3.

3. Jonathan Crary, "Response to Visual Culture Questionnaire," *October* 77 (Summer 1996): 33.

4. "Cinema/Sound," ed. Rick Altman, special issue, *Yale French Studies*, no. 60 (1980); John Belton and Elisabeth Weis, eds., *Film Sound: Theory and Practice* (New York: Columbia University Press, 1985); Rick Altman, *Sound Theory, Sound Practice* (New York: Routledge, 1992); Michel Chion, *Audio-Vision: Sound on Screen* (New York: Columbia University Press, 1994), and *The Voice in Cinema* (New York: Columbia University Press, 1999).

5. Rick Altman, "Sound Studies: A Field Whose Time Has Come," *Iris* 27 (Spring 1999): 3–4.

6. The rare exceptions to this in the field of Russian and Soviet cultural history are Amy Nelson's excellent book *Music for the Revolution: Musicians and Power in Early Soviet Russia* (University Park: Pennsylvania State University Press, 2004), Michael Urban (with Andrei Evdokimov), *Russia Gets the Blues: Music, Culture and Community in Unsettled Times* (Ithaca, NY: Cornell University Press, 2004), and Michael S. Gorham, *Speaking in Soviet Tongues: Language Culture and the Politics of Voice in Revolutionary Russia* (DeKalb, IL: Northern Illinois University Press, 2003).

7. Ian Christie's essay "Soviet Cinema: Making Sense of Sound," *Screen* 23, no. 2 (July–August 1982) later revised as "Making Sense of Early Soviet Sound," in *Inside the Film Factory*, ed. Richard Taylor and Ian Christie (London: Routledge, 1991), for a long time remained the only piece of scholarship in English on this topic. More recently, see Lilya Kaganovsky, "The Voice of Technology and the End of Soviet Silent Film: Grigorii Kozintsev and Leonid Trauberg's *Alone*," *Studies in Russian and Soviet Cinema* 1, no. 3 (2007): 265–81.

8. Robert Robertson, *Eisenstein on the Audiovisual: The Montage of Music, Image, and Sound in Cinema* (London: I. B. Tauris, 2009); Nancy Condee, *Imperial Trace: Recent Russian Cinema* (New York: Oxford University Press, 2009); John MacKay, "*Disorganized Noise*: Enthusiasm and the Ear of the Collective," *Kinokultura* 7 (2005), http://www.kinokultura.com /articles/jan05-mackay.html; Irina Sandomirskaia, "A Glossolalic Glasnost and the Re-tuning of the Soviet Subject: Sound Performance in Kira Muratova's *Asthenic Syndrome*," *Studies in Russian and Soviet Cinema* 2, no.1 (2008): 63–83, and Mikhail Yampolsky, "Chekhov/Sokurov: Repetition and Recollection," *New Formations* (May 1994): 48–58. Two out of the three essays on Soviet-related material included in *Composing for the Screen in Germany and the USSR: Cultural Politics and Propaganda*, edited by Robynn Stilwell and Phil Powrie (Bloomington: Indiana University Press, 2008), deal with the canonical subjects of Eisenstein and Prokofiev.

9. Trudy Anderson, "Why Stalinist Musicals?" *Discourse* 17, no. 3 (Spring 1995): 38–48; Richard Taylor, "But Eastward, Look, the Land Is Brighter: Towards a Topography of Utopia in the Stalinist Musical," in *100 Years of European Cinema: Entertainment or Ideology?*, ed. Diana Holmes and Alison Smith (Manchester, UK: Manchester University Press, 2000), 11–26;

Thomas Lahusen, "From Laughter 'Out of Sync' to Post-Synchronized Comedy: How the Stalinist Film Musical Caught Up with Hollywood and Overtook It," in *Socialist Cultures East and West: A Post-Cold War Reassessment*, ed. Dubravka Juraga and M. Keith Booker (New York: Praeger, 2002), 31–42; John Haynes, *New Soviet Man: Gender and Masculinity in Stalinist Soviet Cinema* (Manchester, UK: Manchester University Press, 2003); Rimgaila Salys, *The Musical Comedy Films of Grigorii Aleksandrov: Laughing Matters* (Bristol, UK: Intellect, 2009).

10. Eldar Riazanov's musical comedies are an exception to this tendency. See David MacFadyen, *The Sad Comedy of El'dar Riazanov: An Introduction to Russia's Most Popular Filmmaker* (Montreal: McGill-Queen's University Press, 2003), and Alexander Prohkorov, "Cinema of Attractions versus Narrative Cinema: Leonid Gaidai's Comedies and El'dar Riazanov's Satires of the 1960s," *Slavic Review* 62, no. 3 (Fall 2003): 455–72. David Gillespie's "The Sounds of Music: Soundtrack and Song in Soviet Film," *Slavic Review* 62, no. 3 (Fall 2003): 473–90, and his contribution to *The Directory of World Cinema: Russia*, ed. Birgit Beumers (Bristol, UK: Intellect, 2011), address this gap by discussing the use of songs in popular films from the 1970s; however, his analysis focuses primarily on the lyrics.

11. Katerina Clark, "Aural Hieroglyphics? Some Reflections on the Role of Sound in Recent Russian Films and Its Historical Context," in *Soviet Hieroglyphics: Visual Culture in Late Twentieth-century Russia*, ed. Nancy Condee (Bloomington: BFI/Indiana University Press, 1995), 3; Tatiana Egorova, *Soviet Film Music: An Historical Survey* (London: Routledge, 1997).

12. There are some exceptions, of course. For example, two recent publications reflecting such approaches are James Krukones, "Peacefully Coexisting on a Wide Screen: Kinopanorama vs. Cinerama, 1952–66," *Studies in Russian and Soviet Cinema* 4, no. 3 (2010): 283–305, and David MacFadyen, "Cinematic *Abuse* as Self-Affirmation: Russian Video Mash-Ups, Illegal Social Networking, and the Rise of Bekmambetov's 'Office Plankton,'" *Kinokultura* 27 (2010), http://www.kinokultura.com/2010/27-macfadyen.shtml.

13. Mikhail Yampolsky, "Cinema without Cinema," in *Russian Critics on the Cinema of Glasnost*, ed. Michael Brashinsky and Andrew Horton (Cambridge: Cambridge University Press, 1994), 12.

14. *Iskusstvo kino* 3 (1962): 63. Quoted in Tomas Korganov and Ivan Frolov, *Kino i muzyka* (Moscow: Iskusstvo, 1964).

15. E. Averbakh, ed., *Rozhdenie zvukovogo obraza: Khudozhestvennye problemy zvukozapisi v ekrannykh iskusstvakh i na radio* (Moscow: Iskusstvo, 1985); Yuri Lotman and Yuri Tsivian, *Dialog s ekranom* (Tallin: Aleksandra, 1994).

16. James Lastra, *Sound Technology and the American Cinema* (New York: Columbia University Press, 2000); Emily Thompson, *The Soundscape of Modernity: Architectural Acoustics and the Culture of Listening in America, 1900–1933* (Cambridge, MA: MIT Press, 2002); Jonathan Sterne, *The Audible Past: Cultural Origins of Sound Reproduction* (Durham, NC: Duke University Press, 2003).

17. See Nora M. Alter and Lutz Koepnick, eds., *Sound Matters: Essays on the Acoustics of Modern German Culture* (New York: Berghan Books, 2004).

18. Emma Widdis, "*Faktura*: Depth and Surface in Early Soviet Set Design," *Studies in Russian and Soviet Cinema* 3, no. 2 (2009): 5–32.

19. S. Eisenstein, V. Pudovkin, and G. Aleksandrov, "Budushchee zvukovoi fil'my: Zaiavka" [The Statement on Sound], *Zhizn' iskusstva*, August 5, 1928. The "Statement on Sound" and other important documents chronicling the transition to sound are translated in Richard Taylor and Ian Christie, eds., *The Film Factory: Russian and Soviet Cinema in Documents 1896–1939* (London: Routledge, 1988).

20. Belton and Weis, *Film Sound*, 83–86.

21. On the attempt to look at early Soviet sound cinema from the point of view of counterpoint, see Kristin Thompson, "Early Sound Counterpoint," *Yale French Studies* 60 (1980): 115–40.

22. Michel Chion, *Film: A Sound Art*, trans. Claudia Gorbman (New York: Columbia University Press, 2009), 203.

23. Nataša Ďurovičová, "Vector, Flow, Zone: Towards a History of Cinematic Translation," in *World Cinemas, Transnational Perspectives*, ed. Nataša Durovicová and Kathleen Newman (London: Routledge, 2006), 90–120.

24. See Jacqueline Reich, "Mussolini at the Movies: Fascism, Film, and Culture," in *Re-Viewing Fascism: Italian Cinema 1922–1943*, ed. Jacqueline Reich and Piero Garofalo (Bloomington: Indiana University Press, 2002), 3–29, and Giorgio Bertellini, "Dubbing *L'arte muta*: Poetic Layerings around Italian Cinema's Transition to Sound," in *Re-Viewing Fascism: Italian Cinema 1922–1943*, ed. Jacqueline Reich and Piero Garofalo (Bloomington: Indiana University Press, 2002), 30–82.

25. Oksana Sarkisova explores this in "Folk Songs in Soviet orchestration: Vostokfil'm's Song of Happiness and the Forging of the New Soviet Musician," *Studies in Russian and Soviet Cinema* 4, no. 3 (2010): 261–81.

26. See, in particular, Rashit M. Yangirov, "Talking Movie or Silent Theater? Creative Experiments by Vasily Goncharov," in *The Sounds of Early Cinema*, ed. Richard Abel and Rick Altman (Bloomington: Indiana University Press, 2001) and Rick Altman, *Silent Film Sound* (New York: Columbia University Press, 2004).

27. For an overall approach to *oralité*, see Germain Lacasse, *Le bonimenteur de vues animées: Le cinéma muet entre tradition et modernité* (Quebec City, QC: Nota Bene, 2000). For a Soviet instantiation of this, see Valérie Pozner, "Le bonimenteur 'rouge': Retour sur la question de l'oralité à propos du cas soviétique," *Cinémas* 14, nos. 2–3 (2004): 143–78.

28. Smeshnye perevody Goblina ot studii Bozh'ia Iskra (Funny translations by Goblin from the Bozh'ia Iskra studio), http://oper.ru/trans/?bi.

29. Abé Mark Nornes, *Cinema Babel: Translating Global Cinema* (Minneapolis: University of Minnesota Press, 2007).

30. Similar issues have recently been picked up in Wolfgang Beilenhoff and Sabine Hänsgen, "Speaking about Images: The Voice of the Author in *Ordinary Fascism*," *Studies in Russian and Soviet Cinema* 2, no. 2 (2008): 141–53.

31. For a seminal account of Hollywood film music, Claudia Gorbman, *Unheard Melodies: Narrative Film Music* (Bloomington: Indiana University Press; London: BFI Publishing, 1987). For a discussion of the role of songs in scoring practices in Soviet cinema, see Andrei Petrov and Natalia Kolesnikova, *Dialog o kinomuzyke* (Moscow: Iskusstvo, 1982).

32. *How the Beatles Rocked the Kremlin* (dir. Leslie Woodhead, TV 2009).

33. Vita Ramm, "Kinorezhisser Karen Shakhnazarov: 'V raspade sovetskoi imperii kliuchevuiu rol' sygrali 'bitly' i 'rollingi.'" *Izvestiia*, February 11, 2008.

34. For a discussion of the different varieties of Soviet and Russian pop and rock music, see Artemy Troitsky, *Back in the USSR: The True Story of Rock in Russia* (London: Faber and Faber, 1988), and *Tusovka: Who's Who in the New Soviet Rock Culture* (London: Omnibus, 1990); David MacFadyen's "trilogy": *Red Stars: Personality and the Soviet Popular Song after 1955* (Montreal: McGill-Queen's University Press, 2001), *Èstrada?! Grand Narratives and the Philosophy of the Russian Popular Song, 1982–2000* (Montreal: McGill-Queen's University Press, 2001), and *Songs for Fat People: Affect, Emotion and Celebrity in the Soviet Popular Song, 1900 to 1955* (Montreal: McGill-Queen's University Press, 2002); and Birgit Beumers, *Pop Culture Russia!* (Santa Barbara, CA: ABC-CLIO, 2005).

35. For different aspects of this issue, see Georgia Born and David Hesmondhalgh, eds., *Western Music and Its Others: Difference, Representation and Appropriation in Music*

(Berkeley: University of California Press, 2000); Paul Gilroy, "Sounds Authentic: Black Music, Ethnicity, and the Challenge of a *Changing* Same," *Black Music Research Journal* 11, no. 2 (Autumn 1991): 111–36; Kodwo Eshun, *More Brilliant Than The Sun: Adventures in Sonic Fiction* (London: Quartet Books, 1998); Veit Erlmann, *Music, Modernity and the Global Imagination* (Oxford: Oxford University Press, 1999).

36. Peter Schmelz, *Such Freedom, If Only Musical: Unofficial Soviet Music during the Thaw* (Oxford: Oxford University Press, 2009).

37. For recent scholarship on this topic, see Kay Dickinson, *Off Key: When Film and Music Won't Work Together* (Oxford: Oxford University Press, 2008).

PART I
FROM SILENCE TO SOUND

1 From the History of Graphic Sound in the Soviet Union; or, Media without a Medium

Nikolai Izvolov

Translated from the Russian by Sergei Levchin

TYPICALLY, THE TERM *cinema* is reserved exclusively for moving images captured on a filmstrip by means of a photographic (i.e., positive-negative) process, capable of reproducing physical reality. Until now very little has been written about another, equally expressive and significant cinematic technique of the "optical period," designed to synthesize a new and wholly novel audiovisual environment.[1] Perhaps the most widely recognized name in this field of drawn animation is that of Canadian animator Norman McLaren, though he was neither the originator of this technique nor its sole practitioner.[2]

Notably, the possibility of this technique was never discussed in early theoretical writings on cinema. In 1945, one of the most insightful theorists of film, Béla Balázs, wrote: "Sound cannot be represented. We see an actor's likeness on the screen, but never his voice. Sound is reproduced, rather than represented; it may be manipulated in some manner, but even then it retains the same reality."[3] Thus, the ontology of sound was equated with that of the voice or of music; no distinction was made between its acoustic and communicative aspects. One wonders whether Balázs's actor was actually represented on film or merely reproduced there. This attitude seems especially perplexing when we take into account that Balázs collaborated on at least two films that made use of drawn sound.

There has been some writing on the subject of graphic sound, however, including S. Bugoslavsky's chapter in the volume *Mul'tiplikatsionnyi fil'm* (The Animated Film) and a chapter in I. Ivanov-Vano's *Kadr za kadrom* (Frame by Frame): unfortunately, neither offers more than a technical overview of the basic principles of the synthetic soundtrack.[4] My own article, titled "Moment ozhivlenia spiashchei idei" (A Sleeping Idea Comes to Life), represented one attempt to set out the philosophical principles behind the idea of graphic sound.[5]

And so, who were the pioneers? Clearly, these could not be filmmakers—until the advent of sound, no one ever thought about sound theory. Instead, the most significant contribution to the invention and development of "drawn sound" was made by just four individuals: Arseny Avraamov (a composer and musical theoretician, and inventor of the forty-eight-tone universal musical system known as the Welttonsystem, or universal tone system; Evgeny Sholpo (an engineer and inventor who developed a device for the artificial performance of music); Boris Yankovsky (an acoustics engineer); and Nikolai Voinov (an animation cameraman).

Drawing directly on film stock opened up possibilities not just for the image track but for the sound track as well. The Soviet pioneers of graphic sound made the most significant contributions to the invention and development of this technique, also known as designed, drawn, paper, animated, synthetic, or artificial sound. With remarkable unanimity, all the early practitioners note the date of the invention as October 1929, even Yankovsky, who was not actually there to witness it. None of them claimed sole authorship of the idea, possibly because the first person to mention it casually in conversation was yet another cinéaste, animation director Mikhail Tsekhanovsky:

> The three of us were sitting in the studio—myself, E. A. Sholpo, whom I had invited to be my assistant, and artist-animator M. M. Tsekhanovsky (the maker of the first Soviet sound animation film, "The Postal Service" [*Pochta*, Tsekhanovskii and Timofeev, 1929], based on the work of Samuil Marshak). With immense interest we were using a magnifying glass to examine the very first, fresh print of the soundtrack, still moist, which had just arrived from the lab.

Tsekhanovsky enthused about the beauty of the ornamental waveform traced on the film. He fantasized:

> "Interesting, if you were to trace an Egyptian or ancient Greek design on the soundtrack—would we hear some hitherto unknown archaic music?"
>
> Sholpo and I brought his fantasy back down to earth. As the ornament itself is strongly periodical in form, depending on its shape, we would hear only single tones of one timbre or another. Whether they would be "Greek" or "Egyptian" is hard to say, but there would certainly be nothing resembling a melody....
>
> But the word had been spoken. The idea of reproducing a synthetic, "artificial" soundtrack on the film strip with all its brilliant possibilities—this idea had taken firm hold of us all.
>
> After the film was finished, each of us pursued it in his own way.[6]

With these words, an idea was born—that of writing predesigned phonograms directly onto a film soundtrack—opening up remarkable new aural opportunities, which all participants in the discussion would later realize.

Синтетическое мажорное трезвучие (4 : 5 : 6)

Профили разных нот синтетической скрипки

Figures 1.1–1.2. Illustrations to Arseny Avraamov's article "Synthetic music," *Sovetskaia muzyka* 8 (1939).

Unlike his three colleagues, Arseny Avraamov was not particularly interested in the technical side of the invention. Rather, he was attracted by the prospect of studying how visual forms could be transformed into the sound of music and voices. The underlying fundamentals of this process were the basic shapes of Euclidean geometry—squares, triangles, and circles—from which all visual forms are constructed, including those found on the optical soundtrack portion of the filmstrip (figures 1.1 and 1.2). Using the standard animation technology of the day, in the summer of 1930 Avraamov became the first person to create drawn sound; he demonstrated the results of his experiments at a conference on sound in Moscow the following autumn.

Each of the three remaining creators of drawn sound invented his own original device designed to facilitate the drawing of sound on film. Evgeny Sholpo called his the Variophone, though his colleagues at Lenfil'm Studios invariably referred to it as the Sholpograph in their various memoirs (figure 1.3).[7] This device enabled the cinematic capture of sound on the moving filmstrip. Templates for the sounds were prepared on disks with the appropriate patterns cut into them.

Figure 1.3. Sholpo at work on the Variophone.

Depending on the number and configuration, the cuts could result in single sounds or chords. By means of prisms, a ray of light would penetrate the cuts on the rotating disks, which was reflected onto the film, which moved continuously (rather than spasmodically, as is more usual in film cameras). The disk could rotate at different rates relative to the film, thus producing various tempos.

Interestingly, a mechanical television technology was also being developed at the same time: the Nipkov disk, which recorded and reproduced an image using a spiral pattern of holes. In response, Avraamov proposed another idea related to the reception of a television signal. If it was possible to transform an optical signal into sound, then the opposite must also be true: one could turn a sound signal into a visual representation. This hypothesis became the subject of his article "Sintonfil'm i Metamorfon" (Synthofil'm and Metamorphon). Though the "Metamorphon" proposed therein was never built, the idea of a rotating disk with openings through which light penetrates was nevertheless inherited from Sholpo's Variophone (figures 1.4 and 1.5).

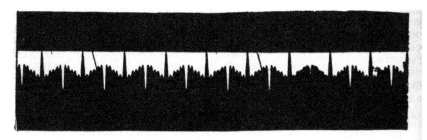

Профиль синтетического кларнета: имеет 3, 5, 7, 9 и 11-й обертоны, причем ампли-
туды у всех одинаковые. Синтез Б. Янковского—в 1935 г. Зазвучал в 1938 г.

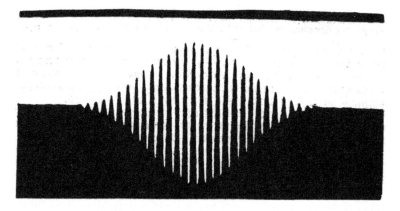

Тембр, наиболее контрастный синусоидальному, состоит из 5 высших обертонов,
без низших, что придает ему резкий и яркий характер колокола или трубы с сур-
диной (в зависимости от разного извлечения звука)

Figures 1.4–1.5. Illustrations to Arseny Avraamov's article "Synthetic music,"
Sovetskaia muzyka 8 (1939).

Boris Yankovsky's device, the Vibroexponator, was devoted to creating sounds of varying timbres, a sonic aspect that had been largely underdeveloped in the other inventions (including those of Sholpo and Voinov). As a professional acoustic engineer, Yankovsky's work in this field is particularly interesting and significant. From 1930 to 1932, he worked alongside Avraamov in his laboratory, conducting a great deal of research that would later prove essential for the graphic representation of sound. In 1932, the ambitious researchers announced that they were preparing to synthesize the sounds of human speech. Avraamov wrote that all consonant sounds could be conveyed in four types of graphic representations and that vowel sounds could be conveyed in only two. But this "homunculus" (as the idea was called by Avraamov's colleagues) was not fated to be heard.

Nikolai Voinov, who also began his experiments with Avraamov, created a device to make a kind of paper "comb," which could serve as a standard template for fragments of future phonograms.[8] His method was based on the traditional technique of paper cutout animation. The soundtrack would be photographed alongside the image, frame by frame. This was a practical but restrictive method, as it reduced to a minimum the rich set of acoustic possibilities available to drawn sound. In the credits of the film *Vor* (Thief, 1934), Voinov's method is credited as "paper sound," though obviously the templates could have been made of any number of other materials. In contrast to the other inventors, Voinov was not inclined to theorize his approach, and did not leave any written texts. But his four finished cinematic works with designed sound have been fully preserved.

Unfortunately, most of the works by the inventors of drawn sound have not survived to the present day. Arseny Avraamov's experiments were kept at his house and were accidentally destroyed. Boris Yankovsky's inventions never left the laboratory stage and may have existed only in single copies. Nikolai Voinov's films were much more fortunate. Some of them were released in theaters and exist in multiple copies. Four of his films are preserved in the Russian film archives. Probably the most well preserved archive is Evgeny Sholpo's. Several dozen of his movies, along with fragments of those by other inventors, were shown for the first time at the animated film festival in Utrecht in November 2008.

By and large, the pioneers of graphic sound maintained friendly relations with one another on the basis of professional camaraderie and goodwill. Debates, when they arose, were mostly over theoretical differences. Thus, according to one legend, when the article "Na avantpostakh tekhniki" (At the Vanguards of Technology) appeared in the May 1931 issue of the journal *Izobretatel'* (The Inventor) attributing the invention of drawn tone film (graphic sound) to Sholpo, and a few months later Soiuzkino recognized Avraamov's contribution to the development of "graphic animated sound recording" using Sholpo's technique,[9] the composer was absolutely furious. On Sholpo's next visit to Moscow Avraamov sought out the inventor and demanded an explanation. Evidently, Avraamov believed that Sholpo intended to take full credit for the idea of graphic sound. Fortunately, the matter did not come to blows, and the two men parted as friends.

One assumes that it was the relative minimalism of Voinov's acoustic experiments that prompted the dismissive tone that is readily detectable in the writings of the ultra-sophisticated acoustic engineer Yankovsky.[10] The group known as IVVOSTON (A. Ivanov, P. Sazonov, N. Voinov) was quick to respond in kind. The late A. Sazonov (son of P. Sazonov) told me about a decade ago that Yankovsky was an object of light mockery among the animators—though, having been very young at the time, he could not remember why.

He also recalled a remarkable incident: after finishing their very first film using Voinov's technique (*Preliud Rakhmaninova*, or Rachmaninoff's Prelude), the team of animators went to screen it at a theater where the Pushkin Theater now stands. The image came on, but—for the first second or so—no sound followed. To those who attended the screening, that second lasted an eternity: it was a violent shock, and it stayed with them for the rest of their lives. A moment later the sound broke in—they had not known about the nineteen-frames rule, or the frame offset required by the optical sound reader—and had printed the sound in sync with the image. The print of the *Soiuzkinozhurnal* (Union Cine-Journal) held at the Russian State Archive of Film and Photo Documents (RGAKFD),[11] which includes the animated film, has preserved this error for posterity. The team learned their lesson, however, and the soundtrack was properly adjusted on their next film, *Tanets vorony* (Crow's Dance).

An earlier version of *Vor*, which was never released and therefore does not appear in any filmography, also made its way to the RGAKFD, where it was discovered a few years ago by film historian A. Deriabin. The script, written by the recently transplanted Balázs, grew out of one of Stalin's exhortations: "Let's keep the fascist pig out of the Soviet backyard!" The film features a suitably vile-looking pig, marked with a swastika, whose attempts at sabotage are easily thwarted.

In the final 1934 version of the film, the pig remains virtually unchanged; however, this time it menaces a *kolkhoz* (a Soviet collective farm) and meets resistance in the form of a young pioneer named Vasia and his dog Druzhok ("Buddy"). Balázs considered Vasia, his brainchild, to be the perfect Soviet cartoon character. (Recurring animated characters had become the norm in the United States at that time, but all efforts to fashion a Soviet equivalent, such as Tip-Top or Bratishkin, had failed to capture the popular imagination). According to Balázs: "This lad is armed with a pencil, which he uses to intervene in the action itself. By drawing he can alter the drawn world around him. (Wherever he must cross a river he will draw a bridge across it.) The boy draws all kinds of things directly into the film frame."[12] Balázs reiterates this formulation nearly verbatim in 1934, at the time of the film's release, and again in 1945 in his book *The Art of Cinema*. Nevertheless, the young pioneer, drawn in Ivanov's characteristically grotesque style, was not a great hit with the audiences.

Another legend describes how Sholpo recorded the soundtrack for the film *Sterviatniki* (Vultures) on his own machine in the late summer of 1941. The sound department at Lenfil'm had already been evacuated, and only Sholpo remained behind to save the day.[13] That recording, alongside several dozen reels containing Sholpo's experiments, is now held at the Cinema Museum in Moscow. The film itself, however, has not survived, and existing catalogs list its production studio as Soiuzmul'tfil'm (i.e., Moscow rather than Leningrad), an inconsistency that warrants investigation.

The creators of graphic sound faced considerable difficulties in realizing their ideas, as the Soviet film industry had little use for theorists, amateur inventors, and audio perfectionists. Indeed, the inventors of color cinematography encountered the very same problems, until a government decree was issued that required studios to produce films in color. The proponents of graphic sound, however, were less fortunate, since by the mid-1930s traditional sound recording was already well established in cinema. As a result, their work was mostly confined to research institutes, where they got by with minimal funding and the help of fellow enthusiasts.

Rumors and legends have obscured the actual events to such a degree that one finds fantastical distortions of the facts even in respectable publications devoted to music and cinema to this day:

> Well before the first experiments with synthesizers and sound processing (or noise processing, in the case of *musique concrète*), just after the end of the First World War, we find the first efforts to generate sound artificially, by means of so-called "graphic music," i.e.[,] graphic representation of sound. These experiments were first carried out by L. Moholy-Nagy, followed, after 1930, by Ernst Toch and the Soviets— A. Avraamov, N. Zelinsky, N. Voinov, G.M. Rimsky-Korsakov, E. Sholpo, who founded an experimental studio at the Leningrad Conservatory; in Germany there were R. Pfenninger and O. Fischinger; in England—Jack Elliot, and later K.E. Boeckl; in Canada—N. McLaren.[14]
>
> Yankovsky was the first to trace a continuous stripe along the edge of the filmstrip, while the idea of composing a "soundtrack" out of discrete geometrical patterns belongs to Avraamov; this produced remarkably interesting audio effects. Using the same principle, Moholy-Nagy traced fingerprints, human profiles, letters of the alphabet, etc. along the edge of the frame; Oskar Fischinger did the same with geometrical drawings, etc. These patterns, "translated" into acoustic events, yielded wholly novel audio effects. The first of such films—i.e. animated with "graphic music"—was made in 1932 in Munich by R. Pfenninger and titled *Sounding Handwriting*. N. Voinov drew sound diagrams, corresponding to the traditional tonal system, and created musical compositions directly on the filmstrip. Thus, in 1934, he was able to reproduce purely graphically the whole of *Rachmaninoff's Prelude*. Similar experiments were undertaken in England in 1933 by Jack Elliot and later by K. Boeckl, and in California by the Whitney brothers.[15]

Despite the confusion of names, dates, and creative principles pervading these passages from Z. Lissa's book, the mark left by the Soviet inventors on the history of world cinema is clear. I. Ivanov-Vano's book, cited earlier and containing several interesting details and anecdotes, recounts one particularly curious incident. Evidently, the author had once asked Norman McLaren directly if he was "familiar with the Soviet animators' experiments with graphic sound or had read our book *The Animated Film*. McLaren intimated that he knew the book very well, having translated it, and that the chapter on graphic sound had considerably advanced his own work."[16] It is hard to know whether McLaren really could translate from Russian to English, but he may have been familiar with the various articles on "graphic sound" that had appeared in English-language publications.[17]

The phenomenological idea of cinema was not entirely cut off from the rest of world culture. Just as technology (the motion picture) doubled philosophy (phenomenology) and the two were synthesized in the "phenomenological aesthetics" of Maurice Merleau-Ponty, so too did the phenomenological understanding of cinema enter at times into some rather unlikely alliances with concurrent historical and cultural (though not necessarily aesthetic) trends. The history of graphic sound offers an interesting example of one such union.

We know that Russian futurism as an artistic movement had almost no formal or ideological influence on cinema. Relations between futurism and the cinema appear to have been marked by outward rejection (e.g., *Drama v kabare futuristov, No. 13* [Drama at the Futurist Cabaret No. 13, 1913];[18] Vladimir Mayakovsky's screenplays; Lev Kuleshov's early experiments) rather than mutual attraction. However, if we consider futurism as a worldview (which is what it purported to be first and foremost) and as a method of knowledge acquisition, we discover some remarkable parallels. The futurist tradition turns out to be capable of productive development while operating with seemingly improbable materials.

In literature, futurism effected a radical transformation of rhyme, rhythm, and the word itself. But paronymism (*korneslovie*) and word creation (*slovotvorchestvo*) are outward signs. What is their inner significance? A montage of Khlebnikov's pronouncements, arranged chronologically to reflect the evolution of the poet's thinking, may give us some indication:

1. "There is an ocean of books written about sound, called Boring. A lonely island in their midst—the opinion of the Manchurian Tatars: the 30-29 sounds of the alphabet are the 30 days of the month, and that the sound of the alphabet is the creaking of the month, heard by the earthly ear. . . . The Manchurian Tatars and Pythagoras are shaking hands" (1914).[19]
2. "It is up to the artists of thought to construct an alphabet of concepts, an order of the primary units of thought—the building of the word is built from these. The task for the artists of paint is to find graphic symbols corresponding to the fundamental units of reason" (April 13, 1917).[20]
3. "(a) In every language V means the rotation of one point about another, whether in a complete circle or along some section or arc, up and back.
   (b) . . . X means a closed curve, dividing the position of one point from the movement of another toward it (a protective barrier).
   (c) . . . Z means the reflection of a moving point away from a mirror plane at an angle equal to the angle of incidence. A ray striking a rigid surface. . . .
   I see V as a circle with a point on it. . . .
   X as a combination of two lines and a point. . . .
   Z as a fallen K, a mirror and a ray" (April 13, 1919).[21]
4. "Consequently, the transrational [*zaumnyi*] language is the future world language in embryo. It alone can unite men. Intelligent languages are already dividing [them]" (May 1919).[22]

5. "[W]hy the spells and the incantations of so-called magical speech, the sacred language of paganism, these '*shagadam, magadam, vygadam, pits, pats, patsu*'—are but strings of syllables, unaccountable to reason, the transrational language of the popular word. . . . The Old Slavonic language is unintelligible to a Russian, as Latin is to the Pole and the Czech. But a prayer written in Latin is no less effective than a shop sign. Consequently, the magical speech of spells and incantations refuses the judgment of quotidian reason" (1919–20).[23]

6. "If we distinguish within the makeup of the soul the rule of reason and the unruly masses of emotions, then spells and the transrational language bypass the rulers and speak directly to the masses of emotions, a clarion call to the twilight of the soul or the apogee of popular rule in the life of word and reason, a legal strategy rarely employed" (1919–20).[24]

A curious general line emerges. Neologisms start to resemble archaisms, and vice versa. A magic spell is equated to a Latin or Slavonic prayer in its effect. New incantations appear in the form of the transrational word, operating directly—that is, without the mediation of morphology, syntax, symbol, and so on, without the instruments of evolved "word culture." Magic spell and incantation: this is the unmediated transrational language of the future, the language that will unite all of mankind. This foundation determines an idea, encapsulated in sound, and it finds its expression in the graphic representation of sound, thus paving the way for the invention and cognition of a universal language of the future and its "writing system"—that trinity of an idea expressed as sound, expressed as image, which in turn expresses an idea. Futurism accelerates natural evolution, pushing the present into the future, thought into emotion, art into engineering at this very moment.

Of course, none of this bears directly on the cinema, unless we count Roman Jakobson's witty, albeit superficial, observation that Khlebnikov's dramatic poem "Mirskontsa" (Worldbackwards) is a filmstrip projected in reverse.[25]

The early career of Arseny Avraamov coincides roughly with the rise of Russian futurism in the early 1910s and culminates in 1917 with the founding of the Leonardo da Vinci Society for Arts and Sciences. Sholpo recalled:

Needless to say, in assuming da Vinci's name we had in mind strictly the scientific and aesthetic (and more scientific than aesthetic) ideology of that brilliant man. Faith in the power of science and mathematics, the drive toward the objective cognition of the "mysterious" laws of art—these compelled the Society to take on that historic name. . . .

Our sights were set on the revolution in music theory and technology, stemming from a fusion of art and science. . . .

Each member had his own distinct sphere of activity: Sergei Dianin undertook a mathematical analysis of acoustics and music theory; Arseny Avraamov focused on the philosophy and sociology of music, with occasional forays into physics and history, as needed; my own particular project was the invention of a recording device for the piano. . . .

Armed with this research—so we imagined—we could penetrate into the mysteries of art (limited, for the moment, to the art of performance), and armed with mathematical formulae, smash the pervasive mystical and idealistic tendencies used to explain music and art. . . .

We were going to tear down the performing artist. This "caste of middlemen" that had insinuated itself between the composer's idea and the listener's sensation seemed to us superfluous. We despised the acrobatics of miserable conservatory students, who poured all of their individuality into exercising the neuromuscular mechanism of their hands. We wanted them to work with their heads. . . .

Sound film changed everything.[26]

At last, a universal performer was found in the sound film, allowing for the unmediated realization of an artistic idea. What was that idea, according to Avraamov?

At this point an incident occurred that bears the indelible markings of history. In the fall of 1929, the sound recording sessions for Abram Room's film *Plan velikikh rabot* (*Piatiletka*) (The Plan for Great Works [Five-Year Plan], 1930) brought Avraamov, Sholpo, and M. Tsekhanovsky together. The first Soviet experiments with sound film were conducted in Leningrad, in the laboratory of A. Shorin. There is no telling what might have become of graphic sound (e.g., animated sound, synthetic music, the artificial soundtrack) if Shorin had forgone the "transversal" method (variable area optical recording where the soundtrack appears as a jagged curve) in favor of the "intensive" method (variable density optical recording in which the soundtrack appears as alternating stripes of varying density and width), like E. Tager was doing in Moscow, or the magnetic method, which was also being experimented with at the time, particularly in Germany. Had the film studio not invited Tsekhanovsky to produce animation inserts for the picture, had the three men failed to meet, had the idea of "performer-free" music not become overripe—whatever might have been, the following episode took place and was subsequently recounted by both Sholpo and Avraamov. I defer to Avraamov's version of the events, since he does not claim full credit for himself and seems generally more objective in his account:

We [Avraamov's team] worked on an animation stand, photographing a (miniaturized) "soundtrack" hand-drawn with ink, one frame at a time. . . . We made use of the ready notes of Euclidean geometry: triangles, trapezoids, squares, semi-circles, etc.

From the very outset we were searching for sounds that had never been heard before, new tonal systems, complex polyrhythmic effects.[27]

Is there anything especially "futuristic" about it—the wish to see *technology subjected wholly to the creative impulse, and not vice versa?*[28]

Do we not stand dumbfounded before the great diversity of Eastern rituals, without a satisfactory means of pinning them down, because in our mathematics of rhythm we have gotten no further than $2 \times 2 = 4$ (whole notes, half notes, quarter notes, eighth notes, etc.)?[29]

What follows is an attempt to demonstrate that in less than two or three years the Soviet composer will lay his hands on a flawless and obedient mechanism for the realization of his boldest artistic visions, a sort of universal "super-orchestra, conducted by the composer himself," unlimited in its virtuosity, expressiveness, accuracy of tuning, assortment of sounds (including wholly invented sounds)—a veritable "world of tomorrow" in music.[30]

"Synthemusic" knows no technical limitations—neither in tuning, nor in timbre, nor in degree of virtuosity: it masters with *uniform facility* the Javanese equally-tempered five-note scale (just try singing it!), the 22-note Indian scale, my own 48-note Welttonsystem or any absolutely pure mathematical tuning, and all sorts of Busonian "thirds" or "sixths," because the whole "problem" comes down to a series of "arithmetical operations" or—in extreme cases—a logarithmic table (for tempering).[31]

Synthetic music requires no arrangements: you could write a piece for a *tari* (using the 17-note scale as the basis for melody and harmony) as complex as you like—with modulations and variations spanning the full register of the piano—perhaps for an imaginary quartet of variously tuned *tari*. So long as you have managed to transcribe your music properly (in terms of intonations) Sholpo and Yankovsky will "synthesize" it for you in three to four days, and you will be able to hear today what—given the normal progress of historical evolution—you might not have heard for another half century.[32]

What we are doing amounts to a bona fide *revolution* on the musical-technological front."[33]

To be sure, what emerges is a familiar theme: the technical limitations of human musicians and their instruments stand in the way of a universal tonal system, which can be truly expressed only with the assistance of a device designed specifically for the task. The sound synthesizer is capable of giving voice to a musical composition, providing an unmediated (i.e., performerless) realization of a musical idea. The idea resides in the graphic representation of sound, in its geometrical form. Thus, the search for sounds not found in the established "sound culture" of the time, but that nevertheless occur everywhere in the natural environment, points toward the geometrical forms. Consequently, the first order of business would be to investigate the sounds of the Euclidean shapes: the circle, the triangle, the rectangle, the trapezoid.

In other words, we are dealing with a universal system, capable of accelerating the evolution of musical culture, combining all existing achievements of East and West, allowing for an immediate and unmediated (i.e., unhampered by human and technological limitations) realization of an aesthetic idea of un-limited complexity, built up from only a handful of basic sound elements, whose meaning is embedded in their graphic (geometrical) form. By the 1930s, this purely futurist way of thinking would require a certain measure of rhetorical camouflage, as in, "Is this futurism?" Indeed, it was.

Each of the three men, as we have mentioned, followed a different path to-ward the realization of "unmediated" sound. But for all the differences in their technical solutions and practical results, the essence of the project was shared. In cinema, the idea of performance had always been opposed to that of synchrony. The mechanical synchronization of "naturophotographic" cinema (a disparaging term, coined by Tsekhanovsky) would invariably produce a dual overtone: either by synthesizing the outward mechanical synchrony with the intra-filmic asyn-chrony or by attaining absolute synchrony at the level of instant photography by combining the phenomenological balance of forces operating within the "frame" with certain photogrammic processes.

The first approach found perfectly adequate realization in the "Sound Mani-festo" of Sergei Eisenstein, Vsevolod Pudovkin, and Grigori Alexandrov, which appeared as early as 1928. The asynchrony of image and sound as an aesthetic principle, promulgated in that document, reduced sound to the status of a mere constituent, no more than a mechanical device, in the overall montage structure of the film. This method—a fundamentally conservative one, aimed at preserv-ing the earlier achievements of montage in the silent era—was appropriate for the very brief transitional period from silent to sound film. Its aesthetic potential hardly exceeded that of monochrome color-separation plates.

It took someone with a daring imagination and disdain for common wisdom to discover the powerful reserve of driving forces in the absolute synchrony of image and sound, and to prove that it alone stands as the foundation of the "dy-namic structure" of cinema.

Using his experience as an animator, Tsekhanovsky went on to make two "naturophotographic" sync-sound films: *Pacific 231* (dir. Mitry, 1949) and *Gopak* (Hopak), though little is known about the latter film. The expressive use of the sound-image combination in these films is rivaled only by A. Alekseev's *Noch' na Lysoi gore* (Night on Bald Mountain). Evidently, Tsekhanovsky was also the first to write about the potential of Avraamov's approach, though he did not experi-ment with it directly. In 1930, the journal *Kino i zhizn'* (Cinema and Life) pub-lished his article "O zvukovoi risovannoi fil'me" (On the Animated Sound Film). He writes:

> The other strictly cinematographic advantage [of animation over "naturophoto-
> graphic" cinema]—one stemming not from the method of production but from the
> material specificity of the animated film—is the absolute freedom it affords the artist

to transform and manipulate the visible object, not only with respect to its outward appearance, but (far more importantly) with respect to the *dynamic* structure of the film itself (i.e.[,] the very heart of the film art). It is true that naturophotographic cinema sometimes resorts to slow-motion or time-lapse photography to compensate for this deficiency, but such mechanical surrogates are manifestly devoid of any aesthetic significance.

Likewise, the animated film has all the advantages when it comes to cinema's fundamental structuring principle—i.e. *montage*.[34]

Tsekhanovsky justly contends that even the most successful of montage juxtapositions in naturophotographic cinema are 95 percent accidental, lacking figural precision. For this reason, the most inventive directors use mirror-image inversions or cut together relatively static shots (see *October* or *The Old and the New* for the former, and *Arsenal* and *Earth* for examples of the latter[35]) to minimize the accidental nature of the cut:

The editing of the animated film is an entirely different process. At the highest level, we might not even consider montage as a distinct element of animated film production. There is no fundamental distinction between the juxtaposition of two shots in an edited sequence and that of two animation cells. Montage begins with the second cell: consequently, the entire editing process of the animated film may be *devised upfront* and *executed* with utmost precision.

. . . In other words: the animated film goes beyond the mere synchronization of image and sound, attaining an extraordinary degree of rhythmic cohesion between the sound track and the image track—something that is hardly attainable in photographic cinema.

. . . With the advent of the so-called "animated" or graphic method of sound recording (presently being developed by Arseny Avraamov in Moscow and comrades Sholpo and Rimsky-Korsakov in Leningrad), we are given an even more perfect means of creating sound animated films: now the visual track and the sound track will be composed in parallel, from the first frame to the last.[36]

Avraamov's method could accommodate, naturally and systematically, the universalist-cosmogonic aspirations of the artistic movements of the 1910s; the futurist efforts to "compress time" through the unmediated language of thought-sensations, composed of graphic-symbolic representations of the sounds of transrational speech and oriented at once toward the past and the future; and the communist idea of a revolutionary science. This conceptual atmosphere was remarkably fertile ground for the cinema of the early 1930s, or the age of sound exploration.

In contrast to the synchronously reproduced "asynchrony" advanced in the aforementioned manifesto by Eisenstein and others, Avraamov proposed an alternative revolutionary trajectory for the development of sound film, based on the principle of synchrony between the basic elements of film image and film sound, with the latter assuming an archaic photogrammic form (recorded without the mediation of a microphone). This approach literally materializes the balance between the three primary movements of objects inside the frame: horizontal, vertical, and perpendicular to the plane of the frame (i.e., the sum of the first two movements, represented by the object's increasing or decreasing in size). Even the main attraction of sound cinema—synchronously filmed human speech—was subjected to a phenomenological dissection.

Avraamov narrated his accomplishments in the article "Sintonfil'ma" (Syntonefilm), which appeared in a 1932 issue of the journal *Proletarskoe kino* (Proletarian Cinema):

> At this time there can be no doubt that the three-dimensional spatial coordinate system is absolutely coincident with the sound coordinate system. Music distinguishes sounds with respect to pitch, intensity, duration and timbre. What happens when we translate these qualities into the language of visual images? [NB: materialized through a technological device! —N.I.]
>
> 1. A subject's movement directly toward the viewer (i.e. along the axis perpendicular to the plane of the screen) corresponds to a rise in *volume* of the accompanying sound.
> 2. Movement along the perpendicular (vertical) axis in the plane of the screen corresponds to changes in *pitch*.
> 3. Movement along the horizontal (left to right or right to left) or the temporal axis corresponds to the *duration* of the sound.
> 4. The change of the object itself corresponds to a change in *timbre* or the coloration of the sound (this variable assumes even greater dimension in color cinema).
>
>   Taking as our starting point this simple and perfectly objective system (since its correspondences are universally true), we can even develop a purely "subject-less, ornamental" screen, corresponding to any musical composition (in a manner quite different from Ivens' treatment of Brahms' dance).[37] [Evidently an error: the author is surely referring to Oscar Fischinger's 1931 film *Hungarian Dances— Study #9*, which made use of Brahms's music. —N. I.]

Responding to widely circulated rumors that his team had been able to artificially re-create Lenin's voice, Avraamov remarks:

> To be sure, we are still far from "resurrecting Lenin," just as we are far from hatching a homunculus in a test tube and asking it to deliver a speech at the Udarnik. Our little one is still working on "mama" and "dada": we are carrying out a graphic analysis of the discrete elements of human speech, and solving problems along the way that reach beyond *syntonecinema*. It turns out that no systematic analysis of this sort has been carried out in linguistics, and very little of it in acoustics; for the most part we are starting from scratch and discovering (genuine!) Americas in "language science":

for example, a reclassification of classic "vowels" (hard, soft) and "consonants" (spirants, sibilants, etc.) considerably simplifies the problem, reducing all "consonants" to four graphic types and all "vowels" to just two. All others are derived from the combination of these six primary elements.[38]

And for all the "universality" of these discoveries, they were also well suited to the social mandate of the day: "The 'Symphony of Sirens' is being constructed out of right triangles, and it will be more harmonious and more powerful than my 'documentary' siren symphonies, performed in Moscow and Baku (for the 5th and 6th anniversaries of the Revolution). For the 'International' we especially like the timbre of squares and rectangles—no natural recording could produce such singular and forceful sounds. Trapezoids and isosceles triangles produce softer, more 'lyrical' colors: they will be used in the 'Funeral March.'"[39] No social mandate was ever issued, however.

Even in the West, the technology of graphic sound never developed past the artisanal stage. Rather, some time later, electronic instruments proved more practical in the creation of artificial sound.

Notes

1. Drawn-on-film animation, also known as direct animation or animation without a camera, is an animation technique whereby footage is produced by creating images directly on film stock, as opposed to other forms of animation in which the images are photographed frame by frame with an animation camera.

2. The best-known practitioners of drawn-on-film animation include Len Lye, Norman McLaren, and Stan Brakhage; later artists who produced numerous animated films using these methods include Steven Woloshen, Richard R. Reeves, and Baerbel Neubauer.

3. B. Balázs, *Iskusstvo kino* (Moscow: Goskinoizdat, 1945), 133.

4. S. Bugoslavskii, in *Mul'tiplikatsionnyi fil'm* (Moscow, Kinoizdat, 1936), 276–86; I. Ivanov-Vano, *Kadr za kadrom* (Moscow: Iskusstvo, 1980).

5. N. Izvolov, "Moment ozhivleniia spiashchei idei," *Kinovedcheskie zapiski* 15 (1992): 290–96.

6. A. Avraamov, "Sinteticheskaia muzyka," *Sovetskaia muzyka* 8 (1939): 70–71; reprinted in *Kinovedcheskie zapiski* 53 (2001): 324–33. All citations refer to the original publication.

7. See, e.g., V. Grigor'ev, "Pionery leningradskoi mul'tiplikatsii," in *Iz istorii Lenfil'ma*, 2nd ed. (Leningrad: Iskusstvo, 1970), 207; T. Likhacheva, "Iz vospominanii proshlykh let," in *Zhizn' v kino: Veterany o sebe i svoikh tovarishchakh*, 4th ed. (Moscow: Iskusstvo, 1994), 27.

8. Bugoslavsky's article, mentioned earlier, contains fairly detailed accounts of the different technologies.

9. Ven. Vishnevskii, *25 let sovetskogo kino* (Moscow: Goskinozdat, 1945), 52.

10. See B. Yankovskii, "Akusticheskii sintez muzykal'nykh krasok," *Kinovedcheskie zapiski* 53 (2001): 353–68.

11. *Soiuzkinozhurnal*, no. 28 (sound version), 1933, RGAKFD, fond no. 4336.

12. Balázs, *Iskusstvo kino*, 111.

13. During the Second World War and the Siege of Leningrad very few cinematographers remained active in the besieged Leningrad and made film documentaries about the heroic fight against the Nazis. Most personnel and production units of the Lenfil'm studio were evacuated to cities in Central Asia, such as Alma-Ata (in 1942) and Samarkand. There Lenfil'm temporarily merged with other Soviet film studios into the Central United Film Studio (Tsentral'naia Ob'edinennaia kinostudiia, or TsOKS, 1941–44). Lenfil'm returned to Leningrad in 1944.

14. Z. Lissa, *Estetika kinomuzyki* (Moscow: Muzyka, 1970), 340. (The book first appeared in Polish in 1964; a German translation was published in 1965.) The cited passage preserves the orthography of the Soviet edition.

15. Lissa, *Estetika kinomuzyki,* 346.

16. Ivanov-Vano, *Kadr za kadrom,* 92.

17. V. Solev, "Absolute Music by Designed Sound," *American Cinematographer* (April 1936): 146–48, 154–55.

18. "Conceived and performed by a group of Futurists calling themselves The Donkey's Tale, the film *Drama in the Futurist Cabaret, No. 13* (no extant prints known) was, to believe the leading Futurist figure David Burliuk (who may have been one of those involved in the production), 'a drastic parody of the cinematic Grand Guignol, a widespread genre in those years.'" See Yuri Tsivian, "Russia 1913: Cinema in the Cultural Landscape," in *Silent Film,* ed. Richard Abel (New Brunswick, NJ: Rutgers University Press, 1996), 209.

19. V. Khlebnikov, *Tvoreniia* (Moscow, Sovetskii pisatel', 1987), 646–47.

20. Ibid., 621.

21. Ibid., 621–22.

22. Ibid., 628.

23. Ibid., 633–34.

24. Ibid., 634.

25. See Roman Jakobson, *Noveishaia russkaia poezia. Nabrosok pervyi: podstupy k Khlebnikovu.* (Prague: Politika, 1921).

26. E. Sholpo, "Iskusstvennaia fonogramma na kinoplenke kak tekhnicheskoe sredstvo muzyki," ed. N. A. Izvolov, with A. S. Deriabin, *Kinovedcheskie zapiski* 53 (2001): 334–35, 340.

27. Avraamov, *Sinteticheskaia muzyka,* 71–72.

28. Ibid., 68.

29. Ibid.

30. Ibid., 68–69.

31. Ibid., 74.

32. Ibid., 73–74.

33. Ibid., 72.

34. M. Tsekhanovskii, "O zvukovoi risovannoi fil'me," *Kino i zhizn'* 34–35 (1930): 14.

35. Eisenstein's *Oktiabr'* (October [Ten Days That Shook the World], 1928) and *Staroe i novoe* (The Old and the New, 1929), and Dovzhenko's *Arsenal* (1929) and *Zemlia* (Earth, 1930).

36. Tsekhanovskii, "O zvukovoi risovannoi fil'me," 14–15.

37. A. Avraamov, "Sintonfil'ma," *Proletarskoe kino* 9–10 (1933): 49.

38. Ibid., 50–51.

39. Avraamov, "Sintonfil'ma," 47.

2 Silents, Sound, and Modernism in Dmitry Shostakovich's Score to *The New Babylon*

Joan Titus

ALTHOUGH WIDELY REGARDED by scholars and general audiences as one of the greatest of the last "silent" films, *Novyi Vavilon* (New Babylon, dir. Kozintsev and Trauberg, 1929) was initially a surprising failure. Even with its original score by the celebrated composer Dmitry Shostakovich, the film failed to fully satisfy audiences and critics at the time of its premiere. Since then, the musical score has been blamed for this initial failure, even though it was intended to be a significant contribution to a work that was designed to be innovative, properly socialist, and entertaining. This narrative, still spun in recent writings about the score, rarely acknowledges that this failure involved intertwining cultural and political issues related to the restructuring of the Soviet film industry and the establishment of a new relationship between sound and image.[1] The score to *New Babylon* was created to explore this new relationship, which signaled the reevaluation of the musician's role in music for cinema. Since *New Babylon* was the first Soviet film to have a full original score written by a professional Russian composer, Shostakovich's compositional process was closely observed and necessarily required a collaborative effort between the composer and the directors Grigory Kozintsev and Leonid Trauberg. The composer's process was therefore a central issue during the film's production.[2] Examining this collaborative process, through the directors' and composer's writings about the music for *New Babylon* and the film's reception, reveals much about perceptions of modernism and socialism in the whole work.

Changes in Soviet film policy in 1928 and the modernist inclination of the directors both played significant roles in the creation of *New Babylon* and its score. The Party Conference on Cinema of March 1928 limited the scope of film politics and required cinema to be profitable, entertaining, and socialist while also being "intelligible to the millions."[3] This conference and other official declarations also addressed the integral role of music for moving pictures, requiring it to be created by "highly qualified musicians."[4] In August 1928, the well-known

"Statement on Sound" followed, in which directors Sergey Eisenstein, Grigori Alexandrov, and Vsevolod Pudovkin argued for the integration of sound and image; it also revealed their fear of sound's potential to rob the images of their privileged ability to create meaning.[5] *New Babylon* was released on the heels of this statement, in March 1929. It marked Shostakovich's first experience in writing a film score and the last silent film by the Factory of the Eccentric Actor (FEKS), a group formed by Kozintsev and Trauberg that engaged modernist trends in the visual arts.[6] The film was representative of its time. The directors used some of the same modernist techniques of their past films while also attempting to develop a story deemed applicable to current Soviet art politics.[7]

Shostakovich and the directors desired a musical counterpart—that is, an "integral" score—that would support the techniques and narrative of the visual component of the film.[8] They each theorized how the music should be integral in their writings and revealed how they collaboratively dealt with musical form and film editing, the creation of recurring motifs, and the usage of musical styles to represent characters. Broadly speaking, this collaboration and Shostakovich's innovative score helped to shape the role of the composer in early Soviet film scoring.

The pre- and post-premiere reception adds another layer of complexity to the production politics of the film. Articles in the press and unpublished discussions from Lenfil'm studio meetings and screenings revealed multiple perspectives on *New Babylon*'s success and how it related to current concerns for socialist themes in cinema. This reception was also dependent on the quality and level of cooperation of the cinema conductors and performers, some of whom were hesitant to accept a newly composed score. Such documents illuminate how the film's codification as a formalist failure was dependent upon its perceived immediate success and failure, as determined by the studio, cinema houses, and the press.

The creative process of the film and its score, together with the issues of its reception, were therefore deeply affected by contemporaneous art politics. My discussion in this chapter addresses how *New Babylon* musically and cinematically represents FEKS's last "eccentric" film while also pointing to future socialist realist trends in both filmmaking and film music. A focused analysis of notable moments in the score to the film, guided by the writings of Kozintsev, Trauberg, and Shostakovich, and informed by studio documents and press reception, forms the core of the discussion. This reading of the eccentric socialism of *New Babylon* ultimately reveals that things modernist and socialist were closely connected throughout this period—instead of opposed to one another—illustrating the complexity of the politics of Soviet music written specifically for film.[9]

Inspired by the work of Émile Zola, Friedrich Engels, and Karl Marx, Kozintsev and Trauberg designed a story using the Paris Commune of 1871 as a metaphor for the proletarian struggle of the late 1920s.[10] The story of the commune was well known at the time and has been referred to as the "official mythology."[11] Their primary aim was to provide a positive portrayal of the "dictatorship of the proletariat" by comparing it with a corrupt French bourgeoisie. The result was a historical drama and proletariat lesson that attempted to educate and entertain its viewers—a tall order in a time when few Soviet-made educational films existed, the majority of which lacked the entertainment value of a Charlie Chaplin or Harry Piel film. The comparison of the bourgeoisie and the Communards was achieved through character typage and Soviet montage, techniques common to such films of the time, including *Bronenosets Potemkin* (Battleship Potemkin, dir. Eisenstein, 1925). Since historical films had "predictable *fabula* [story] with unpredictable narration," the innovation of *New Babylon* would be found in its presentation.[12] This presentation includes typing and montage, which help to define the two central characters (Louise and Jean) and classes (workers and bourgeoisie) of this eight-reel film. Louise is a saleswoman at the New Babylon department store who later becomes a passionate Communard; the soldier Jean is an average peasant-farmer who finds himself enlisted in the National Army to fight in the Franco-Prussian War and, eventually, the bourgeoisie's battle against the Communards.[13] Initially apolitical and romantically interested in each other, both characters eventually become involved in opposite sides of the class war and act as its typed representatives. In the last scene, Jean does nothing but watch Louise's judgment and execution by firing squad while digging her grave. Although finally executed at the Père Lachaise Cemetery, the Paris Commune is celebrated in this film as a symbol of the struggle of the working class.

New demands in film policy required "intelligibility" both in film and in scoring. As a response to the 1928 Party Conference demands that highly qualified musicians be used for film scoring,[14] the Lenfil'm studio branch of Sovkino specifically set out to hire Shostakovich for *New Babylon* because he was a young professional composer of international repute, and one of the "most talented and interesting young Soviet composers" of his time.[15] At this point, Shostakovich had already experienced worldwide success with his Symphony No. 1 (1924–25), and had finished his Symphony No. 2, *Dedication to October* (1927).[16] Regardless, the members of the studio administration were unsure of his skills as a film composer and hired a consultant, film-theater director and compiler Mikhail Vladimirovich Vladimirov, to ensure a "competent showing" of the score.[17] Kozintsev related an alternate perspective on Shostakovich's hiring, in which he focused on how he and Shostakovich musically fit together.[18] After reportedly having seen a rehearsal of the *The Nose*, an opera that revealed the composer's ability to musicalize the grotesquerie of Nikolai Gogol's story, Kozintsev decided that Shostakovich would be the perfect composer for *New Babylon*.[19]

In their writings, Kozintsev and Trauberg highlighted the collaborative process between themselves and the composer:

Our thoughts were the same: not to illustrate the frames, but give them a new quality and range. The music should be composed to go against the action of the film, revealing the inner meaning of the occurrences. That was not the only thing we thought up! The *Marseillaise* should shift into *La belle Hélène*, great tragic themes contrast with bawdy cancans and galops.[20]

In an interview from 1984, Trauberg confirmed that there was an agreement between the composer and himself regarding the alignment of musical and cinematic ideas:

He [Shostakovich] knew where the cancan and the funeral march should be. . . .
I thought of mixing the cancan with the *Marseillaise* and Shostakovich just wrote it
down like that. . . . [A]ll he needed was a list with the length of the scenes.[21]

The three appeared to agree that music should specifically complement the film, as echoed in the "Statement on Sound." This statement, written in August 1928 by Eisenstein, Pudovkin, and Alexandrov, sought to theorize a role for sound in film that would allow the integrity of the Soviet montage style to be preserved and offered suggestions on how to synthesize image and sound. Such ideas led to new concepts such as the film composer and montage score, as a contemporaneous musicologist noted.[22] Kozintsev, Trauberg, and Shostakovich were clearly aware of these arguments and sought to craft an original score that played an integral role in the creation of meaning, even if it was for a silent film.[23] Having a specially composed original score for a Russian film written by a professional composer was therefore relatively exceptional at the time. As far as the directors, the composer, and the administration of the Lenfil'm studio were concerned, *New Babylon* was intended to represent the new future of cinema and music.[24]

Kozintsev's writings evince a desire for a meaningful original score that avoided the contemporaneous practices of individual improvisation or orchestral compilations, and attempted to portray what he designated as the "inner meaning" of a film.[25] A parallel is found in Shostakovich's own words and music. In an article published just before the premiere of the film, Shostakovich protested against musical hackwork in the cinema, where pieces of music were cobbled together to illustrate the film.[26] He declared, "Lack of space does not allow me to write further about so-called film music manuals (musical bits for tears, uprising, corrupt bourgeoisie, love, and so forth). I will say one thing: that this is such hackwork [*khaltura*], if not worse."[27] Instead of *khaltura*, he suggested that music should reflect and be guided by the individual film, and should strive to portray its "inner meaning":

The only correct path was to write special music, as it has been done, if I am not
mistaken, in one of the first instances with *New Babylon*. When composing music to
Babylon, I was guided least of all by the principle of mandatory illustration of every

shot. Mainly, I began from the principal shot in each sequence of shots. [Take,] for example, the end of the second part.[28] The primary moment is the attack of the German cavalry on Paris. The part ends with a deserted restaurant. Total silence. But the music, despite the fact that the German cavalry is not shown on the screen, comes from the cavalry all the same, reminding the viewer of the impending menacing force.[29]

Shostakovich proposed two principles in this article, which was the first of his writings to elaborate his theory of composing for film. The first, the principle of the shot or scene, involves music that symbolizes the general meaning of an entire scene; the second, his principle of contrasts, requires music that closely follows the rhythms of the shots, which may contradict the overall tone of the scene. Shostakovich demonstrated each principle with examples of original and borrowed music related to image and narrative.

Shostakovich's examples for the first principle show various approaches to music as a dominant narrative force within a scene. The first example concerns the attack of the German cavalry on Paris, as related earlier. The music associated with the German cavalry guides the scene, first appearing with images of the cavalry at the beginning and reappearing at the end without these images. Having this music for the German cavalry reappear without its initial referent was intended to conjure the image of the cavalry and to represent war, thus making music the primary agent of meaning that drives the scene. The second example concerns the musical depiction of "the somber sentiments of the soldier" in part 7, wherein Jean attempts to find Louise but instead encounters the partying bourgeoisie.[30] The music for this scene is anempathetic: it contrasts significantly with the musical characterization of the bourgeoisie, but it aptly evokes Jean's mental state after he fails to find his beloved.[31] By concentrating on Jean's emotional state or generalizing the concept of war, Shostakovich actively employed the principle of the shot or scene, avoiding the objective and disconnected associations that were typically found in the technique of musical "illustration."

The elements of contrast and contradiction found in Shostakovich's first principle similarly permeate Kozintsev's essays. Kozintsev often emphasized how contradiction and "visual 'alliteration'" underscore the themes of this film:

> The frames not only engage semantic synthesis, but many elements of the plastic arts (distinctive visual "alliteration"): lace on the counter and soap suds in the washtub of the laundresses; the dancing galop and the rotation of the day in the store; the fog of the garden and the steam of the laundry. Similarity of some elements are presented to contradict with contrasts of others: the abundance of "sales" and of emptiness, and the poverty of the [worker's] shops.[32]

The alliterative images that Kozintsev listed are entirely visual, with the exception of the galop. He realized the visual counterparts of the "dancing galop" and the "day in the store" through crosscutting between the cabaret and the New

[A] Train station → [B] New Babylon Department Store and its customers → [C] Manager (Boss) → [B] New Babylon Department Store and its customers → [D] Saleswoman (Louise) → (Invitation to the ball) → [B] The New Babylon store and its customers → [A] Train station

Figure 2.1. Part 1 in "blocks" as it corresponds to events in the film *New Babylon*.

Babylon store. Shostakovich found a direct musical realization of Kozintsev's visual crosscutting, emulating its structure using musical blocks, each of which represented the chaotic New Babylon store, the train station attendees, or the cabaret and contained the same busied galops every time these images appear throughout part 1. These musical blocks correspond to characters or events in separate locales, including Louise and the busy store, the manager deciding on Louise as his "dessert," and Louise receiving an invitation from the manager. The events as they correspond to musical sections appear in figure 2.1.

This part of the film is symmetrical and self-contained, corresponding to a block form, which can be expressed as ABCBDBA.[33] Both A ("Train Station") and B ("New Babylon Store") recur, acting as structural signposts throughout the part. Although they contain different sections of music that seamlessly segue into each other, both "Train Station" and "New Babylon Store" have the features of a galop, that is, 2/4 meter with offbeat rhythms. The "Train Station" section is also a galop simply by association—this galop has the same melody and key, offbeat rhythms, and meter of a musical number titled "Galop" from Shostakovich's contemporaneous satirical theater work, *Klop* (The Bedbug, 1929).[34] Shostakovich therefore added another layer to Kozintsev's alliteration by applying the principle of the shot or scene and using music that he stylistically signified as a galop.

The second half of Kozintsev's statement concerns contradiction and contrast, another parallel to Shostakovich's second principle of contrast. In his writings, Shostakovich discussed two specific scenes that exemplify this principle, the first of which is a waltz. There are only four waltzes in the score, three of which are musically different from one another; the fourth is a repetition.[35] Of these three waltzes, two are quotations from preexisting works. One waltz and its restatement in parts 2 and 4, in connection with the bourgeoisie's operetta performance, are built from quotations from Jacques Offenbach's *La belle Hélène*.[36] The third waltz, from part 6, in which the bourgeoisie are located in Versailles, is an identical quotation from Shostakovich's *The Bedbug*.[37] Since the waltzes from *La belle Hélène* and *The Bedbug* were written to be satirical, they can be read intertextually within the film as a socialist critique of bourgeois decadence and wealth.[38]

Example 2.1a. The first example corresponds to the "train station" block.

A different form of satire operates in the final appearance of the waltz, which Shostakovich described as "frantic" and "obscene."[39] In this instance, a collision of multiple meanings to create the "satirically grotesque" results from the depiction of two events: Jean's internal crisis at the end of the battle and the celebrating bourgeoisie.[40] In tandem with the film's crosscuts between the battle in Paris (where Jean is situated) and the bourgeoisie in Versailles (who watch the battle like it is an operetta to be enjoyed) the music incrementally builds into a crescendo, hitting a climax as Jean turns to the distant bourgeoisie "filled with despair."[41] Until that point, the music had been characterized by asymmetrical phrase groupings and rhythms, internal cadences, and all the signifiers of *waltz* that had been presented earlier in the film. These textures and meanings build and finally coincide with the image of Jean turning to face the applauding bourgeoisie, who are too far away to see his internal crisis.[42] The editing and music, however, encourage the viewer to empathize with Jean, resulting in an effect of the satirical grotesque that represents the composer's and directors' objective of moving beyond the usual illustration of standard compilation scores.

Example 2.1b. The second example corresponds to the "New Babylon Store" block. Segment from Manashir Yakubov, ed., *Dmitrii Shostakovich, Novoe Sobranie Sochinenii tom 122, "Novyi Vavilon," Muzyka k nemomu kinofil'mu, op.18* (The New Collected Works, *The New Babylon,* Music to the Silent Film, Op. 18) (Moscow: DSCH, 2004), 12 and 28.

The second example of the principle of contrast mentioned by Shostakovich is considerably more ambiguous but has another parallel to contemporaneous filmmaking:

> An interesting method is used in the Fourth Part. There is a rehearsal of the operetta. The music plays a rather well-known exercise by Hanon, which takes on different nuances in relation to the action. Sometimes it has a gay mood, sometimes boring, sometimes terrifying.[43]

This variation approach that Shostakovich used operates both on a large scale—that is, through the entire fourth part—and in some cases, on a small scale, such as a brief ten-measure vignette (measures 44–54) that corresponds to the dancers at the rehearsal and an officer in the countryside.[44] As Shostakovich described, he varied the "well-known exercise by Hanon" (measures 44–54), which was likely borrowed from one of the piano exercises from *The Virtuoso Pianist*, by French composer and pedagogue Charles Louis Hanon (1819–1900).[45] It may have also been borrowed from a recurring motif in act 1, no. 3, of Offenbach's *La belle*

Example 2.2. An example of Shostakovich's principle of contrast—the first three measures of the waltz that appears when the bourgeoisie applaud the solider from Versailles (strings double and are omitted). From Yakubov, *"Novyi Vavilon,"* 455.

Hélène, known as "Song of Oreste," to reflect the mood and actions of the images.[46] This small section represents the whole; it is a correlate to the multiple styles and themes used as recurring motifs within part 4 and throughout the entire score to represent specific characters or moods. The section begins with the cue "People dance at a rehearsal," with rhythms, intervals, and melodic contour most similar to Hanon's exercises 2 and 3 from *The Virtuoso Pianist,* and somewhat similar to "Song of Oreste."[47] The tonal center shifts from C to E-flat (measure 50) at the midway point of the section, where the designation "Officer smiles" appears. This cue corresponds to a visual cut to images of the countryside, where the officer smiles at his soldiers while they prepare the cannon. This specific moment and part 4 as a whole have a parallel in contemporaneous filmmaking: what Shostakovich described closely resembles a musical version of Soviet montage technique of the 1920s. Shostakovich insisted that his music had contrasts, meaning that his score follows the nuances of the action, as revealed in the film editing that corresponds to measures 44–54, rather than following the overall tone or action of a scene. His discussion directly referred to the juxtaposed images of the soldiers in the countryside (who eventually meet the Communards) and the operetta rehearsals; a montage between two different groups of people in two different locales, who are eventually brought together in Versailles. This montage is reminiscent of both D. W. Griffith's crosscutting and the "Kuleshov effect," techniques that influenced the editing processes of many filmmakers of the 1920s.[48] It is also reminiscent of the crosscutting that Kozintsev used to create the "alliterative" comparisons between the shop and the workers, described earlier. Shostakovich's music and its "different moods"—that is, its various musical styles—correspond to the cinematic montage. Shostakovich's discussion of part 4 can therefore be read as a brief moment (measures 44–54) in which the nuances of the music indicate that he emulated the editing of the scene; and it can be read more broadly as describing the multiple juxtapositions of place represented musically by juxtaposed leitmotifs or allusions to musical styles throughout the entire fourth part.[49] This approach to musical juxtaposition resonates with Shostakovich's principle of contrasts and implies that he followed the rhythm of the film (i.e., its editing style) instead of the scene's tone or mood. Read either on a micro or macro level, this is the first written document by Shostakovich that suggests a direct influence of the cinematic montage techniques of the period on his music.

Shostakovich's two main principles were similar to the ideas about music's role in sound film that would permeate most film theory in the decades to follow, such as Siegfried Kracauer's oft-cited notions of parallelism and counterpoint.[50] Shostakovich's principle of the shot or scene involved music that embodied the meaning of the shot or scene, whereas his principle of contrasts created music to follow the rhythm or editing of the scene and/or to contradict the primary mood a central character, as with Jean and the applauding bourgeoisie. The theorizing of these principles set Shostakovich apart from the musical-illustration improvisers and compilers, demonstrating that a composed score was indeed integral to the narrative of a film.

Following the discussion of his principles, Shostakovich reiterated his desire to avoid empty musical illustration and discussed how he chose leitmotifs to maintain what he called a "continuous symphonic tone."[51] He saw the primary goal of his music "to be in the rhythms and tempi of the film and to augment its impact"; borrowed music played a part in that continuity.[52] This conception had a parallel to Kozintsev's concept of the symphony:

> The episodes were formed in a bundle of feelings and thoughts as parts of a visual symphony. Each of these, first and foremost, has distinguished emotional [and] rhythmic character. The sinister scherzo [for] the collapse of the Second Empire;

Example 2.3. Shostakovich's variation of a "well-known exercise of Hanon." From Yakubov, "*Novyi Vavilon*," 225 (measures 44–54).

slow and sorrowful andante (siege of Paris); the gleeful theme of liberation (of the Commune); the stormy melody of the struggle; the requiem of the end. Thus, the real contour of the conception gradually appears.[53]

Although Kozintsev's musical conceptualization of the film-as-symphony refers to the dramatic tone of the work, it has resonance with Shostakovich's notion of his score-as-symphony. Shostakovich strove to maintain the "continuous symphonic tone" that he associated with the symphony as a genre.[54] What results is either continuous music or a fragmented, montagist approach to the music's form that directly mirrors the action, the pacing and editing, the character development, and the emotional content in every reel of the film.[55] To maintain this continuity, Shostakovich stated that he used the "leitmotif," implying a nineteenth-century and specifically Wagnerian practice, quarrying from "dances of the epoch (waltz, cancan), a few of which use melodies from Offenbach's operettas," among other tunes.[56] These statements are verified in the score; he utilized specific tunes and excerpts from Offenbach's operettas.[57] The waltz, for example, was a "dance of the epoch" that he evoked several times to represent the partying bourgeoisie, whereas other melodies were borrowed from Offenbach's *La belle Hélène* and his *The Bedbug*.

Shostakovich also used "French folk and revolutionary ('Ça ira' and 'La carmagnole') songs" throughout the score to maintain a link to both the French revolutionary past and to common 1920s Soviet theater practice.[58] He asserted that "La Marseillaise" represents Versailles (the bourgeoisie), while "La carmagnole" and "Ça ira" appear in strong connection with the Communards.[59] Of the three French songs, the "Marseillaise" is prominent throughout and, as Shostakovich wrote, "sometimes appears in the most unexpected interpretations (cancan, waltz, galop, and so forth)."[60] The "Marseillaise" appears in partial statements in parts 3 and 4 to symbolize the defeat of the Communard Army and in a full statement in part 5 to foreshadow the battle.[61]

This statement of the "Marseillaise" is a clear example of Shostakovich's principle of the shot or scene, whereby the music aligns itself with the scene, "anchoring" the meaning—that is, using *ancrage*, to borrow Roland Barthes's terminology.[62] In the scene set in Versailles just before the battle, an actress-singer at the bourgeoisie's operetta climbs upon a table, rifle in hand, to lead the bar full of the National Army and the bourgeoisie in a rendition of the "Marseillaise," as indicated by italicized intertitles that quote the lyrics of the song. Yet after a full orchestral statement is made to accompany the actress-singer, the horns begin a second statement of the tune in C major layered over a string statement of Offenbach's "Cancan in B-flat Major" from *Orphée aux enfers*, thereby colliding associations of war (horns, the "Marseillaise") with associations of decadence and the bourgeoisie (cancan) that had already built up separately throughout the score.

Example 2.4. Continuation of *Marseillaise* quotation from part 5. At this point, the *Marseillaise*, in the horn, is layered over a statement of Offenbach's cancan in the strings (flute, oboe, and lower strings are tacet or doubling in this section, and are omitted). From Yakubov, "*Novyi Vavilon*," 349 (measures 286–89).

These two quotations merge into a variation based on both musical ideas. Shostakovich used instrumentation (brass versus strings) and key (bitonality) to differentiate between the tunes, calling attention to their differences and their meanings, while creating a musical transition from the full statement of the "Marseillaise." The music of the cancan and the "Marseillaise" was likely composed to coincide with the images and intertitles of "Paris the gay" and "Paris the carefree" intertwined with images of the legs of cancan dancers cut from earlier reels of the film and shots of the singer at the bar. The musical equivalent of this crosscutting, or montage of images of different locales, is reflected in Shosta-kovich's sensitive reworking and layering of the "Marseillaise" and the cancan. The superimposition of these tunes acts as an aural complement to the visual segue from the specific space of the bar scene to the general idea of the bourgeoi-sie. The simultaneity of, yet stark difference between, both tunes emulates the ed-iting and the juxtaposition of the images while also representing the main idea of the scene, thus illustrating Shostakovich's principle of the shot or scene and prin-ciple of contrast. The resulting effect is the mirroring of the horizontal montage on the screen with vertically layered musical ideas. At the same time, the music abides by Kozintsev's notion of contrast and irony; he wrote, "Great tragic themes contrast with bawdy cancans and galops."[63] The "Marseillaise" and the cancan are both firmly associated with the defeat of the Paris Commune and the cor-ruption of the bourgeoisie by this point in the film, but the contrast between the two themes themselves—a patriotic idea and a tune associated with the evocative dancing of Parisian music halls—could be read as a commentary on the insincer-ity of the bourgeoisie. The layering of these two themes therefore serves several functions: it cyclically refers to the party scenes from the earlier reels of the film while also representing the images of the current scene, thus anchoring the im-ages on the screen while simultaneously foreshadowing the eventual victory of the bourgeoisie, whose sense of patriotism is insincere and misdirected. Layered music, which references specific musical codes associated with the themes of the film and comments on the actions of characters, ably reflects Shostakovich's in-tentions of an actively engaged musical score.

As the writings by Shostakovich and the directors have shown, the score was in-tended to be "integral" instead of merely illustrative. Although, similar to compilers, Shostakovich borrowed music from the past, his desire was to attend to the image with greater specificity—to integrate image and music—as opposed to producing spontaneous and generalized responses to the images. These efforts, however, did not guarantee an overwhelmingly positive reception for the music or the film.

Recent and contemporaneous writings alike have claimed that Shostakov-ich's music was the source of the film's failure, whether it was copying errors, lack of rehearsal and eventual alignment with the film, or the musical complex-ity of the score.[64] These factors, however, were not the only reasons for the film's presumed failure. Contemporaneous arguments about the appropriate "Soviet" quality or the intelligibility of cinema were applied to *New Babylon*; as a result, its reception was complex and varied. As Kozintsev retrospectively related in his book *Glubokii ekran* (The Deep Screen), there were multiple points of view on the usefulness, intelligibility, and success of the film.[65] The variety of opinions about the content and the style of the film revealed that critics, film workers, and the public at large were still unclear as to whom the cinema served and what was "intelligible" and permissible in Soviet cinema.

The issue of intelligibility was no doubt clouded by the terrible performances of Shostakovich's score in the premiere of the film in certain theaters. As Yuly Vainkop related:

> An overly enthusiastic cinema entrepreneur was too hasty in sounding the alarm about Dmitry Shostakovich's music to the film *New Babylon*, by ascribing the film's failure to the young composer's supposedly unsuccessful music. This classic maneuver of shifting the blame onto someone else's shoulders should have met with the appropriate rebuff, particularly since this accusation is supported by many cinema conductors deprived of "royalties" for their musical-illustrational compilations due to the presence of a ready score. . . .
>
> This music is played horribly everywhere, although to be fair we should say that M[ikhail] V[ladimirovich] Vladimirov (conductor at the Picadilly cinema) treated it with more care than the rest, achieving the most piquancy and expressiveness and the fewest mistakes and [least] tempo confusion.[66]

Others also related that the performances at theaters in Leningrad and Moscow were unsuccessful. Lev Arnshtam related how badly Shostakovich's music was performed, claiming that the composer ran from theater to theater only to find that orchestras were nearly destroying his score.[67] As Vainkop suggested, however, Shostakovich's music was not necessarily to blame. Since the music was given to theater orchestras, like those of the Picadilly and Gigant cinemas, only days before the premiere, conductors were generally unable to rehearse the orchestras well.[68] Orchestras such as these were unaccustomed to performing specially tailored scores of this level of difficulty, which left much work to be done on the part of the conductor. The music itself was otherwise deemed to be intelligible and of high quality. The administration of Sovkino screened the film almost a month before its premiere and recommended evaluating Shostakovich's music through a performance of it with the screenings of the film. As Sovkino related:

> His music is distinguished by its considerable closeness to the style and rhythm of the film, by great emotional strength and expressivity. The effect of the picture is greatly heightened. Furthermore, despite the originality and freshness of the form, the music is sufficiently simple and can be appreciated by the mass viewer.[69]

After the film's premieres in Moscow and Leningrad, most critics found the score to be successful, especially in fulfilling the party's directives for the new Soviet film. As reviewer M. Gartsman claimed, "Dmitry Shostakovich carried out the instructions of the Party assembly: his music is an integral part of the film. And we will add, one of the best parts."[70] This reviewer and others also praised Shostakovich for his ability to fuse image and sound. They also positively noted his ability to evoke the ideology of the film specific to the historical era through revolutionary songs, such as the "Marseillaise." The idea of the music being "one of the best parts" is further supported by surveys taken by Sovkino at workers' clubs, which are currently housed in the Gosfil'm archive.[71] Most of the audience at these clubs enjoyed the film and its music, ranking the music alongside their usual favorite elements: cinematography and the performances of the actors. Shostakovich's music was therefore received well and considered intelligible by the studio and by audiences at some venues before and after the film's premiere screenings.

Yet, critic Kliment Korchmaryov found fault with the score, claiming:

> Shostakovich, a very talented person, came to this work without enough care; he obviously wrote the music hurriedly, [and] as a result of that, it emerged uneven in quality and style; among the simple, even primitive presentation of the borrowed material (the "Marseillaise," the "Carmagnole," fragments from the operettas of Offenbach), there was much muddled atonal music, which was difficult to perceive. The most successful music [belonged] to the first part, where the composer emphasizes the dynamics of the film language well.[72]

Korchmarev's mixed review focused mostly on the "uneven quality" of the work, its "primitive borrowing" of musical material that led to "atonal muddle" and the "extraordinary technical complexity." He did credit Shostakovich with emphasizing the dynamics of the film language well—that is, the film's editing. Korchmarev mainly concentrated on the first part, which is likely the most easily understood reel of the film, since the blocky quality of the music mirrored the crosscutting of the reel and reflected the symmetry of the film's language, thereby resulting in montagist-sounding music. But a negative tenor dominates this review. This negative language continued into the 1930s, when film music critic Ieremia Ioffe discussed the score to *New Babylon* in connection with the "formalism" and "constructivism" of the late 1920s.[73] This criticism is also similar to that directed at the film, for multiple critics representing the Communist Youth International and from *Komsomol'skaia Pravda* described the film as "formalist," "aestheticist," "art for art's sake," and "expressionistic," all pejoratively referring to earlier modernist art practices that they felt were represented in the film's lighting, mise-en-scène, and editing.[74] Despite the generally positive reception and the attempts by the studio, directors, and composer to create an intelligible and socialist work, the aspects of cinematic and musical style initially resulted from a mixed reception that eventually became wholly negative.

Although *New Babylon* was intended to be "intelligible," its perceived stylistic modernism generated varied reactions. Reviewers complained that the film was too "formalist" or "aesthetic," using language that foreshadowed the criticism of the following decades. This often meant that the film editing was too quick and fragmented, and the shooting and lighting too dark and impressionistic for reviewers who were looking toward a new era of intelligibility and, inevitably, socialist realism. The music followed the film quite closely, as reviewers and Sovkino noted, emulating the tone, mood, tempo, and rhythm of the film editing. This approach to the composed score was relatively new for this time, since the intent of both the composer and the directors was to depict the "inner meaning" of the film, instead of merely providing simplistic musical illustration. The music was therefore as sophisticated and innovative as the music of future sound films.

Although the requirements for creating music that was integral to the film had been met, Shostakovich's score, like the film, was nonetheless received as difficult and formalist. This reception might be explained by his principle of contrast, or more specifically, his grotesque manipulation and development of borrowed material, including Offenbach's waltzes and French revolutionary songs. Shostakovich's main goal was to "intensify [the film's] impression" with his score; therefore, he also paid special attention to the interaction of aspects of film form and musical material.[75] Shostakovich managed to create a score "in the [same] tempo and the rhythm of the film," which was reflected in the montagist approach to musical form and the layering of motifs throughout the film.[76] The superimposition of the "Marseillaise" and the cancan is one example of how he created a multivalent musical equivalent to the montagist editing, realizing an approach that he theorized in both of his principles.

Some of the socialist aspects of this film are found in its content, in particular its treatment of the well-known topic of the Paris Commune. Although FEKS had made earlier films that broached socialist topics, this film was the first to use the concept of a commune and to fulfill the new requirements for film discussed in 1928. As David Bordwell has argued, *New Babylon* was one of the "historical-materialist films [that] paved the way for socialist realism in [its] use of referentiality [and] exemplary heroes."[77] Yet the "negative" topic of the Paris Commune and the manner of reinforcing a socialist agenda in *New Babylon* was not the way in which socialist realist films would develop in terms of plot.[78] Instead, the positive hero, as seen in the *Maxim Trilogy* (1934–38), was to become the stereotype for socialist realist film.[79] The mixed reception of the film and its music shows that critics, filmmakers, and the public at large disagreed as to what "Soviet" film should become.

Though *New Babylon* was one of the last modernist films of the 1920s, it had characteristics that subtly pointed to socialist realist trends that would appear several years in the future. The unsettled reception of the film and its music show that ideas about how Soviet film should be defined were quickly changing toward a new aesthetic that consciously deviated from modernism. It is no surprise that *New Babylon* was deemed one of FEKS's last modernist film experiments. Yet it was Shostakovich's first opportunity to negotiate moving image and sound and, importantly, the politics of the film industry and its developing relationship to the film composer. His next score, for the film *Odna* (Alone, dir. Kozintsev and Trauberg, 1931), was a stylistic departure from *New Babylon* and allowed him to continue to negotiate his role and to develop as a film composer, gradually adopting aspects of socialist and realist aesthetics as part of his approach to film scoring.

Notes

All translations are mine unless otherwise noted. My sincere thanks to Alexander Burry, Arndt Niesbisch, Peter Schmelz, and Gillian Anderson for their assistance and suggestions.

1. Laurel Fay, *Shostakovich: A Life* (Oxford: Oxford University Press, 2000), 50; Tatiana Egorova, *Soviet Film Music: A Historical Survey*, trans. Tatiana A. Ganf and Natalia A. Egunova (Amsterdam: Harwood Academic Publishers, 1997), 10; Elizabeth Wilson, *Shostakovich: A Life Remembered* (Princeton, NJ: Princeton University Press, 2006), 86; John Riley, *Dmitri Shostakovich: A Life in Film* (London: I. B. Tauris, 2005).

2. For a discussion of earlier attempts at original scoring in Russia and Shostakovich's role in that history, see Joan Titus, *Hearing Shostakovich: Music for Early Soviet Cinema* (Oxford: Oxford University Press, forthcoming).

3. "Party Cinema Conference Resolution: The Results of Cinema Construction in the USSR and the Tasks of Soviet Cinema," in *The Film Factory: Russian and Soviet Cinema in Documents 1896–1939*, eds. Richard Taylor and Ian Christie (London: Routledge and Kegan Paul, 1988), 208–15.

4. Ibid., 212.

5. See Sergei Eisenstein, Vsevolod Pudovkin, and Grigori Alexandrov, "Statement on Sound," in Taylor and Christie, *Film Factory*, 234.

6. For a discussion of FEKS, see Vladimir Nedobrovo, *FEKS, Grigorii Kozintsev, Leonid Trauberg* (Moscow: Kinopechat, 1928); "Introduction" and Barthelemy Amengual, "Conversation with Trauberg," in *Futurism/Formalism/FEKS: Eccentrism and Soviet Cinema 1918–1936*, ed. Ian Christie and John Gillet (London: British Film Institute, 1978): 7, 28–29; Grigorii Kozintsev, Leonid Trauberg, Sergei Yutkevich, and Grigorii Kryzhitskii, "Eccentrism," in Taylor and Christie, *Film Factory*, 58–64; Sergei Yutkevich, "Teenage Artist of the Revolution," in Luda Schnitzer, Jean Schnitzer, and Marcel Martin, *Cinema in Revolution* (New York: Da Capo Press, 1973), 11–42; Joan Titus, "Modernism, Socialist Realism, and Identity in the Early Film Music of Dmitry Shostakovich, 1929–1932" (PhD diss., Ohio State University, 2006), chap. 2.

7. According to Trauberg, the directors likely intended *New Babylon* to be "intelligible," even though they may have misunderstood what that meant. Their film style was dependent on montage technique, which was considered modernist by 1928. Leonid Trauberg, "An Experiment Intelligible to the Millions," in Taylor and Christie, *Film Factory*, 250–51.

8. The reception and performance history of *New Babylon* has been complex and controversial, and has led to multiple versions, all of which are considered here. For a detailed performance history and detailed analysis of the overall film score, see Titus, *Hearing Shostakovich*.

9. Titus, "Modernism, Socialist Realism, and Identity."

10. The development of the scenario was complex and inconsistently discussed. See Grigorii Kozintsev, *Glubokii ekran* (Moscow: Iskusstvo, 1971), 105; Leonid Trauberg, "Comment est

né 'La Nouvelle Babylone' (1978)," an extract from a letter to Miriam Tsoukandais reprinted in *L'avant-scene du cinema* 217 (December 1978): 8; "Novyi Vavilon," Gosfil'mofond: section 1, fund 2, work 1, storage unit 597 (Belye Stolby, Russia); Theodore van Houten, *Dmitri Sjostakovitsj, een leven in angst* (Westervoort, The Netherlands: Van Gruting, 2006), 67; Titus, *Hearing Shostakovich.*

11. See David Bordwell, *Narration in the Fiction Film* (Madison: University of Wisconsin Press, 1985), 250.

12. Ibid., 235.

13. Kozintsev, *Glubokii ekran*, 113.

14. "Party Cinema Conference Resolution," in Taylor and Christie, *Film Factory*, 212.

15. *Sovkino*, a shortened word for "Soviet Kino," was the state organization for film, a consolidation of local film institutions under one government-controlled organization. "Letter to Sovkino," December 7, 1928, in TSGALI SPb, f. 257, op. 5, d. 31, p. 12. See also Nina Gornitskaia, ed., *Iz istorii Lenfil'ma. Stat'i, vospominaniia, dokumenty, 1920-e gody* (From the History of Lenfil'm Studio: Articles, Reminiscences and Documents of the 1920s) (Leningrad: Iskusstvo, 1968), 252–53.

16. See Fay, *Shostakovich*, 32.

17. "Dogovor" [Agreement] from Lenfil'm Studio, January 31, 1929, in TSGALI SPB, f. 257, op. 5, d. 31, p. 29.

18. Kozintsev, *Glubokii ekran*, 120. For details on the process of the hiring of Shostakovich, see Titus, "Modernism, Socialist Realism, and Identity," chap. 3.

19. Kozintsev, *Glubokii ekran*, 120. For his impression of the rehearsal of *The Nose*, see also Grigorii Kozintsev, "Deriuga i dudochka" (Sackcloth and a Fife), in *D. Shostakovich, Stat'i i materialy* (D. Shostakovich, Articles and Materials), ed. G. M. Shneerson (Moscow: Sovetskii kompozitor, 1976), 122. See also Wilson, *Shostakovich*, 86–87.

20. Kozintsev, *Glubokii ekran*, 120. See also Wilson, *Shostakovich*, 87–88, for her translation and interpretation of this passage.

21. Interview with Trauberg, July 10, 1984, in Theodore Van Houten, *Leonid Trauberg and His Films: Always the Unexpected* ('s-Hertogenbosch: Art & Research, 1989), 150–51.

22. Vladimir Messman, "Sound Film," in Taylor and Christie, *Film Factory*, 236–37. See also Titus, "Modernism, Socialist Realism, and Identity," chaps. 2 and 3, esp. 199–20.

23. Kozintsev, "Deriuga i dudochka," 122.

24. See "New Babylon," TSGALI SPb, f. 257, op. 5, d. 31.

25. Kozintsev, *Glubokii ekran*, 120.

26. Dmitrii Shostakovich, "O muzyke k 'Novomu Vavilonu'" (On Music for *New Babylon*), *Sovetskii ekran* 11 (1929): 5. For a full translation of and essay about this article, see James Wierzbicki, Nathan Platte, and Colin Roust, eds., *The Routledge Film Music Sourcebook* (New York: Routledge, 2011), 61–64.

27. Shostakovich, "O muzyke," 5. The word *khaltura* is often translated as "trash" or "garbage." For alternate translation of this word, see Manashir Yakubov, ed., "Muzyka D. D. Shostakovicha k nemomu kinofil'mu 'Novyi Vavilon'" (Dmitrii Shostakovich's Music to the Silent Film *New Babylon*), in *Dmitrii Shostakovich: Novoe sobranie sochinenii*, vol. 122, "Novyi Vavilon" (Moscow: DSCH, 2004); Marek Pytel, *New Babylon: Trauberg, Kozintsev, Shostakovich* (London: Eccentric Press, 1999), 26.

28. I translate this as "part," but it can also be translated as "reel."

29. Shostakovich, "O muzyke," 5.

30. Ibid.

31. *Anempathetic* describes how music contradicts or plays against the meaning of the image, thus creating irony. This term was coined by Michel Chion and has been used by Claudia

Gorbman. See Claudia Gorbman, *Unheard Melodies: Narrative Film Music* (Bloomington: Indiana University Press, 1987), 159–61.

32. Kozintsev, *Glubokii ekran*, 114.

33. This form breakdown includes the "Invitation to the Ball" as part of "Saleswoman," that is, part of "D."

34. For a brief mention of this connection, see John Riley, "Myth, Parisity, and Found Music in *New Babylon*," *DSCH Journal* 4 (Winter 1995): 27; Hélène Bernatchez, *Schostakowitsch und die Fabrik des Exzentrischen Schauspielers* (Munich: Martin Meidenbauer Verlagbuchhandlung, 2006).

35. For these waltzes, see Yakubov, "Muzyka D. D. Shostakovicha," 83, 222, 388, 455. For a more detailed discussion of each of these waltzes and their origins, see Titus, *Hearing Shostakovich*.

36. See act 2, entr'acte of Jacques Offenbach, *La belle Hélène*, Chatelet Theatre Musicale de Paris/Marc Minkowski (EMI Records/Virgin Classics, 7243-5-45477-2-0, 2001), approximately forty seconds into track 1. This recording is based on the critical edition by Robert Didion, which contains sections, as in act 2, that do not appear in other editions.

37. The voicing (instrumentation) and form are different between the two works, but the key is the same (D minor and G major). Compare Yakubov, "Muzyka D. D. Shostakovicha," 387–90 (measures 109–40) and "waltz" (track 9) on Shostakovich, *Theatre Music*, which corresponds to the piano reduction of the waltz made by the composer, and "Waltz," in Dmitry Shostakovich, *Muzyka k dramaticheskim spektakliam* (*Music to Plays—For Piano*), ed. Lev Solin (Moscow: Sovetskii kompozitor, 1977), 16. Bernatchez also mentions that this waltz is like a galop from *The Bedbug*, but she fails to specify any further details. See Bernatchez, *Schostakowitsch*, 145–46.

38. Titus, *Hearing Shostakovich*; Jean-Claude Yon, liner notes to Offenbach, *La belle Hélène*; Eric Roseberry, liner notes to Dmitri Shostakovich, *Theatre Music*, Rustem Hayroudinoff (Chandos, 9907, 2001).

39. Shostakovich, "O muzyke," 5.

40. Esti Sheinberg notes that Shostakovich distorts dance genres in concert works to become relentless, clumsy, violent, and/or heavy, that is, a "satirical grotesque." Esti Sheinberg, *Irony, Satire, Parody, and the Grotesque in the Music of Shostakovich: A Theory of Musical Incongruities* (Aldershot, UK: Ashgate, 2000), 63, 210, 233–38.

41. Shostakovich, "O muzyke," 5.

42. For greater detail on the musical nuances of this scene, see Titus, *Hearing Shostakovich*, chap. 4.

43. Shostakovich, "O muzyke," 5. This particular section has been often mistranslated with the word *galop* instead of "exercise by Hanon." See Pytel, *New Babylon*, 26; Bernatchez, *Schostakowitsch*, 123, 252.

44. Yakubov, "Muzyka D. D. Shostakovicha," 225. In Yakubov's edition of the score, this music corresponds with directions from Shostakovich's manuscript, which are "People dance at a rehearsal" and "Officer smiles." See ibid.

45. Charles Louis Hanon, *The Virtuoso Pianist, in Sixty Exercises*, trans. Theodore Baker (New York: G. Schirmer, 1928).

46. The designation "act 1, no. 3" refers to the edition of *La belle Hélène* as it appears in Offenbach, *La belle Hélène* (Chatelet Theatre Musicale de Paris/Marc Minkowski). This melody from "Song of Oreste" reappears twice, for "March and Couplets for the Kings" and in the finale of act 1. See also Bernatchez, *Schostakowitsch*, 123–24.

47. Compare Yakubov, "Muzyka D. D. Shostakovicha," 225, with Hanon, *Virtuoso Pianist*, 3–4.

48. See Kuleshov's discussion of this "effect" in "Lev Kuleshov: The Origins of Montage," in Luda Schnitzer, Jean Schnitzer, and Marcel Martin, *Cinema in Revolution*, 70.

49. Yakubov, "Muzyka D. D. Shostakovicha," 225.

50. Siegfried Kracauer, *Theory of Film: The Redemption of Physical Reality* (New York: Oxford University Press, 1960).

51. Shostakovich, "O muzyke," 5.

52. Ibid.

53. Kozintsev, *Glubokii ekran*, 109.

54. Shostakovich, "O muzyke," 5.

55. Ibid.

56. Ibid.

57. Ibid.

58. Ibid.

59. Ibid.

60. Ibid.

61. See Titus, *Hearing Shostakovich*.

62. Roland Barthes, "Rhetoric of the Image," in *Image Music Text* (New York: Hill and Wang, 1997), 32–51.

63. Kozintsev, *Glubokii ekran*, 120. See also Wilson, *Shostakovich*, 87–88.

64. Fay, *Shostakovich*, 50; Egorova, *Soviet Film Music*, 10; Wilson, *Shostakovich*, 86. See also "V pravlenie Sovkino" (To the administration of Sovkino), April 8, 1929, in TSGALI SPB, f. 257, op. 5, d. 31, p. 79; David Robinson, "When Filmmaking Was All about Circus and Scandal," *London Times*, January 20, 1983, 8.

65. Kozintsev, *Glubokii ekran*, 101–2.

66. Iulii Vainkop, "Muzyka k 'Novomu Vavilonu," *Rabochii i teatr*, April 1, 1929, 9. Translation modified from Yakubov, "Muzyka D. D. Shostakovicha," 545.

67. L. Arnshtam, "Bessmertie," in *D. Shostakovich, Stat'i i materialy* (D. Shostakovich, Articles and Materials), ed. G. M. Schneerson (Moscow: Sovetskii kompozitor, 1976), 115–16.

68. Fay, *Shostakovich,* 50; Wilson, *Shostakovich*, 86.

69. Cited as "Protokol muz. soveshchaniia pri khud. biuro k/f.," February 20, 1929, TSGALI SPB, f. 257, op. 16, ed. 67, in Fay, *Shostakovich*, 50, 298 (translation by Fay).

70. M. Gartsman, "Ne plokho, no i ne sovsem eshche khorosho," *Sovetskii ekran* 15, April 9, 1929.

71. Sovkino report from "Novyi Vavilon," Gosfil'mofond: sektsia 1, f. 2, op. 1, ed. khr. 597, ll. 50–54. Although the report does not directly state that Shostakovich's music was used for the showings of the film, Shostakovich was asked to write alternate versions for piano and small ensembles for smaller venues. See "Letter to Sovkino," December 7, 1928, in TSGALI SPB, f. 257, op. 5, d. 31, p. 12; and "Pis'mo zam. direktora leningradskoi kinofabriki 'Sovkino' tov. Bykova v pravlenie 'Sovkino' (Letter from the Deputy Director of the Leningrad Film Studio Sovkino Comrade Bykov to the Management of Sovkino), in Gornitskaia, *Iz istorii Lenfil'ma*, 254–55.

72. Kliment Korchmarev, "Muzyka k fil'me 'Novyi Vavilon,'" *Izvestiya*, April 4, 1929.

73. I. I. Ioffe, *Muzyka sovetskogo kino* (Leningrad: State Musical Scientific-Research Institute: 1938), 33.

74. DEBE, "Novyi Vavilon—Kankan v Tumane ili kak Sovkino oposhlilo parizhskuyu kommunu" (The New Babylon—Cancan in the Fog or How Sovkino Debased the Parisian Commune), *Komsomol'skaia pravda*, March 21, 1929.

75. Shostakovich, "O muzyke," 5.

76. Ibid.

77. Bordwell, *Narration in the Fiction Film,* 269.

78. See Clark, *Soviet Novel,* 46–67.

79. The *Maxim Trilogy* is a series of films including *Iunost' Maksima* (The Youth of Maxim, dir. Kozintsev and Trauberg, 1935), *Vozvrashchenie Maksima* (The Return of Maxim, dir. Kozintsev and Trauberg, 1937), and *Vyborgskaia storona* (The Vyborg Side, dir. Kozintsev and Trauberg, 1939).

3 To Catch Up and Overtake Hollywood

Early Talking Pictures in the Soviet Union

Valérie Pozner

Translated from the French by
Andrée Lafontaine

ONE GENERALLY ASSOCIATES Hollywood's influence on Soviet cinema with the musical comedies directed by Grigori Alexandrov after 1934, or with the grandiose plans conceived in 1935—following Boris Shumyatsky's trip to Hollywood—of a studio built in the Crimea, entirely outfitted with American equipment (e.g., lighting, recording, mixing), with the potential to produce six hundred films per year. Hollywood's influence on Soviet cinema, however, did not begin in the 1930s; it goes back to the mid-1920s, when American films dominated Soviet screens. For the Soviet film industry during the second half of the 1920s, Hollywood represented, above all, a competitive branch of the industry: a modern unit bringing together all aspects of production, synonymous with efficiency and productivity. When Sovkino launched its grand project to build a new studio (at the time, still referred to as a "factory") in 1927, the press labeled it "Red Hollywood" and "Soviet Hollywood."[1]

The increasing presence of American products (e.g., automobiles, tractors, military equipment) in the world market and in the film industry in particular began to manifest itself more clearly in official Soviet discourse. With Stalin's ascent, the Soviet Union abandoned its utopian visions of global revolution and reoriented itself toward the construction of "socialism in one country"; in this context, the United States personified both a reference and a rival, a figure simultaneously to emulate and to reject: hence the double meaning of Stalin's 1928 slogan, to "catch up and overtake America."[2] Denounced for its capitalist ideology, the United States was nevertheless cited as a model for the efficiency of its management, productivity, technology, entrepreneurial pragmatism, product quality, the training of its managers, and perhaps above all else, for its implementation of Taylorism.

In March 1928, the All-Union Party Conference on Cinema was held in Moscow, during which a new slogan was launched: "cinema for the millions." When interpreting this instrumental moment, film historians generally emphasize the party's takeover of the film industry and its decision to favor political education films over commercial productions, both domestic and foreign. I wish to propose a different reading: cinema for the millions also meant an increase in the number of movie theaters, in the number of films and prints produced, and an improvement of their quality and shelf life. More important, it meant a profitable cinema ("for the millions" . . . of rubles!). Galvanized by Stalin's wish expressed at the fifteenth Party Congress, the authorities established a goal: that "cinema [take] the place of vodka as a source of revenue in the State budget."[3] The same conference saw the realization of cinema's industrial dimension. The traditional model, wherein various studios were linked to the Commissariat of Enlightenment and were entirely dependent on foreign exports for film stock and equipment, was outdated. The development of cinema required the improvement of its "technical base." And while Hollywood was not specifically cited as a model, its presence was evoked indirectly. Still, the conference refrained from determining which structure was best suited to facilitate the technical developments required for Soviet cinema to become competitive in the world market. It seems logical, in this context, to ask ourselves if the Hollywood model effectively served as a reference and, if so, how it was adapted in the Soviet Union.

Despite the successful presentation of the German Tri-Ergon sound-on-film system in Leningrad and Moscow in January 1927, it was the Soviet media's coverage of *The Jazz Singer* (dir. Crosland, 1927) in 1928 that made the transition to sound a reality. Soviet film professionals realized that Hollywood had become the leader of this global transition. With the advancement of talkies in Europe, commercial distribution officials and filmmakers were concerned about a possible decrease in Soviet film exports. The realization that Soviet cinema had really fallen behind occurred in 1929, at which point the Soviet Union had to decide whether to continue the tests that were being conducted in two laboratories since 1926–27 or whether to seek technical help from the United States.

This decision fell to cinema authorities and their governing institutions and primarily affected the tests being conducted in the Soviet Union. Film professionals (e.g., producers, technicians, actors) of course had their own ideas about the coming of sound, which would directly challenge their know-how, while the general public, informed as they were of the developments in Europe and the United States, nourished high hopes for the future of sound film. How and to what extent did these groups affect the transition to sound in the Soviet Union? More importantly, how and when did the technical advancements manifest themselves in the equipment of theaters and studios? This chapter seeks to answer these questions by looking at institutional changes, technological challenges, reactions to the transition, and its eventual impact, with particular attention to how Hollywood served as a model for the Soviet film industry's transition to sound.

The Challenge of Vertical and Horizontal Concentration

Following the 1928 conference, Soviet cinema entered a period of prolonged crisis. While Sovkino's commercial policy had been denounced, profits, nevertheless, would need to be generated to finance modernization. While Sovkino, as the largest film producer, had a monopoly on distribution, it included only the territories of the RSFSR (Russian Soviet Federative Socialist Republic), which often resulted in conflicts with other studios, notably VUFKU (in Ukraine) and Goskinprom (in Georgia), both of whom distributed films within their territories but were expected to give Sovkino back its share of the profits. Another problem arose in the area of exhibition. In the 1920s, the film theater network was handed over to various parties answering to the education sectors, local executive committees, and more recently, to Tsentrosoiuz—the cooperative network responsible for the distribution of goods in the provinces. Incidentally, these various bodies rented copies for a low price, generating increasing revenues, while Sovkino's revenues stagnated. Moreover, the network (especially in the countryside) could not be extended because of the high cost and poor quality of equipment, the lack of replacement parts, and the heavy burden of taxation. These financial questions occupied the discussions of a commission created in September 1928.[4] In December, the commission produced a series of proposals, the most urgent of which concerned the creation of the Film Committee, dependent on Sovnarkom, whose mandate would be to reflect on these questions. This committee was officially established in January 1929.[5]

Attesting to the fact that cinema was not (yet) a priority for the party or the government, the committee's first meeting would not occur until May 1929, wherein discussions resumed over which institutional structure Soviet cinema should adopt. Among the arguments in favor of concentration, the Hollywood model was presented as the most efficient and rational: the resources required for the transition to sound would be available thanks to the joining of the laboratories, the strength of the electrical industry, and the capacities of the studios. The profits generated by the extensive theater network in the United States financed production; in the Soviet Union, however, the body in charge of organizing this concentration—at that point, Sovnarkom's Film Committee—did not have access to this type of revenue, or any other funds. The heads of studios who, seeing the creation of a new governing body, rushed forward with new funding requests, were quickly disappointed: the million rubles allocated on paper in June 1929 had already been halved by July.[6] Nevertheless, the idea that an industrial revolution was impossible without a concentration of resources and the joining of forces was starting to make headway.

After lengthy discussions, the creation of Soiuzkino was finally approved in February 1930. Cinema became a dependent of VSNKh, the Supreme Soviet of the National Economy, although the implementation of this decision would occur over the spring and summer, partly a result of resistance coming from the studios in the republics that interpreted this centralization as a form of vassalization. Following the example of other industries, this new governing body was to have a unique structure that encompassed all sectors of activity: production (i.e., all studios except for Mezhrabpom, which managed to remain a distinct entity), distribution (the issue of exhibition being postponed), and all industrial aspects (production of film stock and equipment, photographic chemistry, laboratories), as well as training centers and cinema schools, including the new NIFKI Institute, which was responsible for the research and development of new technologies (e.g., sound, color, 16mm).

Among the first initiatives emanating from this giant trust was the elaboration of an overview of the "cine-photographic industry in the USSR and the USA," addressed to the Sixteenth Congress of the Bolshevik Party, held between June 26 and July 13, 1930.[7] Hollywood served both as a profitable business model and, pragmatically, as an agency that could grant financial requests. The same could be said of the negotiations around the Five-Year Plan in the spring and summer of 1930. The first plan for cinema, initiated in 1928, had not taken this industrial dimension into account, nor had it foreseen the urgency of the transition to sound. Consequently, no funds had been allocated to the development of the "technical base." Sovnarkom's Cinema Committee, Gosplan, and subsequently VSNKh all asked, in early 1930, that Soiuzkino revise its budget to take the reorganization, the construction needs (e.g., factories devoted to the production of film stock and film equipment, studios to be built or renovated), the importation of film equipment and stock, and so on, into account. In these documents, Hollywood's voluminous output, the number of sound-equipped theaters, and the funding required for the transition to sound are reiterated like a litany.

Unforeseen and Long Insuperable Difficulties

In 1930, the sector's reorganization, briskly, if belatedly, initiated, quickly met with financial difficulties, both at the institutional and the industrial levels. To begin with, one of the guiding ideas—the takeover of distribution and exhibition to generate revenues quickly—was met with the same problem faced earlier by the heads of the former Sovkino: unlike the network in the United States, the Soviet network was deficient and underequipped. The availability of film equipment increased only in the countryside, which was considered a political priority, but yielded insignificant profits. And with the importation of cheap foreign films severely curtailed after the March 1928 conference, profitability became problematic. To garner profits, one must first have movies and a sufficient number of copies to distribute; otherwise, the multiplication of exhibition venues and screens is pointless.

The grouping together of the various enterprises to ensure a technological base resulted in failure and chaos. The laboratories remained dependent on the electrical company (the Pansoviet Electrical Society, or VEO) and were not attached to Soiuzkino. Their main priority was not to develop new technology for cinema but to facilitate liaisons for the army. Though this may have also been the case in the United States, Western Electric's development of the new sound technology had given rise to a new sector of production. In the Soviet Union, talking pictures remained a peripheral sector of activity for the laboratories: the material and human resources were both sorely lacking, and their leaders did not feel the need to answer to Soiuzkino. In contrast, the factories used for the production of film stock and equipment were taken from the army and reallocated to Soiuzkino. Institutional wars lasting for months ensued, at the end of which (December 1930) the film equipment factories were reassigned back under the tutelage of the Defense Commissariat, resulting in contracts being either only partially met or not honored at all. Moreover, the studios themselves and their equipment were in shambles. Though the need was dire, financing, most notably for the importation of equipment, was reduced to almost nothing following the "special" trimester of October–December 1930.[8] The Hollywood model appeared more and more as an inaccessible chimera.

Furthermore, Soiuzkino quickly revealed itself to be an unstable organization: some of its administrators were arrested, including its first director, M. Ryutin, in the fall of 1930; assistants were questioned; internal tensions within management led to inquiries by the Workers' and Peasants' Inspectorate, the Central Control Commission, local party organizations, and professional organizations (e.g., ARRK, or the Association of Revolutionary Film Workers; Rabis, the Trade Union of Art Workers); and an air of suspicion became increasingly pervasive. When Shumyatsky took the helm in the end of 1930, the situation was far from calm. On the contrary, problems had accumulated: the system needed to be reappropriated from the various controlling organizations, new theaters required construction, distribution had to be reorganized, film stock and film equipment needed to be secured. This is to say nothing of production issues: reinforcement of censorship led, in the previous year, to a multiplication of bans that resulted in a net loss.

Finally, VSNKh ordered frequent modifications to Soiuzkino's organizational structure, which was meant to increase productivity but only resulted in further instability. In January 1932, following VSNKh's split into two entities, cinema found itself attached to the newly formed People's Commissariat of Light

Industry, which entailed further modifications to Soiuzkino's internal structure. Within the commissariat, cinema and photography became part of the same sector responsible for the production of matches, which speaks volumes about the status of "the most important of all the arts." A few months later, taking advantage of Shumyatsky's absence, the commissariat's management attempted to demote cinema to the rank of "simple direction," with limited powers and much diminished resources,[9] the intent of which was to eliminate Soiuzkino's special status as a distinct entity. Shumyatsky fought battles at the highest levels to counter these attacks and managed to maintain the status quo, which consequently attracted the attention of the Central Committee's Orgburo. Soiuzkino's line of defense sought to keep the branch's unity—the production of both films and the means of production—without which film production would remain dependent on other commissariats that had no interest in producing film stock and equipment, which was both complex and of limited application. In October 1932, Orgburo once again reexamined cinema's future. A new reorganization was just around the corner.

Meanwhile, starting in 1928, Mezhrabpom was also being shaken up, following the suppression of the last sources of private capital. With an aim to suppress Mezhrabpom, Konstantin Shvedchikov was financially strangling the studio through an overtly aggressive campaign on behalf of Sovkino. Mezhrabpom's survival was achieved with the removal of its founder and production organizer, Moisei Aleinikov, and the subsequent appointment of an associate director by the party's Central Committee, a relatively unknown Chervov, who quickly entered into open conflict with Francesco Misiano, the director appointed by the Workers International Relief's Central Committee.[10] The purges, reduction of personnel, and internal reorganization had further deleterious effects. Shvedchikov's policy did not end with his departure in July 1932; indeed, Shumyatsky repeatedly asked the Central Committee to order the closing and reallocation of the resources (e.g., sets, venues, means of production, personnel) of its rival studio—a desire that was granted in 1936.

Soviet or American Technology: A Cornelian Dilemma

In 1928, the Soviet commercial representation in New York (Amtorg) began to send Moscow clear signals. The key player, cinema administrator Lev Monoszon, thought it was unnecessary to "rediscover America," that it was better instead to import American equipment. The Soviet Union would thereby quickly catch up and find itself capable of producing films that would generate enough revenue through foreign export to rapidly make up for the initial investment.

In fact, contrary to Monoszon's account, the Soviet Union did not stay idle: two laboratories (Pavel Tager's in Moscow and Alexander Shorin's in Leningrad) launched into research as early as 1927, the first mainly following the Tri-Ergon principle, while the latter followed the Photophone principle. Despite frequent statements in the press denouncing competition as a Western—or even, an American—phenomenon, the parallel work of the two laboratories quickly led to a confrontation between two models, two cities, and two studios. Tager was in fact contractually tied to Mezhrabpom, whereas Shorin in Leningrad worked for Sovkino (at the time, Soiuzkino). The attempts at establishing the *zvukovaia piaterka* (the so-called Sound Five), comprising the country's largest studios, meant to put pressure on the authorities and to obtain the funds required for a technological revolution, soon came to a dead end as conflicts and rivalries quickly overshadowed cooperation. Each studio signed treaties, hired its own inventors, and developed its own system, including VUFKU (Ukraine) and Belgoskino (the Belorussian studio located in Leningrad).

Throughout 1929, both the press and the studio authorities remained ambivalent: on the one hand, Soviet inventions were praised; on the other hand, American technological advances were constantly the subject of detailed articles and of discrete requests for information. Theater equipment logically constituted the other subject of preoccupation: the specialized press devoted numerous articles to the benefits and inconveniences of the different systems (sound-on-disc and sound-on-film), to the amplifying systems, and so on, and published worried accounts regarding the increasing number of American and European theaters already equipped for sound.

On the laboratories' side, Monoszon's suggestion to import American sound technology through an agreement with RCA Photophone was clearly interpreted through the lens of American-Soviet competition. Some asserted the superiority of Shorin's invention, even going so far as to hope for the acquisition of an American patent.[11] For its part, Mezhrabpom claimed that such an agreement was both too expensive and unnecessary at a moment when Soviet technology was about to see the light of day. Monoszon offered to organize a presentation of both Photophone technology and Hollywood's first talkies in Moscow for the October anniversary. At the same time, Shorin declared that his system was operational and that he would present it officially, this time in Leningrad.

In the end, it was Leningrad's theater, equipped with Shorin's invention, that first opened its doors, on October 5, 1929, for an elite audience composed of party members, official representatives, the press, and the diplomatic corps. The following day, the venue was to open its doors to the general public; however, the work was not quite finished, the tests were not successful, and the opening was postponed. While Shorin's sound quality left much to be desired, the Soviet press nevertheless applauded it as a success: "Behind scratchy voices, what was heard was the sound of history being made."[12] Film director Abram Room stressed that Shorin's equipment was developed without any foreign help, "without any imported screws." And contrary to that of the United States, this equipment would be used for the benefits of the proletarian masses.

A few weeks later in Moscow, Photophone's sound-recording technology proved superior. Even though the press was more discreet, the public (composed of professionals) was justifiably impressed. So much so that VUFKU (Kiev) immediately sent a projectionist and an official to Moscow to study the screening techniques and theater equipment.

Monoszon arrived with a Photophone offer to outfit Soviet theaters and studios with its equipment—for exorbitant fees, to be sure.[13] His proposition was examined during a meeting of the Sound Five. A timely intervention by Monoszon detailing the advantages and urgency of a deal with the Americans finally brought agreement in October 1929.[14] His arguments were as follows: first, those in charge of production were wrong in believing that such an agreement would be unnecessary and detrimental to Soviet advances; filmmakers and technicians who went abroad did not learn anything, since they went to Europe, where nothing was happening in the realm of sound—it was not in Germany but rather in America that sound was invented. An agreement would allow the manufacturing in the Soviet Union of American-modeled equipment. From that point, Soviet-produced films would be allowed to reach foreign markets; Soviet inventors and engineers would benefit from American help to improve their prototypes; and directors, operators, technicians, and projectionists would receive valuable training. In a document addressed to the Cinema Committee by the Sound Five, the conclusion was simple: "We are currently spending money to commit errors already solved elsewhere. We discover with great difficulty an America discovered long ago by Americans." The urgency of the situation was quantified: in the United States, seven thousand theaters were already equipped for sound. It was decided that Amkino would be the main body to lead talks with the Americans and would then report on its advances to the Sound Five. Moreover, Photophone would be a privileged interlocutor, given its already-existing contacts.[15] On December 6, a meeting of Sovnarkom's Cinema Committee ratified this decision and allocated a budget of one million rubles for the development of talking pictures.[16]

Endless discussions took place throughout 1930 and until the spring of 1931. Since the creation of Soiuzkino in February 1930, the issue of an agreement with the Americans figured prominently among its priorities and was regularly debated during meetings of its management and parent organizations (namely VSNKh, but also Gosplan and the Commissariat for Finance for budgetary forecasts).[17] During the elaboration of the new Five-Year Plan for the development of the branch presented to Gosplan in August 1930, Soiuzkino presented the grandiose project of a three-month training period, in the United States, of twenty-six film directors, nineteen screenwriters, and twenty-one technicians.[18] But in the end, an overall agreement with the American firm never took shape.

In fact, this failure concerned the Five-Year Plan as a whole, something that manifested itself as early as the end of the summer of 1930. Kuibyshev, under questioning during an investigation by the Workers' and Peasants' Inspectorate, came up with a trick: at that moment in Russia, the fiscal year started in October. To give the industry a break, and to improve the year's results, an additional "special" trimester (*osobyi kvartal*), from October to December 1930, would make the fiscal and the civil year coincide. However, the financial disaster could not be avoided, and Kuibyshev was removed in December. As early as the end of summer, the cinema administrators were made aware of drastic cuts to their resources and, more particularly, to foreign currency. Under these new circumstances, priority was given to the importation of film stock, which was desperately needed. As for sound, a document stated: "We will limit importation to equipment parts of the utmost necessity and 2 or 3 recording devices and sound-proofing boxes, in order to fulfill the 1931 plan. These devices will be acquired for experimental purposes. In order to ensure their maximum profitability, they will be left to the disposal of Soiuzkino's management rather than being assigned to specific studios. The production sector will be charged with organizing their use so that various studios and Mezhrabpom can use them alternatively."[19] Already in September 1930, Soiuzkino's management decided to reject Photophone's offer and instead to invite five specialists to Russia to educate film professionals about the new technology. Monoszon was charged with proposing candidates and of communicating the terms.[20]

Producing Sound without any Equipment

Given the institutional instability and lack of funding, the Soviet belatedness in the area of sound film production could not be made up for quickly. The first sound films were produced for Sovkino at Shorin's Leningrad laboratory and for Mezhrabpom-film with Tager's team at the Radio Theater, respectively, thanks to an agreement between the Electrotechnical Research Institute and the Commissariat for Posts and Telegraphs, which were directly interested in the development of a technology to record sound on film for the recording and broadcasting of "radio films." Work toward outfitting a first set at the Leningrad factory took place between the spring and winter of 1929.[21] Lacking funds as early as mid-September, Shorin was able to build only two recording devices, with which Room began shooting his first sound film, *Piatiletka* (A Plan for Great Works). A month later, Shorin had finished five devices, three of which were acquired by the Ukrainian VUFKU, to Sovkino's chagrin. At this point, the famous Sound Five was dissolved, with each studio pursuing its own experiments and launching the outfitting of its own sets in a general atmosphere of secrecy and open competition. In May 1930, Soiuzkino began to outfit its studio in Moscow: construction of the new Potylikha studio (the future Mosfil'm) was considerably delayed as a result of a lack of financing, and the project, which had been approved back in 1927 and had not taken the transition to sound into account, seemed impossible to modify. As a result, it was also decided that the old Second factory on Lesnaya Street would be outfitted for sound and visual recording. Again, work was slow to start and met with numerous technical difficulties. Mezhrabpom, for its part, submitted its first sound studio plan to the Cinema Committee in August 1929,[22] before deciding to acquire and renovate a new building.[23] Meanwhile, sound recording went on at the Radio Theater, where the dialogue for *Putevka v zhizn'* (Road to Life, dir. Ekk, 1931), for example, was recorded.

Sound quality remained problematic for a long time. A month after a difficult inauguration in Leningrad, the screening of Shorin's experimental films in the only Moscow theater equipped by Americans was a fiasco.[24] Shortly thereafter, the presentation of Tager's first experimental tracks also resulted in failure.[25]

What to See, and Where?

The theater where the first screenings using Shorin's equipment were held in October 1929 closed down almost immediately. The same thing happened with the Pervyi Sovkino Theater in Moscow, thus fueling the press's questions: why was the general public not allowed to see American films screened for film professionals and authorities, and, more important, why could it not be the judge of the Soviet experimentations? In February 1930, Konstantin Feldman painted an alarming portrait: while talking pictures had swept cinema worldwide, the Soviet Union responded with carelessness, bureaucracy, rivalries between studios, and (at the highest levels) indifference in regard to cinema's future. All the while, two fully equipped theaters had been waiting for two months to be seen by the general public. While the United States had invested $200 million domestically, the 100,000 rubles promised by the Cinema Committee in spring 1929 had still not been allocated, just like the 1 million rubles that had been promised in December. Tager did not even have quality speakers with which to test his equipment (they were not produced in the Soviet Union but could be bought abroad for a few hundred rubles). Feldman suggested making do with the radio speakers already in use in villages, which would limit the importation needs to photocells.[26]

On March 3, 1930, Room's film *A Plan for Great Works* was finally screened at the Pervyi Sovkino Theater. The program, which was entirely produced at Shorin's laboratory, also included *Tip Top*, a short animated political satire, as well as three musical shorts, two singing numbers, and an "eccentric" talkie. Hopes of a speedy takeoff were, alas, short-lived: the program remained practically unchanged until early August! As a reporter for *Moscow Evening* remarked: "The studios are not producing sound films because the theaters are not equipped, hence profitability is not guaranteed. Exhibitors are not outfitting their venues since they do not know which system is preferable. Shorin and Tager have not received funding since we do not know whether or not sound technology will be completely developed in the Soviet Union or through an agreement securing technical help from abroad. The cinema school is not offering appropriate training, since the studios are not yet producing sound films."[27]

Grandiose plans to outfit theaters and to manufacture recording devices as elaborated by Gosplan (based on VSNKh's objectives) were entirely dependent on an agreement with the equipment manufacturer VTOMP and the electrical company VEO, which was not yet settled.[28] In April, VEO proposed a run of fifty recording devices within a year but holding off on mass production until a special plant was built, which would be impossible before 1932. In any case, certain parts could not be produced in the Soviet Union. The main difficulty seemed to reside in coordinating VEO's efforts, on which laboratories and electrical parts (amplifiers and speakers) depended, with those of equipment manufacturer VTOMP, Soiuzkino, and Mezhrabpom. Goldman, who was in charge of the case at Gosplan, complained bitterly to Kuibyshev about these difficulties and asked him to personally intercede.[29]

Meanwhile, unrealistically high forecasted costs threatened the goal of outfitting fifty theaters before October 1. As a result, VEO and VTOMP were asked to go back to the drawing board. By the end of June, VEO bluntly explained that a plan for thousands of sound devices was not achievable. While its Profradio factory would be in a position to produce five hundred to six hundred devices the following year, the first fifty would be difficult to manufacture, as the prototype was still not yet production ready.[30]

The reshuffling of 1930 succeeded in causing still more confusion. While VEO took a long time to develop an industrial model, and therefore postponed signing a contract with Soiuzkino, the military was putting pressure on VSNKh to regain hold of the VTOMP group. VEO's inability to act, moreover, had kindled the ambition of Narkompochtel' (Commissariat for Post and Telegraph), which publicly requested that cinema's transition to sound be made its responsibility (laboratories as well as equipment manufacturing). In the summer, this commissariat, which specialized in radio broadcasting, launched an institute of radio transmissions that included, following an agreement with Soiuzkino, an experimental laboratory devoted to artistic radio broadcasting and sound film.[31] Meanwhile, disputes between the commissariats led to paralysis: meetings multiplied and resolutions remained on paper only. State investments, initially projected at fifteen million rubles for the entire branch, of which one million rubles were to be allocated to Mezhrabpom-film, were constantly decreased, which made studio renovation and modernization perilous endeavors, to say nothing of the still unresolved theater-equipment issue.

The October deadline set for outfitting the first fifty theaters for sound had already passed when drastic cuts to the budget and, more significantly, to foreign currencies were announced, forcing an in-depth revision of the program. A summit meeting on November 12 revealed a situation that was, to say the least, delicate:[32] the Profradio factory, on which VEO depended, was now under the control of the Commissariat for Posts and Telegraphs and was not able to produce the photocells anyway, which were the specialty of another VEO branch. By contrast, the mandate for the Commissariat for Post and Telegraph was to produce lamps. Unfortunately, the manufacturing process was not yet ready. For its part, the VEO declared itself incapable of supplying the amplifiers and speakers with which it had been charged. The Soiuzkino authorities, whose initiative it was to organize the meeting, discovered that even had the devices' mechanical parts been provided, they still would have been unusable, thus spelling economic failure for Soiuzkino, which had been ordered to be immediately profitable. The two-page minutes of the meeting offer a glimpse of the general tone of the discussions and of the protagonists' nervousness. Soiuzkino's representatives found, to put it plainly, that most participants had been "[taking] them for a ride" for months, always asking for prerogatives and funds that the cinema administrators could secure from the governing authorities only with great difficulty; in the end, none could deliver on its promises. VEO, which had just lost the Profradio factory, suggested that Soiuzkino make a direct agreement with the Commissariat for Posts and Telegraphs, since its factories were already overloaded with military orders.[33] The plan was thus revised.

The fatal blow came on December 5, 1930, when VTOMP returned to the hands of the military: Shumyatsky, who had just taken office, almost resigned after being informed of the decision, as is confirmed by his correspondence with Ordzhonikidze.[34] After this, VTOMP officials abandoned Soiuzkino, claiming more pressing orders and leaving it with no choice but to manufacture the devices on its own.[35]

By this time, the Soviet Union could rely on a total of four theaters equipped for sound, one of which was outfitted with American technology. The second sound program, which finally began its run on August 12, combined tracks from Soiuzkino and Mezhrabpom and received mixed reviews, particularly for its singing numbers and *The Talking A-B-Cs*, a short film to teach the rudiments of reading. Nevertheless, it ran until October 17 in the only Moscow theater equipped for sound. The third program appeared on October 21. It included Vladimir Erofeev's *Olympiad of Arts* and Mikhail Tsekhanovsky's sound animation *Post*. In the meantime, Dziga Vertov's first version of *Entuziazm: Simfoniia Donbassa* (Enthusiasm, 1931) screened to a select audience on November 6 and was quickly pulled from release: the film required further editing and cuts that would take months to complete. Thus ended the cinema industry's second year of "reconstruction."

Pressure from the Press

In 1929, the Soviet public began to be fed announcements of sound film shootings, utopian equipment production forecasts, and details regarding advancements in the number of sound-equipped theaters, and the production of sound films in Europe and the United States. The gap separating this picture and reality was striking. Following harsh articles by K. Feldman in *Moscow Evening*, the daily organized a meeting on March 29, 1930, to which filmmakers, technicians, inventors, and, more important, studio and institutional authorities from Gosplan, VSNKh, and VEO were invited. Luminaries such as Lunacharsky were not forgotten. On all fronts, the press clamored: "Soviet cinema must produce sound!"[36]

With the assembly's inability to notice anything but the deplorable situation at hand, press editorial boards decided to spearhead the transition by organizing inspection brigades of the various organizations concerned and by vowing to report back every ten days to worried readers on the progress of the work.[37] Admittedly, *Moscow Evening* was hardly alone in conceiving such initiatives: other periodicals and professional organizations launched similar campaigns, either concurrently or shortly after.[38] Nevertheless, the case of the popular, high-circulation Moscow daily is, as we shall see, of particular interest.

The authorities' reactions to this initiative were mixed: Kirill Chutko penned an article claiming that Americans were still producing silent films, and he put the ball in the court of the seemingly passive Society of the Friends of Soviet Cinema (ODSK).[39] After a few months, however, Soiuzkino's authorities no doubt saw the benefit of this mobilization. During a meeting of VSNKh held on January 24, 1930, Shvedchikov, evoking the governing organizations' procrastination with regard to a technical aid contract, fulminated: "Now is not the moment to draft resolutions! If we want help, we must make noise!" and, more gravely: "There is no unified voice able to tell the government: shoot us if you wish, but solve this issue!"[40]

Even so, the journalists' and the general public's mobilization was not necessarily welcome. Soiuzkino preferred acting differently: while providing the press with reassuring information and soothing declarations, it organized an exhibit at the Kremlin titled *Cinema as Agitprop*, which opened at the end of June during the sixteenth party congress.[41] Work during the congress was filmed and debates were recorded. The same exhibit, which in fact was devoted to Soiuzkino's latest five-year plan, opened a few days later at the Park of Culture, featuring a backlit map of the country showing studios, theaters, and film agencies to be built, as well as diagrams, film screenings, equipment, lit movie sets, and a schedule of discussions with the public. The outcome of this public relations mission was most likely unsatisfactory, as Soiuzkino's management decided to organize a major conference around the issue of sound, to which the press was invited in addition to authorities, inventors, and filmmakers. The pretext for the conference was the arrival in Moscow of American engineer Joe W. Coffman, who had just signed a contract to act as adviser. Interviewed by *Moscow Evening*, Coffman claimed, "No silent films are produced in the United States today." This assertion, printed in bold characters in the paper, was alarming.

The conference, held between August 25 and August 31, 1930, was covered for *Moscow Evening* by Lev Vaks, who was already critical of Soiuzkino's authorities. Judging by comments made by David Morskoi, who was employed by Mezhrabpom-film, the various interventions highlighted frictions and contentions, with each group laying the blame on someone else.[42] But while VEO emerged as one of the main culprits, Vaks directed his attacks against Soiuzkino's management.[43] This didn't go unnoticed: the journalist was promptly excluded from the conference and Soiuzkino's head of production, Andrei Sutyrin, mobilized an internal supporting committee and submitted a formal complaint to the paper against Vaks. This offensive failed, since the plenum of the journalists' organization held on September 8 at the Press House determined that his harsh articles were justified.[44] The conclusion was that the press and the public at large should add more pressure to overcome the "chaos."[45]

Given the available resources, it is difficult to establish any direct link between these public denunciations and the subsequent arrests of at least three of Soiuzkino's administrators—its first director, Marteman Riutin, and also E. Brokman and A. Ardatov, both of whom were in charge of the technical aspects of the transition to sound—between November and December 1930.[46] To this, we must add a trial "by comrades" against those in charge of the laboratory, who were accused of neglect resulting in the loss of thousands of meters of film stock at a moment when its short supply was becoming a problem.

Moscow Evening proudly reminded its readership that it was the first to condemn the crisis, to talk of "rightist opportunism"—a term used in Riutin's official accusation. As for Sutyrin, he found it very difficult to justify himself at the regional party's office, during a meeting in which Vaks's articles were brought against him as evidence. The documents, as the newspaper boasts, had just been sent to the Central Revision Committee.[47] The delay in the transition to sound was exacerbated by the evident failures of Soiuzkino's industrial and financial plan to produce as many films as it had projected. These new inquiries into cinema affairs added to the first purges occurring at the same time and contributed a whole new dimension to the scandal. Within a few months, the general public's worries, conveyed by the press, took on a different nature, just as attacks focused on different targets. Though the consequences for those involved would be tragic, a concrete solution to the problem of underfunding in the film industry never surfaced.

Who Is to Be Trained, and How?

The general public and the press were not as badly affected by the situation as were professionals in the industry: the lack of equipment and, consequently, the inability to experiment with technical innovations had led to helplessness and rivalry within the profession. Why had Room been chosen for Sovkino's first experiments, and Pudovkin and Obolensky for those at Mezhrabpom? What were other filmmakers to do in order to remain "relevant"? In early 1929, ARRK (the professional association representing filmmakers founded in 1924) decided to act by creating its own "sound group." Established in July, this "sector for training and experimentations in sound film" requested funding from the Cinema Committee on October 1 to organize classes that would commence on October 21.[48] The ARRK archives and the press attest to the great variety of topics discussed by invited specialists, professors working at Moscow University, and highly specialized scientists. Filmmakers (directors, operators, and screenwriters) hence received basic training in musicology, electricity, and acoustics; Tager himself lectured on various principles of sound-on-film and on his own devices.[49] A memo addressed to the Cinema Committee, dated December 30, stressed the importance of this training, given the disastrous situation of the studios, and requested that another 11,606 rubles be allocated so that the classes could be adapted for filmmakers from the republics, who were in even greater need of training.[50] It was thus that the group conducted the first concrete experiments in February 1930.[51]

Obviously, ARRK was not the only party interested in the issue, which concerned the entire profession from production management to exhibition staff. But it ignited the latent conflict between Soiuzkino's management and ARRK, the latter blaming Soiuzkino for the lack of equipment and for the general atmosphere of rivalry and secrecy between the studios.

Soon, more training was established at studios in Moscow, Leningrad, and Kiev. Even so, however, debates over the program continued. Who was to be trained first: up-and-coming filmmakers; sound engineers; or projectionists, whose training was imagined to become much more specialized as difficulties in the equipment's manufacturing increased? From which field were these new specialists to come: were they to be chosen from among musicians, radio technicians, or acoustics graduates? How long was training to take? Finally, what was to be included in the syllabus? For at least two years, industry press ran numerous proposals, counterproposals, polemics, and critiques. As was the case for aesthetic theories regarding the new art that was to be sound film, a preponderance of material on paper betrays a complete inability to act.

The July 30 vote to transform Leningrad's Technical College (Kino-tekhnikum) specializing in cinema into the Technical Institute of Higher

Education (Tekhnicheskii VUZ)—with a department specifically devoted to sound film—also met with serious financial difficulties. A year later, the department still had no equipment and its training remained merely theoretical since no relationship had been secured with either Shorin's laboratory or the studios. Furthermore, students did not receive scholarships, and delays in the payment of salaries ultimately compromised the entire project.

While there was still no equipment, there was also no choice but to continue to produce silent films. On October 7, *Moscow Evening* organized a new debate titled, "The Ways of *Silent and* Sound Film." This time, Room and many other participants—Goldman from Gosplan among them—criticized directors for "deserting silent film." On November 28, 1930, F. Kon, recently appointed head of the Commissariat for Enlightenment Arts' Sector, declared that regardless of the delay, sound film was still much too experimental to serve as a vehicle for feature-length films with ideological content (i.e., the bulk of the thematic plan).[52]

Hard Beginnings and New Rivalries

The first days of January 1931 were marked by the release of a feature-length newsreel devoted to the Industrial Party Trial, *13 dnei* (Thirteen Days, dir. Ya. Poselsky and I. Venzher). Then, starting in April, shorts and feature-length films began to be released more and more quickly: in April, Vertov's *The Donbass Symphony* (a new version of *Enthusiasm*), produced by the Ukrainian studio VUFKU, and Ilya Kopalin's Soiuzkino-produced documentary *Odin iz mnogikh* (One of Many); in May, the much celebrated *Road to Life,* released by Mezhrabpom. October saw the release of *Mekhanicheskii predatel'* (The Mechanical Traitor, dir. Dmitriev, Mezhrabpom) and the dubbed silent film *Odna* (Alone, dir. G. Kozintsev and L. Trauberg), followed by Mezhrabpom's *Tommy* (dir. Protazanov), the newsreel *Krasnyi sport* (Red Sport, dir. Poselsky), and *Zlatye gory* (Golden Mountains, dir. Yutkevich) in November, the last two of which were produced at Soiuzkino's Leningrad factory. Finally, the year ended with the December release of Soiuzkino-Moscow's *Buria* (The Tempest, dir. Levkoev).

With the increase in sound film production, the number of sound-equipped theaters grew. On February 7, 1931, a second theater opened its doors in Moscow: the Koloss, located at the Conservatory's Large Hall and belonging to Mezhrabpom. The equipment cost two hundred thousand rubles and was produced by Tager's team, as was the case for most theaters opening in Moscow in 1931. The theater celebrated its opening by showing two documentaries, though the program in the following weeks featured only two sound shorts following a silent main feature, accompanied, as before, by an orchestra conducted by David Blok.

While a third theater opened its doors in Moscow in May 1931, the Conservatory took action to regain its spaces, and the Koloss survived only after fighting arduous battles. The closure of many city-run theaters was announced throughout the summer in Moscow. In October, only seven Muscovite theatres were equipped for sound, with only one belonging to a factory club. The largest movie theater in the country, the prestigious Udarnik (meaning "shock worker") opened its doors to celebrate the October anniversary. Featuring modernist architecture by B. Iofan, it was equipped with Shorin's systems. By the end of December, the number of sound-equipped theaters in Moscow was up to eleven (out of forty-five); in the Soviet Union, fifty-five theaters were sound ready. Out of these, two in Moscow and twenty-seven in the country were part of the Soiuzkino network, along with three traveling cinemas; more than half of the sound-equipped Soviet theaters were still under municipal control. Despite these openings, the figures were still much lower than the projections published in the press.

While progress was made in outfitting the studios, the Lesnaya Street studio was still not operational by September 1931. The plan to equip the Potylikha studio was not ready either, and other studios were still drafting their own plans. More generally, the equipment produced was technically deficient to the point that newly opened theaters had to promptly close down following audience protests.[53] The work to outfit the Soiuzkino administrators' projection room was delayed for months. But even when theaters did exist, they often had no films to show.[54]

The results of the inquiry launched at the end of 1930 were, unsurprisingly, disastrous for Soiuzkino. It prompted a meeting of the presidium of the Central Control Commission in September 1931,[55] and then of the Orgburo, where Kaganovich took charge of the case and asked a commission to draft propositions. Officially summarized in a memo on December 8, the resolutions would once again remain on paper only.

But it is not these criticisms—which are recurrent in the functioning of the Soviet state, especially after Stalin's Great Turn—which occupy us now. It is more surprising to see that the competitive strategies developed by studios at the dawn of the transition, discussed earlier with regard to technologies, are maintained throughout. The rivalries between Soiuzkino and Mezhrabpom are evident in advertisements and accounts appearing in *Moscow Evening*. For instance, at the exact moment when Mezhrabpom was heavily promoting *The Road to Life,* Soiuzkino was promoting the sound version of *Zemlia zhazhdet* (The Earth Thirsts, dir. Raizman, 1932) with printed ads claiming that the film was "the first cineplay of fiction, containing dialogues, sound, and sound-effects."[56] A few days later, the newspaper bitterly noted that advertisement for the film was dishonest since the movie was in fact a dubbed silent film whose sound seemed forced and artificial. On June 1, the Pervyi Soiuzkino Theater replaced the film with a copy of *The Road to Life.*

While Mezhrabpom was garnering success, publishing, month after month, the number of spectators who had already seen the film (eight hundred thousand in only three months), and had already announced the upcoming release of many feature-length fiction talkies (such as *Tommy* and *The Mechanical Traitor*), Soiuz-kino struggled to keep up with its rival. Its successes were modest by comparison: neither *Red Sport* nor *Riadom s nami* (Close to Us, dir. Bravko, 1931) was success-ful, and *Alone* was unanimously rejected by the general public, who in some cases asked for their money back, requesting "real dialogue." Open competition re-sumed in November 1931, when *Tommy* and *Golden Mountains,* released simulta-neously, had to share sound-equipped theaters in Moscow. This time, Soiuzkino came out on top: quickly, *Golden Mountains* blew *Tommy*, which was considered too boring, out of the water. Maybe more important, Soiuzkino's management promoted Yutkevitch's film to an unprecedented degree, placing articles in all general and trade media outlets, staging debates and promotional evenings, pro-viding interviews with filmmakers, and the like. To counter this publicity stunt, Mezhrabpom brought back new copies of *The Road to Life,* which one Moscow theater even presented as a sequel.[57] The subsequent failure of *The Tempest* with both critics and the general public tempered Soiuzkino's enthusiasm.

Conclusion

The rivalry between Soiuzkino and Mezhrabpom did not limit itself to a com-petition for better films and attendance; it added to an already existing one be-tween Tager and Shorin for recording devices and, more importantly, for theater equipment. Despite Soiuzkino's attempts to discredit Tager in the press and with authorities, his system was chosen in most cases by city-controlled theaters. It is nevertheless surprising to see such "liberal" competition in a country and at a time when it was counter to the official ideology. This competition was respon-sible for behavior and actions reminiscent of certain moments of the American transition to sound. This logic was enough to counterbalance—and even derail— the attempted centralization by the authorities and only added to the existing institutional rivalries.

In conclusion, it may be useful to note the ambivalent function of Hollywood as a reference point for various observations presented here. First, it served as a model in financial negotiations between cinema authorities and their respective governing bodies. Second, attempts at importing American technologies reveal a facet of the Soviet transition to sound unknown until today: the Soviet sound systems' autonomy was relative and resulted from budgetary restrictions. Finally, investment in and the progress of sound film in the United States were constantly reported by the general press and served as a reference for what the Soviet Union was expected to accomplish. These numbers fueled the expectations of both cin-ema professionals and the general public, which translated into hostile reactions and mobilizations against Soiuzkino. That studio, though hardly bearing the main responsibility for the difficulties and delays, was nevertheless at the fore-front of the transition to sound and had done nothing to establish a good rapport with these groups. This situation turned Soiuzkino into the perfect scapegoat when it came time to "sanction those responsible." Shumyatsky would have much to do to reverse this very negative perception of the film industry: his repeated efforts to explain Soiuzkino's responsibilities and mandates to the press were per-sistently negated by the ongoing crisis.

Notes

1. See *Sovetskii ekran* 47 (1927): 14.
2. See, for example, Stalin's speech at the Central Committee Plenum on November 19, 1928. Lenin's statement—"To catch up and overtake" (developed capitalist countries, and later, America), from "The Impending Catastrophe and How to Fight It" (September 1917)—was cited so frequently that it turned into a political cliché. The slogan acquired additional popu-larity in the late 1950s in connection with the statements of the head of the Communist Party Nikita Khrushchev.
3. B. S. Ol'hovoi, *Puti kino. Pervoe vsesoiuznoe partiinoe soveshchanie po kinematografii* (Moscow: Teakinopechat', 1929), 17.
4. The Council of Labor and Defense's (Sovet Truda i Oborony, or STO) Shotman Com-mission was created on September 21, 1928. See GARF 5446/10/2192/l. 29; GARF 5446/10/2196v/ l. 31, ll. 35–38; l. 43; GARF 5446/10a/2496v.
5. GARF 5446/10/2186. Its statutes were approved on January 29, 1929.
6. GARF 7816/1/9/l. 13.
7. RGALI 2497/1/7 (Obzor k XVI s"ezdu VKP/b "Kinofoto-industriia v SSR i SASSh).
8. RGALI 2497/1/2/l. 35 and passim.
9. RGALI 2497/1/64/l. 185; RGALI 2497/1/67/l. 61.
10. Conflict would become even more violent with Chervov's successor, Samsonov, whose direction would drive many directors to desertion.
11. The document is dated May 1930 (RGALI 2496/3/11/l. 35).
12. *Kino* (Leningrad), no. 40, October 6, 1929.
13. The amount required for rental equipment fluctuates between $300,000 and $900,000.
14. GARF 7816/1/9/ll. 34–40.
15. RGALI 2617/1/50.
16. GARF 5446/11/2496; GARF 7816/1/3/l. 70 and passim.
17. GARF 7816/1/9/l. 67.
18. RGAE 4372 /28/408/l. 21.
19. RGALI 2496/2/1/ll. 48–48 ob-49.
20. RGALI 2497/1/3.
21. RGALI 645/1/366, l. 315: details on May 23, 1929; a decision dated April 11. However, the work apparently did not start until September—see *Kino* (Leningrad), no. 36 (September 7, 1929): 4—and would have concluded in November (*Kino*, no. 46 [November 19, 1929]: 5).
22. GARF 7816/1/12/l. 67.
23. GARF 5446/11/2953.
24. See Nikolai Anoshchenko, "Nasha zvukovaia fil'ma," *Kino i zhizn'*, no. 4, 1929.
25. RGAE 4372/28/401/l. 66.

26. *Vecherniaia Moskva*, no. 41 (February 19, 1930): 3.

27. *Vecherniaia Moskva*, no. 69 (March 26, 1930): 3.

28. On March 26, 1930, Gosplan set the goal of equipping 39,010 theaters by the end of 1932 (RGAE 4372/28/403/l. 62).

29. RGAE 4372/28/401/ll. 22–29, April 1930.

30. June 26, 1930 (RGAE 4372/28/401/l. 26).

31. RGALI 2497/1/2/l. 51. See also declarations made by Smirnov, NKPiT's associate director, who accused VEO of sabotage and requested the reintegration of all weak-current industries (chiefly, Shorin's laboratory) to effect cinema's industrial transition with Soiuzkino (*Vecherniaia Moskva*, no. 200 [August 28, 1930]: 3).

32. RGAE 4372/28/402/ll. 20–21 ob.

33. RGAE 4372/28/402/l. 12.

34. RGASPI 85/28/29/1.

35. RGALI 2497/1/49; RGALI 2497/1/18/l. 196 (April 1931). On May 30, 1931, VOOMP still had not delivered anything for the previous two trimesters (RGALI 2497/1/18/l. 166). On June 30, 1931, the order was moved to the first trimester of 1932 (RGALI 2497/1/18).

36. *Vecherniaia Moskva*, no. 75 (April 2, 1930): 2. This kind of title is repeated with few variations in various outlets: "Why Is the Cinema Still Silent?" "Adding Speech to Facts," "The Silent Must Start to Speak," and the like.

37. *Vecherniaia Moskva*, no. 75 (April 2, 1930): 2. See also the April 8, May 12, June 2, and June 10 editions. The information is presented under the rubric "News from the Front," with clear military overtones.

38. Among them are *Za kommunisticheskoe prosveshchenie*, *Sovetskoe iskusstvo*, *Izvestiia*, and the professional organization of artists, Rabis.

39. *Vecherniaia Moskva*, no. 76 (April 3, 1930): 3.

40. RGAE 4372/28/401/ll. 64–65 ob.

41. See speech delivered by Riutin, head of Soiuzkino: "Kino-delo reorganizuetsia," *Vecherniaia Moskva*, May 24, 1930. We can contrast the alarmist tone of Ardatov, head of Soiuzkino's technical branch, when addressing VEO's administration (RGAE 4372/28/402/ll. 24–25, August) with his attempt at reassuring *Vecherniaia Moskva* (August 11) by alluding to a productive collaboration between various organizations.

42. RGALI 2698/1/21/ll. 49–109.

43. "Slova i dela," *Vecherniaia Moskva*, no. 202 (August 30, 1930): 3. See also the September 3 and September 13 articles.

44. *Vecherniaia Moskva*, no. 215 (September 15, 1930): 3.

45. "Ot slov k delu. Nashi predlozheniia po zvukovomu kino," *Vecherniaia Moskva*, no. 218 (September 18, 1930): 3.

46. Brokman and Ardatov were convicted of sabotage and counterrevolutionary activities and were executed a few months later. It was not possible to access their files or to find archival documents detailing their arrests, just as this case was never given a detailed account in the press. Their arrest was the beginning of a trial against "wasters in the film industry," which was somehow linked with the trial against the "Industrial Party." Riutin, for his part, was quickly released for lack of proof. He was executed after being arrested once more during the Great Purge a few years later.

47. *Vecherniaia Moskva*, no. 291 (December 15, 1930): 3. See also a letter sent from Sutyrin to Molotov in December, in which he justifies his actions, diverts accusations toward Shvedchikov, and asks to be appointed to a different position, one in the field of literature. RGALI 3107/1/88.

48. GARF 7816/1/9/ll. 23–27.

49. GARF 7816/1/9/l. 32.

50. GARF 7816/1/9/ll. 53–56.

51. *Kino*, no. 7 (February 5, 1930): 6.

52. *Vecherniaia Moskva*, no. 275 (November 28, 1930): 2.

53. RGAE 4372/28/402/ll. 1–5; *Vecherniaia Moskva*, November 17, 1931; RGALI 2497/1/67/l. 189; see also for 1932, RGALI 2497/1/67/l. 141.

54. This was the case for Ukraine's only sound-equipped theater, in Kharkov: see a telegram sent to *Kino*'s editorial board on June 1931 by the Society of Friends of Soviet Cinema (OZPKF, or Obshchestvo "Za Proletarskoe Kino i Foto," the Society for Proletarian Cinema and Photography) of Ukraine, published in *Kino*, no. 32, 3. See also an article requesting the distribution of *Enthusiasm*, which had been ready for four months, in the context in which sound films were sorely lacking, *Kino*, no. 10 (February 1931): 3.

55. RGALI 2497/1/42/ll. 1–7, 34, and passim.

56. The pre-release screening of *The Road to Life* was held on May 16 (the film was released on June 1), and *The Earth Thirsts* was released on June 18. Both were advertised side by side on May 15.

57. Incidentally, its director was reprimanded for false advertising. See *Vecherniaia Moskva*, no. 304 (December 26, 1931): 3.

4 ARRK and the Soviet Transition to Sound

Natalie Ryabchikova

In the middle of 1931, four years after *The Jazz Singer* (dir. Crosland, 1927) premiered in New York and three years after the first public demonstration of Soviet experiments with sound film, an editorial of the Soviet journal *Proletarskoe kino* (Proletarian Cinema) reproduced a dialogue with an imaginary reader:

> Sound cinema is a powerful weapon of the socialist construction. . . .
>
> We have learned this a long time ago—a reader will reasonably say—they've talked about this and written about this a thousand times, but we do not feel it; we have not been able to verify the force of sound cinema in practice, because for us, tens of millions of Soviet citizens, sound cinema is a nonexistent thing.
>
> The situation with sound cinema in the Soviet Union is highly unfavorable. We are at least three years behind the capitalist West in this area; we have not been fast enough. . . .
>
> And this we have also heard a thousand times—the reader says—but what is the matter, why have we been going around in circles?[1]

The journal was simultaneously criticizing members of the film community and film administration, and implicating its mass readership, tens of millions of Soviet citizens, in the task of creating a Soviet sound cinema. The conflated *we*, the mass effort that was required for this monumental task, is indicative of the times of rapid industrialization and the first Five-Year Plan. There is one possible answer as to why Soviet sound cinema has been "going around in circles," but this answer would surely earn anyone who dared to voice it a number of nasty epithets, such as *saboteur*. The task of mass mobilization and "proletarization" of Soviet cinema set before the film community in the period 1929–31 interfered with its own efforts of mastering the new technology and stalled the development of sound cinema for several crucial years.

The period 1928–32 in the Soviet cinema was transitional in so many ways that it is almost impossible to touch upon one set of "before" and "after" without referring to the others: silent film to sound, the New Economic Policy to the first Five-Year Plan, avant-garde montage cinema to "cinema, accessible to millions," formalism to socialist realism, an import-based industry to a self-sustainable one, and so on.[2] The transition to sound so far has been described either from an institutional point of view or from the aesthetic one. Institution-based accounts of the period usually focus on the technical and organizational upheaval of the whole industry, whereas the aesthetic approach examines individual filmmakers and films that can be considered products or victims of the transition.[3]

Combining the two approaches to describe the Soviet transition to sound has proved fruitful as well. For example, in the early 1990s Russian film scholars began to use the combination of the organizational and the aesthetic approach as a way to make sense of the limitations and distortions of the traditional Soviet film historiography. Historian Viktor Listov expressed an opinion that the established division of Soviet film history into two separate periods of silent and sound cinema was essentially invented to cover up the severe organizational crisis in cinema during the early 1930s. According to Listov, the crisis developed because the whole cinema industry was transferred in early 1930 from Narkompros (Commissariat of Enlightenment) to VSNKh (Supreme Council for National Economy) as part of the general process of Stalinist industrialization. This decision was called for by the desire to strengthen the technical bedrock of film production and distribution. Meanwhile, artistic problems were moved to the background, and emphasis on aesthetics and form became suspect. Ironically, the post-factum explanation of the break between Soviet cinema of the 1920s and the 1930s emphasized, most of all, aesthetic problems in the transition to sound. Listov suggested that the "pause" in the work of famous film directors, explained previously by the difficulty of adapting to the sound cinema or by "individual factors," should also take the turbulent state of the film industry in general into account.[4]

Another way of "making sense of Soviet sound," to borrow Ian Christie's formulation, is to take the middle ground between these two extreme positions—that is, to look at the period from the point of view of both the film community and the creative and administrative personnel, who had to deal with ideological, technical, and aesthetic problems on a daily basis. Looking at a representative sample of the Soviet film community in terms of its practical response to the coming of sound can provide us with a more accurate portrayal of the process and will at least partly explain why the period of transition was so long winded.

The most representative sample of the Soviet professional film community during the 1920s and the early 1930s was ARRK (Association of Workers in Revolutionary Cinematography), of which *Proletarian Cinema* was an official organ.[5] This professional organization was established in 1924 as ARK, or Association of Revolutionary Cinematography. After the renaming in 1929 it became closely associated with the notorious RAPP, or Russian Association of Proletarian Writers. When RAPP was disbanded in 1932, and most of its leaders executed, the subject of ARRK became a sore spot for Soviet historians. Although it was not dissolved alongside other "proletarian" organizations and continued to exist under the name RossARRK until 1935, for Soviet film scholarship its whole history became suspect because of its relatively short-lived association with RAPP. As a result, Soviet *kinovedy* largely avoided any serious discussion of ARRK, with little change in recent years.[6] While Western scholars tend to see RAPP and ARRK as essentially antagonistic, they, too, usually mention ARRK's role during the period of transition to sound only in passing.[7]

The first years of this long transition coincide with the height of RAPP's influence on cinema affairs. During this time, specifically because of the introduction and implementation of sound, ARRK attempted to play its most active role in the Soviet film industry. Its subsequent "proletarization" quickly put an end to that and, as a result, to ARRK's activity in general. ARRK was sufficiently weakened in the purges of the period 1929–31, so that the Party Decree of 1932 disbanding RAPP did not even need to mention the association, whose influence on the film community had already ceased to exist. During this time, however, ARRK managed to consolidate the efforts of the Soviet filmmakers in mastering sound and to make a significant contribution toward educating the first sound film specialists.

The First Professional Film Organizations

To explain the unique position that ARRK came to occupy by 1929 and 1930, we first need to look back to its history, as well as that of earlier Russian and Soviet professional film organizations. In spite of the recognition it posthumously achieved in Western discourse on Soviet cinema, ARK (later ARRK) as an institution was not quite so novel or unique at the time of its inception. Professional organizations of filmmakers started to appear in Russia in scores right after the February Revolution of 1917, which proclaimed the freedom of speech and assembly. Most of the unions were based in Moscow, the cinema capital of prerevolutionary Russia.

The closest counterpart and precursor of ARK was formed on March 6, 1917. The Union of the Workers of Art Cinema was divided into five profession-based sections: actors, directors, cameramen, artists, and scriptwriters and journalists. The main reason for its existence, as was the case with any professional film organization at the time, was mostly to protect its members from unemployment. While they were not officially recognized as trade unions, film unions aspired to have a self-regulatory function, setting tariffs, rates, working hours, and basic contract forms. The Union of the Workers of Art Cinema (commonly known in the film world by the name of its main premises, the café the Tenth Muse) also held discussions about the artistic development of cinema as well as lectures about new cameras and editing techniques. Most of its prominent members went on to work in the Soviet film industry, both as practitioners and as executives.[8]

As time went on, small professional unions started to merge together on the basis of their "class position." By the middle of 1918 the major ones were included in the system of the Moscow City Council of Proletarian Unions. In February 1919, the combined Union of Film Workers entered, as a section, the newly formed All-Russian Art Workers' Union, which was also known as Vserabis or simply Rabis. Other sections of the union included former unions of musicians, ballet dancers, circus performers, and stagehands.[9] This legitimate trade union could boast a substantial number of seventy thousand members countrywide by 1924, but its tendency to be all-inclusive led to individual sections and their concerns being all but lost within the giant organization.

A new, more compact organization of filmmakers was formed in 1922, soon after the introduction of the New Economic Policy. The Society of Cinema Personnel was a resurgence of the early spirit of the Tenth Muse during the new, less vigilant times. Led by Valentin Turkin, a journalist, scriptwriter, and former member of the Tenth Muse, the society was envisaged as a professional community where aesthetic and technical problems could be discussed. It could also serve as a grounds for exchanging knowledge, educating new personnel, and promoting cinema as art.[10]

One of the young communist journalists interested in cinema, Nikolai Lebedev, felt the need for a more politically and aesthetically up-to-date professional organization of filmmakers. He was opposed to the Society of Cinema Personnel's political indifference and its close ties to the émigré part of the prerevolutionary film community. This attitude led Lebedev to become the main force behind the creation of another professional organization of film workers, the Association of Revolutionary Cinematography.[11]

ARK's Mission and Scope of Activities

The list of signees of ARK's declaration in 1924 included, in addition to new names like Sergei Eisenstein, a lot of people with prerevolutionary experience. Many of them had been members of old unions such as the Tenth Muse and the Union of Film Workers. As was the case with the early film organizations, the main task of ARK was to promote cinema and prove that it was indeed an industry, not a "street show" or *kustarshchina* (amateur work). In new terms this agenda was expressed as "drawing the attention of broad Party and Soviet public opinion to cinema questions."[12] The "revolutionary" part of the association's name and agenda was expressed in the intention to exert "pressure on film-producing organizations with a view to correcting their ideological and artistic line." Notably, there was no agreement within the association as to "what a politically committed, communist cinema should be."[13] The correct "artistic" line was even less clear, but these points were something that ARK doggedly worked on in subsequent years. To develop and maintain a correct "ideological and artistic line," numerous film screenings, discussions, lectures, and debates were organized. This side of ARK's activities became most widely publicized.[14]

The association also attempted to carry several research projects. For example, audience polls were conducted to study their reactions and preferences. Another of the tasks that ARK set before itself was taking "measures in order to improve the knowledge of existing filmmakers and the emergence of new personnel."[15] At this time, skilled prerevolutionary artistic, technical, and administrative personnel constituted a relatively small fraction of the new Soviet film community. The State College of Cinematography, or GTK, which had opened in 1919, held classes only for would-be actors, directors, and cameramen.[16] As a result, professional education ranked very high on the association's list of priorities. Before the coming of sound, however, it never attempted to organize a long-term educational program.

In the early years of its existence, the number of ARK members rose significantly, reportedly because of a large influx of "incidental people," so that the organization had to get rid of its "ballast." After the re-registration of 1926 the number dropped to a meager 196.[17] By October 1, 1928, the number had reached 365. The association claimed that the quantitative jump was achieved through the admission of recent graduates from GTK. Just like the Tenth Muse of 1917, the organization was divided into sections based on professional divisions. The majority of the members were actors (ninety-two) and directors and their assistants (eighty-nine). There were fifty-five cameramen and assistant cameramen, thirty-five scriptwriters, sixteen journalists, twenty-six projectionists and lighting technicians, eleven musicians, fourteen set designers, and twenty-seven members of administrative personnel. The section of *kino-molodniak* (cinema youngsters) combined all recent graduates.[18]

ARK was essentially a Moscow-based organization, although it aspired to have republic-wide and union-wide influence. A Leningrad branch was established early on, but it quickly became so disorganized that a new, more independent branch, LenARRK, was set up in 1928.[19] If we consider that most of ARK's members lived and worked in Moscow, then it was indeed highly representative of at least the Russian film community. For example, in *Kino-spravochnik* (Film Guide), compiled by Grigory Boltiansky at the end of 1928, ninety-nine Moscow filmmakers designated themselves as directors and assistant directors, and seventy-two as cameramen and assistant cameramen. This is, respectively, just ten and seventeen people more than the membership of the corresponding sections of ARK.[20]

While the organization was growing, changing, and fighting for truly "revolutionary" cinematography, it still remained, Jamie Miller argues, just "an association of cinema professionals, not a trade union."[21] Rabis continued to be in charge of general organizational and economic matters, and especially of various questions of labor regulation within the film industry; however, "as the decade wore on, cinema personnel felt increasingly neglected by the trade union." The same problem of inflated membership and a disproportional amount of attention directed to the other arts that had brought such smaller organizations as the Society of Cinema Personnel and ARK into existence forced the association to expand its role within the film community. For example, as Miller asserts, it "began to adopt functions that would normally have fallen within the remit of Rabis, without having the powers of that union." These forays into the "territory" of Rabis even brought some tension between the two organizations.

In 1929 and 1930 the Soviet film industry experienced a unique situation, a highly disruptive moment, when ARRK could no longer simply remain an organization lobbying for revolutionary cinema. It had to assume more responsibilities in order to realize this cinema. Political, organizational, technological, and aesthetic problems plagued the industry, and ARRK, as the main professional organization, was caught in the middle. The most significant implication of these problems was the fact that there was suddenly no one before whom the association could successfully lobby, particularly for sound cinema.

Soviet Film Industry in 1929–30 and Its Response to Sound

Even before the film industry's absorption by VSNKh, which accounts for many of the problems the industry experienced during the early 1930s, the symptoms of organizational crisis were apparent. From January 1929 until February 1930, Soviet cinema was headed by the Cinema and Photo Committee, which was subordinate to Sovnarkom (Council of Peoples' Commissars). Although officially its task was to oversee all questions pertaining to the general development of cinema and photography in the Soviet Union, it served only as an advisory body, and not as an administrative one, since it did not have its own administrative apparatus and was not entrusted with economic functions.[22]

Prior to this, no unified planning had been introduced into the film industry. In particular, the first Five-Year Plan had been devised before the coming of sound in the Soviet Union and did not include any practical measures for its development. The ever-mounting criticism of the general production and distribution organization, Sovkino, made its position more and more precarious even within the boundaries of the Russian Republic.[23]

On February 13, 1930, the Cinema Committee and Sovkino were both superseded by a new organ, Soiuzkino (All-Union Combine of the Movie-Photo Industry).[24] Since technical matters had been an increasing concern among filmmakers for at least half a year prior to that, this new body was integrated into the system of VSNKh. As Viktor Listov noted, cinema was simply lost in the giant apparat of the Council for National Economy, and none of the pressing questions (e.g., production of Soviet film stock, cameras, sound projectors) was adequately resolved during this period.[25] By the end of 1930 the situation was still very difficult, especially in terms of sound implementation. An editorial in the journal *Kino i zhizn'* (Cinema and Life) complained that "in *Soiuzkino* alone no fewer than eight people 'answer' for sound cinema (one member of the board for production, another for supplies, a third one for cadres, a fourth one for the cinema network, and so on). In other words, there is complete chaos and a complete absence of responsibility."[26]

Soviet production companies were left to their own devices. On the one hand, the major film studios Sovkino and Mezhrabpom-film hastened to secure the services of the two Russian engineers who worked on sound technology (Alexander Shorin and Pavel Tager, respectively). On the other hand, their research was not sufficient to launch the mass production of sound films or sound equipment; as a result, film organizations felt the need to pool their resources to create some sort of a unified planning body devoted solely to sound. In early August 1929, the All-Union Conference of Film Organizations on Sound Cinema decided to create such a body. Zvukovaia Piaterka (the Sound Five), as it came to be known, included five high officials of the major Soviet film organizations: Moisei Aleinikov from Mezhrabpom-film; Ilya Trainin from Sovkino; and representatives of the Ukrainian film concern VUFKU, of the Belorussian Belgoskino, and of the Caucasian republics.[27]

Trainin was understood to be the head of the Sound Five, since its meetings were held under the Sovkino roof. It soon became apparent that the initiative failed to evolve into anything more than tea parties. In spite of the group's decision to pool resources and work on acquiring sound devices together, VUFKU went on and bought a recording device from Shorin's laboratory.[28] In December 1929, ARRK member, director, and cameraman Nikolai Anoshchenko noted: "The chaos is mounting, and the Sound Five that was supposed to be the only guide for the right way of developing sound film in the USSR has quietly . . . fallen apart."[29] The next month Alexander Razumnyi, cameraman, artist, director, and a prominent member of ARRK, expressed hope that the Cinema Committee would soon solve the problems of sound cinema, but a month later the committee itself ceased to exist.[30]

In the absence of any regulatory body or any supervision of the activities of individual studios and filmmakers, ARRK became the main forum for discussion, where anyone interested in the new technology and its repercussions could meet to debate organizational, technical, and aesthetic questions of sound cinema. Soon it aspired to be more than that.

ARRK's Sound Group

In August 1929, a special conference dedicated to sound cinema was held in Moscow. Its participants agreed that the future mass-scale implementation of the new technology demanded that certain educational measures be taken. Since the first sound films intended for general distribution were most likely to come from abroad (Germany or the United States), qualified projectionists were needed before anything else. The conference suggested organizing a six-month course for sound projectionists. The proposed curriculum included six hundred academic hours dedicated to electrical technology, radio technology, general film technology, and sound film technology, as well as acoustics, optics, and draftsmanship.

Members of ARRK opposed this idea, insisting that education had to start from the production side, namely with educating directors and cameramen. Ilya Trainin, however, expressed the firm belief that it was too early to talk about educating artistic personnel, since there was not anyone who could teach them anything about sound film.[31] The most that the Sound Five was prepared to do was to send one film director to Berlin to study sound film technology—and the Berlin experience was already considered secondhand at best.

Trainin was also against the idea of teaching the technology and methodology of sound film production simultaneously, arguing that technology had to come first. At the same time, the general view of Soviet filmmakers on sound cinema was that sound film abroad was a slave to technological novelty and that commercial reasons overshadowed the artistic development of sound film in the West. According to this view, only Soviet artists could bring it to full realization, just as they had done with silent film.[32] ARRK activist and film director Yury Genika lamented that the cinema administration wanted to, first of all, "set up film projectionist courses" instead of providing its subordinates with the opportunity to master the artistic side of sound film production. Meanwhile "film directors are left to search for ways to master sound cinema on their own, at their respective studios."[33] The Trainin-ARRK conflict over the question of sound education was the immediate impetus behind the Association's decision to organize the Educational-Experimental Group of Directors and Cameramen for Studying the Sound Film, otherwise known simply as the ARRK Sound Group.

The association's active preoccupation with sound can be traced to the report that member and journalist Vatslav Solsky made before the Central Committee of Rabis in 1928. In the same year, an ARRK group devoted to the theoretical study of sound cinema was established under the leadership of Grigori Alexandrov, co-author of the "Statement on Sound" with Eisenstein and Pudovkin, but "the group's activity was low and it soon dispersed."[34] During 1928 and 1929 several reports on sound cinema were read at general meetings of the association, and its members published a number of articles explaining and advocating sound cinema. Almost everyone who was writing about sound or making the first sound films during this period (Sergei Eisenstein, Vsevolod Pudovkin, Vladimir Erofeev, Ippolit Sokolov, and Nikolai Anoshchenko, to name just a few) was a member of ARRK.[35]

All of this fell in line with ARRK's previous activities. The Sound Group, however, was its boldest venture into the practical matters of film production. The association's leaders considered the organization of the group to be "the practical measure taken by ARRK in the business of sound cinema's creation, which constitutes the conclusion of the large political campaign for sound cinema accomplished by ARRK."[36] Since the association included professionals from all film organizations, it could help avoid "parallelism in the work of different studios (with inevitable 'secrets') and pointless searches for something that has already been found at another studio." This exchange of experience and knowledge could prevent competition between Soviet filmmakers and direct all their combined efforts to the task of "catching up and overtaking" the United States and Europe instead.[37]

Initially, the plan was to divide the work into four directions: introduction into radio technology; acoustics and music theory; acquaintance with the existing methods of sound reproduction; and colloquia on the sound projects of individual members, with reports on problems of technology, methodology, and organization of production. Members of the group were also supposed to conduct experiments, to collect and systematize all the information pertaining to sound technology and methodology, and to promote further development of sound cinema in the Soviet Union. It was proposed that the experimental part would dominate, "since the group includes the best directors and cameramen."[38]

Just like the proposed film projectionist courses, the educational program at ARRK was to last six months. The first official meeting of the Group was held on October 21, 1929. The group included twenty-five people who were chosen from eighty-seven applications proposed by the studios.[39] It was organized specifically for the education of directors and cameramen, but the majority of its participants were directors, with only three cameramen initially present.[40] Some people declined invitations to participate in the group's activities. Abram Room, who was in Leningrad working on his first sound film (*Plan velikikh rabot* [The Plan for Great Works, 1929]) at the time, allegedly answered that he was already filming, thus implying that had no need for classes, unlike his less fortunate colleagues.[41] Nevertheless, Room's co-writer for the film, director Vladimir Legoshin, became one of the members, together with cameramen Anatoly Golovnya and Grigory Kabalov, and noted film directors like Alexander Razumnyi, Viktor Turin, Nikolai Shengelaia, and Nikolai Okhlopkov.

The small number of students was expected to be advantageous for conducting experimental and practical work, although some members of the association expressed disapproval that they had been excluded from the group. Oleg Leonidov, a prominent scriptwriter working at Mezhrabpom-film, later lamented the complete absence of scriptwriters in the group. By January 1930 the number of students had reached thirty-five. At least some of the new members were journalists, who were entrusted with the task of publicizing the group's activities.[42]

The members of the initial group were expected to serve later on as the first sound film experts, who would be able not only to do practical work but also to train new "echelons" of future sound professionals. It was reported that several working groups on sound were set up around them at film studios. ARRK itself planned to organize several more groups and to regulate subsequent large-scale activities across the country. In the summer of 1930 there were still talks about the second sound group for cameramen and directors, and the first group for scriptwriters, but these plans did not materialize.[43]

When ARRK set up its Sound Group, there were very few people in the Soviet Union who had firsthand experience with sound film. These lucky few could at best boast about their trips to Berlin. As one of the ARRK members noted, however, Russians were not actually welcomed in German sound studios, and doors were politely but firmly closed in their faces.[44] As a result, even these fortunate travelers had to rely mainly on hearsay and those examples of American sound productions that reached Berlin. For those who remained in the Soviet Union, their only exposure to sound technology was through demonstrations of the German sound system, Tri-Ergon.[45] Some people familiarized themselves with the new technology through foreign magazines and books, which had only started to make their way into the Soviet Union. The talks and the articles of the few initiated were nowhere near enough to satisfy the anxiety that was rapidly spreading among the film community.[46]

It appeared that Ilya Trainin was right in saying that there was no one within the film industry who could teach sound cinema. Just like sound projectionists, however, sound directors and cameramen could gain knowledge from radio engineers and music specialists. The Sound Group curriculum thus relied heavily on these resources. Both Tager and Shorin presented their respective sound systems at the group's meetings. Sergei Bugoslavsky, a composer and a critic who at the time was heading the musical section of the Soviet radio, gave a course on musical analysis. Composer Arseny Avraamov reported on his work with Abram Room on *The Plan for Great Works*.[47] The other lecturers included the head of the radio division of Narkompochtel' (Commissariat for Post and Telegraph), A. M. Vasiliev, and Professor Samuil Lifshits, a student of the famous Russian radio and telephone inventor Alexander Popov.

The curriculum was continuously adjusted during the process of implementation. In the end, about 80 percent of the outlined program was fulfilled. The proposed number of classes on musical analysis was cut in half. Six hours of classes on voice training for sound film were added, as were six more hours on sound imitation. Several directors and cameramen who had been able to start implementing sound technology gave reports, including actor, director, and sound engineer Leonid Obolensky, documentary filmmaker and one of ARRK's organizers Vladimir Erofeev, and cameraman Yury Stillianudis. The group organized several general symposia on sound, including a meeting with members of the association's screenwriting section. The participants read and discussed the sound script for the Hollywood film *Broadway* (dir. Fejos, 1929).[48] Although sound experimentation was envisaged as an essential part of the group's activities, only four "practical" classes were held: two at the Radio Center with engineer Garon and two with Shorin on his system. When the theoretical part of the curriculum was over in March 1930 and the question of practical sessions arose, the group had to be disbanded simply because there were no facilities where these sessions could be conducted.[49] The experimental part of the group's work failed to materialize as well. Plans to buy a recording apparatus from Tager's laboratory were thwarted when the price the association was ready to pay turned out not to include any amplifiers, accumulators, or other necessary devices. Still, even though no more lectures were given after March 1930, after the initial six months had ended, individual talks and discussions continued, as did occasional meetings. Thus, even with this abridged experience, the group's graduates still had more knowledge of sound cinema than the general film population. Studying sound at ARRK was declared to be more beneficial than going to Berlin.[50] Members of the Sound Group considered themselves among the first Soviet sound filmmakers and expected to be treated accordingly.

Effects of the Sound Group's Activity on the Industry at Large

Despite the importance that ARRK's members attached to their work on sound, the association's initiative met with the general indifference of the industry and its executives. At the moment of the Sound Group's inception, Sovkino's Sound Five agreed to assist with acquiring, multiplying, and distributing stenographic records of the lectures, but it did not provide any other material support or ideological and practical guidance.[51] After its dissolution, no other production or administrative cinema organization oversaw or supported the Sound Group's activity.

By the summer of 1930 only twelve members of the group were reportedly working on sound projects at different film studios.[52] Not all of them were able to fully implement their knowledge into practice and finish their projects. N. Prim, a director of *kul'turfil'my* (educational films) and one of the most active members of the group, complained in December 1930 that the sound film he was supposed to make, *Den'* (Day), was passed on to the "silent director" Eduard Pentslin. The "sound director" Prim was offered to work on silent shorts instead.[53]

In May 1930, member of the ARRK Sound Group Nikolai Ekk started work on what was to be lauded in a year as the first Soviet sound film, *Putevka v zhizn'* (The Road to Life, 1931), at *Mezhrabpom-film*. Cameraman Grigory Kabalov was working on Vsevolod Pudovkin's *Ochen' khorosho zhivetsia* (It's a Beautiful Life), released in 1932 as *Prostoi sluchai* (A Simple Case; see figure 4.1). In contrast,

Figure 4.1. On the set of Vsevolod Pudovkin's first sound film *Ochen' khorosho zhivetsia* (Life Is Beautiful), later renamed *Prostoi sluchai* (A Simple Case). The filming began in the summer of 1929 but was released in 1932. *Left to right*: sound engineer Leonid Obolensky, inventor Pavel Tager, assistant Shchipanovsky, and cameraman Grigory Kabalov. Photo by S. Karasev (*Sovetskii erkran*, no. 35 [1929], back cover).

Alexander Razumnyi, who was determined to add the profession of sound engineer to his already-impressive list of credentials, had the production of his sound film *Pesn' o Kamenke* (A Song about Kamenka) suddenly stopped by Soiuzkino in February 1931. By that time the film had already been half completed, but the recently introduced "regime of economy" made the studio reluctant to put more money into its two sound projects. It was less costly to simply cut its losses and leave the films unfinished, so the films were shelved despite protests from ARRK and the studio's party cell.[54] Razumnyi then turned to radio and, after several months of preparation, directed a "radio film" about the celebration of the fourteenth anniversary of the October Revolution. He was finally able to re-establish his position as a film director in the late 1930s, but not before another of his projects, based on Alexander Serafimovich's novel *Zheleznyi potok* (The Iron Stream), had been stopped before even reaching the filming stage, and the next one, *Kara-Bugaz* (1935), was shelved.[55]

Director Vladimir Kasianov similarly moved to a related field and made the first Soviet television film, *Litso mezhdunarodnogo kapitalizma* (The Face of International Capitalism) in 1932;[56] after that he stopped working as a director altogether. At a meeting of the Sound Group he complained that film studios invited people from the theater, music, and fine arts to direct sound films while the clearly more experienced members of the Sound Group were left idle.[57] Nikolai Anoshchenko made several documentaries, experimented with color film in 1931, and then concentrated on teaching future cameramen at VGIK (the former State College of Cinematography, and later the All-Union State Film Institute). The thwarted careers of these people, who took every measure to prepare for the coming of sound, confirm Viktor Listov's thesis, mentioned at the beginning of the chapter—namely, that organizational and administrative chaos (and not aesthetic or technological impediments) was the primary factor of the deferred development of sound cinema in the Soviet Union.

In the politicized parlance of the day, Konstantin Feldman, a journalist and a former film executive, termed this attitude of the film studios as "right-wing opportunism," whereas director Victor Turin called the Soiuzkino actions "bordering on wrecking."[58] Although the level of discussion in 1930 tended to be more politically charged than the previous year, at that point there was little ARRK or its Sound Group could actually do to change the situation. The meeting in which the sound directors' grievances were discussed passed a modest resolution, protesting against Soiuzkino's attitude and asking the ARRK Secretariat to pay attention to the disruption of production work of the group's members.

ARRK's Last Years

The changing language of the discussions surrounding sound indicated changes that were both external and internal to the organization. In 1929 and 1930, the years of ARRK's most active involvement in all matters of sound cinema, were also the most turbulent for the association. As organizational, technical, and economic crises rocked the film industry in this period, ARRK remained the only stable institution. This stability, however, had already begun to be questioned and undermined.

By the late 1920s the association was perceived as an elite organization, since it was essentially restricted to Moscow and Leningrad and included only some categories of personnel. At the same time it was considered too liberal, because it allowed relative aesthetic freedom to its members and did not impose many limitations on their ways of thinking or on their practices. It was, instead, a genuine forum for debates within the film industry. This got the organization into trouble during the Cultural Revolution that was in full swing by 1930. As Peter Kenez has noted, the Cultural Revolution "represented a resurgence of utopian notions about the nature of culture and politics and a demand for a complete break with the past. More specifically, the cultural pluralism that had existed in the 1920s was to be rejected. Under these circumstances the enemy was no longer an abstraction, but flesh and blood: anyone who aimed at protecting the tiniest bit of cultural autonomy."[59]

In 1929 the association had already changed its name from ARK to ARRK, adding the word *workers* to its title. The attack on ARRK was most violently lodged by RAPP several months after that, in September 1929, right before the Sound Group's classes began. RAPP demanded that the association purge "obviously hostile elements" and train film workers from a "proletarian background."[60]

Turning ARRK into a proletarian mass organization proved impossible, but the purges of 1929–31 were quite successful in terms of eliminating the "obviously hostile element." By the end of January 1931, 40 percent of the total 428 members had been purged. As a result, the number of party and Komsomol members went up from 18 percent to 28 percent.[61] Some active members, such as the critic Mikhail Shneider, were expelled. One of the organizers of the Sound Group, Anatoly Ardatov, a scriptwriter, director, and Sovkino and Soiuzkino executive, was among the few ARRK members who received capital punishment. He had been "a sixth member" of the Sound Five and had tried hard to lobby in the Sound Group's interests. By the summer of 1930 he had become the head of the planning and economic division of Soiuzkino. As such, he was arrested on December 7, 1930, and shot half a year later on charges of wrecking and counter-revolutionary activity.[62]

The years following the purges also witnessed a drastic change in ARRK discussions, of which sound debates provided only one, but the most obvious, example. Initially, questions of "sound methodology" (i.e., of aesthetics) were heatedly debated.[63] The Trainin-ARRK debate in the summer of 1929 was indicative of the shift from methodology to technology. Later, organizational problems came to the fore, since Soviet technology so noticeably lagged behind that of the United States and Europe. By the end of 1930, neither technological nor organizational problems were considered principal. Film critic Ippolit Sokolov, who had spent 1928 and 1929 writing on various topics connected to sound and had presented a paper at a meeting of the Sound Group in 1930, remarked mockingly: "Our filmmakers have spent the whole year in a one-sided obsession with the technical side of sound equipment or, rather, with elementary technical aspects of electrical and radio engineering and have dreamed of becoming sound mixers. . . . Bare technology has overshadowed questions of ideology and questions of content and form of sound film." The questions of content and form were subordinated to ideology and were not identical to the earlier problems of "methodology." If anything, technology became closer to aesthetics, since they were both related to form and, according to the logic of the times, to formalism. Sokolov stated, "The substitution of bare technology for content and form is the most extreme kind of Formalism."[64] This was a serious assault. As Peter Kenez put it, "In film polemics the term [formalism] came to describe any concern with the specifically aesthetic aspect of filmmaking, any deviation from a simple narrative line, and any artistic innovation."[65] Sound cinema was all about technical and formal innovation; and the purpose of ARRK's Sound Group was to prepare filmmakers for future production work. Instead, after the purges they were urged to focus on political education and working with the masses.[66]

When *Proletarian Cinema* was launched in 1931, its editorial stated that the "socialist reconstruction" of the Soviet film industry was in fact "the complete and final overcoming of the experience of our class enemy—bourgeois cinema."[67] The prerequisite for this was "a correct political line, created solely on the basis of very great experience of the struggle of the working class, the experience condensed in the teaching of Marx, Engels and Lenin." The new main task of the journal and, by extension, of ARRK, was to elaborate a Marxist-Leninist theory for cinema, and to make hegemonic that theory and its method of dialectical materialism. The advocated cinematic practice was to be a social one, defined as a violent class struggle. ARRK and its journal were no longer concerned with creating a small number of reliable professionals for the rapidly changing industry, but with politically large numbers of "proletarian cadres," the only possible driving force behind the socialist reconstruction of the industry. Organizational, technical, and economic problems were declared important too, but they could not be "an end in themselves. . . . [T]heir correct resolution will be achieved only if everything is seen in the light of the tasks of *socialist* reconstruction, i.e. on the basis of a definite political line." Now ARRK was more concerned with rallying in support of children's cinema, rural cinema, military cinema, and Stakhanovism. These demands no longer rose from within ARRK or the film community in general; they were imposed on them from above.

Conclusion

In 1929 and 1930 ARRK was the only organization in the Soviet Union that was active in consolidating scattered resources and facilitating the exchange and dissemination of knowledge on sound cinema. Following the period of "proletarization" and the purges, in 1931 the association's members continued to appeal in vain for any organization to take up this task. Dziga Vertov's cameraman Boris Tseitlin noted that while sound films were being made in three different cities of the Soviet Union (Moscow, Leningrad, and Kiev), their studios still did not know or simply did not want to share their experiences or to exchange their knowledge. As a result, according to Tseitlin, each of them still had to go through the same processes of trial and error, repeating each other's mistakes and thereby needlessly wasting time and money. "Who can stop all this nonsense and how? Who will organize a regular and immediate exchange of experience that we already have and that we are acquiring daily?" he asked.[68] Ironically, this question was voiced on the pages of the ARRK publication, at a time when the organization itself could only print these pleas and did not yet have the power to act on them.

In a sense, the efforts of the Sound Group paid off. Its graduates, such as Nikolai Ekk, Grigory Kabalov, and Grigory Levkoev, became the first professional sound filmmakers of the Soviet Union. Several others, like Alexander Razumnyi and Vladimir Kasianov, with the help of knowledge acquired through ARRK, made important contributions to other nascent media, such as radio and television. Some went on to teach future generations of filmmakers who only had sound cinema to work with.

The efforts of the film community to build a pool of creative and technical personnel for sound film production and to lobby for sound before the film administration were both thwarted in favor of ideological education and immediate mass mobilization. This hindered and decelerated the process of the transition to sound. The other effect of the purging and "proletarization" of ARRK was the dissolution of the community spirit of Soviet filmmakers. Despite an attempt at organizing a new professional organization in the mid-1930s, it was not until the 1950s that the filmmakers were able to start lobbying successfully for a cinema-specific union that could represent their community before the authorities and be instrumental in resolving organizational, technical, and aesthetic problems of the industry.

Notes

I would like to thank Lilya Kaganovsky and Masha Salazkina for their comments and suggestions. I am indebted to Lidia Zaitseva for encouraging my initial interest in ARRK and the period of the transition to sound. Naum Kleiman and Armen Medvedev have sustained this interest and have helped in innumerable ways over the years. I am also very grateful to Natalia Chertova for many happy hours of browsing through old film periodicals and archival materials kept at the Russian State Film University (VGIK).

1. "V chem zhe delo," 1. The first public demonstration of the system invented by Pavel Tager happened in Moscow in March 1928.

2. For a summary of the traditional Western approach to the "break" between the cinema of the 1920s and the 1930s, see Richard Taylor, "Soviet Socialist Realism and the Cinema Avant-Garde," *Studies in Comparative Communism* 17, nos. 3–4 (1984): 185–202.

3. For an example of the former approach, see Vance Kepley Jr., "The First *Perestroika*: Cinema under the First Five-Year Plan," *Cinema Journal* 35, no. 4 (1996): 31–53. For examples of the latter approach, see Ian Christie, "Soviet Cinema: Making Sense of Sound," *Screen* 23, no. 2 (July–August 1982): 34–49; Kristin Thompson, "Early Sound Counterpoint," *Yale French Studies* 60 (1980): 115–40.

4. Viktor Listov, "Kino: iskusstvo ili promyshlennost'? (Iz opyta kommentariev k gosudarstvennym aktam 20-30-kh godov)," in *Teoreticheskie chteniia pamiati S. I. Iutkevicha* (Moscow: VNIIK, 1992), 74–75.

5. Since 1924 the association had a number of newspapers and magazines. For a quick list, see Taylor, "Soviet Socialist Realism," 191–92.

6. The dominant Soviet point of view is expressed most eloquently in the entry for "Assotsiatsiia rabotnikov revoliutsionnoi kinematografii (ARRK)," in Sergei Iutkevich's *Kino: Entsiklopedicheskii slovar'* (Moscow: Sovetskaia entsiklopediia, 1987).

7. The exact nature of ARRK's complicated relationship with RAPP is beyond the scope of this text. For an introduction to the subject, see Taylor, "Soviet Socialist Realism," 192; Denise Youngblood, *Soviet Cinema in the Silent Era, 1919–1935* (Ann Arbor: University of Michigan Research Press, 1985), 59–60; and Richard Taylor and Ian Christie, eds., *The Film Factory: Russian and Soviet Cinema in Documents 1896–1939* (London: Routledge and Kegan Paul, 1988), 249. For the discussion of 1928 to 1932, see Youngblood, *Soviet Cinema in the Silent Era*, passim; Jamie Miller, *Soviet Cinema: Politics and Persuasion under Stalin* (London: I. B. Tauris, 2010), 56–57, 76–78, and 105–9.

8. For a general history of professional film organizations in the period 1917–21, see Natalia Ryabchikova, "Sorokhuki i desiataia muza," *Menedzher kino*, no. 49 (2008): 34–41. On the Tenth Muse, see also Aleksandr Razumnyi, *U istokov . . . : vospominaniia kinorezhissera* (Moscow: Iskusstvo, 1975), 28–51.

9. "Privet Vserabisu!" *Kino*, June 3, 1924, 1.

10. Redaktsiia (editorial), *Kino: dvukhnedel'nik obshchestva kinodeiatelei*, October 20, 1922, 1.

11. Miller, *Soviet Cinema*, 105–6. Lebedev went to become one of the leading Soviet film historians. Unfortunately, his books sometimes presented his early views and attitudes as unequivocal truth, which led to distortions and misrepresentation of certain historical facts and tendencies.

12. This and the next quotation are from "Declaration of the Association of Revolutionary Cinematography," in Taylor and Christie, *Film Factory*, 103.

13. Miller, *Soviet Cinema*, 106.

14. For example, see Youngblood, *Soviet Cinema in the Silent Era*, 119–24.

15. Grigorii Boltianskii, ed., *Kino-spravochnik* (Moscow: Teakinopechat', 1929), 325; Miller, *Soviet cinema*, 106.

16. Vishnevskii, "Istoriia Gosudarstvennogo Instituta Kinematografii," 8–10.

17. Boltianskii, *Kino-spravochnik*, 325. Denise Youngblood considers this event the first purge in film industry (*Soviet Cinema in the Silent Era*, 61).

18. Boltianskii, *Kino-spravochnik*, 326–27.

19. Razumnyi, *U istokov*, 108; Youngblood, *Soviet Cinema in the Silent Era*, 253.

20. The numbers are based on the address book in Boltianskii, *Kino-spravochnik*, 412–41.

21. This and the next two quotations are from Miller, *Soviet Cinema*, 107–8.

22. Kepley, "The First *Perestroika*," 42.

23. Taylor and Christie, *Film Factory*, 285; Aleksandr Razumnyi, "Usilim tempy," *Kino i zhizn'*, no. 1 (1930): 7; Youngblood, *Soviet Cinema in the Silent Era*, 157–62, 169–71.

24. Taylor and Christie, *Film Factory*, 283.

25. Listov, "Kino," 75–77.

26. "*Kino i zhizn'* Editorial: Is There a Soviet Sound Cinema?" in Taylor and Christie, *Film Factory*, 310–11.

27. Valerii Fomin and Aleksandr Deriabin, eds., *Letopis' rossiiskogo kino: 1863–1929* (Moscow: Materik, 2004), 668.

28. RGALI, f. 2494, op. 1, ed. kh. 220, ll. 9–10.

29. Nikolai Anoshchenko, "Nasha zvukovaia fil'ma," *Kino i zhizn'* 4 (1929): 15.

30. Razumnyi, "Usilim tempy."

31. Iurii Genika, "Uchebno-eksperimental'naia gruppa pri ARRK," *Kino*, August 20, 1929, 5.

32. N. Prim, "Neobkhodim perelom," *Kino*, October 29, 1929, 1.

33. Genika, "Uchebno-eksperimental'naia gruppa," 5.

34. RGALI, f. 2494, op. 1, ed. kh. 292, l. 9.

35. For explorations of theoretical views of the association's members see, e.g., Christie, "Soviet Cinema," 176–92; Youngblood, *Soviet Cinema in the Silent Era*, 222–23; and Thompson, "Early Sound Counterpoint," 115–40.

36. This and the next quotation are from "Nachali uchit'sia," *Kino*, October 29, 1929, 1. These words, allegedly said by ARRK's chairman, Konstantin Iukov, are absent from the stenographic record of the meeting.

37. On the importance (and implications) of this pronouncement, made by Stalin, see R. W. Davis, *The Soviet Economy in Turmoil, 1929–1930* (Cambridge: Cambridge University Press, 1989), 139–42.

38. "Nachali uchit'sia," 1; "V ARRKe," *Kino*, September 24, 1929, 3.

39. Prim, "Neobkhodim perelom," 1. ARRK's chairman, Konstantin Iukov, at one point gave the figure of 150 applicants, but this was probably exaggerated for polemical reasons. See RGALI, f. 2494, op. 1, ed. kh. 219, l. 1.

40. Prim, "Neobkhodim perelom," 1.

41. RGALI, f. 2494, op. 1, ed. kh. 220, ll. 32–33.

42. RGALI, f. 2494, op. 1, ed. kh. 219, l. 1; ed. kh. 220, l. 28; ed. kh. 292, l. 10.

43. "Nachali uchit'sia," 1; Anoshchenko, "Nasha zvukovaia fil'ma," 15; Prim, "Neobkhodim perelom," 1; RGALI, f. 2494, op. 1, ed. kh. 219, l. 1 and ed. kh. 292, l. 10.

44. RGALI, f. 2494, op. 1, ed. kh. 219, l. 2.

45. Fomin and Deriabin, *Letopis' rossiiskogo kino: 1863–1929*, 560.

46. Christie, "Soviet Cinema," 177–78.

47. The lecture was published as "ARRK. Stenogramma lektsii tov. Avraamova v gruppe zvukovogo kino ARRKa," *Kinovedcheskie zapiski*, no. 53 (2001): 300–313.

48. RGALI, f. 2494, op. 1, ed. kh. 292, l. 9.

49. Ibid.

50. Ibid., ed. kh. 219, ll. 3–4.

51. Anoshshenko, "Nasha zvukovaia fil'ma," 15; RGALI, f. 2494, op. 1, ed. kh. 292, l. 9.

52. RGALI, f. 2494, op. 1, ed. kh. 292, l. 10.

53. Ibid., l. 8.

54. The second film was *Shtorm* (The Storm) by Grigory Levkoev, another member of the ARRK Sound Group. His film was later completed and released in 1931. See "Roscherkom pera unichtozhaetsia trud mnogikh dnei," *Kino*, February 11, 1931, 2; Razumnyi, *U istokov*, 122; Valerii Fomin and Aleksandr Deriabin, eds., *Letopis' rossiiskogo kino: 1930–1945* (Moscow: Materik, 2007), 91.

55. Razumnyi, *U istokov*, 122–24.

56. On May 1, 1931, the Soviet Union held its first experimental mechanical television broadcast without sound. The first television programs with sound were broadcast on medium radio-wave frequency on October 1, 1931, in Moscow (with broadcasts from Leningrad and Odessa coming later). Moscow began regularly broadcasting programs twelve times a month for sixty minutes; and in October 1932, it showed a film on opening the Dnieper hydroelectric power, filmed only a few days before. In December 1933, Moscow broadcasting ceased, in anticipation of the development of electric television. However, since the industry had not yet mastered the new television equipment, transmission again resumed on February 11, 1934, with the formation of the All-Union Committee for Radiofication and Radio Broadcasting of the Soviet Union. Regular television broadcasting in the Soviet Union started in 1938, first in Moscow and Leningrad only. Mechanical television finally ceased broadcasting April 1, 1941.

57. RGALI, f. 2494, op. 1, ed. kh. 292, l. 8.

58. Ibid.

59. Peter Kenez, "The Cultural Revolution in Cinema," *Slavic Review* 47, no. 3 (1988): 415.

60. "RAPP Resolution on Cinema," in Taylor and Christie, *Film Factory*, 275–80. On the purges in ARRK, see Miller, *Soviet Cinema*, 76–78; Youngblood, *Soviet Cinema in the Silent Era*, 191–92. Many scholars have perceived it as an attempt to rebuff claims that the association was not revolutionary or proletarian enough. While the word *rabotniki* is commonly translated as "workers," it applied more to personnel than to factory workers, and the numbers of true proletarians in the film industry were always regrettably low. Since 1919 the same word has also been included in the name of the art workers' trade union, Rabis, which could accept anyone from the best-known actors and directors down to the last set builder. Since there was talk of parallelism between Rabis and ARK at the time, it is possible that the name change was designed to further reflect this parallelism and to show ARRK's broader scope of membership rather than to simply prove ARK's compliance with the demands of "proletarization."

61. "Vyvody komissii po chistke ARRK," *Kino*, February 11, 1931, 3; Youngblood, *Soviet Cinema in the Silent Era*, 192.

62. RGALI, f. 2494, op. 1, ed. kh. 220, l. 32; Leo Mur, "Zvukovaia konferentsiia ARRK," *Kino i zhizn'*, no. 24 (1930): 20; V. Tikhanova, ed., *Rasstrel'nye spiski, vypusk 2: Vagan'kovskoe kladbishche, 1926–1936* (Moscow: Memorial, 1995), 160.

63. The "Statement on Sound" by Eisenstein, Pudovkin, and Alexandrov is the most famous example of these debates. See, e.g., Christie, "Soviet Cinema," 180–83.

64. This and the previous quotations are from "Ippolit Sokolov: The Second Sound Film Programme," in Taylor and Christie, *Film Factory*, 308. For the stenographic record of Sokolov's presentation at ARRK, see RGALI, f. 2494, op. 1, ed. kh. 292, ll. 7–8.

65. Kenez, "Cultural Revolution in Cinema," 417.

66. "Vyvody komissii po chistke ARRK," 3.

67. This and the next two quotations are from "*Proletarskoe kino* Editorial: What Does 'Proletarian Cinema' Mean?" in Taylor and Christie, *Film Factory*, 318–19.

68. Boris Tseitlin, "Zvukovaia bestolkovshchina," *Proletarskoe kino*, nos. 2–3 (1931): 57–58, 60.

5 Making Sense without Speech

The Use of Silence in Early Soviet Sound Film

Emma Widdis

Abram Room's 1936 film *Strogii iunosha* (A Severe Youth), with a screenplay by Yury Olesha, opens in silence. Its credits run to an entirely silent sound track, as does the first visual sequence, which comprises a succession of filmed objects. The camera eye moves through venetian blinds to a table set with a vase of flowers, viewed through a transparent curtain. The scene changes to a shot of a woman diving into the sea; only then does a musical sound track quietly begin. This music accompanies the scene of the swimming woman until a long still shot of a Dalmatian dog's head returns the sound track to silence.

This opening sequence is the first of several striking uses of silence in *A Severe Youth*. In this film, Room exploits what Hungarian critic (and contemporary of Room and Olesha) Béla Balázs identified as the specific and vital power of the sound film: the ability to reproduce silence. For Balázs, this reproduction of silence was "one of the most specific dramatic effects of the sound film."[1] As is well known, *A Severe Youth* was banned by the censors and criticized for "chasing after external beauty."[2] Film historians have largely followed the censors in blaming the film's fate on the formalism of its visual style.[3] This has obscured full consideration of the film's use of sound. By the time that Room made *A Severe Youth*, sound film was well established in the Soviet Union; the second of Grigori Alexandrov's well-known musicals, *Tsirk* (Circus, 1936), appeared in the same year. But Room's use of sound in his film is unusual; in places—and in its frequent recourse to a "dead" (silent) sound track in particular—it can appear clumsy. Yet Room's creative use of sound and silence can and should be considered part of the film's broader formal experiment.

A Severe Youth, however, is not only of interest to Soviet cinema historians as an example of political censorship or formal experimentation. In both its theme and its style, this film engaged with a core question that preoccupied Soviet filmmakers throughout the 1930s: the shape of the new Soviet cinematic hero. In *A Severe Youth*, that question was directly linked to a self-reflexive inquiry into the place of cinema—and of art more generally—in forming the contours, and specifically the *sensibility*, of that Soviet self. The creative use of the technical possibilities of sound film was central to this inquiry, in particular in the use of silence as a challenge to speech. The dominance of dialogue—of the voice—in sound cinema has preoccupied film theorists and practitioners since the inception of sound technology and has been intensively explored by Michel Chion. Chion writes: "In actual movies, for real spectators, there are not *all the sounds including the human voice. There are voices, and then everything else.*" The presence of the human voice, he suggests, sets up "a hierarchy of perception."[4] I argue that in *A Severe Youth*, Room made a conscious challenge to this "hierarchy of perception." In this film, sound and silence create a space for working through core questions. First, and perhaps inevitably, these questions relate to the nature of cinematic communication itself: how did the transformation to sound change or challenge the nature of spectatorial engagement with, and experience of, a film?

This inquiry into the potency of different sensory modes in cinema—seeing, speaking, hearing, feeling—was crucially linked in *A Severe Youth* to broader questions about the nature of Soviet subjectivity itself. Debate and practice in Soviet cinema during the 1930s were distinguished by the search for a viable shape for the new Soviet cinematic hero: the search for individual, "real" characters to replace the "mass heroes" of the cinema of the 1920s. There was a call for what critic Nikolai Iezuitov called a cinema "of socialist *feelings* [*sotsialisticheskikh chuvstv*]" to replace the cinema "of concepts/abstractions [*poniatii*]" that had dominated the previous decade.[5] But the nature of these "socialist feelings" was by no means clear. In this essay, I analyze *A Severe Youth* in relation to two other key examples of early Soviet sound cinema, both by director Alexander Macheret: *Dela i liudi* (Men and Jobs, 1932), one of the first Soviet sound films, and *Chastnaia zhizn' Petra Vinogradova* (The Private Life of Petr Vinogradov, 1934). Between them, these three films straddle four core years in the development of Soviet sound film, from its beginning to its relative maturity. They all exploit the relationship of sound, silence, and image to explore the sensory relationship between their protagonists and the material world. Specifically, these films question the nature of *verbal* communication. *Men and Jobs* features a hero who cannot speak; it appropriates the new technology of sound to its inanimate characters, to the machinery of production; *The Private Life of Petr Vinogradov*, in contrast, features a hero who needs to learn to speak less, who needs to learn to feel. And finally, *A Severe Youth* explicitly links its youthful heroes to the mute statuary of classical antiquity. In all of these films, although in different ways, explicit challenges to spoken language are part of a two-fold inquiry—into the nature of cinema itself and into the shape of Soviet "feelings." How would sound technology transform, damage, or enrich cinema's contribution to the production of a new sensory regime for Soviet Russia?[6]

Men and Jobs: Feeling Soviet?

Macheret's *Men and Jobs* was much discussed in the Soviet film press and was hailed as one of the first successful Soviet sound films: successful, that is, in that it succeeded—according to Iezuitov—in making good use of all of the existing sound technology. Iezuitov bemoaned the fact that the coming of sound technology had, in many cases, meant a neglect of the importance of visual material—"as if the art of Tisse, etc., had never existed."[7] By contrast, he suggested, Macheret's film used sound to enhance the impact of the film's visual track. Most reviewers praised actor Nikolai Okhlopov for his performance as the film's hero, brigade leader Zakharov, and in particular for the creation of Zakharov as a "real" character, with both flaws and strengths.[8] In its plot, the film treats a core slogan of the first Five-Year Plan: the assertion that the Soviet Union's industrial productivity would "catch up and overtake" the United States. It tells the story of the arrival of an American specialist, Mr. Kleins, at the Dneprostroi construction site and his judgment that the Soviet work brigades do not work effectively. Through the narrative of the personal evolution of brigade leader Zakharov, and the improvement of his team's productivity, Macheret's film was an object lesson in workplace discipline and efficiency.

With the figure of Zakharov, Macheret and Okhlopov responded to growing calls for "real," three-dimensional characters on the Soviet screen. There were, Macheret later recalled, two key problems that dominated the debate in the film industry during the early 1930s: "the search for contemporary heroes, and the working out of the principles of a rounded presentation of character."[9] Who were the heroes of the new Soviet Union, and how could they be represented on-screen? He described *Men and Jobs* as both a search for a route through the complex and contradictory messages that framed discussions of the shape of the new Soviet subject on film and a reconciliation between the "individual/personal qualities" of a character and his or her "social role."[10] Here Macheret was echoing some of the key terms and questions of the day: according to film critic Piataev in 1933, "The individual is emerging." He went on to ask, "Which individual?" His answer: "The individual builder of Socialism, the many millions of individuals who make up the collective of builders of socialism."[11]

In *Men and Jobs*, the attempt to represent the inner life of a character on-screen was certainly carried out with the help of sound technology, but it was not, crucially, dependent on monologue, dialogue, or the straightforward representation of speech. Indeed, one of the distinctive weaknesses of Zakharov's character is his lack of facility with words. He speaks badly—especially as an orator. We first see him struggling to make himself heard against the ambient noise of a public meeting. He is trying but failing to speak the Soviet word. In another scene, he stages a drunken debate with himself in front of a mirror, his language marked

by rhetorical interjections, ambivalence, and false starts: "Now, I . . . Now, I . . .
I am a worker. . . . Right, right, right. . . . That's what I'm saying. . . . But not like
that, not like that." This fractured language carries a message about Zakharov as
an individual, but it also extends beyond him into the film's broader thematics,
which stage an inquiry into the value and nature of the spoken word in the revolutionary project. In *Men and Jobs*, the human voice is often struggling to make
itself heard amid a sound track full of other sounds, including music, industry,
transport, and conversation.

Macheret's response to the "problem" of the voice in sound cinema, then,
was to create a central protagonist who could not speak.[12] There are several other
instances in the film in which speech and words are challenged. First, through
the film's multilingualism: the presence of American engineer Kleins and his
translator creates a gap between language and meaning that has resonance in
several ways.[13] First, like other sound strategies in the film, it challenges the su-
premacy of the spoken word within the film's soundscape. Second, it allows key
words to be considered critically. Mr. Kleins fails to understand two terms that
were central to the discourse of the first Five-Year Plan: *sotsialisticheskoe sorevnovanie* (socialist competition) and *udarnik* (shock worker). This failure is a mark
not just of his linguistic foreignness but also of the terms' conceptual originality:
it is not that the translator is incompetent, but there simply is no equivalent to
sotsialistichestkoe sorevnovanie; it cannot be equated to capitalist "competition."
This estranging of the phrase does not equate to straightforward praise, however;
rather, the film's plot interrogates the real successes of "socialist competition" and
reveals its failings. Kleins misunderstands the term: "you mean that these people
do not know how to work; I saw that immediately." His lack of comprehension
prompts a fresh look at the reality of Soviet labor.

More broadly, the challenge to the primacy of dialogue in this film is part
of its interrogation of the impact of sound on the creation of cinematic meaning. Although dialogue is challenged in *Men and Jobs*, the film exploits the full
potential of other forms of sound technology. Sound increases the impact of
Macheret's "production sequences": the machines rumble and click, drills grind,
gravel tumbles noisily. These sounds of technology are enhanced by a musical
score that echoes their mechanical rhythms. A synchrony between sound and
visual material is used as a means of anthropomorphizing machinery; indeed,
the machines speak more eloquently than Zakharov. In one scene, for example,
a dialogue between Kleins and his translator is interrupted by the moaning of an
enormous excavator, its metallic jaws apparently baying in pain. When Zakharov is rendered mute, shocked by Kleins's brutal dismissal of the achievements
of Soviet labor, it is the metallic screeches of machines that express his anguish.

This rich manipulation of sound is directly linked to the film's overarching
challenge to the dominance of speech. As Chion suggests, "The use of different

sensory effects and the presence of various sensations and rhythms . . . gives us the feeling that the world is not reduced to the function of embodying dialogue."[14] But it also holds part of the message and meaning of *Men and Jobs*. Macheret emphasized his desire that the film link the iconic production sequences, which had become characteristic of Soviet cinema during the first Five-Year Plan, with the development of the new model of cinematic hero. He aimed to show machinery not "in abstract terms" but as it was perceived by real people. The film was a "struggle against the fetishization of external frameworks [*vneshniaia obstanovka*] as something that exists independently, without any relationship to the inner world of people."[15] These humanized, vocal machines are operated by people, and the film focuses on the relationship between man and machinery. It suggests that the "inner life" of workers shapes their participation in the collective project. The machines of the power plant are only as efficient as the bodies that operate them, and the undisciplined bodies of the Soviet workers in Zakharov's brigade are in no position even to catch up with, let alone "overtake," the Americans. Kleins's division is marked by more efficient physical labor.

The key message of the film, however, is that the Soviet worker can be reeducated, and his body regulated. In a later sequence, when Zakharov is attempting to "teach" his brigade about the functioning of their machinery to encourage more efficient labor, he is unable to make himself heard over the machines themselves: noisy bursts of steam punctuate his speech. As the lesson continues, he implicitly absorbs the energy of the machines and the train; he begins to speak in time with the technology, increasing his vocal pace with the rhythm of the train, until he is eventually able to utter a stream of words that mirror its spinning wheels. This montage blurs into a sequence of the dam construction itself, now absorbing the new, energized pace of its workforce. The strength of the Soviet worker lies not in language but in energy: it is *felt*.

This triumphant harmony between Zakharov and technology is central to the film's message. *Men and Jobs* is a film about the regulation of the Soviet body, its transformation into an efficient instrument for industrial production. Two key moments mark the final transformation of the undisciplined worker's body. First, a residual lack of harmony between the human body and technology is marked by the final dance of the last remaining drunken worker in the brigade. His reeling body is almost hit by the swinging weight of a crane; the increasingly uncontrolled swinging of its pendulum and its eventual fall mirrors his collapse. The message is unambiguous: as long as the human body is undisciplined, it cannot hope to control the world of machines. In what follows, Zakharov's second triumphant moment of transformation comes as he carefully learns to operate the machines himself: he moves the levers of the plant; cogs and pulleys respond to his touch. This is a symphony of machines as controlled by man, and its finale is marked by a striking moment of total silence, which is more eloquent and powerful than any celebratory speech.[16]

Like many early Soviet sound films, *Men and Jobs* frequently draws the spectator's attention to the act of listening.[17] In its opening sequences, we see a man listening intently to American jazz on his gramophone. It becomes clear that he is traveling by train, and the sounds of the train appear faintly in the background. He stops the record, stands, opens a window, and the sound of the moving train (and its steam) enters through the window. When he subsequently closes the window again, the faint sound of the train can now be heard more distinctly. This encounter with the sounds of the mechanical world marks the arrival of the American Kleins at the construction site: Soviet reality is signaled by its affiliation with a soundscape that is radically distinct from that of American dance music. This scene is directly echoed in the film's closing sequences, where Kleins is again listening to the same American song. The needle sticks, and he is irritated. He turns off the gramophone, removes the record, and moves to the window. The sound of the song gives way to silence, and then to the very faint sound of a distant whistle before the sound track becomes dominated by industrial noise (accompanied by orchestral music). Looking at the movement of machines, Kleins throws his record out of the window and symbolically embraces the new sound track.

In his important article on early Soviet sound film, Ian Christie describes the transformation of the American protagonist as brought about by the sticking of the gramophone needle, which changes the English word *darling* into the Russian *udarnik*, repeated emphatically as Kleins moves across the room to stop the record. For Christie, Kleins's "moment of commitment is signaled by a 'symptomatic' interruption in routing and 'slippage' between languages"; his soundscape mutates to reflect his new ideological framework.[18] The bourgeois endearment *darling,* with its sentimental emphasis, transmutes into a term that emphasizes a distinctively *Soviet* emotional commitment: to the collective project of labor. *Udarnik,* we recall, is the word that Kleins so markedly failed to understand at the beginning of the film; though there continues to be no adequate translation, he now grasps the word's meaning instinctively. And in parallel, Kleins and Zakharov are able to communicate without the need for a translator at the end of the film, as if united by Soviet "revolutionary *razmakh*" (sweep, or fervor). This *razmakh,* innate in Zakharov, is a greater gift than linguistic fluency, and one that film is able to convey without language. It is embodied in a nonverbal energy that is a core part of Zakharov's heroism at the end of the film. In the final scenes, he makes a speech, announcing that the Soviets have in fact outstripped Kleins's production record. At a crucial moment, however, his apparently triumphant verbal fluency falters; he stumbles and cannot find the word that he needs. Exhorted by the audience, however, he pronounces that "enthusiasm" is the secret ingredient. It is this intangible, nonrational quality—which can be *felt* but cannot be spoken—that distinguishes the Soviet labor brigade; Kleins, implicitly, is convinced.

The Private Life of Petr Vinogradov: Sounding Soviet?

Macheret's next film, *The Private Life of Petr Vinogradov*, as the title makes clear, engaged even more directly with the question of the shape of the new Soviet hero, with the relation between public and private life, and here, too, the question of language was central. Macheret described the film as another attempt to show complex characters on screen. As such, it responded to growing calls for film to offer three-dimensional heroes: as the critic Popov wrote in 1934, Soviet filmmakers had created images of the mass but not of the individual; the shape of the "real" individual communist was still not clear.[19] For this film, Macheret worked with a dedicated scriptwriter: Lev Isaevich Slavin (notably also the writer of *Vozvrashchenie Maksima* [Return of Maxim, dir. Kozintsev and Trauberg, 1937], another film that sought a clear shape for the new Soviet cinematic hero). In pre-release articles about the film, Macheret praised Slavin's screenplay for its representation of the complexity of human emotions. Indeed, there was much for the critics to praise in the final film: E. Gabrilovich saw the film as part of a quest for "full-blooded" art, describing the eponymous Petr Vinogradov as one of the first "complex, temperamental, sharp, multidimensional" characters in Soviet cinema.[20]

The particular "complexity" of Petr Vinogradov, however, bears subtler consideration. He is an inventor, a self-made man in progress, an autodidact: he speaks loudly and often, proclaiming the value of science and endeavor in the revolutionary project. The walls of his Spartan room are decked with photographs of scientists and "learned men" (*uchenye*), who he celebrates for their "thinking" (*myshlenie*). He has a rigorous daily timetable dedicated to self-improvement, within which there is explicitly no space for pleasure. Petr Vinogradov is engaged in a process of *self-regulation*, of transforming himself into the ideal Soviet hero. The plot of the film, however, complicates this picture, for it shows that the particular form of Petr's self-regulation leads, in some sense, to his downfall. He may be a successful inventor, but within the film's romantic plotline, he doesn't get the girl. And his romantic failure represents a much larger lack. Petr is revealed as *nekul'turnyi* (uncultured), with culture understood here broadly, as a sense of beauty, pleasure, and sentiment. He disrupts classical music concerts; he is unable to appreciate the pleasures offered by his various potential relationships; he cannot join in the leisure of his friends. The plot suggests that, in addition to his self-discipline, Petr needs to learn to appreciate the sensory pleasures of life.

Macheret's interest in the capacity of film to reveal his characters' emotional inner lives can be clearly traced in the evolution of his work from *Men and Jobs* to *The Private Life of Petr Vinogradov*. But the difference between these two films can also be attributed to a more widespread shift in Soviet cinema, mirroring a growing emphasis on the necessity of emotion and sensibility in the ideal Soviet hero. Macheret described Petr Vinogradov as suffering from a fatal combination of the enthusiasm of youth and of *tekhnitsizm* (an excessive focus on the technical).[21] Petr Vinogradov tries to fit both love and heroism into his rigid timetable, and that project is doomed to failure. In the context of the early 1930s, he might also be seen as an outmoded Soviet hero, a type that needs remodeling, with emotions, for the new age.

For my purposes, it is significant that Petr Vinogradov is characterized by one thing in particular: he is too loud. He speaks in a booming bass; he performs and does not listen. For all its admiration for his technical prowess as an inventor, the film mocks his bombastic poetry readings in the (implicitly outmoded) style of Vladimir Mayakovsky. However genuine his commitment to the revolutionary project, we understand that these impassioned, declamatory statements are no longer the required genre for Soviet culture. In remarkably similar terms, Igor Savchenko's *Sluchainaia vstrecha* (A Chance Encounter, 1936) presented a challenge to the value of bombastic rhetoric in its own presentation of new heroic ideals. When that film's antihero, Grisha, visits his factory director to make a case for a co-worker to be released from duties in order to train for an athletics competition, he is asked to "speak more quietly." The factory director seemingly cannot *hear* the bombastic words of the old-style Soviet message. When Irina's other co-workers return to plead the case again, they do so without words; instead, they demonstrate their own productivity in a silent, visually stunning display of the pleasures and wonders of the toys that they have made.

In both of these films, then, noise—and in particular, the noise of speech—is interrogated as part of an investigation of models of Soviet subjectivity. *The Private Life of Petr Vinogradov* and *A Chance Encounter* launched a different kind of challenge to speech from that that which we identified in *Men and Jobs*. In that first early sound film, the human voice ceded its authority to the noise of machines—the revolutionary *razmakh* and the "enthusiasm" of the Soviet worker were marked not by words but by the absorption of the noise and the energy of technology. In these later films, as the technology of sound films was more established and the ideological agenda of Soviet cinema shifted, that "enthusiasm" underwent a further moderation: Grisha and Petr Vinogradov, I suggest, embodied a type of socialist hero that was becoming increasingly problematic and outmoded in mid-1930s culture: they were both too loud. And, as the films suggested, they needed to learn to feel, not just to speak. Both of these films made a case for a model of Soviet subjectivity where there was a place for both sentiment and sensory pleasure, albeit reconfigured in Soviet socialist terms. They used sound technology, uncharacteristically, to challenge the primacy of dialogue, to make a case instead for the quieter value of *feeling*. And to make that case in part through the visual, silent potential of film itself: the textural impact of filmed objects.

A Severe Youth: The Silence of Sensation

Made in the same year as *A Chance Encounter*, and in the same Kiev film studio, Room and Olesha's *A Severe Youth* also raised core questions about the shape of the new Soviet subject. Toward the end of the film, its hero—another Grisha—enumerates the "complex of spiritual qualities" that any *komsomolets* (Komsomol member) must have: alongside humanity, humility, sincerity, and generosity, he adds, intriguingly, *sentimental'nost'* (sentimentality). Sentimentality, he elaborates, "that they might love not only marches, but also waltzes." Yet the film's broader narrative, which tracks Grisha's possible love story with a young woman, Masha, who is married to an older and eminent surgeon, suggests that there is no place for sentiment: as Grisha's love suffers in the face of Masha's decision to stay with her husband, Stepanov, the plot proclaims the victory of the scientist as a scion of rationality and learning.[22]

For all this apparent certainty at the level of plot, however, Room's inquiry into the place of sentiment in Soviet subjectivity is continued, and rendered more complex, through the visual and formal style of *A Severe Youth*. This is a film in which material matters, in which the camera dwells with evident pleasure on the formal properties of *stuff*: of wrought-iron railings, of light and water, of the marble of statues and bodies. As such, it can be read as a manifesto for sentience; and the use of silence in the film has a key part to play in the cinematic presentation of this sentience, for it is in these moments of silence that the act of looking acquires a particular potency. Siegfried Kracauer, discussing *Modern Times* (dir. Chaplin, 1936), described how Chaplin's "undermining" of naturalistic sound could turn the audience "from naïve listeners to engaged spectators."[23] Silence, then, is one strategy through which Room compels his spectators not only to listen but also to look. And this *looking* is central to the film's thematic purpose, its consideration of the moral and emotional framework that was necessary for the new Soviet subject.

Through the characters of Stepanov, Masha, and Grisha, *A Severe Youth* stages an encounter between generations, between the old and new worlds (figure 5.1). And this encounter is coded in part through an opposition between looking and being looked at, between observing and acting. Tsitronov, a permanent guest in the home of Masha and Stepanov, is a corpulent representative of the old world, of bourgeois greed and passivity. And he is a constant observer: he watches, but he does not act. Indeed, Tsitronov's role as spectator has overt shades of voyeurism: returning from her swim, Masha is uncomfortable to find his eyes upon her; later, he watches her alone in her chamber. As a representative of the older generation, Tsitronov is pictured alongside Masha's husband, Stepanov, and his intervention turns that man into an observer-voyeur too: Tsitronov hands him a pair of binoculars so that he can see the meeting between Grisha

Figure 5.1. Frame capture from *Strogii iunosha* (A Severe Youth, dir. Room, 1936).

and Masha properly, and his commentary about the two young people provides a voice for the other man's fear of cuckoldry. These men as *observers* are differentiated from the younger generation, who are the constant objects of their gaze. When Grisha arrives at the home of Masha and Stepanov, and she goes to meet him (watched by the older men), the two young people greet each other without dialogue (but with the accompaniment of a musical track). Here, Room makes his sound film into a silent film, as if in a conscious gesture to the narrative associations of the romantic silent rendezvous. But the significance of this silence goes further. Grisha and Masha do not speak because they do not need to. Theirs is principally a world of action and feeling, rather than language, and as such it is differentiated from the world of Stepanov and Tsitronov.

The inquiry into different modes of looking in *A Severe Youth* is not limited to plot, however; it is part of the film's broader consideration of the role of the musical and plastic arts and, through them, the nature and purpose of beauty in the new Soviet world.[24] The kind of voyeuristic spectatorship that Tsitronov represents is crucially distinguished from the act of looking that the film itself explicitly invites from its spectator. This is a film preoccupied with surfaces, and its engagement with those surfaces is directly linked to its treatment of sound. This essay began with an account of its opening sequence, in which the camera's initial lingering gaze onto the surface of a venetian blind, and then through a diaphanous screen to a table set with flowers and crystal, is carried out in silence. The black-and-white markings of the large head of a dog are also viewed in silence. The film abounds in semi-still images of patterned, material surfaces, and these images are often viewed to the accompaniment of an empty sound track. When, in one of the film's most memorable scenes, the discus player Diskobol moves through an underground room populated by classical statues of naked youths, he does so in silence. Walking among the mute statuary in a theater basement, this man—whose name consciously evokes a famous Greek statue (the Discobolus, or Diskobólos, of Myron)—moves through what the spectator experiences as a potent force field of visual and tactile communicative modes.

Béla Balázs memorably described the capacity of silent film to reveal "the hidden common language of mute things, conversing with each other, recognizing each other's shapes and entering into relations with each other." In the potent silences made possible by the sound film, he suggested, this impact could be still stronger: "In this mutuality of silence, this community of objects turns inwards and pays no further heed to the human world."[25]

In this respect, the statues in *A Severe Youth* function powerfully as *voiceless* bodies, or mute figures. In his persuasive analysis of the centrality of the voice in cinema, Chion suggests that mute figures hold a particular power in sound cinema. As voices that do not and cannot speak, mute figures reference cinema's "primordial secret."[26] They recall the original and originary silence of cinema. This, I suggest, is part of the self-reflexive inquiry into the nature of cinematic looking that *A Severe Youth* undertakes. The mute statues challenge the spectator not to listen but to see and to feel their material presence. As such, they call forth a mode of spectatorship that was perhaps at risk in sound film; they recall the *faktura* of the silent medium, its ability to reveal material *texture*.[27] The significance of this goes beyond film, however, and into a broader consideration of the nature of art. Diskobol's silent walk, the film's first presentation of statuary, takes place in the backstage spaces of a ballet theater: in ballet, as in sculpture, the human body is transformed into a plastic work of art. And it is not only the statues, of course, that are looked at here; Diskobol himself, a fine exemplar of Soviet youth and vitality, becomes an object of silent contemplation. Statuary, indeed, is a constant reference point throughout the film: Diskobol's toned body, throwing his discus, explicitly assumes the harmonious balance of the statue that provides his name.

As an object of contemplation, Masha herself is implicitly a work of art, and the film's emphasis on framing and staging underscores this: when Masha and Grisha first meet, without words, they are framed by, and viewed through, the ornamental patterning of iron fretwork that surrounds Stepanov's mansion.[28] Masha, too, is explicitly linked to statuary: in her absence, Stepanov gazes at a statue of Venus, positioned alongside a photograph of her. As she moves amid the waves in the film's opening sequence, she is like Venus Anadyomene (Venus Rising from the Sea), an iconic image of the birth of Aphrodite, eternally renewed by the waves.

The youthful characters in this film, then, are bodies to be admired. In a later scene, after a stunning display of athletic prowess, Grisha, Diskobol, and friends are in their changing room, still in their sports clothing, talking about the moral qualities of the ideal *komsomolets*; they are surrounded by incongruous classical statuary. Diskobol, the most magnificent of them all, lies on a couch, waiting to be massaged. The equation of these fine physical forms with those of the statuary is particularly overt: both are objects to be contemplated. But the young protagonists, crucially, are art made *real,* given flesh. Here, and elsewhere in the film, there is a provocative and important tension between stillness and immobility (between the flowers and crystal glasses of the opening sequence and the powerful body of Masha that succeeds them, for example): this tension draws our attention to the new *embodied,* animate, aesthetic ideal of the Soviet youth.

This realization of the aesthetic ideal in flesh lies at the center of the film and provides a link between its formal preoccupation with surface(s) and the thematic investigation of the moral and emotional frameworks of the new Soviet youth. It provides an important corollary to critical accounts of *A Severe Youth*, which consider its formal elements as a subversive counter to the emerging narratives and styles of Soviet socialist realism. In the censors' report, Room was accused of "chasing after external beauty," while the film was accused of having a "mystical insubstantiality of form."[29] In her reading, Oksana Bulgakowa follows the latter accusation of "insubstantiality" in describing the space of the film as "unreal" and "surreal."[30] The film's interest in "external beauty" need not, however, be linked to such claims of pure formalism, insubstantiality, or unreality. Rather, *A Severe Youth* reveals the plastic, textural beauty of material objects, as well as their tangible *presence.* This emphasis on the texture, materiality, and surface is vitally linked, however, to the film's consideration of human form. All of the filmed objects—animate and inanimate alike—in *A Severe Youth* are given powerful physical presence by the camera's lingering gaze.

This discovery of the film's interest in material prompts further consideration of its perplexing and apparently clumsy sound track. In addition to its silences, *A Severe Youth* makes several other challenges to the "reality effect" of sound technology and frequent challenges to the primacy and communicative potential of the spoken word. Jerry Heil lists no fewer than twelve occasions when the phrase "Don't you understand?" is used by one character, so drawing the spectator's attention to the inadequacy of language.[31] Dialogue is often nothing short of absurd and out of step with action (a discussion of souvenir hats during an emergency operation, for example). And throughout the film, the artificiality and staged quality of dialogue is emphasized rather than smoothed over. Such aspects of the soundscape must be considered part of Room's broader purpose— particularly in light of his experimental work with sound in the 1930 documentary film *Plan velikikh rabot* (Plan of Great Works), which consisted of found footage, edited and sequenced with a complex sound track of speech, noise, and music.[32] According to Room's collaborator Vladimir Legoshin, in an article coinciding with the release of that film, work on *Plan of Great Works* led Room to the understanding that the real potential for the future sound film lay in the use of sound to create additional levels of independent "meaning" (*smysl*): the potential of a combined visual and sound track to maximize the multisensory impact on the spectator.[33] Five years later, in *A Severe Youth*, Room's soundscape represents a core element of the film's overarching "meaning": the film's use of silence, and its revelation of the artificiality and inadequacy of screened dialogue, presents a new mode of being-in-the-world as a model for Soviet subjectivity.

In this film, the bodies of the "new" Soviet man and woman inhabit the world in ways that are radically distinct from those of the older generation. As the young athletes sit surrounded by statuary (and as Masha emerges from the water, or as Diskobol moves among statues in silence), they not only are objects of physical beauty themselves but also exist in a kind of mute communion with the material world. This mute communion—powerfully emphasized by the silence of Room's sound track—is implicitly unavailable to representatives of the old world. In this sense, the film echoes a core idea of Olesha's 1929 novel *Zavist'* (Envy), whose protagonist Kavalerov exists in a disjunctive relationship with the material world ("Things don't like me") that distinguishes him from those characters who have easily embraced the new Soviet ideal.[34] A renewed, reanimated relationship with objects is a precondition for the new Soviet subject.

This is not to suggest, of course, that Room and Olesha present a straightforward or unproblematic celebration of the ideals of the Soviet 1930s, but rather that the use of visual and sound material in *A Severe Youth* might be viewed as a working through of core questions relating to the sensory or emotional formulation of the new Soviet subject. In a sense, the young people in this film embody an ideal of aesthetic beauty in the world—what Bliumbaum describes as "statues brought to life and music made flesh." They enact a shift of the category of beauty from the ideal to the real. This can be explicitly linked to the film's own sensory challenge to the spectator. The spectator's eye is drawn into a material encounter with the viewed surfaces of the film. Through the textural intensity of the film's call to *look*, and the voiceless space in which this call so often takes place, the film seeks to transform the act of spectatorship into something *embodied* and multisensory.

Conclusions

This essay has provided a three-stop journey through one "story" of early Soviet sound film, examining three films that, in distinct ways, challenge the dominance of the spoken word. This challenge to language can be viewed in two related ways. First, it is an investigation into the sensory hierarchies of cinematic spectatorship, an attempt to exploit the technologies of sound film without sacrificing silent cinema's ability to create an intensified visual and sensory relationship between the spectator and the material world. Second, it is part of an inquiry into the particular "sensibility" that might characterize the emergent Soviet cinematic hero—and, more broadly, the Soviet subject in the world. Roland Barthes's evocative essay "Writers, Intellectuals, Teachers" approaches the "dominance" of language in different terms from those which preoccupied early filmmakers, but it nevertheless provides a striking statement of the same fear: "Nothing to be done: language is always a matter of force, to speak is to exercise a will for power; in the realm of speech there is no innocence, no safety."[35] This emphasis on innocence has important resonances for us here: all three of my case studies argue against language and for an appreciation of a sensory plenitude that is accessed in part through silence, and they link this sensory plenitude explicitly to the new generation of Soviet man and woman. In comments made at the first Congress of Soviet Writers in 1934, Yury Olesha recalled the impact of the revolution in revealing terms as a return of youthfulness: "Suddenly, I don't know why, I felt young again. I can see the young skin of my hands; I'm wearing a vest; I had become a child."[36] It is notable that this youthfulness (*molodost'*) is figured in sensory, visual terms first: the texture of skin, the feeling of a vest. Revolution brings with it a return to innocence, a renewal of sensation. *A Severe Youth*, Olesha's collaboration with Abram Room, sought to bring about a similar renewal of sensation in its spectators and to do so in two ways: first, through an intensified sensory encounter with material objects; second, through a return to what Barthes calls the "innocence" of silence. In that film, as in a number of key sound films produced in the Soviet Union during the 1930s, the relationship between silence and sound was used to explore how the new, non-silent art form might retain the core purpose of its silent predecessor, that is, its capacity to provoke a reanimated engagement with the material world, to give its spectator a heightened ability to see and to feel. It was also, perhaps, a way of questioning whether that purpose could continue to be part of the Soviet revolutionary agenda.

Notes

1. Béla Balázs, *Theory of the Film: Character and Growth of a New Art* (London: Dennis Dobson, 1952), 205.
2. "Postanovlenie tresta Ukrainfil'm o zapreshchenii fil'ma 'Strogii iunosha," *Kino*, July 28, 1936, 2.
3. Arkady Bliumbaum has written the most extensive consideration of this film from an aesthetic standpoint. See "Ozhivaiushchaia statuia i voploshchennaia muzyka: konteksty 'Strogogo iunoshi," *Novoe literaturnoe obozrenie* 1 (2008): 138–89.

4. Michel Chion, *The Voice in Cinema*, trans. Claudia Gorbman (New York: Columbia University Press, 1999), 5 (italics in original).

5. N. Iezuitov, "O stiliakh sovetskogo kino," *Sovetskoe kino* 5–6 (1933): 44. This was a continuation of an article published in the previous edition of the journal: "O stiliakh sovetskogo kino: (Kontseptsiia razvitiia sovetskogo kinoiskusstva)," *Sovetskoe kino* 3–4 (1933): 35–55. The publication was a transcript of a speech presented to the Komakademiia on April 22, 1933. The article worked in dialogue with another series of key articles by Mikhail Bleiman: "Chelovek v sovetskoi fil'me 1: istoriia odnoi oshibki," *Sovetskoe kino* 5–6 (1933): 48–57; "Chelovek v sovetskoi fil'me 2: fil'ma obozrenie," *Sovetskoe kino* 8 (1933): 1–60; and "Chelovek v sovetskoi fil'me 3. V poiskakh novogo stilia," *Sovetskoe kino* 9 (1933): 27–42.

6. This essay is part of a broader project that explores how, in the first decades of Soviet power, cinema was conceived as a medium that had the potential to "transform," or reinvigorate, the human sensorium, thus creating a heightened engagement with the material world. Specifically, I explore the significance of cinema as enabling a textural, material, and even tactile experience. See, e.g., Emma Widdis, "Socialist Senses: Film and the Creation of Soviet Subjectivity," *Slavic Review* 71, no. 3 (fall 2012), 590–618.

7. N. Iezuitov, "Dela i liudi sovetskoi kinematografii," *Proletarskoe kino* 15–16 (1932): 11. The many energetic debates about sound in Soviet cinema have been extensively documented and are discussed elsewhere in this volume, so I do not treat them in detail here. Kristin Thompson notes the uses of the "dead" sound track in Vsevolod Pudovkin's *Dezertir* (Deserter, 1933) and Nikolai Ekk's *Putevka v zhizn'* (Road to Life, 1931). See Kristin Thompson, "Early Sound Counterpoint," in "Cinema/Sound," ed. Rick Altman, special issue, *Yale French Studies* 60 (1980): 115–40. In Grigory Kozintsev and Leonid Trauberg's 1931 film *Odna* (Alone), the sound track also cuts to total silence when the heroine receives a letter informing her that she is to be posted to Altai.

8. Iezuitov, "Dela i liudi," 16. See also M. Tsekhanovskii, "Dela i liudi kak professional'nyi urok," *Proletarskoe kino* 19–20 (1932): 15.

9. A. V. Macheret, *Khudozhestvennye techeniia v sovetskom kino* (Moscow: Iskusstvo, 1963), 151.

10. A. Macheret, "Dela i liudi," *Proletarskoe kino* 13–14 (1932): 12.

11. A. S. Piataev, 'Chto takoe individual'nost'? V diskussionnom poriadke', *Kino* 40 (1933): 3.

12. In *Dve vstrechi* (Two Meetings, dir. Urinov), another film of 1932, we see the character Rybakov failing in the middle of a speech. This man, a "hero" of the revolution, is celebrated for his facility with words. But at the beginning of the film, this facility leaves him; his body is weak, and he needs to heal. It is not accidental, I suggest, that he is carried off to a sanatorium to heal at a moment when he (and the spectator) are explicitly surrounded by the presence of the Soviet word (*logos*)—in this case, none other than the supreme logos that is the name of Lenin himself.

13. Siegfried Kracauer points to the value of "bilingual" films in shifting the emphasis of language from "the meanings of speech to its material qualities." See Siegfried Kracauer, "Dialogue and the Sound Film," in *Theory of Film: The Redemption of Physical Reality* (Oxford: Oxford University Press, 1960), 110. Evgeny Margolit has written with great insight about multilingualism and heteroglossia in early Soviet cinema. See chapter 6 in this volume.

14. Michel Chion, *Audio-vision: Sound on Screen*, trans. Claudia Gorbman (New York: Columbia University press, 1994), 183.

15. Macheret, "Dela i liudi," 11.

16. This is one of several moments when Macheret uses silence for dramatic effect. When the translator finishes reading a newspaper article in English that mocks Soviet industrial productivity, Macheret inserts a piece of empty sound track; even the sound of the moving train is interrupted. This expression of the workers' outrage emphasizes a clamorous eruption of almost choral noise on the part of the workers who have been listening; the shouting of individuals, which merges into a collective shout, marks the workers' commitment to new study and self-regulation.

17. Lilya Kaganovsky, "The Materiality of Sound: Esfir Shub's Haptic Cinema" (unpublished manuscript).

18. Ian Christie, "Soviet Cinema: Making Sense of Sound. A Revised Historiography," *Screen* 23, no. 2 (1982): 46.

19. F. Popov, "Obraz kommunista na ekrane," *Sovetskoe kino* 1–2 (1934): 6–14.

20. E. Gabrilovich, "Problema geroia," *Kino* 22 (May 1935): 3.

21. A. Macheret, "Realizovannyi optimizm," *Sovetskoe kino* 1–2 (1934): 60.

22. There is some ambiguity in the ending, but the most common interpretation of both film and screenplay is that Masha's final decision involves renouncing Grisha's love and returning to her husband.

23. Kracauer, "Dialogue and the Sound Film," 108.

24. Bliumbaum provides a very strong reading of this film in relation to aesthetic theory.

25. Balázs, "The Sound Film," in *Béla Balázs: Early Film Theory—Visible Man and the Spirit of Film*, trans. Rodney Carter, ed. Erica Carter (London: Berghan, 2010), 191.

26. Chion, *Voice in Cinema*, 100.

27. This important term *faktura*, a commonplace in Soviet cinematic discourse during the 1920s, has no single translation into English: it is best understood as "texture" or "materiality," but it also refers to the working of that material in an artistic context. For the Soviet avant-garde, *faktura* acquired a particular meaning, signaling the revolutionary proximity between art and reality. The constructivist theorist Alexei Gan distinguished the avant-garde view of *faktura* from what he called a traditional "artistic" understanding. Where the term might traditionally describe simply "the handling of a surface," for the avant-garde it meant "the selection and processing of the raw material" and "the organic condition of processed material" (Alexei Gan, *Konstruktivizm* [Tver': Tverskoe Izdatel'stvo, 1922], 62–64). Thus, *faktura* was part of a broader emphasis on the sensory rediscovery of the material world.

28. As Milena Michalski discusses, and as Bliumbaum explores in considerable detail, Grisha's dream sequence envisages Masha as "music made flesh." M. Michalski, "Promises Broken, Promise Fulfilled: The Critical Failings and Creative Success of Abram Room's *Strogii iunosha*," *Slavonic and East European Review* 82, no. 4 (October 2004): 820–46.

29. "Postanovlenie tresta Ukrainfil'm o zapreshchenii fil'ma 'Strogii iunosha'," *Kino* 28 (July 1936): 2.

30. Oksana Bulgakova, *Sovetskii slukhoglaz: kino i ego organy chuvstv* (Moscow: NLO, 2010), 163, 160.

31. Jerry T. Heil, *No List of Political Assets: The Collaboration of Iurii Olesha and Abram Room on "Strogii Iunosha" [A Strict Youth (1936)]* (Munich: Verlag Otto Sagner, 1989), 11.

32. *Plan velikikh rabot* was released as part of *Zvukovaia sbornaia programma no. 1* (Sound Programme No. 1) in March 1930.

33. V. Legoshin, "Zvuk kak smysl," *Kino i zhizn'* 10 (April 1, 1930): 14. The same issue of the journal featured another article on the film, which detailed its technical "devices" (including asynchronous sound recording): I. Sokolov, "Plan velikikh rabot," *Kino i zhizn'* 10 (April 1, 1930): 5–6.

34. Iurii Olesha, "Zavist', in *Zavist*," in *Tri tolstiaka, ni dnia bez strochki* (Moscow: Khudozhestvennaia literature, 1989), 13.

35. Roland Barthes, "Writers, Intellectuals, Teachers," in *Image Music Text*, ed. Stephen Heath (London: Fontana, 1977), 192.

36. Iurii Olesha, "Zavist'" in *Zavist', Tri tolstiaka, Ni dnia bez strochki* (Moscow: Khudozhestvennaia literatura, 1989), 13.

PART II
Speech and Voice

6 The Problem of Heteroglossia in Early Soviet Sound Cinema (1930–35)

Evgeny Margolit

LET ME START with a clarification: the problem of heteroglossia or multilingualism (*raznoiazychie*) in early Soviet sound cinema is a problem for today's film historians; the filmmakers and film critics of the period did not consider it as such. Indeed, one of the artists who used multiple untranslated languages as a principal device in his early sound films—Ivan Kavaleridze, a prominent figure of the Ukrainian avant-garde—and even coined the term, devoted no more than a few paragraphs to the practice in his memoirs, which were written some thirty years after the fact.[1] And yet those first years of sound cinema saw the release of about a dozen films—Soviet film studios produced about twenty sound films a year on average in the first half of the 1930s—that showcased a broad range of heteroglossic strategies.

Outside of the Soviet Union, we also find the practice of heteroglossia in German cinema of the same period, just prior to Hitler's rise to power (e.g., in Georg Wilhelm Pabst's *Kameradschaft* [1931]; in *Das blaue Licht* [The Blue Light, 1932], directed by Arnold Fanck and Leni Riefenstahl from a script by Béla Balázs; in *Niemandsland* [No Man's Land, 1931], directed by Victor Trivas, himself a Russian émigré), as well as in the experimental work of the Czech novelist, screenwriter, and director Vladislav Vancura (e.g., *Marijka Nevernice* [1935]). Yet even in the well-known *Kameradschaft*, in which bilingualism is an integral element of the dramatic plot, a translation of the foreign dialogue appears in subtitles. By contrast, Soviet cinema rejected translation in such cases as a matter of course. This holds true not only for Kavaleridze's *Koliivshchina* (By Water and Smoke, 1933) and *Prometei* (Prometheus, 1936), or Boris Barnet's classic *Okraina* (The Outskirts, 1933), but also for a broad range of lesser-known films that share at least one thing in common: typically these are significant works of art, situated (from a modern perspective) in one way or another outside of the contemporaneous cinematic mainstream. I emphasize "modern perspective" because many of these films went unnoticed at the time (e.g., *Tommy* [1931], the first sound film by the patriarch of Russian cinema, Yakov Protazanov), disappeared from view because they were banned (e.g., *Moia rodina* [My Native Land, 1933], by Iosif Heifits and Alexander Zarkhi, and, once more, *Prometheus*), or were never considered in terms of their heteroglossia (e.g., *Putevka v zhizn'* [Road to Life, 1931], directed by Nikolai Ekk, the first Soviet "fully talking picture").

One possible explanation for this phenomenon may be that the Soviet screen was supposed to present an ideal reflection of a world moving toward communism. This model emerges with absolute clarity precisely at the start of the 1930s. The preceding decade had proffered two ideals, two competing utopian visions. One was the industrial utopia, based on the idea of absolute mastery over the primal and unpredictable "natural principle." Its principal doctrine was the total mechanization of society, whereby man became one component of a flawless mechanism, and himself a mechanism, a "man-machine"—a term coined by the 1920s writer-philosopher Alexei Gastev. In cinema, this vision reaches its practical and theoretical peak in the films of Dziga Vertov. The alternative view envisions a return to a "natural society," emphasizing nature as the generative, life-giving force. Aided by science and technology, the new man attains maturity; after mastering the language of nature, he evolves into nature's creative partner. This is the tradition of Velimir Khlebnikov, taken up in poetry by Nikolai Zabolotsky (e.g., the narrative poem "Torzhestvo zemledeliia" [The Triumph of Agriculture, 1933]), and that finds its fullest cinematic expression in the works of Alexander Dovzhenko.

By the end of the 1920s, it was the industrial utopia that had come to dominate the creative imagination. In cinema, this is especially evident in the proliferation of the agitprop film, with its outright paganistic deification of industrial production at the expense of the individual and nature. At the same time, films espousing the alternative vision—including such major works as Dovzhenko's *Zemlia* (Earth, 1930), Vsevolod Pudovkin's *Prostoi sluchai* (A Simple Case, 1930), and Mikhail Kalatozov's *Sol' Svanetii* (Salt for Svanetia, 1930)—were either censured in the official press (in the first two instances) or passed without notice (in the third). The world of the agitprop film, ideologically (over)saturated with emblems and slogans, professed to be the sole reality. And within this reality the word assumed a frankly sacred function: it was the word of the masses, nameless, faceless, and dissociated from any concrete speaker; it was the word as divine utterance, as directive, and as slogan. The agitprop film, with its conflation of newsreel and staged action, was the word's cinematic incarnation.

With the advent of the sound film, the word attained its ultimate form of cinematic expression in the off-screen voice of the newsreel narrator. Yet at the same time, a wholly opposite trend emerged: the objectification or reification (*opredmechivanie*) of the word. Just as the impulse to capture an object in motion, or movement as such—undifferentiated as yet between its natural and social aspects—had been the subject of the earliest moving pictures, so too was early sound cinema driven by the impulse to capture the sounding object.[2] And even here, the primary sounding object of the early Soviet sound film is not the human being but rather the radio: it is the word alienated from its speaker and made wholly mechanical, whereas the soundtrack as a whole is dominated by industrial sounds.³ The peculiar stylistic features of the early Soviet soundtrack can be traced back to the fact that sound arrived by way of the nonfiction film in the Soviet film industry, in contrast to its Western European or American counterparts: hence the peculiarly "laconic" dialogue of Soviet sound films of the early 1930s and their preference for industrial noise over natural sounds. Radio becomes one of central characters in Vertov's *Entuziazm* (Enthusiasm, 1930), as well as in the semistaged agitprop film about preparing for war, *Vozmozhno zavtra* (Maybe Tomorrow, 1931), directed by nonfiction filmmakers Dmitry Dalsky and Lidia Snezhinskaya. Meanwhile, in fiction film the radio quickly assumed a fascinating and highly indicative role as the "embodied voice of bureaucracy."⁴ In Grigory Kozintsev and Leonid Trauberg's *Odna* (Alone, 1931), as well as in Dovzhenko's *Ivan* (1932), radio intervenes directly in the lives of the characters, reprimanding or praising them, exposing their activities and deviations from prescribed norms, and generally functioning as an all-seeing eye of the state (in some ways similar to the factory camera in Chaplin's *Modern Times* [1936]). Needless to say, this approach was severely limiting: the universalized official word effectively eliminated the hero's right to speak as an individual; individualized speech became an attribute of the "negative" characters, making their roles unwittingly more dramatic. This is precisely what happens in *Ivan* to the character of Stepan Shkurat, a former peasant unable to accept new working standards who is denounced by his own son. This character's key phrase is "I am an inimitable individuality!" (*Ia nepovtorimaia individual'nost'*). Such individuality is suppressed by the universalized, prescribed word. No other kind of word is available to the characters of early Soviet sound film.

In such circumstances the possibility of an individual's liberation is communicated through inflection, which operates as a kind of desacralization of the official word. Vocal inflection comes to carry more weight and substance than the word's lexical meaning. This perception is conditioned by how the cinema used sound in its early stages, which was already evident to the prominent theorist and critic Adrian Piotrovsky, the de facto ideologue and cinematographic leader of the Lenfil'm Studios of the 1930s, in 1929. He writes: "Sound film is the marriage of optical continuity and cinefied [*kinofitsirovannaia*] music, understood here as a complex of sounds: noises, articulation of inflections. . . . Evidently, for reasons of novelty and expressive potential, noise and various kinds of non-harmonized sounds will be given preference. Music and song stand in second place, followed by human speech—primarily in the form of emotional exclamations and intense inflection rather than meaningful dialogues."⁵

Consequently, the individualization of the word is closely linked at this initial stage to an acute, emphatic departure from the standards of pronunciation, often to the point of incomprehensibility—a turning toward the materiality of language, to use Siegfried Kracauer's formulation. In such circumstances, speech begins to resemble natural sounds; with the advent of sound, the doctrine of a natural society returns to the Soviet screen. It seems reasonable to suppose that heteroglossia—with its tendency toward natural sound—acts as a kind of counterbalance to the overwhelming predominance of industrial noise in the Soviet cinema of the early 1930s.

We find a ready example of this dynamic in *The Road to Life*. In the final scene the main character, young Mustafa—formerly a lumpen, now a fully fledged member of the new Soviet society—rides along the railroad tracks a handcar that he himself had built with his friends; overcome with emotion on this moonlit night, he sings a song in his native Mari tongue. The structure and pathos of this episode are reminiscent of another hero's dance (also by night and on the eve of his death) in Dovzhenko's *Earth*. Both the song and the dance signal each hero's perfect union with the cosmos, with nature. Thus, in the first sound film, the singing hero is accompanied by a chorus of frogs! And, just as in *Earth,* the scene of Vasily's murder is followed by a shot of a horse flinging back its head, the death of Mustafa in *Road to Life* is followed by a sunrise and the singing of birds. The death of the hero elicits a response from nature: both speak a universal language. Characteristically, throughout the film Mustafa speaks Russian with a comical accent, but on the eve of his death-union he sings in his native tongue, as though returning to his origins. (Similarly, in *Moia rodina* [My Native Land, dir. Kheifits and Zarkhi, 1933], the mortally wounded hero-soldier Katz abruptly switches to Yiddish in his delirium).

Foreign speech compels the viewer to concentrate on the speaker's face, thus emphasizing his or her individuality and humanity, and triumph over the tyranny of the word. Characteristically, this device is often used in war-themed films to heighten the humanist-internationalist pathos, of which *The Outskirts* offers the most prominent example. But Protazanov had already made the film *Tommy* in 1931—an adaptation of the famous "bell tower scene" from the play *Bronepoezd 14-69* (Armored Train 14-69, 1927) by Vsevolod Ivanov—in which Siberian partisans try to "propagandize" a captured British soldier. The actions of the partisan, portrayed brilliantly by the famous actor Ivan Chuvelev, who had previously played the peasant boy in Pudovkin's *Konets Sankt-Peterburga* (The End of St. Petersburg, 1927), are motivated not so much by the wish to make contact with the foreign proletariat as by the instinct to save the life of another man who is himself equally weary of bloodshed. The key word in this film is not the pass code *Lenin*, but a pleading *Understand!* Answering this plea, the soldier saves himself from death.

Films produced at the Lenfil'm studio as early as the 1920s portrayed a material world, a world of things in conflict with the individual: the material versus the spiritual principle. The young soldier Vas'ka from *My Native Land*—the film that virtually laid the foundations for the "Grand Lenfil'm" tradition (as seen in films such as *Chapaev* [dir. Vasiliev and Vasiliev, 1935], *Iunost' Maksima* [The Youth of Maxim, dir. Kozintsev and Trauberg, 1935], and *Granitsa* [The Border, dir. Dubson, 1933–35])—never masters the Chinese phrase for "The Red Army is a friend of the poor" (the story is built around the Manchurian Railway conflict of 1929). But the Chinese youth Wan, dressed in the enemy's uniform, can nevertheless understand him through his inflections and facial expressions. The same tactic is echoed in *The Outskirts,* released a month later: in this case, all communication between the German boy-soldier Müller and various Russian villagers takes place outside of spoken language.

At the same time, Zarkhi and Heifiz's film demonstrates how "another" language in a different context could be interpreted as the language of the "other," that is, the enemy. This happens when the speaker of "another" language is seen as a bearer of the official word and is principally identified with it. In this particular case, a technical difficulty leads to a fascinating aesthetic solution. In the role of the Chinese boy Wan, the filmmakers cast Boris Khaidarov, a young Central Asian actor who did not speak Chinese (neither did the prominent screen and theater actor Gennady Michurin, who played the owner of the inn that shelters the youth). The only character heard speaking Chinese in the entire film is the captain, Wan's warmongering commanding officer; the boy himself remains silent. In this case, his silence identifies him with the lowest social order, marking him as a pariah. Notably, in the titles he is invariably referred to as Vagrant Wan (Van-bosiak).

In the Soviet films of this period, the "official word" is always equated with falsehood and deceit; its high pathos conceals corrupt intentions. The captain's confiding tone, which seduces Wan into fleeing with him from Soviet captivity (the title card reads, "It is sweet to hear words of Home"), turns despotic as soon as the fugitives cross over into Chinese territory. The captain's self-betraying inflections (and actions: he promptly appropriates Wan's bread) push the young hero to murder the officer with a bayonet and then make his own way back to the Red Army outpost.

The heroes' youth is as significant as their social status. More accurately, they are two sides of the same phenomenon, the same principle. The marker "childhood" (and this is especially emphasized in *My Native Land*) is associated with the "natural state," that is, with the unformed, the coming-into-being. Young heroes are depicted in the act of mastering the language of international communication. And this is also the language of the new communist world, which shall be founded on radically new relations among men. The childlike qualities of the "positive heroes" are consistently emphasized in *My Native Land*, which contrasts these characters with the passing world of "adults," the world of the fathers, which traditionally embodies the social or civic principle as opposed to the natural, maternal principle.

Heteroglossia evolved as a direct response to the rigid schematization of both story and character in the Soviet cinema of the early sound era, as a highly effective method of circumventing the schema, and as a means of individualizing increasingly conventional characters. Needless to say, this technique gained popularity thanks in no small part to the widely circulating theory of the class character of language, propagated by Nikolai Marr and his disciples (this doctrine was not denounced by Stalin until the very last years of his rule). Accordingly, no single language—including Russian—could claim official status in an emerging classless society. (Another characteristic example from *My Native Land:* in their conversation, Vas'ka and Wan enlist the interpreting services of a Russian prostitute who is lodged at the inn.) Young heroes, destined to erect a beautiful new world, find themselves at the threshold of a fundamentally new language: they exist in anticipation of its emergence. Almost unwittingly, early sound cinema tries to produce (or perhaps intuit) a language of that future that is consistent with the principles of the "musical" period. First and foremost, it is a language of musical melodies. Various multinational characters in Mikhail Dubson's *The Border,* set in an impoverished Jewish settlement along the border of Soviet Russia and bourgeois Poland, come together in the finale to sing a song that one of them had heard among the Soviets. A similar incident occurs in an earlier film by Boris Shpis and Rashel Milman—*Vozvrashchenie Neitana Bekkera* (The Return of Nathan Becker, 1932), in which an African American who had come to work in the Soviet Union (he is played by Kador Ben-Salim, the star of *Krasnye d'iavoliata* [Little Red Devils, dir. Perestiani, 1923], a hit of the previous decade), diligently reproduces a melody taught to him by the main character's father, an old Jew (played by the great Solomon Mikhoels).

We find a more elaborate version of this hypothetical "language of the future" in a Georgian film, Siko Dolidze's *Poslednie krestonostsy* (The Last Crusaders, 1935), which is truly remarkable in its use of heteroglossia. The story revolves around the efforts to end an age-old clan feud between the Chechens and the Khevsurs in the new socialist society. *The Last Crusaders* was made as a silent film in 1934, with the soundtrack added a few months later. Typically, such soundtracks comprised music, some ambient sounds, and a handful of spoken lines. For *The Last Crusaders,* however, the filmmakers hit upon a radical solution: Russian-language intertitles would be left in place, and the lines spoken by various Khevsur characters would be spoken in Georgian, giving the impression of an off-screen chorus (some thirty years later Tengiz Abuladze would make use of a similar technique in his celebrated *Vedreba* [The Plea/*Mol'ba*, 1967]). Throughout the film, the Chechens speak Russian both among themselves and with the Khevsurs. It is evident that the authors were more interested in heteroglossia than they were with achieving a sense of verisimilitude.

As the story unfolds, we learn that the elders of both tribes have conspired, in plain Russian, to continue stoking the conflict on both sides. But in the scene in which a *komsomolets* Khevsur and a *komsomolets* Chechen come together for "peace talks," communication takes a very different form.[6] The young Khevsur removes his dagger from its sheath and lays it on the ground; he then produces a small pipe and plays the first measures of the "International"; finally he exclaims, "Komsomol!" and raises his hand in a salute; the young Chechens respond with "Komsomol!"; the two parties embrace and exit the frame. The language of the future turns out to be a combination of gestures, words, and melodies—with melody (or, more broadly, inflection, as understood in the previously cited article by Piotrovsky) taking precedence over the other components of speech.

All of these various techniques spring from cinema's desire to escape the confines of lexical meaning, to expose the word's inadequacy. It is altogether characteristic that the official, socialized language is attributed to a character possessing absolute power over the story's hero in virtually every case (e.g., the captain in *My Native Land;* the "warring" kulak elders in *The Last Crusaders;* Zhigan, ringleader of the criminal gang in *The Road to Life;* and the pseudo-revolutionary yes-man in *The Outskirts,* whose off-screen oration, calling for a reconciliation with the German soldiers, plays over the scene of the hero's execution. It is hardly an accident that in the very first scene of *Prometheus*—a film that brings this period to its conclusion—the peasant addresses the landowner in Ukrainian: "You are our master; we are your children." The hero reproduces the formula instilled in him by a social order, against which he will eventually revolt. The word of the master-father in this film, set in mid-nineteenth-century Russia, is presented as the ultimate embodiment of the official word: the language of the Russian Empire. The hero, robbed of his bride on his wedding night and conscripted into the army operating in the rebellious Caucasus, will find a "common language"—one which is, again, extra-lexical—with the defiant tribespeople and will return to his native village as a steadfast fighter and avenger. Like Vagrant Wan in *My Native Land,* the hero of *Prometheus* and his bride are virtually mute. Those in positions of power (e.g., the landowner, his steward, the merchant, the madam of a brothel), however, converse in Russian, but all of their tirades serve only to disguise the true nature of their actions. Speech functions as a mask, hiding the true intentions of the ruthless oppressors. In the film's finale the hero, having returned to his native village, discovers his compatriots whipping the waters of the landowner's pond with twigs on a summer night. This is done, it turns out, to frighten away the frogs, whose croaking troubles the master's sleep. The hero exhorts the peasants to revolt, but we do not hear his words; instead, the import of the scene is reflected in the sound of croaking frogs, which are no longer being disturbed by the peasants, who are captivated by the hero's speech. In the following scene the landowner and his wife, awakened by the din, are terrified to discover the mutinous Ukrainian and Georgian serfs, led by our hero, inside their very bedchamber. The chorus of frogs thus represents the voice of oppressed nature in revolt. The hero, meanwhile, rehearses the phrase he had heard from his friend, an executed Russian revolutionary, like a magic incantation: "This is the dawning of our freedom," a phrase entirely uncharacteristic of the lexicon of a Ukrainian serf.

"Every character in the film speaks his own language. But there is one common language—that of the coming Revolution."[7] In thus summing up of *Prometheus,* Kavaleridze effectively resolves the problem of heteroglossia in early Soviet sound cinema. In this context any existing language is understood as deficient, as something to be made whole in the imminent future. The deficiency, the irregularity of language, invariably carries within it an element of spontaneity. We have already seen the hero's affinity with the primal forces of nature. But official language, dissociated from the hero in its hyper-regularity, is likewise gradually transformed into its own antithesis. It is the language of social forces, alien and antagonistic to the hero. In Kavaleridze's *Koliivshchina* and *Prometheus,* the language of the Orthodox service functions analogously to the Chinese language spoken by the captain in *My Native Land,* discussed earlier; the same may be said of the Hebrew service in Dubson's *The Border.*

Characteristically, *Prometheus,* completed in the fall of 1935, was rejected by the party leadership, headed by Stalin, and was subjected to a scathing critique in a *Pravda* editorial in early 1936. In a certain sense, the film stands as the ultimate example of heteroglossia in Soviet sound cinema of the first half of the 1930s. Officially, the last heteroglossic film was Grigori Alexandrov's *Tsirk* (Circus), which was released in mid-1936. It was at once the official apotheosis and the swan song of heteroglossia. The abdication is first enacted in the famous "Lullaby" sequence, in which all languages come to pay tribute to the infant of the future world, and again in the final episode, where all of the major positive characters march in formation to the familiar "Song of the Motherland" (composed by Isaak Dunaevsky, with words by Vasily Lebedev-Kumach). This song had been considered an alternative Soviet national anthem alongside the "International"; with the adoption of the new anthem (music by Alexander Alexandrov, words by Sergei Mikhalkov and Harrold El-Registan) in 1943, it served as a kind of "invariant": its opening measures became the identifying signal of the state radio network, and thus invariably preceded the daily broadcast of the national anthem. Its lyrics spawned countless slogans and catchphrases, gracing the surfaces of everything from state holiday banners and placards to students' copybooks. If the Soviet Union still positioned itself as the ideological home of the international proletariat (this is precisely the meaning of *rodina*—with a lowercase *r*—in the title of Heifiz and Zarkhi's film) in the first half of the 1930s, from then on it would be construed as a concrete state, with very precise geographical borders, as *Rodina* with a capital *R*. And the official language of this state, for all its proletarian citizens, would be Russian. It is no accident that the American circus performer, played by Lyubov' Orlova, picks up the *words* of the song—in contrast to films we considered earlier, in which characters speaking different languages would be united through melody—and responds to Raechka, her Soviet counterpart, in grammatically incorrect Russian. Her meaning is nonetheless clear: in response to the question, "Now do you understand?" (*Teper' ponimaesh'?*), she happily declares, "Now understand!" (*Tip'er' ponimaesh'!*).

After the debacle of *Prometheus* and the release of *Circus*, heteroglossia and multilingualism disappear from the Soviet screen for about twenty years. "Those colors added finishing touches to the characters! They enriched the sound palette! . . . And how outrageously tasteless and shortsighted were the demands of the editors after '37!" complains Kavaleridze in his memoirs. "According to them the language of the film ought to resemble that of the papers. Dialogues like headlines. And how often I hear the dreaded 'The people won't understand . . .' or 'It won't reach the broader audiences . . .'"[8]

From this point on, any foreign (*ino-strannyi*) language is interpreted as the language of the enemy, of an alien social sphere, and a foreign accent identifies its bearer with that milieu. It is the language of a potential aggressor (predominantly German, but also Japanese or Polish). In certain rare cases it appears as a symbol of potentially remediable social "immaturity." Orlova's American circus performer in *Circus* falls into this category, as does the speech of other characters belonging to the various ethnicities inhabiting the Soviet Union (e.g., "younger brothers" in the family of Soviet nations, with the "elder brother"—the great Russian people—at the head). From this point on, the central hero is not simply the bearer of the official word but also represents its direct incarnation. In this context one character emerges as the ultimate embodiment of the word: Stalin, the Father of Nations, who will also have the final word in our story. In the second half of *Oborona Tsaritsyna* (The Defense of Tsaritsyn, 1942), directed by the "Brothers" Vasiliev, a censured Georgian officer (Vladimir Kandelaki), pleading his case before Stalin, switches to their shared native tongue. Stalin (Mikhail Gelovani) interrupts his effusive monologue with the words, "I don't understand Georgian."

In the end, as one would naturally expect, the leader of all Soviet people (with the Russian nation at the helm) endorsed Alexei Dikiy's portrayal of him in *Tretii udar* (The Third Strike, dir. Savchenko, 1949) and *Stalingradskaia bitva* (The Battle of Stalingrad, dir. Petrov, 1949), speaking in perfectly unaccented Russian.

Notes

1. See Ivan Kavaleridze, *Sbornik statei, vosponinanii* (Kiev: Mistetsvo, 1988).

2. Cf. eyewitness accounts of first experimental viewings of foreign sound films. Khrisanf Khersonsky, *Stranitsy iunosti kino* (Chronicles of Cinema's Youth) (Moscow: Iskusstvo, 1965), 271–72; Tat'iana Likhacheva, "Iz vospominanii proshlykh let" (Memories of Years Gone By), in *Zhizn' v kino* (A Life in Cinema) (Moscow: n.p., 1994), 23; recall that the synchronous

quacking of a duck in the nature film (*Na dvore usad'by*) had made a most striking impression, while M. Bleiman, *O kino—svidetel'skie pokazania* (Of Cinema—Witness Statements) (Moscow: Iskusstvo, 1973), 133–34, refers to a piece of music by Offenbach, captured onto an optical soundtrack, as the "materialization of sound."

3. "The earliest efforts in sound cinema made abroad centered largely around music, while here in the USSR we have different preoccupations. First of all, our sound pictures made extensive use of various kinds of noise and rumble. This approach was determined by the so-called 'industrial style,' which many of our directors considered compulsory, for some reason. Just as silent cinema signaled 'industrialization' with a handful of utterly naïve devices, boiling down (with rare exception) to some spinning wheels, clanging hammers, flying sparks and the perennial piston-rod, swinging toward the viewer, so sound cinema took to 'doing' industrialization as an insufferable cacophony of various clangs and thumps," wrote Alexander Andrievsky in his book *Postroenie tonfil'ma* (The Structure of Sound Film) (Moscow: Gosudarstvennoe izdatel'stvo khudozhestvennoi literatury, 1931), 21.

4. See Sabine Hänsgen, "'Audio-vision.' O teorii i praktike rannego sovetskogo zvukovogo kino na grani 1930-x godov," in *Sovetskaia vlast' i media*, ed. Hans Günther and Sabine Hänsgen (St. Petersburg: Akademicheskii proekt, 2006), 350–64.

5. "Tonfil'ma v poriadke dnia" (Sound Film on the Agenda), in *Teatr. Kino. Zhizn'* (Theater, Cinema, Life), by A Piotrovsky (Leningrad: Iskusstvo, 1969), 230.

6. Editor's note: *Komsomolets* refers to a member of the All-Union Leninist Communist League of Youth—Vsesoiuznyi leninskii kommunisticheskii soiuz molodezhi, or Komsomol.

7. I. Kavaleridze, "My raznoschiki novoi very" (We Are Peddlers of a New Faith), *Iskusstvo kino* 12 (1966): 33–34.

8. Ibid., 33.

7 Challenging the Voice of God in World War II–Era Soviet Documentaries

Jeremy Hicks

I n 1943, a documentary of the battle of Moscow (*Razgrom nemetskikh voisk pod Moskvoi*) titled *Moscow Strikes Back* won the Soviet Union its first Oscar. This version of the film had discarded the original voice-over and added a new one, written by Albert Maltz and read by Edward G. Robinson. This was not an unusual practice, and it has been repeated many times since. Both during and since the war itself, Soviet World War II black-and-white newsreel images have been recycled to illustrate this or that television documentary about the conflict, stripped of the verbal context provided by the voice-over commentary that first accompanied them in the original films. In removing what are assumed to be pompous voice-of-God commentaries encumbered by encomiums to Stalin and the party, historical filmmakers imply that a new voice-over will provide more informative verbal interpretations than the original, with less distortion and to greater effect.

But what if these images were originally combined with a verbal commentary that increased their power as testimony and their expressive force? What if treating such footage as silent serves to mute and marginalize distinctive and personal commentaries about the Soviet wartime experience? This chapter seeks to explore these possibilities and demonstrate that many Soviet wartime documentaries need to be seen and heard with their original commentaries, as they were not universally dominated by a monolithic voice-of-God style. In a number of cases, they pushed against the impersonal authority of the dominant form of voice-over in an attempt to convey a specific moment and place or a personal story at odds with the common Soviet narrative of the war. Two particularly important cases are the film of the Leningrad Blockade, in its original, uncompleted March–April 1942 version titled *Leningrad v eti dni* (Leningrad during These Days) with a voice-over by playwright Vsevolod Vishnevsky, and Alexander Dovzhenko's film of the successful 1943 battle of Kharkov, *Bitva za nashu Sovetskuiu Ukrainu* (The Battle for Our Soviet Ukraine, 1943). These films test the boundaries of the monolithic voice-of-God style, and as such challenge the hegemonic narrative of the war while also pointing forward to Soviet documentary film's turn toward a new style of personalized, authorial voice-over in the 1960s with Mikhail Romm's *Obyknovennyi fashizm* (Ordinary Fascism, 1965).

Testimonial Power of Voice and Images in Soviet World War II Films

In his influential categorization of the various modes of documentary filmmaking, Bill Nichols saw the voice-of-God commentary as associated with the expository mode of filmmaking, in which there is a "commentary directed toward the viewer; images serve as illustration or counterpoint."[1] While Nichols argues that the expository mode and voice-of-God commentary may incorporate elements of interviews, the "voices of others are woven into a textual logic that subsumes and orchestrates them. . . . The voice of authority resides with the text itself rather than with those recruited to it."[2] As such, the expository mode stands in contrast to other approaches to sound in the documentary, such as the use of long takes with diegetic and overheard speech or sync sound (the observational mode), and likewise avoids reference to the subjective position of the filmmaker or the process of filmmaking (the interactive or reflexive modes).[3] However, Nichols accepted that these modes might overlap or that a given film might employ a combination of approaches.

Michael Renov has argued, with regard to the objective authority of the voice-of-God commentary, that "repression of subjectivity has been a persistent, ideologically driven fact of documentary history; yet subjectivity has never been banished from the documentary ranks."[4] Moreover, as he points out, while the voice-over commentary has been often disparaged, it, too, may be a vehicle of subjectivity.[5]

Michel Chion's theorizations of film sound are also of use in theorizing the documentary voice-over. Chion argues that whatever other noises may be heard in a sound film, the human voice commands the viewer's attention above all other acoustic information.[6] To aid his analysis, Chion invented term the *acousmêtre*, referring to a voice we hear but whose source we do not see in the film's diegetic world.[7] Such a disembodied voice, according to Chion, has God-like powers and suggests "the fantasy of the total mastery of space by vision."[8] He elaborates: "The sound film . . . has an offscreen field that can be populated by acousmatic voices, founding voices, determining voices—voices that command, invade, and vampirize the image; voices that often have the omnipotence to guide the action, call it up, make it happen."[9] While Chion's primary focus is the acted feature film, his comments may also be fruitfully mapped onto the documentary film and the use of the voice-of-God commentary as an authoritative, apparently omnipotent offscreen voice. Yet what interests Chion above all is the play between the presence and absence of voices, such as an offscreen narrator who is or becomes a visible character in the film's diegetic world. In such cases, the effect is to show the narrator's knowledge to be limited and to undermine its power. Chion terms this *de-acousmatization*, when the voice's fate becomes that of ordinary mortals.

As we shall see, the wartime period in Soviet documentary film saw a number of attempts to embody the voice-over commentary, to reference its subjectivity—its local or ethnic particularity—a choice that had the potential to undermine the authority of the form, causing such films to be censored.

Vishnevsky and the Leningrad Project

The Blockade of Leningrad began on September 7, 1941, and the project of making a film about life under siege dates back to October of that year.[10] By the beginning of December, the unimaginably bleak winter conditions—meager food rations, travel on foot to film as public transport ground to a halt, lack of resources to develop their rushes—prevented the Leningrad filmmakers from filming even for the immediate purposes of regular newsreels.[11] As the studio's central control over what they filmed weakened, the cameramen simply began to accumulate hours of footage which recorded the terrible plight of the city, such as the long lines of emaciated citizens dragging sledges with drinking water, fuel, or a corpse. At the end of December 1941, the city authorities (*obkom*) were shown some of the footage and agreed to find the resources to make a film about the besieged city.[12]

As a result of this, in February 1942 all the footage that had been taken since October was developed, and the primary cameramen—Valery Solovtsov, Nikolai Komarevtsev, and Efim Uchitel—began to look for a way of structuring the material. It was soon after this that they approached Leningrad-based dramatist and journalist Vsevolod Vishnevsky; on March 25, he sat with them in an unheated projection room on Obvodnyi Kanal in central Leningrad and watched 3,500 meters of footage.[13] He agreed to come up with a scenario, including a voice-over, for a film made from the fifteen thousand meters of film by the end of April, that is, within five weeks.[14] Vishnevsky was inspired, and he worked night and day to complete a first version of the scenario by March 30.[15]

Besides being associated with Leningrad and the White Sea–Baltic fleet, Vishnevsky represented something of a modernist tendency within official Soviet literature and, like Sergei Eisenstein, was a passionate admirer of James Joyce.[16] His fascination with film as a form dated back to an admiration for Esfir Shub's 1927 compilation film *Padenie dinastii Romanovykh* (The Fall of the Romanov Dynasty). Despite this interest in documentary, Vishnevsky's first foray into screenwriting was the complete rewriting of his play *Optimisticheskaia tragediia* (An Optimistic Tragedy, 1933) into an original screenplay for a fiction film, *My iz Kronshtadta* (We Are from Kronstadt, dir. Efim Dzigan, 1936), which frequently reworked scenes and motifs from Sergei Eisenstein's *Bronenosets Potemkin* (Battleship Potemkin, 1925). However, Vishnevsky's first engagement with documentary came when he collaborated with Shub to produce a scenario about the Spanish Civil War from hours of newsreel footage filmed between 1936 and 1939 by the Republican Spanish as well as Soviet cameramen Roman Karmen and Boris Makaveev. Vishnevsky wrote both the scenario and the voice-over for this film, and he intended to read the commentary himself.[17] Indeed, he did so in the first cut, and to powerful effect, as described by director Vera Stroeva:

> His voice merged with the pictures, it was as if he led the spectator by the hand through the trenches and fields of the war. He was marching alongside the soldiers over the plains and mountains of Spain, and he shouted, along with the defenders of Madrid: "No pasarán!"[18]

However, the final version of *Ispaniia* (Spain, 1939) was voiced by Yury Levitan, the most official of all Soviet voice-over men, and the intensely personal effect that was originally intended was lost in the final film.[19] History now presented Vishnevsky with another opportunity to write for and revitalize documentary film.

As he watched the already-accumulated Leningrad footage, above all Vishnevsky was overwhelmed by how the filmmakers cataloged the town's terrible ordeal. At the center of his nascent conception of the film was the sense of tragic suffering, as is clear from his notes:

> A siege! (all rail and sea routes have been cut) . . .
> Life coming to a halt in December-January (slower rhythm of editing).
> Think through the whole theme of the struggle for life. We've got to be brave and show starvation, the frozen bodies and the wounded. . . . Then—back to the struggle for life and the growing bits of life, movement.[20]

Along with an attempt to convey the depths of the privations and horrors endured by the city's population, Vishnevsky wanted to express the almost indescribably tragic experience of the Leningrad Blockade, something that he felt strongly that an outsider could not convey. He was understandably hostile, then, to the idea that the film could be finished in Moscow by people who had not endured the blockade, as is evident from his March 25 diary entry:

> Discussion about the film. People listened to my ideas about the film. . . . We touched on the issue of deadlines and of editing . . . of Comrade Bol'shakov's "wishes" to take the whole of the Leningrad footage to Moscow and edit it there. How could directors who don't know Leningrad and its struggle make the film? I spoke bitterly.[21]

Consequently, in his scenario for the film, and above all in his voice-over commentary, Vishnevsky attempted to convey a powerful sense of the exceptional experience of the Leningrad Blockade, of a tale explicitly told by someone who had lived through it.

Analysis of *Leningrad during These Days*

One of the provisional titles for the film at this point, *Leningrad during These Days,* is an apt expression of Vishnevsky's conception of a film that emphasizes the insider's point of view, the perspective of someone who has been and is himself undergoing the experience of the blockade.[22] In linguistics, such emphasis upon the particular moment of time and the place specific to the subject of speech is termed *deixis.*[23] This includes the words *here, there, now,* and *today,* as well as the demonstrative pronouns *this* and *these.* Roman Jakobson termed these words *shifters,* and classified pronouns, especially first and second person pronouns, as similarly designating the utterance, the act of speaking, and indexically linking the speaker and the message.[24] Vishnevsky's draft for the voice-over repeatedly uses the first-person pronoun *we,* referring to the narrator as one of those blockaded. It also addresses the city and seems to include it in the *we* too: "City, our beloved, our light, and our youth—you are suffering! But we will hold on!"[25]

The use here not only of the first and second person but also of the present and future tenses further conveys a powerful sense of the ongoing ordeal of the blockade, and it situates the speaker in the blockaded city. Similarly cameraman Efim Uchitel refers in his March 1942 notes to the film as a "film-diary," a generic designation that suggests closeness to the material, and a striving to record and represent experience as it happens without knowledge of the ultimate outcome or how the narrative will be shaped, as is the case with retrospectively structured autobiographies.

The perspective of a witness caught in the worst of the blockade during the winter of 1941 and 1942 also leads to a far greater emphasis in this film on the population's unalleviated suffering, on the ordeal (*ispytaniia*). The film begins with a prologue that shows some of the worst scenes of the first winter of the blockade, including trams abandoned in snowdrifts and a corpse lying in the Summer Garden. After flashing back to the eve of the war and building the narrative chronologically from this point, the sequence then shows a great deal more of the most horrific sights of the complete breakdown of the city's transport, water, fuel, and food supplies, and the corresponding deterioration, destitution, and, in many cases, death of its inhabitants. But unlike other Soviet wartime films that show the aftermath of the Nazis' crimes against Soviet civilians, here the heartrending scenes are of a situation occurring under Soviet rule, and what's more, the suffering is not counterbalanced by victory, and there are no images of the perpetrators. In this respect, Vishnevsky's film anticipated the modern emphasis on the sensory memory rather than on the ideological meaning of the siege, and in this sense prefigures filmmaker Sergei Loznitsa's use of the same footage without any voice-over whatsoever but only sounds emphasizing the actions, in his 2005 film *Blokada* (The Siege).[26]

The way in which Vishnevsky's film catalogs Leningrad's particular and unique suffering, filtered through a voice-over that draws attention to its status as the view of a witness to and participant in the privations, serves to contradict the dominant tone of objectivity to which Soviet-era voice-overs aspired, to undermine that impersonal authority. The overall effect is one of "deacousmatization," as Chion has termed it, the undermining of impersonal, objective, unquestionable authority by showing the voice's fate to be the same as the other inhabitants of the city. In its place, a different kind of authority is proposed: that of the eyewitness, conferred not by the party or by Stalin, but by direct, first-hand experience alone. The subjectivity of the voice-over serves to corroborate the experience by reference to the position of the speaking subject.

Vishnevsky's attempts in the commentary to anchor the film in the concrete time and space of Leningrad during the blockade are likewise supplemented by an emphasis upon the city's heroic traditions, that is, its prerevolutionary military greatness with Peter the Great and General Suvorov, as well as its celebration in the literary works of Pushkin, Gogol, Dostoevsky, Tolstoy and Gorky. Polina Barskova has shown that inserting the siege narrative into that of the city's aestheticized past was a common practice in accounts of the blockade.[27] Above all, though, Vishnevsky's commentary invokes the city's revolutionary tradition as the site of the "first Russian Revolutions," as the city that repulsed Krasnov and Kerensky in 1917, Kaiser Wilhelm II in 1918, and anti-revolutionary figures such as Rodzianko, Iudenich, and Mannheim in 1919.[28] Vishnevsky repeatedly returns to these patriotic and popular traditions, calling to the citizens to defend "the first city of the Revolution" and to man the barricades. This appeal to Leningrad's unique history as the tsarist capital and crucible of the revolution was, like the emphasis upon the perspective of eyewitness, a risky strategy. While it might function as a motivation to defend and fight for the city, it also accentuated the city's separateness from the rest of the country and its exceptional past in a way that could not necessarily be assimilated into the wider narrative of Soviet wartime propaganda.

The repeated use of *we* to refer to Leningrad and its inhabitants defines them as a community separate from Moscow and the rest of the Soviet Union. Thus, in describing the deaths through starvation in 1941, the commentary emphasizes the city of Leningrad as the entity that the victims served, as that which has suffered the loss, and that which must be avenged:

> We know every scar, every wound on the body of our beloved city. The groans and whispers of those who, dying, said goodbye to their native city will remain in our memories forever. They remained faithful to their banner and to their city. . . .
> Hitler will answer to us for all of this!

While the voice-overs in wartime Soviet films generally adopted an impersonal tone, one case in which they typically adopted the collective *we* was in portraying Nazi atrocities. In, for example, the Russian-language version of the film of the battle of Moscow, the voice-over apparently conveys the sentiments of the bereaved and the Red Army eyewitnesses of the atrocities, promising, "We shall not forget[;] we shall not forgive." The personal tragedies are picked up and translated into a universalized Soviet subject that will avenge the Nazi crimes. Vishnevsky's treatment of the Leningrad material was unacceptable because it systematically treated the suffering as separate from the common Soviet experience, as something specific to Leningrad. The Nazi invasion threatened to splinter the Soviet state not only through violent destruction but also because of the way that it treated the peoples of the Soviet Union differently: they appealed to ethnic Germans, the peoples of the Caucasus, and Ukrainians on the one hand, and they annihilated Jews, resisters, and loyal communists on the other hand. Soviet film created a unified subject of suffering, bereavement, and resistance that Vishnevsky's script for the Leningrad film undermined.

Nevertheless, a recording of the Vishnevsky voice-over was made.[29] It was, however, doomed from the outset, as the minister for cinema Ivan Bol'shakov had already lost patience with the Leningrad filmmakers' failure to send material for the Soviet Union–wide twice-weekly newsreel, *Soiuzkinozhurnal*.[30] As a result, he dispatched the most prominent and reliable figure in Soviet documentary, Roman Karmen, to ensure that the Leningrad filmmakers delivered the film about "the defense of Leningrad" that they had promised.[31] It appears that Karmen, although he claimed to have been sent just as a cameraman, was intended as the director of the film from the moment he was ordered to Leningrad.[32] According to his own overwrought account, he left Moscow on March 29, 1942, during the fourth movement of the premiere of Shostakovich's Seventh (Leningrad) Symphony in Moscow, traveling over the "Road of Life."[33] Shortly after his arrival, Karmen met the Leningrad filmmakers and explained Moscow's anxieties:

> We had a talk about the matter in hand. I informed the comrades about the worries the Committee for Cinematography has about the position of the Leningrad newsreel-cameramen. Having decided to make a feature-length film, they had decided no longer to send material for newsreels.[34]

The Leningrad filmmakers themselves in turn explained why they had not been sending any footage to Moscow:

> We really have been accumulating material for a feature film about the defense of Leningrad. . . . We have sent some stuff to Moscow, of course we could have sent more, and more regularly, but problems with the laboratory also prevented us. We weren't able to make double negatives from all the footage. So we didn't dare send the original negative—what if it got lost?[35]

Clearly, the Leningrad cameramen had a different conception of the film from that held in Moscow: as for Vishnevsky, the footage was a priceless trace of an almost incommunicable experience, which they would not risk getting lost. Nor did they want to let an outsider tell the story. For Moscow it was all simply material with which to mobilize the Soviet people and international support. Karmen was committed above all to the imperatives of journalism:

> The film you create will clearly possess tremendous emotional power. But we also need constant information. The central editorial office of newsreel is inundated with requests from countries around the world: "Show us Leningrad in the siege!" To keep the material you have accumulated in a safe is an enormous mistake—let's get together and try to think how to get out of this situation.[36]

Vishnevsky was to write a total of seven variants of the scenario, with the last diary entry relating to the film dating from April 14.[37] Nevertheless, none of them was accepted.[38] One of Vishnevsky's final efforts, entitled *Oborona Leningrada* (The Defense of Leningrad) was discussed following a silent screening in the Smolnyi, home of the city's party authorities, on April 17, 1942.[39] The Leningrad officials objected to the film's emphasis on suffering, and especially to the way in which the film opened with a prologue set at the bleakest point of the winter of 1941–42. Instead, they argued, it should follow a strict chronological order. Thus it was accused of "laying it on thick" (*sgushchaet kraski*) and even flaunting the enormous sacrifices undergone: "it's as if they're saying look, in Leningrad one person, three people, ten are dying, but we're still alive."[40] The city's party boss, Andrei Zhdanov, specifically objected to the invocation of the tsarist past of Peter the Great and the civil war situation of 1919.[41] There were calls for more images of combat and industry, and the city's party authorities themselves.

Consequently, on the night of April 29, 1942, a new version of film, bearing the title *Leningrad v bor'be* (Leningrad Fights On) and with a scenario and voice-over commentary written by Karmen, was shown at the Smolnyi, and was accepted.[42] What had changed?

Leningrad Fights On

Karmen's reworking of the film overcomes the rootedness of the material in the firsthand experience of the blockade. In place of the original voice-over, which filtered the images through a personal, subjective sensibility that strove to speak in the voice of the city, Karmen's film inserts the tragic images of the blockade into the broader Soviet narrative, adding compensatory uplifting images of the first trams running again, of the road of life, of increased bread rations, of the city being cleaned and restored; images of factories working still or again, images of the front. The final voice-over is laconic and dry, where Vishnevsky's had been expressive. In place of the subjective coloring, despite being read by Ruva Vygodsky, who had himself lived through the blockade, there is the impersonal tone of the professional announcer. Instead of the references to *we* and addresses to the city as *you* in Vishnevsky's commentary, the city is referred to in the third person throughout, as from an outsider's perspective: "Steadfastly and bravely the Leningraders underwent the trials and privations caused by the enemy siege. . . . This strengthened their fight, their belief in their own strength and seething hatred for the base foe." Here we once again have the objective, authoritative voice of the *acousmêtre*. Its power endows the suffering with unquestionable meaning: Vishnevsky's commentary treated the citizens' ordeal in simply surviving (*ispytaniia*) as equal in importance to the city's military resistance and struggle. Karmen's film, as its title—which could also be translated as "Leningrad in Struggle"—makes clear, emphasizes and elevates struggle and resistance rather than suffering.

Nevertheless, *Leningrad Fights On* still shows footage of the civilian tragedy of the blockade, including a number of images of corpses being dragged on sledges in the snow. These heartrending images are accompanied by few words in the commentary, whereas Vishnevsky's film, as we have seen, attempted to verbalize the pain and loss. As a writer, Vishnevsky attempted to rise to the challenge of articulating the reality of the blockade in words. Silence might be said to be an appropriate response to what might be called the indescribable, or the unspeakable: certainly, this approach has frequently been seen as the only fitting response not only to the blockade, as with Olga Berggolts's "February Diary," but also to the reality of the Nazis' contemporaneous murder of Jews in Eastern Europe. Here, though, the silence of Karmen's commentary is part of an attempt to downplay and stifle the specific voice of the blockaded city.[43]

The same tendency is evident in Karmen's use of newspaper clippings to make proclamations, appeals to the population, and calls to arms; Vishnevsky, conversely, had intended for the narrator to read excerpts from original speeches and newspaper articles that had appeared at the time in order to heighten the sense of immediacy and to bring the spectator closer to the atmosphere of the besieged city. Karmen's use of newspaper headlines, posters, and signs—shown almost as silent film intertitles—conveys a far fainter trace of the original moment in time, of the town under siege, than the more direct force of voice-over quotations would.

By contrast, Karmen's film mobilizes the greater power of the voice, as opposed to the photographed written word, in his use of the synchronous recording of Stalin's November 7 speech on Red Square.[44] The concluding words of the speech, "under the banner of Lenin, forward to victory," are shown repeated on the front page of the Leningrad daily, *Leningradskaia Pravda,* the following day. Karmen's film shows a message authentically produced during the worst period of the blockade, but one that expressed no Leningrad-specific sentiments: it simply repeated the wooden formulas of Stalin's Moscow speech. Likewise, Karmen's film contains very few references to the specific traditions of Leningrad, including its role in the revolution. Such an emphasis on the city's separate, potentially unruly identity would have been unacceptable for a wartime documentary film.

Karmen's film does, however, use music to evoke a specific sense of place, including a number of recognizable quotations from the works of Shostakovich and the sound of a piece by then-influential Soviet composer Boris Asafiev (1884–1949) as he continues to compose through the siege: the sound functions as proof that he is still composing, that art is still being produced in Leningrad—the same piece of music also accompanies images of scientists continuing their work in the public library. Yet the ideological content of music is inherently more ambiguous than language, and while there is quite a lot of music in the film, Karmen's version limits itself in the use of the voice-over to explaining, describing, and contextualizing the images, not to enhancing their emotional power or authority as a testimony.

It has been said that this is the only historical incidence of a film made from within a besieged town.[45] As such, Vishnevsky's version of the film would have given us a unique insider's insight into the horrific plight of the nearly one million civilians who died during the siege.[46] Had it been made, it would have been comparable in importance to a film made by the inmates of a working concentration camp, affording a great deal of insight into the plight of the Nazis' victims. In its place, we have a film that treats these losses as a meaningful sacrifice compensated for by the ultimately victorious course of the war. Two months after *Leningrad Fights On* was released in June 1942, Vishnevsky wrote Stroeva a letter expressing his frustration over how the film watered down the full extent of Leningrad's tragedy:

> We badly need documentary films. In the 14 months of the war there have only been two, and they were only just made, with great difficulty. Our cinema is working badly.
> You write: "Make some fragments of war for the screen, even if in a compromised way." . . . God help you and the rest of the comrades! You don't seem to understand what that whole "compromise" means. . . . In theater and cinema there have been so many crude things, smug lies, and "average" works. For what? Art should be harsh, tragically direct. . . . People need to learn to look at all our problems, sufferings; they need to think! (The other paths only lead to disillusion . . .)[47]

It is no coincidence that Dovzhenko, another filmmaker who attempted to break free from the formal constraints of the conventional form and tone of the standard Soviet wartime voice-of-God commentary, was also a writer; he, too, tried to convey a greater sense of the enormity of the price paid in human life by the country.

Dovzhenko and *The Battle for Our Soviet Ukraine*

In his 1943 documentary *Bitva za nashu Sovetskuiu Ukrainu* (The Battle for Our Soviet Ukraine, dir. Dovzhenko and Solntseva), Dovzhenko attempted to convey a sense of the enormous price paid for the emergent victory over the Nazis. In contrast to most other wartime Soviet directors, of documentaries and features alike, Dovzhenko went to the front himself and saw the aftermath of Nazi atrocities firsthand. From his diaries and films, it is evident that he was changed utterly by his experiences, initially as a journalist, then as an army political instructor (between February and October 1942), and later when he was appointed a member of the Ukrainian Commission Investigating German War Crimes (beginning in April 1943).[48] There were other Soviet filmmakers who spent time at the front, including 250 or so Soviet cameramen, a quarter of whom were killed in action. They were typically required to produce short items for newsreels that would then be edited to a voice-over and sound track by a director in Moscow, who in turn had no say over the filming process. These films quickly established and then followed conventional patterns for representing Nazi atrocities, showing death and suffering compensated by victories, and they rarely conveyed a personal vision. Yet Dovzhenko's legendary status meant that *The Battle for Our Soviet Ukraine* could articulate a distinctively personal depiction of the Nazi occupation and the genocide in the East, born of his firsthand experience of the front and newly liberated areas. The final film presented both a challenge to the voice-of-God form and the prevailing representations of the war.

Dovzhenko, while credited only as artistic director and author of the commentary in the final release, had—along with his wife, Yuliya Solntseva—an exceptional degree of control over filming. Thus, Dovzhenko's emphasis upon images of destruction—or as he put it, "the price of victory"[49]—was evident from his instructions to frontline cameraman Vladislav Mikosha in 1942, as the latter returned to Moscow after filming the unsuccessful defense of Sevastopol:

> "Show people's suffering unflinchingly . . ." he said to me. "Death, tears, suffering. There lies a tremendous life-affirming force. Show the sufferings of the soldier wounded on the field of battle. Show the hard drudgery of the soldier. Film the death of the soldier. Do not flinch: you can cry, but you must film it. . . . Everyone must see it. Tears can fill your eyes, but you must film it . . ."[50]

The resulting footage, which became *The Battle for Our Soviet Ukraine*, concentrates on the loss rather than the gain. It does this through the use of sound testimony in particular, employing ten synchronously recorded sound sequences (the norm in Soviet wartime film was one).

Overwhelmingly the synchronous sound is in the Ukrainian language, which serves to stress the suffering of Ukrainians in particular under the Nazi occupation. The most poignant of the ten sequences records the testimony of four Ukrainian women as they describe how their loved ones died at the hands of the Germans. Each ends with unanswered and unanswerable questions, such as, "What did you die for?" Such questions are not habitually asked of the dead and are not allowed to remain unanswered in Soviet wartime films. Here the questions are posed in this way in order not to explain, recuperate, or "Sovietize" bereavement. In this sequence, no voice-over intervenes to contextualize or explain the bigger picture, and nor do the hard-won victories in the film narrative sufficiently counterbalance the bereaved women's haunting questions. This sequence prefigures the way in which documentary cinema since the 1960s has employed synchronous sound interviews to supply eyewitness testimony of crucial historical events. Dovzhenko stands out among his contemporaries for his enthusiasm for this dimension of the form, as the recordings were central to his purpose of conveying the extent of Ukrainian suffering. He turned the film's voice-over commentary to the same purpose no less effectively.

One of the film's most powerful sequences shows Drobitsky Yar, the ravine outside Kharkov, where the city's Jews were shot dead and buried. As the film's voice-over puts it: "the Fascists shot fourteen thousand citizens of the town." Accompanying an image of the mass grave, revealing lines of partially decomposed corpses, the film addresses the spectator:

> Look at us, you who are living, do not turn from our terrifying pits. We cannot be forgotten or silenced. We are many. We are an enormous multitude in Ukraine! Do not forget us! Make Germany pay for our suffering!

Here, instead of interviewing the bereaved, Dovzhenko makes the victims themselves speak on their own behalf: they will not be silenced or forgotten. The spectator is told to contemplate the dead as a number of skulls, most notably that of a dead woman apparently disinterred from Drobitsky Yar, are arranged and photographed as if they were staring at the spectator. We are being told to look at the dead, but at the same time, they are looking back at us, addressing us, entreating us not to contemplate passively but to act.[51] The response demanded of the spectator is familiar—contribute to the war effort, exact "vengeance"—and entirely consistent with most Soviet newsreel depictions of atrocities. But the means of achieving it are extraordinary. The impossible dead witness—central to the question of testimony and memory of the Holocaust, the event said to be without witnesses—is made to speak.

Yet this image is also indicative of the problem in both Dovzhenko's film and the depiction of Nazi atrocities in many Soviet wartime documentaries: we know almost nothing of the woman whose corpse addresses us. She speaks in words composed by Dovzhenko, spoken by a professional announcer. Had she been able to, she might well have had a different story to tell, and her intonation certainly would have been different. She was most probably Jewish, but here she is made to articulate a narrative of Ukrainian suffering.

Thus, in an unusual gesture for Soviet documentaries, Dovzhenko again underlines the Ukrainian identity of the dead by getting them, as it were, to say (again using the first-person plural *we*) how many of them there are in such "pits" (*iamy*) in Ukraine. While it is true that there were many dead in Ukraine, this use of *we* also avoids and misrepresents the fact that the majority—more than ten thousand—of the fourteen thousand people killed in Drobitsky Yar were killed for being Jewish, not Ukrainian, and that these pits, which can be found all over Ukraine, were filled overwhelmingly with the Jews shot in 1941 and 1942. Thus, through the combination of a skillfully composed voice-over and shocking images of the mass grave, Dovzhenko grants his audiences a powerful sense of the immense scale of the mass killings in the East. But the identity of the victims is audaciously shifted away from the habitually misleading, description of "peaceful Soviet citizens" to the equally misleading implication that they were ethnic Ukrainians, when they were in fact overwhelmingly Jewish.

This message was also at odds with the overall thrust of Soviet wartime documentary practice, which sought to unify the nation around the ethnically and regionally undifferentiated Soviet victim. This excluded the Leningrad-specific narrative of the blockade, just as it excluded the story of the specific fate of Jews under Nazi occupation, and ultimately, any sense of the exceptional extent of Ukraine's suffering under the Nazis. It likewise toned down the personal and subjective element in documentary: it appears that Dovzhenko had intended to read the voice-over for *The Battle for Our Soviet Ukraine* himself but ultimately had to opt for the standard voice-over man, Leonid Khmara, instead.[52] But the worst was yet to come: within months of the film's premiere in October 1943, Dovzhenko's proposal for a feature film on the occupation of Ukraine, to be entitled *Ukraina v ogne* (Ukraine in Flames), was rejected by Stalin for its even more outspoken treatment of Ukrainian suffering, and the director's voice was effectively silenced.

Conclusion

Any attempt to challenge the clichés of Soviet documentary required exceptional personal authority. It is thus no surprise that these two attempts to depart from the standardized voice-of-God style of commentary were undertaken by figures who enjoyed considerable prestige, personal experience of their subject matter, and strong ideas about the art of cinema: namely the writer Vishnevsky and the writer-director Dovzhenko. In each case there was an attempt to make the commentary serve a purpose other than the habitual discourse of impersonal, universalized, Soviet authority—the *acousmêtre*—but rather to convey the raw emotion of the eyewitness, the sense of first-person testimony. This alternative, vestigially subjective vision, whether conveyed through an authorial voice-over or through synchronous-sound testimony, was in both cases employed to tell the particular story of a special class of civilian victims of the Nazis during the war: the inhabitants of Leningrad or of Ukraine. In both cases the form and the message pushed at the very limits of the acceptable.

Paradoxically, when postwar, post-Stalin Soviet documentary eventually succeeded in breaking away from the voice-of-God commentary, it was once again personal prestige, in this case that of director Mikhail Romm, which was to prove decisive. With the 1965 release of *Obyknovennyi fashizm* (Ordinary Fascism), Romm was successful in discarding the monolithic voice-over style and opening the way for films to be narrated by their directors; this formal innovation also permitted a reassessment of the wartime period: both of Nazism, its ostensible object, but also of Stalinism, its figurative target. By dispensing with the now-suspect authority of the voice of God in favor of a fallible interlocutor— who refers to his own position through the use of deixis, through the pronouns *I* and *we*—Romm was attempting to persuade rather than assert, to respect rather than harangue the viewer, in an implicitly democratic interpellation of our powers of reason.[53] *Ordinary Fascism* is thus rightly regarded as a landmark both in Russian and Soviet documentary film and in de-Stalinization. But Vishnevsky's and Dovzhenko's films were early attempts to achieve something similar, and as such, they grant precious insight into both the extent and limits of "spontaneous de-Stalinization" during the wartime period and the interplay between style and politics in the sound film voice-over.

Notes

1. Bill Nichols, *Representing Reality: Issues and Concepts in Documentary* (Bloomington: Indiana University Press, 1991), 32.

2. Ibid., 37.

3. Ibid., 32. Nichols subsequently added further modes, especially relevant to contemporary documentary, in Bill Nichols, *Introduction to Documentary* (Indianapolis: Indiana University Press, 2001).

4. Michael Renov, *The Subject of Documentary* (Minneapolis: University of Minnesota Press, 2004), xviii.

5. Renov, *Subject of Documentary*, xxi.

6. Michael Chion, *The Voice in Cinema*, ed. and trans. Claudia Gorbman (New York: Columbia University Press, 1999), 5.

7. Ibid., 18.

8. Ibid., 24.

9. Ibid., 27.

10. Nina Vol'man, *Efim Uchitel'* (Leningrad: Iskusstvo, 1976), 25–26.

11. Ansel'm Bogorov, "Nachalo," in *Tsena kadra. Kazhdyi vtoroi—ranen, kazhdyi chetvertyi ubit. Sovetskaia frontovaia kinokhronika 1941–1945 gg. Dokumenty i svidetel'stva*, ed. Valerii Fomin (Moscow: Kanon, 2010), 170.

12. Vol'man, *Efim Uchitel'*, 27.

13. S. Vishnevetskaia, "Dokumental'naia trilogiia Vs. Vishnevskogo," *Iskusstvo kino* 4 (1958): 108; Vsevolod Vishnevskii, *Stat'i, dnevniki, pis'ma o literature i iskusstve* (Moscow: Sovetskii pisatel', 1961), 419 (entry for March 25, 1942).

14. Vishnevetskaia, "Dokumental'naia trilogiia Vs. Vishnevskogo," 110; Vol'man, *Efim Uchitel'*, 27; Vsevolod Vishnevskii, *Leningrad: dnevniki voennykh let: 2 noiabria 1941 goda-31 dekabria 1942* (Moscow: Voenizdat, 2002), 1:121.

15. Vishnevetskaia, "Dokumental'naia trilogiia Vs. Vishnevskogo," 111.

16. See, e.g., Vsevolod Vishnevskii, "Uporno k novomu iskusstvu," (1933) in *Sobranie sochinenii*, 5 vols. (Moscow: Khudozh. literatura, 1954–61), 5:340–46.

17. Esfir' Shub, *Zhizn' moia—kinematograf* (Moscow: Iskusstvo, 1972), 178.

18. Vera Stroeva, "O druge," in *Pisatel'-boets. Vospominaniia o Vsevolode Vishnevskom*, (Moscow: Sovetskaia Rossiia, 1963), 151.

19. Shub, *Zhizn' moia—kinematograf*, 179.

20. Vishnevetskaia, "Dokumental'naia trilogiia Vs. Vishnevskogo," 111.

21. Vishnevskii, *Leningrad: dnevniki voennykh let*, 121.

22. Vol'man, *Efim Uchitel'*, 28.

23. P. H. Matthews, *Oxford Concise Dictionary of Linguistics* (Oxford: Oxford University Press, 2005), s.v. *deixis*, 89–90.

24. Jakobson also classified deictical markers as "indexical symbols": "the word 'I' designating the utterer is existentially related to his utterance, and hence functions as an index." Roman Jakobson, "Shifters, Verbal Categories and the Russian Verb," in *Selected Writings, Vol. 2: Word and Language* (The Hague: Mouton, 1971), 132. Also see Giorgio Agamben's lucid account of this in *Language and Death: The Place of Negativity*, trans. Karen E. Pinkus with Michael Hardt (Minneapolis: University of Minnesota Press, 1991), 19–37.

25. Vsevolod Vishnevskii, "Leningrad v bor'be. Literaturnyi variant stsenariia khudozhestvenno-dokumental'nogo fil'ma otcheta ob oborone Leningrada v 1941–1942 gg," *Iskusstvo kino* 4 (1958): 122.

26. For an account of this shift, see James Clapperton, "The Siege of Leningrad as Sacred Narrative: Conversations with Survivors," *Oral History* 35, no. 1 (2007): 50. For a review of Loznitsa's film that relates it to the material discussed in the present article, see Polina Barskova, "Sergei Loznitsa *The Siege*" (review), http://www.kinokultura.com/2009/24r-blokada.shtml.

27. Polina Barskova, "The Spectacle of the Besieged City: Repurposing Cultural Memory in Leningrad, 1941–1944," *Slavic Review* 69, no. 2 (2010): 327–55.

28. Vishnevskii, "Leningrad v bor'be," 114.

29. Vol'man, *Efim Uchitel'*, 32.

30. Bogorov, "Nachalo," 173.

31. Ibid., 173.

32. Ibid., 175.

33. Roman Karmen, *No pasarán!* (Moscow: Sovetskaia Rossiia, 1972), 111.

34. Ibid., 115.

35. Ibid., 116–17.

36. Ibid., 117.

37. Vishnevetskaia, "Dokumental'naia trilogiia Vs. Vishnevskogo," 112.

38. Ibid., 112.

39. At this point the version shown did not include the full voice-over. Valerii Fomin, ed., *Kino na voine. Dokumenty i svidetel'stva* (Moscow: Materil, 2005), 211.

40. Ibid., 212.

41. Ibid.

42. Vol'man, *Efim Uchitel'*, 33.

43. Ol'ga Berggol'ts, *Stikhi, Proza* (Moscow: Khudozhestvennaia literatura, 1961), 314–20; Claude Lanzmann, in *Au sujet de Shoah: Le film de Claude Lanzmann* (Paris: Belin, 1990), 310.

44. Famously, the speech was actually recorded in a studio the following day, after changes in the timing of the event prevented Soviet newsreel sound engineers from recording it live. For an English-language account of the incident, see Rodric Braithwaite, *Moscow 1941: A City and Its People at War* (London: Profile, 2007), 287–88.

45. Vol'man, *Efim Uchitel'*, 26.

46. Richard Bidlack, "Lifting the Blockade on the Blockade," *Kritika: Explorations in Russian and Eurasian History* 10, no. 2 (spring 2009): 334.

47. Vera Stroeva, "O druge," in *Pisatel'-boets*, 157.

48. George O. Liber, *Alexander Dovzhenko: A Life in Soviet Film* (London: British Film Institute, 2002), 191.

49. RGALI 2923/1/95, l. 13. Stenogram of meeting to discuss *Battle for Our Soviet Ukraine*, October 28, 1943.

50. Vladislav Mikosha, "'Ia ostanavlivaiu vremia.' Vospominaniia frontovogo operatora," *Iskusstvo kino* 5 (2005): 115.

51. Libby Saxton, *Haunted Images: Film, Ethics, Testimony and the Holocaust* (London: Wallflower, 2008), 109.

52. RGALI 2923/1/95, l. 4.

53. As Wolfgang Beilenhoff and Sabine Hänsgen argue, Romm's calm, questioning, critical, ironic voice contrasts with the hysterical performances of Hitler himself; it functions as a countervoice. Wolfgang Beilenhoff and Sabine Hänsgen, "Speaking about Images: The Voice of the Author in Ordinary Fascism," *Studies in Russian and Soviet Cinema* 2, no. 2 (2008): 145.

8 Vocal Changes

Marlon Brando, Innokenty Smoktunovsky, and the Sound of the 1950s

Oksana Bulgakowa

Translated from the German by Katrina Sark

THE BEST STUDIES of voice in film—by Michel Chion or Kaja Silverman—have examined disembodied, formless voices, voices as phantoms.[1] However, signs of social and temporal anchoring of the electric voice—as part of the medial body—have been neglected by film theory. One does not have to be Professor Higgins to distinguish film voices of the 1930s from those of the 1990s, since the manner of speech depends not only on the quality of an individual voice that reveals the age, gender, appearance, and mood of the speaker but also on the historically, culturally, and socially determined speech patterns, on technical conditions of recording practices, and on artistic conventions. Norms, conventions, and parameters change at certain points in time. The history of technology is concerned with microphones and tape recorders, amplifiers and filters; linguistic studies conduct phonetic and prosodic analyses of speech patterns. Can film studies indicate traces of time in the electric voices and merge the historicity of the voice with the history of recording technology?

Much has been written about film voices in the context of the first technological sound revolution, during the initial transition to sound film in the 1930s. The talkies revived the confrontation between the natural and the technologically transformed voice, introduced by the invention of the telephone and gramophone, public microphones, speakers, and radio. Right around that time, philosophers and sociologists (Plessner, Heidegger, Spengler, Adorno) examined such topics as silence, the cry, and the phenomenology of the voice, while the political situation drew attention to the rhetoric of community-building speeches that located the voice in the realm of the sacred and the affective. Much was written, for example, about the vocal changes in the German public sphere after 1945. Albrecht Schöne analyzed the performance style of the contemporary German writers (e.g., Peter Handke, Ilse Aichinger) compared to the prewar generation (e.g., Stefan George, Franz Werfel). Beatrix Schönherr examined changes in speech patterns on stage, using the role of Shylock in Shakespeare's *The Merchant of Venice*, as performed by Fritz Kortner, Fred Düren, and Walter Schmidinger between 1966 and 1984. Johannes Schwitalla examined the presentation styles of German politicians of the 1930s and 1950s. Claudia Schmölders created a physiognomic portrait of Hitler's voice.[2] But this wave barely noted filmic voices, even though the vocal changes of the 1950s were hard to miss.

The Sounds of the 1950s

In the early 1950s, a technological revolution took place in film that altered the shape of cinematic spectacle. Cinerama, 3-D film, widescreen, and multi-channel sound brought new experiences of mediated senses. Stereo sound was recorded onto magnetic tape, which increased the quality of sound; cinemas were equipped with seven speakers.[3] Sound changed not only in the cinemas—radio sound was improved by FM frequencies, and stereo sound became a fixed part of everyday culture thanks to broadcasting and record production, similar to the hi-fi in private homes. The new noise components became an essential part of the musical aesthetic. *Musique concrète* not only split recorded sounds into tiny pieces of montage but also created artificially produced sounds from the lab. The Music Box with American jazz and rock and roll changed everyday listening culture in Europe. "How quickly the ear of the people changes!" noted one chronicler.[4] The new sound experience reoriented the senses away from the centrality of the image. (Perhaps the phonocentric orientation of Jacques Lacan and Roland Barthes should be considered in this context.)

The introduction of stereo sound in cinema revived the motifs that were emblematic for the transition period to the talkies. The gap between the voice and the body was portrayed in split personality and depersonalization stories: a girl working as a phone receptionist gives each of her conversation partners the expected image ("the voice can bear any image," as she says) and in the end does not know whether she is a caring mother, a bohemian, or a romantic lover (*Bells Are Ringing*, dir. Minnelli, 1960). *Singin' in the Rain* (dir. Donen, 1952) plays with the divergence between sound and image enshrined in a plot about the coming of sound. The voice is first given a "wrong" body, and the coincidental meeting of the two is hailed as a "happy marriage" at the end of the film.

Sensibility toward an artificially mediated screen voice was revived also thanks to a new medium: television. Frank Tashlin played with it so brilliantly in *Rock-a-Bye Baby* (1958) and in *Will Success Spoil Rock Hunter?* (1957). His heroes converse with the partners on the television screen and incidentally make a discovery: one can hear better if one can see, and one can speak more freely if one is not seen. On the phone, the uptight hero can vocally claim to be a chief executive officer. The Soviet film heroes knew that as well. In the comedy *Karnaval'naia noch* (Carnival Night, dir. Riazanov, 1958), the shy hero records a declaration of love for his sweetheart onto a record; the medial separation of his voice from his body makes this possible.

The voices—or more precisely, the way they were used and recorded—also changed. Indeed, blond-haired sopranos, with light breaths that marked erotic arousal, could still be found on the screens of the 1950s. But new bodies also appeared, equipped not only with new gestures but also with different voices and modes of speaking. In American cinema, it was Montgomery Clift, Marlon Brando, and James Dean; in Russian cinema, it was Innokenty Smoktunovsky.

Today, Brando's and Smoktunovsky's voices have become trademarks. Electronic Arts developed the computer game *The Godfather* (2006) with Brando's voice. Smoktunovsky's voice is discussed in Russian blogs as "flattering" and "catchy," and is designated as the "voice of an era" for its uncontested appeal.[5] For their contemporaries, both Brando and Smoktunovsky were marked by their unconventional way of speaking, which, among other features, was characterized by gender confusion. Brando's "brooding, inarticulate" heroes suggested a "scandalous sexuality" in contrast to "utterly straight Waynes, Gables, and Pecks," as James Naremore remarked.[6] His biker in tight leather (*The Wild One*, dir. Benedek, 1953) became a figure of homosexual fantasies (compare *Scorpio Rising*, dir. Anger, 1964). His playfully infantile boxer in *On the Waterfront* (dir. Kazan, 1954) had slight and graceful movements and feminine eye makeup. This peculiar appearance accompanied Brando until the role of the homosexual Major Penderton in *Reflection in a Golden Eye* (dir. Huston, 1961).[7] This sexual ambivalence was also associated with his voice, which was breathy, like Marilyn Monroe's, characterized by too much intimate closeness, too much artificiality in low tones, its slowness, and frequent pauses.

Smoktunovsky's voice similarly appeared unmasculine. It was too high, too soft, also with too much breath, and therefore sexually ambiguous. His idiosyncratic intonation, which transformed affirmative sentences into questions and seemed feminine and inconclusive, could easily be connected with homosexual mannerisms. Brando's style was immediately copied by James Dean; Smoktunovsky also found many imitators—not only on stage but especially in everyday life. The male Soviet intellectuals who were sixteen to eighteen years old in the late 1950s to this day speak with a soft Smoktunovsky-type voice.

In the late 1950s, this vocal quality and manner of speaking were first classified as incredibly unprofessional. The voices seemed too quiet for the theater, where both Brando and Smoktunovsky started out. Brando shocked Broadway with his indistinct manner of speaking. Irene Selznick, the producer of *A Streetcar Named Desire* (which premiered on December 3, 1947), complained to

Brando's agent Edith Van Cleve after a performance that he was inaudible.[8] Theater critics criticized Brando's difficult-to-understand mumbling and spoke of a "speech impediment."[9] Brando stammered, grunted, spoke casually and indistinctly, whispered, breathed, and used his voice without rich modulations. The mumbling, a sign of a lack of education, which Professor Higgins eliminated in Eliza Doolittle, was assessed as physical indolence and labeled as a "slouch and mumble style."[10] Brando's performance style was interpreted as an expression of his loyalty to naturalistic principles. This was not (rhetorical) art but total physical relaxation, physiologically calculated spontaneity, soft articulation, an almost sleepy sound: he exhaled words with his breath.[11] Brando's natural voice had a slightly hoarse nasality, but according to his friends, he did not mumble in everyday life. This kind of speaking, which he fully controlled, was reserved for his performances, and he believed that the audience did not follow individual words but their emotional coloration, which was more important than the text.[12]

Brando was not the only actor to use these new speech patterns. Montgomery Clift did it before him, and James Dean after. Clift, too, put in unaccustomed breaks, and he spoke so softly that it was almost impossible to hear him on stage. He, too, had sudden mood swings in syncopated rhythmic speech with high tones and speech breaks.[13] Both Brando and Clift puzzled audiences with this peculiar way of speaking in the plays of Tennessee Williams, who offered new images of masculinity: suddenly it was not women, but the men who would whisper, breathe, scream hysterically, or fall into long silences and incomprehensible mood swings. The vocal changes, in other words, could not be separated from a transformation of masculinity.

Brando made this mannerism into his trademark and used it for film roles. He appeared in Elia Kazan's film version of *A Streetcar Named Desire* (1952) as the vulgar, uneducated Pole, Stanley Kowalski, with grease-smeared fingers and lips, in a dirty, sweaty T-shirt, and was seen as the embodiment of unbridled sexual energy. He spoke with his mouth full of chicken bones, stood with his back to the camera, and obscured his mouth with a beer bottle, which he opened with his teeth. All of these devices motivated his indistinct articulation; it was a part of the costume of the uncultured type who dressed, spoke, and moved casually. Brando's former boxer in *On the Waterfront* also spoke indistinctly, chewed gum, used a lot of slang, and frequently turned away from the microphone. And yet, at the same time, Brando's rhythmization of the sentences through breaks and pauses produced elegant musicality.

The practice of swallowing the second half of the sentence and his interest in accents shaped all of his roles.[14] After his success in the role of Stanley Kowalski, Brando tacked this manner to the ethnic and social habits of his other protagonists. To motivate the speech style, he asked the screenwriter Carl Foreman to change the name of the hero from Williams to Wilcheck (*The Men*, dir.

Zinnemann, 1950), to justify the slurred speech through Polish American roots.[15] Such ethnically inflected sound environments were characteristic of the beginnings of sound film, as, for example, the Berlin dialect of Heinrich George and the multilingualism of early Soviet film and Hollywood.[16] They were maintained only by the French film school until the 1940s—in the raspy voice of Arletty, a voice of the gutter, or in Jean Gabin's proletarian slang. By the mid-1930s, Soviet cinema, like Hollywood, had eliminated accents and enforced a new articulation standard.

Although Smoktunovsky spoke without an accent, his soft voice, too weak for a stage performer, seemed almost unprofessional. When he tried his luck in the capital in 1955, after several years in the provinces, he was rejected by every theater in Moscow, except the studio for film actors, and only thanks to the patronage of Mosfil'm's director, Ivan Pyriev.[17] In his first film role, *Kak on lgal ee muzhu* (How He Lied to Her Husband, dir. Berezantseva, 1956), he attempted to speak with a high and bright voice, just as the young Soviet film lovers did—loud, fast, and clear. But his voice lacked range and flexibility; it had no energy, no strength, and no full sound—a professional stigma. It "broke," and breathing could be heard, as if the actor could not master the technique of exhalation. The standards of the time were clearly formulated in the textbook of elocution: the voice of an actor must be clear, bright, high sounding, loud, lush, and rich in all voice registers. If the breathing technique is not trained and the respiratory organs remain dull and flat, then the sound does not "carry" meaning, words and phrases are lost. A soundless voice, a voice that breaks because it lacks air, has to be trained by the actor; he must make his inhalation inaudible, or he is not suited for the stage.[18]

Yet only two years later, thanks to his new vocal pattern, Smoktunovsky became a huge success on the stage in Georgy Tovstonogov's staging of Dostoevsky's *The Idiot* (1956). His Prince Myshkin stood out because of his low but clear-spoken and decidedly slow pace—he did not use any significant rising or falling pitch movements, no great dynamics from pianissimo to scream, no numbing jumps across octaves, but a monotonous, internalized vocalization. The quiet tone and his ingenious intonation demanded tense attention: the intonation was uncertain, one could not predict which way the melody would go, the last word fell silent, and spectators were forced to catch the words and to follow as the sound died off.[19]

In the film *Vysokosnyi god* (Leap Year, 1961), former theater director Anatoly Efros effectively showcased Smoktunovsky's vocal performance on-screen. At the moment of "entering the screen," Smoktunovsky remained silent for almost a minute, then at the "entry into the role," he emphasized that he first had to tune his voice like an instrument. Cautious and hesitant—in front of the mirror—he looked down his throat, his tongue outstretched, tried different sounds, and cleared his throat to test how his hoarse voice sounded, and whether it "matched" his role. In the scene, these exercises were motivated by an explanation: a cold was mitigating "the naturalization process," like the chicken bones in Brando's mouth.

According to the critics of the time, Brando and Smoktunovsky celebrated the art of the amateur. Of course, dialogues were also written differently, with broken sentences that supported this speech style. However, both actors consciously used controlled and controllable techniques. Both were actors of the Stanislavsky method-acting school, where one worked intensely on articulation techniques. We should not forget that Stanislavsky had actually dreamed of an opera career but had to switch to the theater stage because his voice was too weak. Significantly, Brando and Smoktunovsky—shorty after such astonishingly authentic performances—each played roles in which they could not afford such naturalistic, "unprofessional" deviations: in Shakespeare plays, for example. Joseph L. Mankiewicz was not afraid to cast Brando in his adaptation of *Julius Caesar* (1953) as Mark Antony, next to the famous Shakespearean actor John Gielgud, and then cast him singing along with Frank Sinatra in the musical *Guys and Dolls* (1955) just two years later. Similarly, in 1964, Smoktunovsky appeared in the title role of the film version of *Hamlet*, directed by Grigory Kozintsev.

Brando trained for these roles with vocal coaches, but his Shakespearean monologues sounded still monotonous and "prosy."[20] In *Hamlet*, Kozintsev had to help Smoktunovsky. The film was shot almost like a silent film, and the vocal image of Hamlet was shaped in postsynchronization. The microphone emphasized the loneliness of the speaker, and his whisper was perceived as an inner voice. The few of Hamlet's soliloquies left in the film were presented as his thoughts, as inner monologue. He famously spoke the words "to be or not to be" standing with his back to the camera. Moreover, Kozintsev had asked Anna Akhmatova to rewrite Hamlet's monologues into prose. Akhmatova refused. The editor of Kozintsev's writing, Yakov Butovsky, discovered this and suspected that the request was caused by the director's fear that Smoktunovsky had no sense of how to deal with the verse and the rhythm. When Kozintsev was unable to realize this idea, he made Smoktunovsky copy his intonation and rhythm instead.[21]

But apparently, Smoktunovsky was not the only one who could do little with poetry at the time—Kozintsev was also guilty of preferring prose to verse. Noteworthy in this context is a letter from Olga Freudenberg to her cousin Boris Pasternak (the author of the definitive Russian translation of *Hamlet*), dated April 1, 1954, in which she shared her impressions after a visit to Kozintsev's staging of *Hamlet* at the Leningrad Theater. Freudenberg noted that it was "Shakespeare without Shakespeare," for the actors had forgotten how to recite verses, had no feel for the rhythm, and instead muttered the text to themselves: "There were a lot of omissions. All of Shakespeare's metaphors and aphorisms were erased. Verse was abolished. The actors read it as everyday speech. If we did not live in such a bright and wonderful era, I would have said that such resistance to poetry, rhythm, passion, and temperament could only be brought about by an epoch that pins people down and guts them, an era of downtrodden poetry and puked-on souls. Please explain to me: if rhythm and meter have to be hidden like a perversion, then why write in rhythm and meter? Let's talk instead like we do during dinner."[22]

The preference for prose over verse was evidently still unusual in the 1950s. But what a traditional philologist, such as Freudenberg, felt to be a "must" of poetic recitation had lost its artistic value for Kozintsev, as well as for Smoktunovsky. The actor was guided by a different standard, and this divergence in perception was itself a sign of cultural change. In his review of Kozintsev's film, Alexander Anikst, arguably the most famous Soviet Shakespeare scholar at the time, also noted this peculiarity in dealing with verse that so horrified Freudenberg but was able to justify it. He saw this as a trend, audible also in Sergei Yutkevich's film version of *Othello* (1955). There, too, verse was preserved only before the opening credits, after which the actors began to speak in prose.

"Film characters cannot express themselves in verse," Anikst wrote. "In general, one should speak as little as possible in films because, first of all, one goes to the cinema not to hear but to see, and secondly, the human voice still does not sound natural enough on film. It is not a living voice, but a mechanically recorded one. Film sound has not yet reached that level of perfection that creates the illusion of natural sound." Anikst concluded that while Shakespeare's text loses enormously in film, in the theater, it is still alive—thanks to the live voice. The best film adaptation of Shakespeare, he suggested, could be achieved only in silent film.[23] Kozintsev agreed and noted that in his film, Shakespeare's verse had to be replaced with prose. "If we listen carefully to Kozintsev's film," wrote Anikst, "we'll notice that all of the original prose passages were retained, but that he used only those verses that could be spoken as prose. Naturally, Boris Pasternak's translation was the best for this, because Pasternak had tried to bring the language of Shakespeare's protagonists closest to living, contemporary, everyday speech."[24] For Anikst, this preference for prose was connected to changes in gender roles and a new image of masculinity—"without romance, without virility, without sentimentality."[25]

With his hoarse, breathy voice and his particular way of speaking (with rhythmic breaks and unstable intonation), Smoktunovsky embodied this ambivalent image of masculinity. His greatest theatrical success, Prince Myshkin—the idiot—was a patient in a mental institution. His film heroes were too strange, too headstrong, too playful, childish or foolish. In *Leap Year*, he embodied a very anarchic hero bored with women, work, parents, and enthusiasm; he dressed in black like an existentialist; he slept with a girl and refused to marry her; he wanted to win the lottery, to travel south—all desires criminalized in the film. His portrayal of the physicist in *Deviat' dnei odnogo goda* (Nine Days of One Year, dir. Romm, 1961) was also too ironic, too coldly distancing, too courageous, too convinced by his superior intellect to fully win our sympathy. Thus, in the film, his rival gets the girl.

In all his roles, the unconventional characters Smoktunovsky played motivated his vocal peculiarity. After his very successful Hamlet—received by critics as a fighter against the lies of the fathers, and for which he was awarded the highest national decoration, the Lenin Prize—Smoktunovsky could embody all possible characters with his voice: contemporary, historical, classical.[26] Along with Sergei Bondarchuk, he became the highest paid and the most regarded of film voices. Andrei Tarkovsky cast him in *Zerkalo* (Mirror, 1974), in the role of the invisible narrator, the alter ego of the director, a role created entirely through vocal presence.[27] Smoktunovsky's voice changed slowly as he developed low notes and omitted the high metallic sounds completely. Already in the comedy *Beregis' avtomobilia!* (Watch Out for the Car!, dir. Riazanov, 1966), in which he parodied his Hamlet performance on the stage of an amateur theater, he changed his vocal register from the high tenor of a timid insurance agent to the "velvety" baritone of a noble criminal.

The voices of both Brando and Smoktunovsky acted in strong contrast to the clear articulations of the 1930s and 1940s. Their floating, soft voices produced a different type of communication (intimate, internalized, confidential), that was supposed to forge a secret community and establish a confidential intimacy against an enforced collectivity, and of "amateurism" against the "well-made art" of the previous decades. *Internalization, intimate communication*, and *trust* were the keywords of the post-Stalinist Thaw, but not necessarily of American culture of the 1950s and 1960s. It may not be enough, therefore, to define the changes in voice and speech patterns as exclusively cultural and stylistic—we also need to see them as products of a technical phenomenon, because filmic voices cannot be separated from their recording techniques, which are in themselves tightly connected with aesthetic and cultural explanations.

Recording Technique and Style

The new technological possibilities of the second sound revolution of the 1950s also meant innovations for the voice. The advent of stereo sound did not affect the location of the voice and other spatial effects exclusively. Stereo sound required directional microphones and the placement of the microphones behind the actors; otherwise, there would be distortion.[28] The proximity of the microphone to the mouth meant that the signal became clearer (thus the microphone helped weak voices attain more volume) and background noises such as breathing, voice breaks, slight hoarseness, and spit were "caught" and played back, intensifying the level of realism, as well as the feeling of intimate proximity.

Sound-on-film technology did not permit tones that were either too loud or too quiet, and the differences between cries and whispers had to be avoided. New microphones and the process of recording on magnetic tape had introduced a new dimension especially for soft voices. New resonance quality permitted a wider range of contrasting volume and intensity of sounds, voices were recorded separately with the single adjustment of each channel, and noises were transmitted through several speakers.[29] It was now possible to move freely between whispers (of about thirty decibels) and loud voices (about a hundred decibels), so that actors standing next to each other no longer had to speak equally loudly. Quiet voices, low voices, and whispers were made technically possible.

In the 1930s, certain frequencies could not be faithfully reproduced; the lower frequencies of voices were especially problematic, resulting in incomprehensible dialogue. It was considered a special mastery for sound technicians to single out the voices clearly from the background and to isolate noise. In the 1950s, sound clarity had been achieved, which meant that sound could be "contaminated." Voices could sound deeper, and the indistinctness was no longer considered a "disturbance." The second contamination came later with rock music that rejected the clear metallic sound and allowed for hoarseness and sonic pollution.

Film historians believe that the new realism of sound and voice in feature films was influenced by the contemporaneous development of documentary filmmaking. The appearance of the small synchronized camera and the Nagra equipment for the film industry gave a new impulse to documentary films with direct sound. Direct cinema and cinema verité tolerated indistinctness, unidentifiable noises, and the simultaneity of overlapping voices. Protagonists of documentary films had untrained voices; they spoke with pauses, coughs, hiccups, and stutters; in unfinished, broken sentences, with incorrect pronunciation; they brought with them the peculiarity of intonation, and that vocal aesthetic was also adopted for feature films. The mumbling of real people undermined the transfer of meaning through words—meaning now shifted to intonation, sound, and mood.

Neorealist films and the films of the various new waves utilized the same stylistic devices: streets and original interiors instead of studios; natural rather than artificial lighting; black-and-white film in contrast to Technicolor; long, seemingly uncomposed shots, loose dramaturgy, and indistinctly speaking amateur actors. This aesthetic meant a renunciation of written dialogue, acting, and the professionally trained voice. It favored silence and broken sentences, and not only because the amateur actors could not memorize and perform long, artistically shaped texts. As part of this aesthetic, noise was more important than speech, and the voice was understood not as a bearer of meaning but as a sound phenomenon.

Paradoxes of Cultural Studies

The description of fluctuations within the always-changing patterns of speech is often interpreted as a binary opposition that defines two basic types: the pathetic, romantic, expressive, and the prosaic, sober, artless manner of speaking.[30] These descriptions can be specified through functions: public speaking (pathetic, loud) versus private voice (confiding, quiet). But can one speak of one single norm within a society? Rather, we find a heterogeneous vocal landscape within each cultural group and each period, in which any person can speak with different voices (everyday voice, public voice). Moreover, various spheres offer a wide variety of standard voices (e.g., radio voice; film voice; theater voice; singer's voice; the voice of a politician, a teacher, a therapist). Obviously, there is no uniformity within a society at the same time period, as examples from Soviet and American cultures demonstrate.

German researchers found it easy to explain the vocal changes after 1945: the "skepticism of big words and heroic sounds acquired through painful experience" was great, and thus speech patterns changed.[31] While German politicians of the 1930s overused ecstatic, aggressive speech, using emotionally heightened forms of prose with the maximum pitch, maximum volume, and maximum emphasis, the new political orators after 1945 rejected great sound jumps and climactic increases of volume and speed: they eschewed high frequencies, stretched vowels, and chanting rhythms. Democracy was marked by a soft sound; by monotonous, restrained speech; by a mild, casual, unhurried conversational tone; by a deeper voice and unfilled pauses, slips of the tongue, corrections, repetitions, dialectal sounds, slurring, indistinct articulation—even to the point that certain words became incomprehensible.[32] Albrecht Schöne observed a similar change from the expressionist manner of performance in writers, describing their dry, sober style, and their peculiar "unengaged monotony" as a manner of speaking typical of a time and a generation.[33]

The sound landscape of the 1940s was different in the Soviet Union. Stalin delegated aggressive and emotionally exaggerated forms of prosody to other public actors—such as Attorney General Andrei Vyshinsky and the radio announcer Yury Levitan. They became the vocal representatives of publicly lived emotions (anger, rage, discontent, and triumph) that were associated with loud voices. Levitan had been the main radio announcer since the war years, and his low baritone was named the disembodied "voice of Soviet history." His manner of speech was based on such methods as rhythm, vowel strain, the trembling ups and downs of his voice, and effective pauses. He put emphasis on almost every syllable, on overly clear articulation, on stresses with escalations and slowdowns (and did not differ much from Harry Giese, spokesman of the Nazi newsreels, who had a distinct, rather high voice).

In contrast to Hitler, Roosevelt, or Mussolini, who presented their voices in public, the voices of Lenin and Stalin were often replaced by those of professional actors. Their actual voices could be heard only rarely. Lenin died in 1924, but he withdrew from the political scene even earlier as a result of a stroke that led to paralysis and loss of speech. Although it was customary to release records of political speeches, there were very few recordings of Lenin's voice (eighteen speeches in all).[34] Arseny Avraamov, who was working on the creation of synthetic voices, suggested to "vocalize" Lenin's writings by synthesizing his voice:

> At the all-Union sound conference in 1930, I proposed the idea of a conceivable reconstruction of [Lenin's] voice (using the records that have remained, with the subsequent timbre correction by memory) and, hence, the possible vocalization of mute pieces of the Lenin chronicle, by precise assignment of fragments of the shorthand report uttered by him in each particular moment of speech, and, finally, a general reconstruction of his speeches which were not recorded in any way, except in the shorthand report.[35]

Stalin rarely spoke on the radio; and in the cinema, his body and his voice were replaced by actors. The same was done with Lenin. On the screen, these voices were connected with a familiar intimacy, gentle tones, and domestic physicality. Lenin spoke with a small speech impediment, a softened *r* that would normally have been fixed in childhood. (A soft *r* was a trademark of aristocratic French pronunciation, which in the early talkies signified the enemy, as in *Zlatye gory* [Golden Mountains, dir. Yutkevich, 1931]). Stalin spoke with a Georgian accent at a time when accents and deviations from standard language and pronunciation on the radio and on-screen were unacceptable. On screen, Stalin was generally portrayed by Mikhail Gelovani, with his softer Georgian accent. But after the war, the Russian actor Alexei Diky, with his stretched-out Moscow pronunciation and nasal vowels, was chosen for the role of Stalin as commander (*Stalingradskaia bitva* [The Battle of Stalingrad], dir. Petrov, 1949).

Stalin spoke particularly softly; his manner of speech (in life and on screen) was short and rhetorically unadorned, its pace quiet and rather slow.[36] His vocal screen image contrasted with the clear, loud, sonorous soprano and tenor voices of the film characters from the 1930s and 1940s, who almost sang their lines. American cinema of that time developed a range of genre-specific filmic voices: for westerns, film noir, musical, comedy, melodrama. In the Soviet Union of the 1930s, cinema, along with radio, maintained the tradition of well-trained actors' voices while the Russian stage—Stanislavsky's Art Theater or the Maly Theater—cultivated the old fashioned prerevolutionary prosody, never too loud and never too expressionistically pathetic. The Maly Theater had always understood itself as a museum of the Moscow manner of speech, whereas the Stanislavsky Theater preserved Chekhovian chamber tune.

Russian poets, in contrast, celebrated unusual forms of prosodic speech: Osip Mandelstam, Boris Pasternak, or the youth poets of the 1960s (e.g., Andrei Voznesensky, Evgeny Evtushenko, Robert Rozhdestvensky). In their speeches, all the elements of extensive expressionist manner of speaking were preserved: stressed accents that appeared in patterns, elongated vowels, accented consonants, melodic ups and downs, and a wider range of vocal dynamics. In 1964, this way of speaking was also adopted by the alternative Taganka Theater, under the direction of Yury Liubimov, which made lyrics and songs its main focus. One of the most famous actors of the ensemble was also the most popular singer of that time—Vladimir Vysotsky, who distinguished himself through various voice masks and a hysterically expressive performance style. Another alternative theater, Sovremennik (The Contemporary), founded in 1956, favored a different performance style: quiet, restrained, subdued, with emphasis on the "prosaic." Mockingly, this style was labeled "mumbling" or "whispering" (*bormotal'nyi, sheptal'nyi*) realism. Sovremennik's director, Oleg Efremov, preferred roles in which he remained silent. Sometimes, he cut his text completely—that was his condition, for example, when he agreed to play the role of the painter in the film *Gori gori, moia zvezda* (Shine, Shine, My Star, dir. Mitta, 1972). But of course, this style could already be heard in the early 1950s, as Olga Freudenberg's letter attests.

In the late 1950s, a simple Soviet film hero speaking softly and slowly—as only Stalin could before—was a novelty. However, the soft sounds were understood differently at that time. In Hitchcock's film about East Germany, *Torn Curtain* (1966), the closed society behind the Iron Curtain is realized in very simple details: all the doors are closed and the people with stiff gestures are silent, thus leaving the simplest of questions unanswered. This silence, enhanced by the absence of movement, produced a traumatic effect and appeared as the embodiment of repression. Stalin's daughter, Svetlana Allilueva, wrote that unlike the timid, soft-spoken Soviet people, her Indian husband spoke and laughed loudly. She interpreted this as a sign of unconstrained freedom.[37] In comparison, the loud Americans—as well as people who articulated noisily in public—were described in behavioral books of that time as defective or ill mannered.

Breaking the Code of Conduct

Brando and Smoktunovsky's new ways of speaking were an expression not only of intimate or familiar communication or of a new style but also of new gender images, new norms of behavior, and new forms of expression of subjectivity, all of which were changing radically during this time. Brando's uneducated proletarian slur and Smoktunovsky's bohemian drawl "naturalized" new speech patterns and made the relaxed manner acceptable. Class served as a motivation for why the actors could move and speak differently from the "norm." The transfer of this style onto Shakespeare and onto "positive" heroes quickly followed.

This new way of speaking was associated with a new behavioral norm that was first interpreted as disrespectful toward speaking partners. This refraction of politeness can be confirmed by American, German, and Russian books on manners from the 1950s, which suggested that one should never speak so softly that one could not be understood, but also no louder than good understanding required. Soviet books on manners advised readers not to speak too loudly, not to be ironic, not to stretch out words or to speak too slowly, which was considered bad form.[38] German books on manners from the years 1951 and 1957 recommended: "Speak in a resounding voice. If nature has denied this gift, acquire it through practice. . . . In any case, it is in your power to eliminate the habits of slurred speech, lisping and thrusting of the tongue, the over-extension of the voice in excitement, rushing or swallowing words. Speak evenly and calmly, rather a little slower than too fast. Speak clearly, naturally, and unpretentiously, avoid anything theatrical, bolted and winding. . . . Avoid all unintelligible dialect expressions, and be careful in the use of foreign words." One's voice should not be effeminate or peasantlike, not jarring or too soft, not harsh or crude sounding.[39]

The required standard of conduct could not be separated from speech standards. The manners books condemned these techniques, but Elvis Presley demonstrated how to loosely move shoulders and hips, and Marlon Brando and James Dean's physical casualness became a cult. At first, their heroes were shown as criminal problem cases, until their body language was taken up not just on screen but also in everyday life. Jack Kerouac summed it up: "The 'Beat Generation' has simply become the slogan or label for a revolution in manners in America." After the publication of *On the Road*, Kerouac was "horrified" "to suddenly see 'Beat' being taken up by everybody, press and TV and Hollywood Borscht circuit." Now, he wrote, "they have beatnik routines on TV." Much of this is "a simple change in fashion and manners, just a history crust—like from the Age of Reason to romantic Chatterton in the moonlight—from Teddy Roosevelt to Scott Fitzgerald. . . . So there's nothing to get excited about. Beat comes out, actually, of old American whoopee and it will only change a few dresses and pants and make chairs useless in the living room and pretty soon we'll have Beat Secretaries of State."[40]

Horst-Volker Krumrey, who analyzed German books on manners from 1870 to 1970, defined the set of body techniques as new "standards of conduct appropriate to democratic structures." He claimed that "the waltz initiated . . . a bourgeois revolution and the victory of democracy," whereas the Beat revolution after World War II "united criticism of dusty social rules, long before students went to the barricades against stuffiness at the universities."[41]

Brando's style was perceived as uncultured, just like James Dean's. Dean's on-screen father in *East of Eden* (dir. Kazan, 1955) gave him lessons on how to correctly read the Bible. "Like Dean, [Brando] spoke softly, sometimes departed slightly from the scripted dialogues, used regional or 'ethnic' accents. At the same time, his body was self-consciously loose, and many of the working-class characters he played allowed him to mock the 'good manners' of traditional theaters," Naremore noted.[42] He described Brando's manner of speaking in the same breath as his posture, because one's voice depends on breathing techniques and body postures. Brando barely opened his mouth; Smoktunovsky spoke as if half asleep. Their postures were characterized by complete relaxation and the lazy freedom of slow movements. The muscles were completely relaxed, their exhalation was directed differently; the sound did not make it to the mouth but was formed in the chest, the sound box, and conveyed a velvety tone.[43]

Initially, theatrical standards coincided with the new social norms. But soon the standards began to drift apart, and the ways to describe them also changed. While critics of the late 1950s found the manner of Smoktunovsky and Brando astonishingly authentic and naturalistic, by the 1960s they emphasized the moments of freedom, naturalness, harmony, and spontaneity in both actors' speech. These were keywords to describe romantic individuality. Brando inspired not only a new fashion but also new forms of subjectivity whose expression also changed. For men, it became acceptable to show despair, torment, vulnerability, and sensitivity; a new "thwarted maleness" of this "girl-boy almost, but he needs a shave," as John Dos Passos described James Dean.[44] This change was even more substantial in the Soviet Union. With the lifting of the Iron Curtain, Western cultural novelties and imports began to challenge the previous standards of Soviet imagery. This experience even influenced bodily motion: "The Tarzan series alone, I daresay, did more for de-Stalinization than all Khrushchev's speeches at the Twentieth Party Congress and after," wrote Joseph Brodsky. "One should take into account our latitudes, our buttoned-up, rigid, inhibited, winter-minded standards of public and private conduct, in order to appreciate the impact of a long-haired naked loner pursuing a blonde through the thick of a tropical rain forest with his chimpanzee version of Sancho Panza and lianas as means of transportation."[45]

For Brodsky, the unfettering of thinking was produced by a relaxation of the joints, but this change in motility was only one aspect of a wide-ranging break with tradition. The nonverbal art forms of this period (music, painting, and design) altered the paradigm of perception, both visual and auditory, and film became one of the most powerful conduits of new preverbal physiognomic experience that also influenced the manner of speaking. These "physiognomic" aberrations, markers of an elusive something else, the matter of phonetics, and behavioral plasticity marked a profound change in Soviet subjectivity. In this frame, Smoktunovsky's voice suggested a total contrast to Tarzan's provoking cry: an erotic whisper.

Notes

1. Michel Chion, *La voix au cinéma* (Paris: Éditions de L'Étoile, 1993); Kaja Silverman, *The Acoustic Mirror: The Female Voice in Psychoanalysis and Cinema* (Bloomington: Indiana University Press, 1988).

2. Albrecht Schöne, *Literatur im audiovisuellen Medium. Sieben Fernsehdrehbücher* (Munich: Beck, 1974), 54–67; Beatrix Schönherr, "So kann man heute nicht mehr spielen. Über den Wandel der sprecherischen Stilideale auf der Bühne seit den 60er Jahren," in *Sprache Kultur Geschichte sprachhistorische Studien zum Deutschen*, ed. Maria Pümpel-Madder and Beatrix Schönherr (Innsbruck: Institut für Germanistik, 1999), 145–69; Johannes Schwitalla, "Vom Sektenprediger zum Plauderton. Beobachtungen zur Prosodie von Politikerreden vor und nach 1945," in *Texttyp, Sprechergruppe, Kommunikationsbereich. Studien zur deutschen Sprache in Geschichte und Gegenwart. Festschrift für Hugo Steger zum 65. Geburtstag*, ed. Heinrich Löffler and Karlheinz Jakob (Berlin: de Gruyter, 1994), 208–24; Claudia Schmölders, "Die Stimme des Bösen. Zur Klanggestalt des Dritten Reiches," *Merkur* 581 (1997): 681–93; Claudia Schmölders, "Stimmen von Führern. Auditorische Szenen 1900–1945," in *Zwischen Rauschen und Offenbarung. Zur Kultur- und Mediengeschichte der Stimme*, ed. Friedrich Kittler, Thomas Macho, and Sigrid Weigel (Berlin: Akademie-Verlag, 2002), 175–95.

3. See John Belton, "1950s. Magnetic Sound: The Frozen Revolution," in *Sound Theory/Sound Practice*, ed. Rick Altman (New York: Routledge, 1992), 157.

4. Jean Améry, *Geburt der Gegenwart. Gestalten und Gestaltung der westlichen Zivilisation seit Kriegsende* (Open und Freiburg im Breisgau: Walter-Verlag, 1961), 202.

5. As in the culinary magazine *Kuking* (http://kuking.net/10_940.htm).

6. James Naremore, *Acting in the Cinema* (Berkeley: University of California Press, 1988), 195.

7. In a later interview, Brando spoke openly about his homosexual experiences. See Gary Carey, *Marlon Brando: The Only Contender* (London: Houder and Stoghton, 1985), 250.

8. Ibid., 52.

9. Ibid., 67.

10. Naremore, *Acting in the Cinema*, 201.

11. Ibid., 210.

12. Compare Carey, *Marlon Brando*, 68.

13. Robert La Guardia, *Montgomery Clift: A Biography* (London: W. H. Allen, 1977), 50, 122–23.

14. He played a Mexican in *Viva Zapata!* (dir. Kazan, 1952), a Japanese man in *The Teahouse of the August Moon* (dir. Mann, 1956), Napoléon in *Desirée* (dir. Koster, 1954), a German in *The Young Lions* (dir. Dmytryk, 1958), and a Texan in *The Chase* (Penn, 1966), among others.

15. Carey, *Marlon Brando*, 67–68.

16. See Nataša Ďurovičová, "Translating America: The Hollywood Multilinguals 1929–1933," in *Sound Theory/Sound Practice*, ed. Rick Altman (New York: Routledge, 1992), 138–53; Evgenii Margolit, "Problema mnogoiazychiia v rannem sovetskom zvukovom kino (1930–1935)," in *Sovetskaia vlast' i media*, ed. Hans Günther and Sabine Hänsgen (St. Petersburg: Akademicheskii proekt, 2006), 378–86; for the English version, see chapter 6 in this volume.

17. Elena Gorfunkel', *Smoktunovskii* (Moscow: Iskusstvo, 1990), 14.

18. Elizaveta Saricheva, *Stsenicheskaia rech'. Uchebnik dlia teatral'nykh vuzov* (Moscow: Iskusstvo, 1956), 103–4, 162–64.

19. Gorfunkel', *Smoktunovskii*, 217.

20. Carey, *Marlon Brando*, 87–89, 113–14.

21. Iakov Butovskii, "Monologi prozoi," *Kinovedcheskie zapiski* 94–95 (2010): 307–27, esp. 318–19.

22. Boris Pasternak, *Perepiska s Ol'goi Freidenberg*, ed. Elliott Mossman (New York: Harcourt Brace, 1981), 314.

23. Aleksandr Anikst, "*Gamlet* Grigoriia Kosinzeva," *Iskusstvo kino* 6 (1964): 5–15 (7–8).

24. Ibid., 8.

25. Ibid., 12.

26. During his career, Smoktunovsky starred in more than eighty-four films. He played Mozart (with vocals dubbed by the popular, and openly gay, tenor Sergei Lemeshev) in *Mozart i Sal'eri*, (dir. Gorriker, 1962) and the homosexual Tchaikovsky (*Tchaikovsky*, dir. Talankin, 1969); he played a subversive and childishly playful intellectual (*Beregis' avtomobilia!* [Watch Out for the Car!], dir. Riazanov, 1966), an erotic lover in Turgenev's *Pervaia liubov'* (First Love, dir. Ordynskii, 1968), and Caesar in a screen adaptation of George Bernard Shaw's *Caesar and Cleopatra* (dir. Belinsky, 1979). He portrayed high statesmen like Lenin (*Pervyi posetitel'* [The First Visitor], dir. Kwinichidse, 1974) and Roosevelt (*Vybor tseli* [Choice of a Goal], dir. Talankin, 1976), sadistic despots like the king of the Netherlands (*Legenda o Tile* [The Legend of Till Eulenspiegel], dir. Alov and Naumov, 1977), and refined villains. Then he began reading official commentary in documentary films.

27. For the director, this voice was also autobiographically coded, because it sounded like the voice of his father, the peculiar poet Arseny Tarkovsky. In the film, the poetry was recited by Arseny Tarkovsky himself, whose monotonous, listless manner of performance could be compared with that of Alexander Blok.

28. See Mikhail Vysotskii, *Sistemy kino i stereozvuk* (Moscow: Iskusstvo 1972), 145–46.

29. Ibid.

30. See Reinhart Meyer-Kalkus, *Stimme und Sprechkünste im 20. Jahrhundert* (Berlin: Akademie-Verlag, 2001). He refers to the work of Irmgard Weithases *Geschichte der deutschen Vortragskunst im 19. Jahrhundert*, expanded ed. (Weimar: Böhlau, 1940); *Zur Geschichte der gesprochenen deutschen Sprache*, 2 vols. (Tübingen: Max Niemeyer Verlag, 1961).

31. Schwitalla, *Vom Sektenprediger zum Plauderton*, 222.

32. Ibid., 212, 216.

33. Schöne, *Literatur im audiovisuellen Medium*, 61–65.

34. When Dziga Vertov was ordered to make the first sound film about Lenin, he was in a difficult situation. For *Three Songs of Lenin* (1934), documentary recordings of Lenin's voice were cleaned with filters (the press reported frequently on the restoration of Lenin's voice). See the reprint: Vertov, *Tri pesni o Lenine*, ed. Elizaveta Svilova-Vertova and Vitalii Furtichev (Moscow: Iskusstvo 1972), 117.

35. Arsenii Avraamov, *Sintonfil'm* (1932); reprint published by Nikolai Izvolov and Aleksandr Deriabin, *Kinovedcheskie zapiski* 53 (2001): 313–33 (323).

36. The main Soviet political orator of the 1950s, Nikita Khrushchev, in contrast to Stalin, introduced affective outbursts into his political speeches. His pronunciation betrayed both his origin (Ukraine) and his low level of education.

37. Svetlana I. Allilueva, *Tol'ko odin god*, reprint edition of the 1970 publication (New York: Harper and Row; Moscow: Kniga, 1990), 19–20.

38. Ivan Sadkovskii, *O kul'ture povedeniia sovetskoi molodezhi; stenogramma publichnoi lektsii* (Moscow: n.p., 1958), 10–11.

39. These norms were also formulated in 1885: "In public one lowers one's voice"; "Do not laugh loudly"; "Whoever laughs loudly and roughly, and bends, opens the mouth, and throws one's head back, appears uneducated, uncontrolled, and repulsive." Cited in Horst-Volker

Krumrey, *Entwicklungsstrukturen von Verhaltensstandarden: eine soziologische Prozessanal-yse auf der Grundlage deutscher Anstands-und Manierenbücher von 1870 bis 1970* (Frankfurt am Main: Suhrkamp, 1984), 272, 275–76.

40. Jack Kerouac, "The Origins of the Beat Generation," in *On the Road* (New York: Viking Press, 1979), 363, 366.

41. Krumrey, *Entwicklungsstrukturen von Verhaltensstandarden: eine soziologische Proz-essanalyse auf der Grundlage deutscher Anstands-und Manierenbücher von 1870 bis 1970* (Frankfurt am Main: Suhrkamp, 1984), 187.

42. Naremore, *Acting in Cinema*, 201.

43. The connection between voice and muscle relaxation has been analyzed by Eduard Siev-ers and Otto Rutz, who were particularly popular in Russia. See Meyer-Kalkus, *Stimme und Sprechkünste im 20. Jahrhundert*, 82–103.

44. John Dos Passos. *Midcentury* (Cambridge, MA: Riverside Press, 1961), 480.

45. Joseph Brodsky, "Spoils of War," in *On Grief and Reason* (New York: Farrar, Straus & Giroux, 1995), 8–9.

9 Listening to the Inaudible Foreign

Simultaneous Translators and Soviet Experience of Foreign Cinema

Elena Razlogova

For decades, Natalia Razlogova had a recurring dream: she enters a film translator's booth and puts on the headphones. The audience is clamoring outside—they can hear the film, they demand the translation, but she hears nothing. She cannot translate; the foreign film is completely inaudible to her.[1] This story conveys translators' fears of failure: being unable to cope with shoddy technology, failing to relate to an alien culture, confronting an incomprehensible language. But most of all, it shows the fear of failing in their responsibility to their moviegoing public. Between the 1960s and 1980s, Soviet simultaneous translators made foreign-film screenings possible: at international film festivals, specialized theaters such as Moscow's Illiuzion, and tours of foreign films organized by cultural and propaganda agencies. They simultaneously observed and shaped the Soviet moviegoing experience. The improvised voice of a simultaneous translator was a key element of the foreign-film sound track throughout the Soviet Union.

What follows is an initial investigation into simultaneous translation of foreign films in the Soviet Union, centered on several interviews with and written memories of the earliest surviving simultaneous translators, who began their work in the mid-1960s. Four of the interviewees are my relatives: my grandmother, Kira Razlogova; my father, Kirill; and my aunts, Elena and Natalia. All of them were fluent in French because they had just returned after spending several years in France. Kirill began translating at the Moscow Graduate Director's Program and from there was invited to join Illiuzion's stable of translators. Razlogovs became the main translators from French at Illiuzion when it opened in 1966. I also interviewed Natalia Nusinova, who translated from Italian beginning in the early 1970s; Alexander Bondarev, who started as a translator at a Polish film retrospective in Illiuzion in 1969 while in graduate school in theoretical physics; and Grigory Libergal, who was a first-year college student when he began interpreting films for the Film History Lecture Series at the Filmmakers' Union. He translated from English on the second day of Illiuzion's existence. Many of the original legendary interpreters are now dead, including Nelia Nersesian (English), Maria Dolia (Japanese), and Alexei Mikhalev (Persian and English). But the surviving translators' accounts convey the experience of interpreting and, to some extent, seeing and hearing a foreign film in the post-Stalinist Soviet Union.[2]

To understand the historical specificity of simultaneous translation in the 1960s and 1970s one only has to compare it to contemporary translation standards. Audiovisual translation manuals now focus on dubbing and subtitles.[3] The few practitioners who consider simultaneous screen translation specifically take the existence of subtitles or a script for granted and recommend that translators prepare by previewing the film several times, reading and translating the script, and taking notes. "In eight years of experience of translating films at the Venice Film Festival," David Snelling wrote in 1990, "I have never been required to interpret a film directly from the sound-track without either sub-titles or a copy of the script. I would in any case consider the task impossible for a variety of reasons." Snelling and other translation scholars have also recommended a minimalist approach to interpreting: one should condense phrases to their essential meaning and rely on the visual context to convey local turns of phrase and passions of the moment. "The interpreter is not an artist," Snelling declared. "He is an artisan . . . a modest *comprimario* whose discretion and professional skills are best displayed when he least intrudes upon his listening public."[4]

Not so in the 1960s and 1970s, at least in the Socialist bloc.[5] Translators more often had to interpret the film cold, without a preview, script, or even subtitles. A fully bilingual simultaneous translator from the German Democratic Republic reported in 1975 that in such cases he helped himself by imitating gestures and facial expressions of the movie character he was translating at the moment, to his listeners' surprise. "It is hard for non-translators to understand," he explained, "that my head does not produce automatically (as you have to with speedy translation) the perfect word if I translate two opponents' heated discussion or self-conscious character's meandering interjections in a boring steady voice, without tuning in to the 'wave' of the emotions of the phrases' author."[6] Far from advising minimalism, one Russian specialist insisted in 1978 that an oral translation must be nuanced enough to convey not just meaning but also the "spoken consciousness" of a people.[7] Hardly modest *comprimarios*, translators of that era aspired to be artists.

For their part, moviegoers of the era responded to this expressive technique. In the early 1970s, Nelia Nersesian gesticulated and changed her vocal inflection and facial expression while interpreting for different characters in American films, including all seven protagonists in the famous western *The Magnificent Seven* (dir. Sturges, 1960). Audiences reportedly burst into applause at certain turns of phrases she came up with during screenings, and one spectator remembers her *Magnificent Seven* rendition as "brilliant."[8] As mediators between foreign cinema and the Soviet public, translators like Nersesian resembled not so much the model interpreter of the present but rather an "abusive translator" as defined by Nornes: "willing to experiment, to tamper with tradition, language, and expectations in order to inventively put spectators into contact with the foreign."[9] Yet if Nornes's abusive subtitlers played upon the visual elements and cultural context of a film, simultaneous translators of the 1960s and 1970s explored the aural and affective elements of film spectatorship.

Foreign-film fandom in the Soviet Union rekindled after World War II. From 1947 until the mid-1950s, Soviet moviegoers for the first time encountered dozens of German, Austrian, Italian, American, and French films that were stolen from the so-called trophy fund during the occupation of Germany. These films, which were meant to provide funding for the then-moribund Soviet film industry, were dubbed (most German films were) or subtitled (most American films were) and shown without credits; initially, each copy began with the title "trophy film" but later even that title was omitted because many of the films shown were made by the Soviet Union's allies in the war.[10] Poet Joseph Brodsky remembered that his initial excitement over seeing Western lifestyles in trophy films abated after a few years, and he turned to the journal *Inostrannaya literatura* for more exalted literary examples of Western individualism, an alternative to the Soviet collectivist ideology he found unpalatable.[11] But Soviets who stayed faithful to film experienced the foreign lifestyles differently, in part because the official Soviet ideology led to spectators' contact with non-Western cultures as well.

As the postwar Soviet Union opened up its cultural borders, it aimed to compete with the "first world" Western powers for the attention of the decolonizing and unaligned "third world" countries of Africa, Asia, and Latin America.[12] After Joseph Stalin's death in 1953, international festivals came one after another: the Indian Film Festival in 1954, the International Youth Festival in 1957, the Moscow International Film Festival (MIFF) in 1959, and the first Asian and African Film Festival in Tashkent in 1968. The Moscow and Tashkent festivals took place in alternating years, and both used translators from Moscow. Latin American films were well represented in Tashkent as early as 1974; two years later the festival was renamed as the Asian, African, and Latin American Film Festival. MIFF also publicized and awarded prizes to films from Senegal, Algeria, Iran, and Latin America (especially Cuba), often for political reasons. Although most translators and cinephiles subscribed to a cultural hierarchy that put Western films at the top—a popular joke claimed that "films can be good, bad, and Chinese"—they could not avoid seeing non-Western films, often as part of a double bill with coveted Western pictures. By contrast, in this period Soviet cinephiles had equal respect for highbrow auteur-director fare, such as a Bernardo Bertolucci film, and for what film scholars today consider a lowbrow star vehicle, such as a Jean Marais picture.

The geopolitics of foreign-film spectatorship depended on the practice of two-tiered simultaneous interpreting, which was unique to the Soviet Union. In Russia, simultaneous translation was first used informally during the Sixth Communist International Congress in 1928. Systematic professional simultaneous translation of speeches and testimony dates back to the Nuremberg Trials, where each foreign delegation translated the proceedings into its own language, and the Americans translated into German. Two-tiered interpreting was a Soviet improvement on the Nuremberg system, which was first used during the 1952 International Economic Congress in Moscow. The system delayed the translation and exacerbated errors but used fewer interpreters at once and did not depend on translators fluent in two foreign languages, which made it easier to cover more languages. Speeches at the Twenty-Second Communist Party Congress in 1961 were translated, using the latest equipment, to and from twenty-nine languages, including Vietnamese, Indonesian, Korean, and Japanese, as well as Arabic and several rare African languages:[13] as a result, Nikita Khrushchev's famous announcement at the congress that the current Soviet generation would see the implementation of national communism reached a wider international audience.

While the Soviet Union's imperial ambitions shaped its simultaneous translation practices, they also shaped screen translation at film festivals. At the 1974 Asian and African Film Festival in Tashkent, each film was first translated into Russian, which played through the theater's loudspeakers, and then into the languages of the various foreign guests, who listened through transistor headphones. American film critic Gordon Hitchens complained in *Variety* that his "second-order" translation came up to half a minute later than the original utterance. Yet he also noted that it made it easier to interpret the huge number of languages, many of them rare, represented at the festival.[14] In this respect, the Soviet interpreting setup also benefited foreign filmmakers in attendance. During the 1968 Tashkent festival, Alpha Amadou Diallo, secretary of state for information of Guinea, lamented that because of the variety of local African languages, a Senegalese may have to travel to Tashkent to see a film made in neighboring Guinea. Here the ungainly Soviet screen translation made audible the connection, pointed out by Nataša Ďurovičová, between *translatio studii* (transfer of learning) and *translatio imperii* (transfer of power) in a transnational cinematic landscape.[15]

Soviet foreign-film spectatorship grew in scale and depth with the opening of Illiuzion—an official theater of Gosfilmofond (State Russian Film Archive)—a repository of Soviet film materials, copies of lawfully exhibited foreign movies, and all trophy films. Illiuzion opened in March 1966 with 369 seats, a translator's booth equipped with wartime sound equipment, and a stable of film scholars sent from Gosfilmofond as programmers and lecturers. By law, Illiuzion's repertoire was supposed to consist of at least half domestic films and included thematic film series that sometimes lasted for years. A lecture from a staff member or an invited scholar preceded each film. Screenings started between 9 and 10 a.m., and the last show was at 9:30 p.m. on weekdays, while screenings ran from 8 a.m. to midnight on weekends. Patrons could buy tickets for an entire film series at once. In the 1960s and 1970s, foreign-film screenings, at fifty kopeks a ticket, always sold out, with a certain share of tickets always reserved for privileged officials and creative unions, and long but orderly lines for rush tickets sold immediately before the screening. Scalpers and informal ticket trading proliferated, especially during film festivals.[16] Illiuzion shaped foreign film spectatorship as a key Moscow festival venue and through syndication of its programs to affiliated theaters around the country. It shaped screen translation because most famous interpreters of the 1960s and 1970s were trained at Illiuzion.

Spectators from every strata of society viewed foreign films in the 1960s and 1970s. Illiuzion mostly attracted intelligentsia, but anyone could come to the theater, and affiliated DK (Dom Kul'tury, or "House of Culture"), such as DK "Red Textile Workers," showed the same lectures and screenings for workers. The average Soviet citizen could see foreign films unofficially as well. During his work at Gosfilmofond in the 1970s, Kirill Razlogov routinely translated a racy Swedish film *Jeg - en kvinde* (I, a Woman, dir. Ahlberg, 1965), working from English subtitles, for workers who were building a new theater on the premises. This 35mm copy, stored in Gosfilmofond's archive, was shown informally by the archive staff for workers' entertainment.[17] One typical cinephile of the time, Vladimir Durikin, attended one of the first day's screenings at Illiuzion and remained a faithful patron to the theater throughout the 1960s and 1970s, at the same time as he was building highways for a living.[18] Thousands of *kinomany*—a stronger Russian term for cinephile or movie fan—shared Durikin's passion for film. By the early 1970s, the International Moscow Film Festival used hundreds of screens, from Houses of Culture affiliated with factories to houses of various creative unions, to large first-run movie theaters like Udarnik with 735 seats, and even the Palace of Sports with 13,700 seats.[19] Simultaneous interpreters introduced and translated films for theaters in capital and provincial cities throughout all Soviet republics and the far east of the Russian Soviet Socialist Republic after every Moscow International Film Festival and during traveling programs organized by the national Filmmakers Union, Propaganda Bureau, and Sovexportfilm, the state organization that bought and distributed films nationally. By the 1980s, the Propaganda Bureau was even bringing films to high-security prisons.[20]

By the 1970s, simultaneous translation grew into a lucrative profession that benefited from unofficial relationships between various branches of the Soviet bureaucracy. Simultaneous translators could get five rubles per screening at Sovexportfilm, and seven and a half rubles per screening elsewhere, including at Illiuzion and its affiliates, festival venues, the Moscow Graduate Director's and

Screenwriter's Programs, Dom Kino (House of Cinema, official headquarters of the Soviet Filmmakers' Union), and houses of other creative unions, Gosfilmofond, Goskino (State Committee for Cinematography), and other state agencies, including the KGB (Committee for State Security). Kirill Razlogov remembered his worst interpreting mistake: while interpreting a spy film from French for KGB officers, he wondered why his audience was laughing at odd times. Only later did he realize that, not knowing anything about counterintelligence, he vocalized FBI as "FBI" instead of "FBR," which is the proper Russian abbreviation for the Federal Bureau of Investigation.[21] The New Year's season was the most lucrative, when every creative union and apparatchik organized a foreign-film screening, which was impossible without a 35mm print and a translator, who could demand a fee far above the usual rate. By comparison, a regular student's stipend was 35 rubles a month, and a salary for a white-collar worker, including an academic lecturer at Illiuzion, was 120 rubles a month. A translator could earn a student's salary in a day.[22]

The same Soviet bureaucracy that fed simultaneous translators also made screenings of foreign films politically risky. Party and security officials monitored most interactions with foreigners closely, including foreign-film screenings. They selected only a small fraction of foreign films for general distribution and edited out politically incorrect scenes.[23] Illiuzion's program, controlled by Gosfilmofond and Goskino, escaped close state control—for example, the theater could show many trophy films that were never approved for wide distribution. Yet it, too, operated under close scrutiny. Former Illiuzion director Zinaida Shatina remembers several unpleasant audits of her foreign film screening practices in the 1970s, brought about by a denunciation of an anonymous staff or audience member. One of these audits found that, in violation of state-imposed limits, more than 50 percent of all films screened at the theater were foreign; this finding led to her forced resignation.[24]

During international events, control over foreign-film screenings tightened. Communist Party officials approved all dialogue lists used for screen translation at MIFF. KGB officials required interpreters who worked with international guests to write reports about their conversations. And KGB "curators" watched interactions between Soviet staff and invited guests. Screen translators needed to be aware of this surveillance. At the Congress of the International Federation of Film Archives in Moscow in 1973, Kirill Razlogov, then working at Gosfilmofond, exclaimed how happy he was that Lia van Leer, founder of the Israel Film Archive, was able to come despite the strained relationship between Israel and the Soviet Union. Then he could not help but turn to check if the KGB curator standing behind him noticed his exuberance.[25]

Yet screen translators usually managed to avoid being completely incorporated into the Soviet surveillance system. An interpreter attached to a foreign guest was trained to write reports and often graduated from a higher institution that prepared diplomats and security officials. But even though Kirill Razlogov, as a recent resident of France, did not have the proper ideological background to work as a guest's interpreter, he was hired as screen translator.[26] When Natasha Nusinova interpreted for a film conference, she was informally asked to report on conversations she witnessed. But when she claimed that she could not translate if she tried to memorize what people were saying, her "handler" accepted her excuse and did not press for further information.[27] At the Moscow festival, simultaneous translators were not allowed to mingle with foreign guests. But at the Tashkent festival, where everyone stayed in one hotel and local KGB curators were less invested in surveillance, screen translators could socialize with African, Asian, and Latin American filmmakers and were not asked to write reports.[28] Thus, translators could usually escape the political and aesthetic control exerted by the state over their colleagues who read approved film dialogue lists or interpreters who accompanied foreign filmmakers.

If festival selection committees chose foreign films to represent discrete sovereign nations, ordinary spectators' emotional investment disrupted official political, ideological, and bureaucratic boundaries. Film scholar Maya Turovskaya remembered how she saw a sentimental Mexican melodrama *Yesenia* (dir. Crevenna, 1971), featuring mistaken identities and illegitimate children, while seated next to an ordinary harried Russian woman with a bag of groceries at her feet at MIFF. The woman kept talking to the screen under her breath and at one point started weeping, spreading her makeup all over her face with a large handkerchief. After the film, Turovskaya inquired why the woman found the film so riveting and heard back: "You see, it's all about my life!"[29] This spectator bypassed the national and cultural milieu of the film to relate to its depiction of private life.[30]

Some evidence suggests that spectators used sexual content in films to imagine breaking through ideological and geographic boundaries separating their second world from the first and third worlds. Soviet movie fans sought a glimpse of Western sexual liberation—the cinematic equivalent to kissing "capitalist lips," as Yevgeni Yevtushenko described his most memorable moment of the 1957 Youth Festival in Moscow.[31] Kirill Razlogov remembered how one middle-age schoolteacher from Tashkent, who regularly traveled to Moscow for the festival, kept asking his fellow movie fans whether he really saw a woman lying in bed between her two lovers, comparing the firmness of their penises in Bertolucci's *Novecento* (1900 [translated as *Twentieth Century* in Russian], 1976).[32] Access to such graphic movie images at the festivals acquired double political significance in the 1960s and 1970s, when Soviet censors began to cut more and more sex scenes from Western and even Eastern European films before they went into general distribution.[33]

Some Soviet spectators used sexuality to look for "unexpected points of congruence" between intimate lives at home and abroad.[34] Natalia Nusinova remembers an incident that took place at a Tashkent film festival: during a scene in which a topless Chinese woman emerged from a swimming pool accompanied by dramatic music, a middle-age Uzbek man suddenly rose up and exclaimed, "Ahmed, remember this?"[35] It is unlikely that this spectator had experienced anything like what he saw in the film. More likely, he remembered an instance when he transgressed, in some small way, the tenets of both Soviet and traditional Uzbek morality; both strongly discouraged looking at topless women. When Natalia Razlogova spent a day translating French drama *Loulou* (dir. Pialat, 1980) in Georgia, she noticed that spectators repeatedly applauded a scene that elicited no reaction whatsoever from her Moscow audiences, in which a woman says goodbye to her handsome husband and then says to her friend, who remarks on his beauty, "If only he was as impressive in bed." At the end of the day, she asked her host at the Georgian Filmmakers Union to explain the applause. It turned out that local folk wisdom held that Georgian men were handsome and strong, but past thirty-five years of age, they tended to lose their virility—a point well made by the French female character.[36] To be sure, these stories show how exotic the spectators from Soviet republics in Central Asia and the Caucasus were to screen translators, who overwhelmingly came from families of intelligentsia in Moscow and Leningrad. Yet they also show interpreters' wonder at their audiences' ability to traverse the terrain between their own private experience and the experience of others.

In trying to connect with these audiences, simultaneous translators thought of themselves as self-aware practitioners of an improvisational sound art, invested in but not bound by the ideal of authentic viewer experience. Libergal explained, "When you are watching a film with a simultaneous translation, you, the viewer, have to clearly hear the original soundtrack of the film. If the translator is a master of his craft, he will not 'dominate' the screen, speak on top of the actors. If he is a virtuoso, if he can feel the balance between the film proper and his own voice, after several minutes the spectator in the theater will forget about the translator, feeling that he himself can understand English, French, or Japanese."[37] Soviet screen translators would reject the contemporary standards of dubbed translation, a "domesticating" mode, in Lawrence Venuti's terms, that erases any traces of the original text.[38]

At the same time, they would also reject the contemporary minimalist view on live screen translation. In the 1990s, Venice festival translator David Snelling, for example, would not have had the translator use any verbal inflections at all, making no distinctions between "'Would you like a cup of tea?,' 'What would you say to a cup of tea?,' 'Wouldn't a cup of tea be super?' and 'av' sum tea' as these social distinctions will be abundantly clear from costume and mimicry. 'Tea?'

with an interrogative intonation is the only minimal-disturbance alternative."³⁹ Conversely, translators spent multiple screenings perfecting their rendition of particular phrases and took pride in audience gratitude. Elena Razlogova, for example, most liked to perform films like François Truffaut's *Jules et Jim* (1962), because after multiple screenings she knew exactly how to render each line. Once, she came to translate the French comedy *À nous les petites Anglaises!* (Let's Get Those English Girls, dir. Lang, 1976) at Udarnik, one of the biggest festival venues. At the entrance she heard two cinephiles talking: "Who will translate?" "Razlogova." "Thank God!" She took this as an appreciation of her determination to use precision rather than minimalism in interpreting.⁴⁰ Some translators at the end of the film announced, "This film was interpreted by . . ." But according to Alexander Bondarev, only an incompetent would do that: "Audiences recognized the best ones by their voices."⁴¹

To achieve a perfect performance, translators tested any jokes or turns of phrase with the audience. At Illiuzion, one usually translated the same film six times in a row, and eight times on weekends. As Libergal explains it, "You'll begin with one variant of translation and listen to the audience reaction. At the next screening, you'd use a different word construction—and again, test it by spectators' response. By the evening, you'd work out the most precise Russian text and a perfect intonation that would elicit the strongest emotions from the audience." In the mid-1970s, Libergal used this technique to render *The Godfather* (dir. Coppola, 1972) each time to audience applause.⁴² Alexander Bondarev's first stint at MIFF happened when another translator refused to interpret Andrzej Wajda's comedy *Polowanie na muchy* (Hunting Flies, 1969): "I don't do youth slang," she declared. Bondarev did not have much experience, but he took the job and improvised, making up some jokes for the first few shows. He ended up interpreting every festival screening of the comedy to audience laughter. Bondarev remembered that he used to warn his friends not to show up for early screenings of films he translated.⁴³ Most regular Illiuzion patrons got tickets to a fifth or sixth film show of the day, to enjoy the version perfected during previous screenings.⁴⁴

Rather than ignoring the translators, Soviet foreign-film spectators paid particular attention to them. Over the years, a cinephile would experience a range of translation styles, from painful to inspired. During a festival screening, translator Alexei Mikhalev complained to Libergal that an Iranian film was interpreted from error-ridden English subtitles. At the next screening at Illiuzion, Libergal invited Mikhalev to translate directly from Persian soundtrack. Whether a given spectator would hear the mangled or the corrected version was just a matter of chance;⁴⁵ the audience responded to both. During a screening of the British film *Saturday Night and Sunday Morning* (dir. Reisz, 1960), the excited interpreter translated the character's "That's nice!" after a lovemaking scene, not literally—"Neplokho!"—but with feeling, "Khorosho-o-o!" ("[I feel] go-o-od!").

The audience burst into laughter.[46] A cinephile who frequented festival and club screenings became a translation art critic. During a 1965 MIFF screening of *My Fair Lady* (dir. Cukor, 1964) at the largest festival venue, the Palace of Sports, every time the interpreter tried to speak over a musical number, all 13,700 spectators "stomped their feet and screamed indignantly, 'No translation!'"[47]

Melodrama and epic-film lovers expected dramatic inflections and serious renditions of exalted emotions. Some could do it. Kira Razlogova excelled at rendering epic films such as German two-part production *Kampf um Rom I* and *II* (The Fight for Rome, dir. Siodmak, 1968 and Fight for Rome II, dir. Siodmak, 1969, shown together in Moscow as *The Battle for Rome*) with Orson Welles as Emperor Justinian. "It was especially important to convey the pathos without irony," she remembered.[48] Others could not. Kirill Razlogov remembers his mother's horror when he translated the religious appellation *mother* as *mom* in a respectful French screen adaptation of Denis Diderot's eighteenth-century novel *La religieuse* (The Nun, dir. Rivette, 1966). Elena Razlogova once spent a day interpreting a French film she loathed, *L'éternel retour* (Eternal Love, dir. Delannoy, 1943)—an adaptation of the Tristan and Isolde story that inspired *New York Times* critic Bosley Crowther to advise, "Whenever you find in a movie two persons who are solemnly in love and refer to this state as a 'beautiful madness,' brother, you'd better beware."[49] While she translated every word of the film correctly, by the end of the day she pronounced the main characters' repeated declarations of love in a bored monotone. As she was leaving the theater after the last screening of the day, she heard one weeping spectator tell her friend, "If I could only meet that translator, I would strangle her with my own hands!"[50] Each translator specialized in films compatible with their personalities and aesthetic preferences; still, it was difficult to avoid clashing with spectators' expectations.

Repeatedly, interpreters described simultaneous translation as akin to a battlefield experience.[51] For a simultaneous translator, keeping your wits under pressure was more important than fluency in languages. Mark Kushnirovich, Illiuzion lecturer, remembered sitting in a translator's booth during a screening of a Hungarian film *A ménesgazda* (The Stud Farm [translated as *Horse Stable Owner* in Russian], dir. Kovács, 1978). In the middle of the film, novice translator Misha, bilingual in Russian and Hungarian, forgot both languages and turned to Kushnirovich in a panic: "What do you call a mare's husband in Russian?"[52] Such lapses disappeared only with constant practice, and simultaneous translators took care to convey their practical knowledge to the next generation. Libergal learned the craft by listening to Nelia Nersesian's turns of phrase and pace, and by asking her questions about her word choices.[53] For those films that were hard to hear, translators would get together and compare notes on unclear phrases in the original.[54] Three or four times a year, Illiuzion organized meetings at which veteran translators shared their experiences with novices.[55]

Imperfect audio technology also contributed to translators' anxiety. Take, for example, Kira Razlogova's first interpreting job in 1966, a screening of Truffaut's *Les quatre cents coups* (The 400 Blows, 1959) at a DK for workers at the outskirts of Moscow: in a theater with four hundred seats, she stood leaning against the back wall, without headphones or a microphone, screaming over the sound track, which could not be muted because she had to hear it from the loudspeakers to translate. "I only knew I succeeded in reaching the spectators' ears," she remembered, "when I saw that they stayed in their seats silently, listening to me."[56] Although this is given as an example of the worst possible interpreting conditions, such arduous translation circumstances actually advanced Truffault's attack on traditional narrative of cinema, further enhancing, for the interpreter and the audience, the disorienting effects of direct audio recording that produced French new wave's signature sound.[57]

Ideal circumstances prevailed at Illiuzion, however, which was equipped with a booth, mike, earphones, a soundboard, and a way to see and hear the reaction of the audience. Wartime earphones with limited frequency range would have been terrible for music but worked well for hearing human speech. Still, many trophy films shown at Illiuzion had damaged sound tracks. Libergal remembered how he had to improvise for the first eight minutes of Alfred Hitchcock's *Rebecca* (1940)—luckily he had seen the film previously—because the print could produce nothing but whining noise.[58] Most new wave films used a naturalistic sound track recorded during the shoot, fully audible only on the fifth or sixth viewing.[59] Technology, then, was one contributor to Natalia Razlogova's recurring dream of not being able to translate an inaudible foreign film.[60]

But fear of the "inaudible foreign" reflected not just the state of technology but also translators' constant encounters with unfamiliar cultural contexts. Translating a film live for the first time, interpreters often tripped on its national and political context. When translating a French film about Chilean revolution, *Il pleut sur Santiago* (It's Raining on Santiago, dir. Soto, 1976), Kira Razlogova pronounced the last name of Victor Jara as "Iara," which was correct in French but not in Russian or Spanish. She realized her mistake only later, when her daughter Natalia told her that her dissident boyfriend was appalled that the ignorant translator did not know about the famous poet and revolutionary, well known in Moscow student circles at the time.[61] No amount of preparation could protect against cultural lapses like this, given the variety of films translators had to cover.

A third and related fear of the "inaudible foreign" was related to the risk of working with an unknown, usually non-Western, language. Interpreters were often asked to translate non-Western films in languages they did not know from dialogue lists or subtitles. But these promised lists and titles did not always materialize. At the 1968 Tashkent festival, Kirill Razlogov was supposed to interpret an Iraqi documentary from French subtitles. But when the film began, he saw no subtitles—the only word he could understand was *Baghdad*. He asked the projectionist to run only the first and last reel, to show only twenty minutes out of forty, but had to invent voice-over for the rest. In what he considers an inspired moment, once during the film he turned from describing the natural beauty of water reserves to water as a source of energy—and at the next moment footage of a hydroelectric station appeared on the screen.[62] Kira Razlogova once translated an African film from a French dialogue list during a Moscow film festival. Ten minutes before the end, the script was over. The film goes on, in a rare African language; she has nothing to say; an administrator storms into her booth predicting a diplomatic crisis. To save the situation, she went ahead and composed the dialogue for the rest of the film on the basis of the moving images. She remembers that after the film, the ambassador, made aware that the dialogue list was too short, thanked her for making up the end. He claimed it was quite close to the original.[63]

Such extreme situations recurred with alarming regularity. At the time, simultaneous translation was valued more than translation from scripts or subtitles because dialogue lists made for festival screenings were notoriously unreliable. Working at a Moscow film festival paid well and was prestigious. Many people who translated dialogue lists for the festival got the job through high-placed friends and usually did not know the languages as well as simultaneous interpreters. Natalia Razlogova remembered how a friend asked her to help translate French dialogue lists for the festival: she was able to find everything in the dictionary except a strange phrase, "happi berdeh." Upon examination it turned out that the French "happi berdeh" was actually the internationally known English phrase "happy birthday."[64] As a result of such uninformed translation, sometimes the only solution was to compose the dialogue on the spot.[65] People who could make up lines if a dialogue list skipped a scene or ended early—a frequent occurrence—were in high demand during film festivals.[66]

In such cases, screen translators were forced to assume the role of a *benshi*, who vocally interpreted films for Japanese audiences into the 1930s.[67] Occasionally, such festival "translators" did not know the language at all. Right before the screening of *Onna hissatsu ken* (Sister Street Fighter [translated as *Lady Karate* in Russian], dir. Yamaguchi, 1974) in Illiuzion at the 1975 Moscow festival, the usual translator from Japanese was suddenly called away to an official function. The eagerly anticipated sold-out screening could not be canceled: this was the first martial-arts film shown publicly in the Soviet Union and tickets for the screening at the cinephiles' "ticket exchange" traded for two, three, or more tickets to other films. (Because festival tickets sold out quickly, often to party officials and their friends, to get into a particular screening, average cinephiles had to buy an extra ticket from another patron right before the show or exchange a ticket they had for another one, for a film they actually wanted to see.) Illiuzion lecturer Mark

Kushnirovich had seen the film before but did not know a word of Japanese. He announced that the film would be translated from the dialogue list—expecting the audience, as usual, to attribute any errors to the list's translator—and went on to make up the dialogue based on his memory of previous viewings of the film. Grateful spectators gave him an ovation at the end, and the only Japanese speaker who complained to the administration had to admit that Kushnirovich conveyed the general meaning of the film even though he mangled every single line in it.[68]

Likewise, Kira Razlogova once acted as a *benshi* when she was asked to narrate a documentary about fishermen's work and life in a small village in Iceland without any textual aids. When she pointed out that she did not know the language at all, the administrator replied that she would just announce the presentation as a "spoken accompaniment," not a translation. In the end, the film and the "accompaniment" played to a satisfied audience. In that particular place and time, then, live simultaneous translation by a conscientious and invested commentator, whether by ear or sight, was as acceptable to audiences as an official written script or subtitles, and it was sometimes even preferable. The important thing, Kira Razlogova claimed, was that the audience "felt that it had the experience of understanding the film."[69]

As interpreters fought against the imperfections in sound technology, the difficulties of live translation, and the grueling regimen of having to translate the same film six to eight times a day, they also experimented with and "abused" foreign films, though not always intentionally. Yet their aural and embodied trial-and-error method for understanding a different world may have been useful. Musicologist Ingrid Monson argued, "The human ear . . . has the capacity to reinstate sounds that have been masked by noise or other auditory interference and in the process create a more stable interpretation of the auditory landscape." This ability to intuit missing sounds in music, which she calls "perceptual agency," can be trained by repeated listening and interpretation.[70] Likewise, interpreters and their audiences developed their perceptual agency by struggling with the incomprehensible in foreign films.

In part, translators' practice capitulated to the Soviet hierarchy of languages—translators were invested in rendering American, French, or German precisely, but they took many more liberties with rare and non-Western languages.[71] Yet, in different ways, they applied the trial-and-error method to both types of films. Just as they expected their audiences to intuit, together with the translator, what was said on the screen in the language they did not know, so did translators themselves plunge into the unknown in perceiving foreign speech. During tours to Soviet republics after the festival, each translator was usually given two films to translate live in a language he or she knew, and two films, for instance in an African or Indian dialect, to translate from a script. "I learned," recalls Elena Razlogova, "that when you translate such a film for the twentieth time you begin to soak in that culture and it was useful to not just experience the familiar European culture but something else. Often the dialogue lists were missing several scenes but by the fourth or fifth time I would invent translations of these scenes for myself."[72] The idea of "soaking in" another culture through multiple exposures to it seems to explain why simultaneous translators claimed to "understand" speech in films in languages they did not know and routinely agreed to translate from languages they did not speak fluently. "Knowing the language" acquired a different meaning as each translator usually claimed to "know" half a dozen languages.[73]

In the 1960s and 1970s, a translator and a cinephile learned a language or a culture by interacting with it, not by systematic memorization. Theodor Adorno once compared essay writing with learning a language. A man forced to learn a language in a foreign country derives nuanced meanings from particular contexts; this serves him better than memorizing a dictionary. "Just as such learning remains exposed to error," Adorno argued, "so does the essay as form; it must pay for its affinity with open intellectual experience by the lack of security." Thus an essayist deliberately "abrogates" certainty and proceeds "methodically unmethodically."[74] That seems to describe not only how simultaneous translators approached films but also how they encouraged their audiences to approach films—neither to fear nor to ignore the inaudible and incomprehensible elements of a foreign culture.

Notes

1. Natalia Razlogova, interview by author, April 15, 2012.

2. Vladimir Solov'ev, ed., *Kinoteatr Gosfil'mofonda Rossii Illiuzion: vchera, segodnia, zavtra* (Moscow: RID Interreklama, 2008), is an excellent compendium of recollections by and about Soviet simultaneous screen translators. See also Michele Berdy, Dmitrii Buzadzhi, Dmitrii Ermolovich, Mikhail Zagot, Viktor Lanchikov, and Pavel Palazhchenko, "Kinoperevod: Malo chto ot Boga, mnogo chto ot Goblina," *Mosty* 8, no. 4 (2005): 52–62; M. A. Zagot, "Kinofestival'," *Mosty* 10, no. 2 (2006): 70–75.

3. For an overview and an intervention of the "sub versus dub" debate, see Abé Mark Nornes, *Cinema Babel: Translating Global Cinema* (Minneapolis: University of Minnesota Press, 2007); for a film studies perspective, see Nataša Ďurovičová, "Vector, Flow, Zone: Towards a History of Cinematic Translation," in *World Cinemas, Transnational Perspectives*, ed. Nataša Ďurovičová and Kathleen E. Newman (New York: Routledge, 2010), 90–120; for a translation studies perspective, see Yves Gambier, "Screen Transadaptation: Perception and Reception," *Translator* 9, no. 2 (2003): 171–89. One of the earliest works on the subject is Atom Egoyan and Ian Balfour, eds., *Subtitles: On the Foreignness of Film* (Cambridge, MA: MIT Press, 2004).

4. David Snelling, "Upon the Simultaneous Translation of Films," *Interpreters' Newsletter* 3 (1990): 14; Mariachiara Russo, "Simultaneous Film Interpreting and Users' Feedback," *Interpreting* 7, no. 1 (January 2005): 1–26.

5. Several preliminary studies suggest live screen translation was widespread in Asia, Africa, and the Soviet Union in the silent era and in some cases into the 1950s. See Nornes,

Cinema Babel; Birgit Englert and Nginjai Paul Moreto, "Inserting Voice: Foreign Language Film Translation as a Local Phenomenon in Tanzania," *Journal of African Media Studies* 2, no. 2 (April 2010): 225–39; S. V. Srinivas, "Is There a Public in the Cinema Hall?" *Framework* 42 (2000), http://www.sarai.net/research/media-city/resouces/film-city-essays/sv_srinivas.pdf; Peter Fawcett, "Translating Film," in *On Translating French Literature and Film*, ed. Geoffrey T. Harris (Amsterdam: Rodopi, 1996), 65–88.

6. B. Shtaier, "O mekhanizme sinkhronnogo perevoda," *Tetradi perevodchika* 12 (1975): 105.

7. V. P. Gaiduk, "'Tikhii' perevod v kino," *Tetradi perevodchika* 15 (1978): 93–100.

8. Zinaida Shatina, "Kinoteatr Illiuzion v moei zhizni," in Solov'ev, *Kinoteatr Gosfil'mofonda Rossii Illiuzion*, 62; and Vladimir Golubev, "Zapiski kinomana," *Kinovedcheskie zapiski* 64 (2003): 303.

9. Nornes, *Cinema Babel*, 230.

10. Maia Turovskaia, "Gollivud v Moskve, ili Sovetskoe i amerikanskoe kino," *Kinovedcheskie zapiski* 97 (2011): 51–63; Maia Turovskaia, "Trofeinye fil'my poslevoennoi Rossii" (paper presented at the Hybridität in Literatur, Kunst und Medien der russischen Moderne und Postmoderne, Universität Konstanz, Switzerland, June 2006).

11. Joseph Brodsky, "Spoils of War," *Threepenny Review*, no. 64 (winter 1996): 6–9.

12. On this, see, e.g., Odd Arne Westad, *The Global Cold War: Third World Interventions and the Making of Our Times* (Cambridge: Cambridge University Press, 2005).

13. E. Gofman, "K istorii sinkhronnogo perevoda," *Tetradi perevodchika* 1 (1963): 20–26; Francesca Gaiba, *The Origins of Simultaneous Interpretation: The Nuremberg Trial* (Ottawa: University of Ottawa Press, 1998).

14. Gordon Hitchens, "Mind-Bending, Discomforts at USSR's Fest for Asia, Africa," *Variety*, June 12, 1974. I thank Rossen Djagalov for making me aware of this article and other materials on the Moscow and Tashkent festivals.

15. Alpha Amadou Diallo, quoted in Kirill Razlogov, "Stanovlenie," *Iskusstvo kino* 2 (1969), 135–38; Ďurovičová, "Vector, Flow, Zone." On nation-building empires, see also Paul A. Kramer, "Power and Connection: Imperial Histories of the United States in the World," *American Historical Review* 116, no. 5 (December 2011): 1348–91; Francine Hirsch, *Empire of Nations: Ethnographic Knowledge and the Making of the Soviet Union* (Ithaca, NY: Cornell University Press, 2005).

16. Shatina, "Kinoteatr Illiuzion v moei zhizni," 57.

17. Kirill Razlogov, interview by author, April 15, 2012.

18. Vladimir Durikin, "Illiuzion stal dlia menia vtorym domom," in *Kinoteatr Gosfil'mofonda Rossii Illiuzion: vchera, segodnia, zavtra*, ed. Vladimir Solov'ev (Moskva: RID Interreklama, 2008), 190.

19. Maia Turovskaia, "Zritel'skie predpochtenia 70-kh," *Kinovedcheskie zapiski* 11 (1991): 92–96; Grigory Libergal, interview by author, April 12, 2012.

20. Kirill Razlogov, "Moi festivali" (unpublished manuscript, 2011); Elena Razlogova, interview, April 21, 2012; Natalia Razlogova, interview; Libergal, interview.

21. Razlogov, interview.

22. Libergal, interview; Razlogov, interview; Elena Razlogova, interview; Natalia Razlogova, interview.

23. Razlogov, "Moi festivali"; Golubev, "Zapiski kinomana."

24. Shatina, "Kinoteatr Illiuzion v moei zhizni," 67.

25. Razlogov, interview.

26. Razlogov, interview.

27. Natalia Nusinova, interview by author, April 13, 2012.

28. Razlogov, interview; Elena Razlogova, interview.

29. Maia Turovskaia, cited in Aleksei Gusev, "Nekomu soperezhivat'," *Imperia dramy*, January 2010, http://www.alexandrinsky.ru/magazine/rubrics/rubrics_376.html; for more on *Yesenia*, see Turovskaya, "Zritel'skie predpochtenia 70-kh."

30. On *projection nationale*, see Ďurovičová, "Vector, Flow, Zone." On Soviet spectatorship of Indian melodramas, see Sudha Rajagopalan, *Indian Films in Soviet Cinemas* (Bloomington: Indiana University Press, 2009).

31. Yevgeni Yevtushenko, interview, *National Security Archive Cold War Interviews* 14: Red Spring, The Sixties (January 17, 1999), http://www.gwu.edu/~nsarchiv/coldwar/interviews /episode-14/yevtushenko1.html.

32. Razlogov, "Moi festivali."

33. Golubev, "Zapiski kinomana."

34. The phrase and concept were introduced by Ann Laura Stoler, "Tense and Tender Ties: The Politics of Comparison in North American History and (Post) Colonial Studies," *Journal of American History* 88, no. 3 (December 2001): 829–65.

35. Nusinova, interview.

36. Natalia Razlogova, interview.

37. Grigory Libergal, "Illiuzion—shkola dlia perevodchikov," in Solov'ev, *Kinoteatr Gosfil'mofonda Rossii Illiuzion*, 143; several translators reported that the best compliment to the translator is if the audience exiting the theater discusses the film as if they heard it the original language. Natalia Razlogova, interview; Elena Razlogova, interview; Natalia Nusinova, interview.

38. See Lawrence Venuti, *The Translator's Invisibility* (London: Routledge, 1994).

39. Snelling, "Upon the Simultaneous Translation of Films," 15.

40. Elena Razlogova, interview.

41. Aleksandr Bondarev, interview by author, July 16, 2012.

42. Libergal, "Illiuzion—shkola dlia perevodchikov," 147.

43. Bondarev, interview.

44. Elena Razlogova, interview.

45. Libergal, interview; Elena Razlogova, interview; Natalia Razlogova, interview.

46. Mark Kushnirovich, "Veseloe delo," in Solov'ev, *Kinoteatr Gosfil'mofonda Rossii Illiuzion*, 105.

47. Golubev, "Zapiski kinomana."

48. Razlogov, interview.

49. Bosley Crowther, review of *L'éternel retour*, *New York Times*, January 5, 1948.

50. Elena Razlogova, interview.

51. Natalia Razlogova, interview; Kira Razlogova, interview.

52. Kushnirovich, "Veseloe delo," 105.

53. Libergal, "Illiuzion—shkola dlia perevodchikov," 145.

54. Natalia Razlogova, interview.

55. Kira Razlogova, interview.

56. Ibid.

57. Nataša Ďurovičová, "Vector, Flow, Zone."

58. Libergal, interview.

59. Elena Razlogova, interview.

60. Natalia Razlogova, interview.

61. Ibid.

62. Razlogov, "Moi festivali."

63. Kira Razlogova, interview; Natalia Razlogova, interview. Unfortunately, no one re-membered the year or title of the film.

64. Natalia Razlogova, interview.

65. Elena Razlogova, interview; Libergal, interview; Razlogov, "Moi festivali."

66. Elena Razlogova, interview.

67. Kira Razlogova, interview; on *benshi*, see Nornes, *Cinema Babel*, chap. 3

68. Shatina, "Kinoteatr Illiuzion v moei zhizni," 65–66; Golubev, "Zapiski kinomana," 303.

69. Kira Razlogova, interview.

70. Ingrid Monson, "Hearing, Seeing, and Perceptual Agency," *Critical Inquiry* 34, no. 2 (2008): 40.

71. On the hierarchy of languages, see Ella Shohat and Robert Stam, "The Cinema after Babel: Language, Difference, Power," *Screen* 26, nos. 3–4 (May 1985): 35–58.

72. Elena Razlogova, interview.

73. Libergal, interview; Nusinova, interview, Razlogov, interview, Kira Razlogova, interview.

74. Theodor W. Adorno, "The Essay as Form," trans. Robert Hullot-Kentor and Frederic Will, *New German Critique* (1984): 161.

PART III
MUSIC IN FILM; OR, THE SOUND TRACK

10 *Kinomuzyka*

Theorizing Soviet Film Music in the 1930s

Kevin Bartig

In December 1926, a small German crew disembarked in Soviet Russia. There they entertained audiences with the Tri-Ergon system, a technological curiosity that captured both moving images and the accompanying sound on film. Similar Soviet-made systems soon followed, most notably from the workshop of Pavel Tager.[1] Pondering these developments, Soviet filmmakers felt both excitement and trepidation. The 1928 "statement" issued by Sergei Eisenstein, Vsevolod Pudovkin, and Grigori Alexandrov is justly famous for capturing this mix of emotions. At best, they reasoned, sound offered untold creative possibilities for film. At worst, it reduced the medium to mere filmed theater.[2] These avant-garde directors were not, of course, the only Soviet artists pondering the advent of sound film. *Kinomuzyka,* an entirely new genre, was also on the minds of Soviet composers. A few had already written original music for silent films, and sound on film seemed to confirm the newfound priority of that endeavor. Yet the rapid development of sound technology also raised a critical question: what exactly was film music?

Soviet composers and musicologists hastened to answer, both in practice and in theory. In the latter camp, a specialist literature rapidly appeared in the 1930s, crowned by two full-length monograph studies. Considering its ambitious goal of defining a new musical genre, this body of writing is surprisingly consistent in its basic assumptions. For example, its authors never doubted that film music would have a foundation in older genres with analogous visual and musical elements, such as opera or ballet. In other words, to modernize and to maximize were the guiding principles, rather than to revolutionize or to transform. Such a position might seem rather pedestrian for the musically conservative 1930s, the decade that saw the rise of socialist realism and the ostensible quashing of the avant-garde possibilities of which Eisenstein and his colleagues dreamt. Yet that which smacks of bureaucratically mandated aesthetics can often be traced back well before any "policy" was officially codified, as Marina Frolova-Walker has shown apropos Soviet opera.[3] There was a wide and relatively early consensus among Soviet composers and musicologists that venerable genres such as opera possessed expressive powers that should not be discarded. Seeking continuity with the past would not trivialize or somehow cripple sound film, they reasoned, but rather would appropriate a centuries-old body of dramaturgical and expressive wisdom. As this contention found voice alongside a very different practice, however, it became increasingly polemical and mired in complaints about the sound-film industry. Musician-writers complained about directors who treated music as an afterthought, invariably requesting musical cues to match the actions and emotions of visual images without considering a larger dramaturgical whole. These grumbles attest to a deeper disappointment, namely that film music had become subservient to a narrative forged in images and dialogue. In the end, the avant-garde designs of Eisenstein, Pudovkin, and Alexandrov proved just as elusive as the far more conservative theories of composers and musicologists.

Initial Divisions

While Eisenstein, Pudovkin, and Alexandrov drafted their statement, a composer duo was busy poring over a manuscript that would appear the following year as a book unassumingly titled *Muzykal'noe soprovozhdenie v kino* (Musical Accompaniment in Film).[4] The authors, Sergei Bugoslavsky (1888–1945) and David Blok (1888–1948), were both conservatory-trained musicians. Although their tract is largely devoted to using preexisting music in silent films (even including a chapter titled "Training of the Cinema Pianist"), Bugoslavsky and Blok were the first Russian-language writers to comment on original film scores in any detail.[5]

Their definition of film music as a distinct genre hinged on music's potential to communicate something that went beyond that which the visual image conveyed, be it emotions, psychological states, or ideas. Only when music serves as the "emotional amplification of visual impressions" is it possible "to speak of film music," they argued.[6] As a veteran silent-film musician, Blok particularly detested standard anthologies of stock numbers for all "moods and situations" (as the most popular of them advertises on its title page).[7] These collections meant that a given march might accompany, for instance, the Red Army or a group of Young Pioneers. For Bugoslavsky and Blok, such usage was mechanical and ultimately superfluous, adding little to that which was expressed visually. For similar reasons, the authors summarily dismissed music closely synchronized with the visual image (later known in Hollywood as mickey-mousing), which they felt signaled an equally vapid dramaturgy in which music merely duplicated on-screen actions.[8]

Bugoslavsky and Blok's route away from these dramaturgical pitfalls involved making the composer an equal member of the production team, essentially a partner of the director. The composer would "manage" the emotional reactions various types of music might elicit in listeners with the very same care with which the director handled visual sequences. As they explained, the composer would match visual design with a corresponding musical blueprint. Such a plan would "take into account the overall theme and style of the film, distribute the film's music along the thematic, emotional, and aesthetic (better to say dramatic) characters of its parts, and highlight the plot's most striking and meaningful moments."[9] Bugoslavsky and Blok's simple wish was that film music be dramaturgically sound, that its function be as robust and necessary as that of images and dialogue. In this respect, they never challenged the style or content of the music that had accompanied silent films, only its indiscriminate use.

We might compare this position with that found in V. Solsky's *Zvuchashchee kino* (Sounding Cinema), which appeared in print at nearly the exact moment as Bugoslavsky and Blok's book.[10] Solsky was not a trained musician but rather a high-ranking party journalist with a particular interest in the work of Soviet writers and cinematographers. His primary claim—that sound must not disrupt the achievements of silent film—was a common one at the end of the silent era.[11] Not surprisingly, American sound film, in which spoken dialogue precluded the rapid and sophisticated montage of 1920s Soviet films, was first in line for attack by Solsky. In this respect, his position is not all that different from many European directors who lobbied against the realism of spoken text.[12] Yet music was Solsky's primary concern, and he agreed with Bugoslavsky and Blok, at least on synchronized music, which he called illustrative music. This audiovisual construction, Solsky reasoned, was flawed in its "attempt to repeat the visual image in the music" rather than operating "on the basis of the combination of music and visual image."[13] To illustrate the difference, he imagined a scene in which a character plays the piano, accompanied not by the theater orchestra, but rather by a live pianist who plays in sync with the on-screen counterpart. He argued that the base realism of such source music is wholly unnecessary—better that the orchestra continue playing even if it destroys the illusion of actually hearing what the on-screen pianist plays.[14] To be sure, Solsky likely imagined uses far more avant-garde than those of Bugoslavsky and Blok, something akin to the famous audiovisual "counterpoint" imagined in the 1928 statement noted earlier. Nevertheless, all agreed that the future potential of film music rested on establishing its independent narrative role in sound film.

Solsky disagreed with his composer colleagues on what exactly his hypothetical orchestra should be playing, and it is here that his discussion is perhaps the most illuminating. He predicted an imminent revolution in film music, one that was entirely necessary considering sound film's modernity; what might emerge from the ashes was anyone's guess. Borrowing an analogy from the French critic Léon Moussinac, he suggested that comparing contemporary film music with its postrevolutionary counterpart would be similar to a juxtaposition of early Western music and Stravinsky's *Le sacre du printemps*. But whereas more than half a millennium separated early monophony and modernist ballet, film music's transformation would span mere decades. Solsky only tacitly suggested his more fundamental hope for this musical revolution: that it would sever sound film from the baggage of tradition, with its powerful semiotic codes and intertextual references.[15]

Naive Realism and *Khaltura*

> In filming a picture a director often does not take into account the specific details of sound. He does not consider that sound makes its own demands on the behavior of the actors and, indeed, on the compositional substance of the entire film. . . . The presence of indifferent, unnecessary little sounds is intolerable. Each sound must have a logical and emotional direction.[16]

Or so the prominent Moscow composer Nikolai Kriukov summarized the state of Soviet film music in 1936, only six years after Solsky finished his text. Kriukov's conclusions reflected those of almost all of his composer colleagues who entered into a discussion on the theory and practice of Soviet film music in the mid-1930s, as recorded primarily in two specialist publications: *Iskusstvo kino* (The Art of Cinema) and *Kino* (Cinema).[17] Although Solsky's revolution in film music had not come to pass, his concern for clear function—shared by Bugoslavsky and Blok—had become the central issue. Sound film was no longer new by mid-decade, and the discussion shifted to one of theorized potential versus practical execution. More often than not, writers derided the latter as *khaltura,* or hackwork, heaping blame on unmindful directors who impeded film music's potential.[18]

Dmitry Gachev, a Bulgarian musicologist who immigrated to the Soviet Union in 1926, set the tone for the discussion in a 1934 *Iskusstvo kino* article.[19] He announced that the aesthetic problems seemingly unique to sound film had been around, in fact, for some four centuries. "The problem before us," he wrote, was already posed by the "great German composer." Wagner's *Gesamtkunstwerk*, at least in Gachev's estimation, had been rather "narrow-minded" in restricting a synthesis of the arts to opera.[20] Film-music composers thus sat not on the precipice of revolution but rather near the summit of a hallowed evolution in the synthetical arts. Not surprisingly, Gachev saw sound film as a new musical genre rather than the completely new "art" proclaimed by Solsky and like-minded theorists. Yet Gachev sensed no difference between silent- and sound-film practice, except that a celluloid track had taken the place of live musicians. Sound film, in other words, had become something much more banal than filmed theater: it was, at least from the perspective of music, "filmed" silent film. Illustration via "stock" music—the type condemned by Bugoslavsky and Blok—still pervaded: country people got simple *chastushki* (a short, satirical folk song) and capitalists were bathed in jazz, all of which indicated a certain "sluggishness" on the part of composers and directors.[21] Nevertheless, he proposed no clear solution, holding up Beethoven's incidental music for Goethe's *Egmont* and Bizet's for Daudet's *L'arlésienne* as positive examples of sight-sound interaction, but leaving the reader to infer what was ideal about them. Tellingly, Gachev averred that it would be foolish to simply imitate Beethoven or Bizet, film music being a much "deeper" art than orchestral or incidental music. Thus, he revealed a deep anxiety about film music's status: something had to be new, but building on the high-art status of its art-music predecessors.[22]

Other composers amplified Gachev's assertions, interweaving them with Kruikov's concerns.[23] For example, Vladimir Shcherbachev complained that directors lacked even basic musical facility, let alone the skills to produce complicated counterpoint. Like Gachev, he argued that film music should be something entirely new and free from the constraints of earlier musical genres, yet the only positive examples he could muster came from operatic practice.[24] Composer Lev Knipper, like so many of his colleagues, railed against musical "illustration" at the expense of the emotional potential of music. Knipper also suggested that when such emotional underpinning is unnecessary or impossible, composers should let the scene pass in musical silence rather than drench it in gratuitous tunes.[25]

Clearly articulated goals distinguish the Moscow composer Mikhail Cheremukhin's extensive writings on film music. To be sure, he agreed with the authors noted already, particularly on the topic of illustration.[26] He asserted two dramaturgical possibilities for film music: "its most primitive form, illustration—that is, introducing it into the frame on the basis of similarity, or its true nature as a profound art, as one of the springs of action and the development of the film's plot."[27] For Cheremukhin, the problem of illustration derived from a "naive understanding" of realism, particularly the kind that privileged source music (for example, Solsky's example of the audience "hearing" exactly what an on-screen pianist plays). This mechanical reliance on verisimilitude denies music its own narrative function, Cheremukhin argued. He suggested that his colleagues instead consider an excerpt from Beethoven's *Moonlight Sonata* used in the 1934 film *Chapaev* (dir. Georgy Vasiliev and Sergei Vasiliev), which a certain Colonel Borozdin plays at the piano while sinking deep into his own thoughts. Cheremukhin described:

> [Borozdin's] attendant, scrubbing the floor in the same room, also reflects, but on something different, the death of his brother, whom the colonel had flogged. The music develops, Colonel Borozdin's "reverie" deepens, but the attendant's face grows threatening and the audience perceives the music as a burst of hate.[28]

Cheremukhin's example of source music was ostensibly purposeful, chosen to demonstrate how such seemingly "illustrative" source music was necessary to reveal the scene's full narrative implications.

Discussions that sought to tease out additional instructive examples invariably disintegrated into complaints. Knipper lamented that composers remained subservient to directors who were unqualified to craft coherent, musically supported narratives. In a particularly frank moment, he offered the reader a hypothetical but supposedly typical scene: having written music for a cue, a composer presents his music to the director, who promptly rejects it, requesting something "fashionable, like Prokofiev or Shostakovich." The director reminds the composer that the contract states that "the director and management approve the music." Facing tight deadlines, the composer "hastily writes something 'like' Prokofiev or Shostakovich," perhaps hurriedly turning out a new musical cue as the previous one is being recorded in the next room.[29] Similarly, Cheremukhin complained that composers are "guest artists," participating not in a new synthetical art but rather in a crudely "mixed" one. Knipper exhorted directors to trust composers more, and not treat musical scores as something that can be looped, shortened, or modified and then joined to a carefully edited visual sequence. After all, he added sardonically, nobody would ever dream of chopping up or reordering Beethoven's Fifth Symphony.[30]

The most pointed criticism came not from a composer but from the actor Azary Messerer. Writing for *Kino* under his professional name, Azary Azarin, he cited three films in simultaneous production during 1935, all of which were assigned to the same composer with seemingly no forethought. One film received its music prior to filming (initially a common practice in Soviet sound-film studios), yet multiple revisions to the director's script during filming impaired the thematic and formal integrity of the musical score. The other two films missed their deadlines when the composer struggled to finish his score in the little time allotted him; eventually, a second composer had to come to his aid. Azarin concluded:

> We are used to the idea of a scenario being discussed among various artists long before a film actually goes into production. Often this dialogue results in practical and significant changes that benefit the common cause. But typically these discussions do not involve musicians or bother with musical sketches or even finished scores that are destined for some film. Might not involvement in the process be of benefit not just to the composer but also to the film?[31]

Knipper did not mince words: "I myself work in film and have never enjoyed it." He no longer could turn out *khaltura;* the only solution was for directors and composers to understand each other's arts.[32]

"More Expression of Feeling Than Painting"

The two major theorists of Soviet film music who emerged at the end of the 1930s, Cheremukhin and Ieremia Ioffe, both invoked the foregoing directive, an entreaty perhaps more familiar in its original German: *Mehr Ausdruck der*

Empfindung als Malerei. The words are Beethoven's, who scrawled them on a violin part for his Sixth Symphony in 1808. The line is generally assumed to refer to the titles of each of the symphony's movements (e.g., "Scene at the Brook," "Thunderstorm"), inviting listeners to perceive a spiritual, essential relationship of subject and music rather than mimetic coupling. That the phrase cropped up well more than a century later and in a Soviet context is telling, as it historicized Soviet film-music discourse and invoked the authority of past practice (recall that Beethoven was also Knipper's example of exalted musical practice). More to the point, the phrase reminded readers that history had already posed solutions to the problem of "illustration." By adopting this position, Ioffe's 1938 monograph *Muzyka sovetskogo kino: Osnovy muzykal'noi dramaturgii* (The Music of Soviet Film: Foundations of Musical Dramaturgy) and Cheremukhin's 1939 *Muzyka zvukovogo fil'ma* (Music of the Sound Film) added little to the arguments already noted.[33] More significant, the two texts positioned a decade-long discourse in a broad theoretical context.

A polymath musicologist, art historian, and philosopher, Ioffe had a natural inclination to interdisciplinary approaches.[34] For example, his first major study, *Sinteticheskaia istoriia iskusstv* (A Synthetical History of the Arts), argues that subtle interactions between creative fields generally assumed to be autonomous (e.g., painting and music) were, in fact, the primary driving force behind the historical development of the arts.[35] From this perspective, sound film appealed to Ioffe as an art that would catalyze reciprocal influence between music and cinema. In his 1938 study, Ioffe positioned himself as an analyst rather than a theorist, emphasizing his unprecedented access to scores and special film equipment at the Leningrad Scientific Research Institute of Theater, Music, and Cinematography.[36] Indeed, particularly illuminating are thirteen brief, descriptive chapters devoted to the film music of individual Soviet composers. Bookending them is a trenchant argument for why film music must be seen as the "direct continuation and development of areas of musical culture where music works together with visual forms of art."[37] Ioffe maintained that music's content or emotion—the prickly issue deflected by other contemporary musician-writers—must be understood in the context of music's emergence from and inextricable relation to the phenomenological world.

Ioffe placed film music in the bimodal framework that he argued was common to all synthetical art. His "illustrative" mode, in which music duplicates or mimics visual action, is already familiar. A "revealing" mode is unique to Ioffee's study only in name, as it classifies music that reveals the emotional content of action. Ioffe did not assert the superiority of one or the other, however, but instead reasoned that all art relies on a mix of the two. To gain purchase on this claim, he cited examples such as Eugène Delacroix's *Hamlet and Horatio in the Graveyard* (1839), a painting in which Shakespeare's famous scene is made visual (illustration) but also expresses an emotional content absent from the literary original (revealing). He wished to parse sound film similarly but also to prove the medium's superiority over its predecessors. Ioffe thus argued that the elements of opera and theater—dialogue, action, singing, and music—are inherently illustrative or revealing. In opera, for example, the singer does little but relate the plot while the orchestra handles the essential emotional or "revealing" development of the plot. Sound film's accomplishment, then, was to transcend the rigid delegation of functions to allow each element full expressive potential: image and music share equally illustrative and revealing roles. Accordingly, Ioffe was more permissive of illustration than his composer colleagues, as long as the music supported the film's overall dramaturgy.[38]

But what of musical content? Music is not "arabesques" but rather a language of "intonations," Ioffe asserted.[39] His choice of language is critical, as it evokes two ideological opponents who remain otherwise unnamed in his study. The first is the Austrian music critic Eduard Hanslick (1825–1904), whose 1854 *Vom Musikalisch-Schönen* (On the Musically Beautiful) caused a stir in its own time for arguing that music cannot have concrete referents.[40] Distinct feelings or concrete images, Hanslick contended, were not the content of music; rather it was tonally moving forms, which he likened to animated "arabesques."[41] His vision for what later became known as "absolute" music pitted him against Richard Wagner and the proponents of the New German School, who advocated abandoning conventions to allow music a deeper emotional truth and meaning.

Hanslick's basic arguments were, of course, anathema to theorists of socialist realism: art without connection to the phenomenological world was by definition formalist. One of Ioffe's contemporaries and colleagues, the composer and influential musicologist Boris Asafiev (1884–1949), wrote extensively about this formalist danger, the vapid and essentially anti-artistic nature of art for art's sake. An "intonation," a term appropriated from Asafiev by Ioffe, implied a range of concepts and practice. In its most basic form, an intonation is a discreet, sonic event with a concrete referent (such as a baby's cry or the sound of rain). A musical intonation, though cast in melody, harmony, and rhythm, preserves some essence of the phenomenological intonation such that it conjures a similar meaning in the listener's mind. In Asafiev's words, such is "the emotional ideational pronouncing of sound, as a quality determining the direction of meaning in musical speech."[42] According to him, musical intonations evolved over time as a semiotic set, deriving meaning first from nature and then from embedded in artworks and their audiences, creating a complex system of referential content: thus the pervasive Soviet musicological belief that "the semantics of musical expression are in essence associative and symbolic, not illustrative," as Malcolm H. Brown argued.[43] Put more baldly, intonations furnished music with a "vocabulary" by which it could be subjected to the same content demands as other Soviet arts.[44]

Asafiev (and Ioffe's appropriation) demonstrably influenced Cheremukhin, although he acknowledges neither in his study. His first chapter introduces intonational theory, the main departure from Asafiev here being the degree of agency he grants the composer in the formation of musical ideas:

> We perceive the images a talented composer creates. We respond to the effects of the images he created. The composer's mind captured all that is alive and moving, and that makes an impression on us. He communicates these things because he has the necessary means for this expression.[45]

Cheremukhin later qualifies this assertion, arguing that the essential vocabulary for musical expression in fact dates from the nineteenth century. He opined that the formal cogency of classical-era music works was a product of their emotional one-sidedness and, by extension, the simplicity of their musical images. A true vocabulary came only with increasingly complex music, particularly that of Beethoven, Liszt, and Wagner.[46]

Ioffe filled in some of the detail glossed over by Cheremukhin. He argued that the "heroic" operas of the French Revolution were the point of departure for Beethoven because they established the intonations of "tragic struggle" and "victorious will" that became the basis of the composer's symphonies. Indeed, intonations were the result of a clear historical development:

> [Opera] overtures grew from simple introductory fanfares to orchestral introductions that capture the overall mood of the action. Then they became symphonic expositions of the musical plot's main themes. This development is the formation of symphonism, an instrumental exposition of the dramatic action's essence. It is precisely the symphonies of classical music that contain the deepest and most serious thoughts of internal speech, of struggle and reconciliation, despair and inspiration, suffering and love. The realism and the historical method of Soviet dramaturgy demands that the emotions of specific, real people and actions be the basis of intonations. Symphonic music must fulfill this role in film.[47]

Significant for both Ioffe and Cheremukhin, then, was the "richness" of the past and its ability to accommodate socialist themes. Wagner's "Ride of the Valkyries" is perfect for a scene of "Red-Army men in battle," Ioffe asserted, while the heroic finale of Beethoven's Fifth Symphony should be used when "the squares seethe with meetings" or citizens observe a "solemn people's victory."[48]

By this line of reasoning, composing Soviet film music involved managing inherited intonations and considering, in consultation with the director, the power they could exert over visual images.[49] Moreover, because of the specificity of musical intonations, their interaction with visual images must always be considered a constant dialectical flux. A funeral march paired with a sleeping child, as Ioffe notes, "speaks of the threat of the child's death" and not of the brevity of life, just as a lullaby accompanying an elderly man facing his own demise implies that death brings peace, and not anything more profound, such as the "fateful cycle of life."[50] Directors unaware or uninterested in this fact risked marring their films with ill-considered music. Cheremukhin, seemingly bringing a decade-long discussion full circle, claimed that indiscriminate use of powerful musical images would result in the very audiovisual counterpoint envisioned by Eisenstein and his colleagues a decade earlier: an abstract, dizzying mix of visual and musical images with conflicting content.[51]

* * *

In early 1945, the Committee on Cinema Affairs called a meeting of directors and studio administration to discuss the industry's accomplishments and failings in the previous year. Several of the presentations, particularly one by Kriukov on behalf of film composers, addressed long-standing problems. Evincing a flair for the dramatic, Kriukov likened a film composer to an "epic hero" who must triumph over "dragons." Such fire-breathing opponents included screenplays prepared without composer input, directors not versed in music, and inept sound technicians.[52] These were familiar gripes, ones that had beset composers since the late 1920s. Nevertheless, such consistency is significant, spanning as it does a period of radical change in the Soviet arts. The writings of Ioffe, Cheremukhin, and others reveal an alternate narrative of Soviet film's development, one in which concern for continuity with the past, and thus a privileged place for music in the synthetical arts, remained constant.

Notes

1. Jay Leyda, *Kino: A History of the Russian and Soviet Film* (Princeton, NJ: Princeton University Press, 1983), 278–79.

2. S. Eizenshtein, V. Pudovkin, and G. Aleksandrov, "Zaiavka," *Zhizn' iskusstva*, August 5, 1928, 4–5.

3. Marina Frolova-Walker, "The Soviet Opera Project: Ivan Dzerzhinsky vs. Ivan Susanin," *Cambridge Opera Journal* 18 (2006): 181–216, esp. 188–89.

4. David Blok and S. Bugoslavskii, *Muzykal'noe soprovozhdenie v kino* (Moscow: Teakino-pechat', 1929). Bugoslavsky went on to publish a number of articles on film music as a correspondent for *Kino*: "Za prostotu v muzyke," February 21, 1935, 3; "Muzyka v fone," May 28, 1936, 4; "Formalizm v kinomuzyke," February 16, 1936, 3; and "Zhivoi svidetel' nashikh dnei," February 4, 1935, 4.

5. Bugoslavsky co-authored a pamphlet on film music with Vladimir Messman in 1926, but their discussion does not address original film scores. See Sergei Bugoslavskii and Vladimir Messman, *Muzyka i kino* (Moscow: Kinopechat', 1926).

6. Blok and Bugoslavskii, *Muzykal'noe soprovozhdenie*, 6.

7. Erno Rapée, *Encyclopedia of Music for Motion Pictures* (New York: Belwin, 1925).

8. On mickey-mousing, see Roy M. Prendergast, *Film Music: A Neglected Art*, 2nd ed. (New York: Norton, 1992), 80; Royal S. Brown, *Overtones and Undertones: Reading Film Music* (Berkeley: University of California Press, 1994), 16; Michel Chion, *Audio-vision: Sound on Screen*, ed. and trans. Claudia Gorbman (New York: Columbia University Press, 1994), 121–22.

9. Blok and Bugoslavskii, *Muzykal'noe soprovozhdenie*, 7.

10. V. Sol'skii, *Zvuchashchee kino* (Moscow: Teakinopechat', 1929).

11. Soon after the publication of his book, Solsky became disillusioned with the Soviet experiment and emigrated to Germany. See V. L. Genis, "Nevozvrashchentsy 1920-kh—nachala 1930-kh godov," *Voprosy istorii* 1 (2000): 55.

12. Kristin Thompson, "Early Sound Counterpoint," *Yale French Studies* 60 (1980): 118.

13. Sol'skii, *Zvuchashchee kino*, 51.

14. Ibid., 35.

15. Ibid., 39–41, 47, 52–53.

16. N. Kriukov, "Opyt kompozitora," *Kino*, April 6, 1936, 3.

17. See, for example, A. Shkliarovich, "Chto takoe 'predvaritel'nyi period'," *Iskusstvo kino* 7 (1933): 27–30; N. Volkov, "Na zvukovye temy: Nekotorye osobennosti zvukovoi khudozhestvennoi kinematografii," *Iskusstvo kino* 8 (1933): 61–70.

18. Shostakovich used *khaltura* to describe film music as early as 1929. See "O muzyke k 'Novomu Vavilonu'," *Sovetskii ekran* 11 (1929): 5.

19. D. Gachev, "Muzyka v zvukovom kino," *Iskusstvo kino* 4 (1934): 34–42. Gachev's work also addressed issues in philosophy and literature. His best-known work is a 1936 study of Diderot's aesthetics, *Esteticheskie vzgliady Didro*, 2nd ed. (Moscow: Gosudarstvennoe izdatel'stvo khudozhestvennoi literatury, 1961).

20. Gachev, "Muzyka v zvukovom kino," 35.

21. Ibid., 37–39. Gachev lists a number of 1933 films that use musical typing: *Odna radost'*, *Annenkovshchina*, *Dezertir*, and *Konveer smerti*.

22. Ibid., 41.

23. See, e.g., D. Blok, "Muzyka v kino," *Kino*, January 22, 1935, 3.

24. V. Shcherbachev, "Muzyka v kino," *Iskusstvo kino* 3 (1936): 22–23.

25. L. Knipper, "Kino i muzyka," *Iskusstvo kino* 4 (1936): 42.

26. M. Cheremukhin, "Rol' kompozitora v kino," *Iskusstvo kino* 11 (1935): 50-51. Cheremukhin had been in the class of Nikolai Miaskovsky at the Moscow Conservatory during the 1920s. After earning his degree in 1928, he composed primarily concert music, including two substantial cantatas, a symphony, and a series of songs. Other publications concerning film music include "O realisticheskom stile v muzyke kino," *Iskusstvo kino* 6 (1936): 52–54, and "Na podstupakh k muzykal'noi kinodramaturgii," *Iskusstvo kino* 11 (1936): 51–53.

27. Cheremukhin, "Rol' kompozitora v kino," 51.

28. Ibid., 52–53.

29. Knipper, "Kino i muzyka," 42.

30. Cheremukhin, "Rol' kompozitora v kino," 51, 55–56.

31. A. Azarin, "Muzykal'nye siurprizy," *Kino*, December 11, 1935, 3. Sergei Prokofiev experienced similar, unexpected changes to the script after completing his music for the film *Lieutenant Kizhe*, which forced him to revise at the last minute. See my "*Lieutenant Kizhe*: New Media, New Means," in *Prokofiev and His World*, ed. Simon Morrison (Princeton, NJ: Princeton University Press, 2008), 385.

32. Knipper, "Kino i muzyka," 42.

33. Ieremiia Ioffe, *Muzyka sovetskogo kino: osnovy muzykal'noi dramaturgii* (Leningrad: Gosudarstvennyi muzykal'nyi nauchno-issledovatel'skii institut, 1938), 136; Mikhail Cheremukhin, *Muzyka zvukovogo fil'ma* (Moscow: Goskinoizdat, 1939), 27. Ioffe addressed film music initially in a short chapter in his *Sinteticheskoe izuchenie iskusstva i zvukovoe kino* (Leningrad: Gosudarstvennyi muzykal'nyi nauchno-issledovatel'skii institut, 1937).

34. On Ioffe's biography, see M. S. Kagan's introduction ("O kul'turologicheskoi i esteticheskoi kontseptsii I. I. Ioffe") to *I. Ioffe: Izbrannoe: 1920-30-e gg.* (St. Petersburg: Petropolis, 2006), 6–40, esp. 6–8.

35. Ieremiia Ioffe, *Sinteticheskaia istoriia iskusstv: Vvedenie v istoriiu khudozhestvennogo myshleniia* (Leningrad: Lenizogiz, 1933).

36. Ioffe, *Muzyka sovetskogo kino*, 3–5, 15.

37. Ibid., 23.

38. Ibid., 131–32, 137–38, 145–46.

39. Ibid., 12–13.

40. Eduard Hanslick, *On the Musically Beautiful: A Contribution towards the Revision of the Aesthetics of Music*, trans. Geoffrey Payzant (Indianapolis, IN: Hackett, 1986), originally published as *Vom Musikalisch-Schönen: Ein Beitrag zur Revision der Ästhetik der Tonkunst* (Leipzig: R. Weigel, 1854).

41. Ibid., 29.

42. B. V. Asaf'ev, *Izbrannye trudy* (Moscow: Izd. Akademii Nauk SSSR, 1957), 5:145, cited in Gordon D. McQuere, "Boris Asafiev and Musical Form as a Process," in *Russian Theoretical Thought in Music*, ed. Gordon D. McQuere (Ann Arbor: UMI Research Press, 1983), 224. Asafiev developed his theory of intonations throughout the 1920s; the most detailed discussion is in *Muzykal'naia forma kak protsess* (Musical Form as Process) (1930) and *Intonatsiia* (Intonation) (1947). See also E. M. Orlova, *B. V. Asaf'ev, put' issledovatelia i publitsista* (Leningrad: Muzyka, 1964), and James Robert Tull, "B. V. Asaf'ev's Musical Form as a Process Translation and Commentary," 3 vols. (PhD diss., Ohio State University, 1977).

43. Malcolm H. Brown, "The Soviet Russian Concepts of 'Intonazia' and 'Musical Imagery,'" *Musical Quarterly* 60, no. 4 (1974): 557–67.

44. Music's lack of definable "meaning" was a perennial problem for Stalinist bureaucrats and censors. See, for example, Amy Nelson's discussion in her *Music for the Revolution: Musicians and Power in Early Soviet Russia* (University Park: Pennsylvania State University Press, 2004), esp. chapter 1.

45. Cheremukhin, *Muzyka zvukovogo fil'ma*, 7.

46. Ibid., 83–84.

47. Ioffe, *Muzyka sovetskogo kino*, 143.

48. Ibid., 26.

49. Ibid., 129–30; Cheremukhin, *Muzyka zvukovogo fil'ma*, 84.

50. Ioffe, *Muzyka sovetskogo kino*, 155.

51. Cheremukhin, *Muzyka zvukovogo fil'ma*, 90.

52. "Itogi raboty sovetskoi khudozhestvennoi kinematografii za 1944 g.," published in V. Fomin, ed., *Kino na voine: Dokumenty i svidetel'stva* (Moscow: Materik, 2005), 715–18.

11 Listening to *Muzykal'naia istoriia* (1940)

Anna Nisnevich

ON THE DAY of its Moscow premiere, October 18, 1940, the musical comedy *Muzykal'naia istoriia* (A Musical Story), scripted by Evgeny Petrov and Georgy Munblit, directed by Alexander Ivanovsky and Gerbert Rappoport, and starring Sergei Lemeshev and Zoia Fedorova, had already received warm official welcomes in the leading newspapers *Pravda* and *Izvestiia*. The author of the *Pravda* article, Mikhail Lvov, lauded the film's culture-promoting plot, describing *Muzykal'naia istoriia* as "a very simple and uncomplicated story [of] how a taxi driver Petya Govorkov became an opera soloist."[1] Recounting Petya's meeting with an older, experienced opera singer, Vasily Fomich, his singing of Lensky's part in the staging of Tchaikovsky's *Eugene Onegin* at the Club of Auto Transport Workers, his first artistic failure (a consequence of a heartbreak), and his eventual success (the result of hard work), Lvov emphasized the necessity of "propaganda of the best examples of musical art by way of cinema's lively, accessible means." The stance of the review in *Izvestiia*, by A. Alexandrov, was more overtly political. Comparing *Muzykal'naia istoriia* with Hollywood's *One Hundred Men and a Girl* (dir. Koster, 1937), a musical Cinderella story (starring Deanna Durbin) that had charmed Soviet film viewers earlier that year, Alexandrov pointed to a striking discrepancy between the American Cinderella—an adolescent singer whose successes come by way of a string of pure coincidences—and the Soviet one, who is catapulted to stardom by the system itself. "The script-writers of *Muzykal'naia istoriia* do not imitate the American film, but argue with it," he contended. "The taxi driver Govorkov has a path entirely different [from that of his American counterpart]: his future is open, he can be the hero of a film in which the joys of life are not merely fruits of the comedic skill of the script-writer or of his experience in creating happy endings, but are informed by the life material, the reality itself."[2] By way of classical music, Alexandrov suggested, the film showcased a specifically Soviet way of life.

Although their level of ideological engagement differed, the two reviewers nevertheless joined voices on one key issue: the weight of the film's musicality. Lvov's assertion that "Lenfil'm's new release is a truly [*v samom dele*] musical film, from its first to its last frame" was echoed by Alexandrov, who similarly noted that "the film's plot allowed to infuse it with music organically, without much strain, and make it a truly [*deistvitel'no*] musical film." Therein, the authors seemed to agree, laid the film's worth. Lvov's verdict that the film was the first "Soviet motion picture in which the music appears not as accompaniment or an inserted number, but as the main thing [*glavnoe*]" was capped by Alexandrov's conclusion: the film's "cultural significance cannot be denied."[3]

The claim that *Muzykal'naia istoriia* marked the arrival of nothing less than a new cinematic genre—fully musical, and important precisely because of that—seems like an odd one to make circa 1940: dozens of musical comedies had been produced throughout the 1930s, including such great successes as Ivan Pyriev's *kolkhoz* musicals and Grigori Alexandrov's *Veselye rebiata* (Jolly Fellows, 1934), *Tsirk* (Circus, 1936), and *Volga-Volga* (1938), which were thoroughly suffused with the music of Isaak Dunaevsky.[4] In those films, music—and in particular song—was much more than a mere accompaniment, as it performed several ideological functions: it stood in for the solidity of the Soviet community, portended the profusion of a specifically Soviet talent, and articulated the joyous symbiosis of the singing individuals and the sung-about realm.[5] It came, as it were, as close to the "main thing" as possible. Lvov's bold contention, however, was more than an isolated instance of unruly enthusiasm. The belief that a new genre had been born in *Muzykal'naia istoriia* also underlaid much of the discussion after the film's premiere at the House of Cinema.[6] Diverging in their opinions as to whether the production team had succeeded in realizing the demands of the new genre, the discussion's participants seemed to have little doubt that they had just witnessed the "first production of a musical film" (Boris Leonidov, a scriptwriter), "the first instance of a wonderful coincidence between [the tenor Lemeshev's] effortless acting and brilliant singing" (Evgeny Petrov), or "Soviet cinema's first serious and cultured musical expression of a lyric element" (Khrisanf Khersonsky, a dramatist and critic).[7] Lauding the film as a storehouse of firsts would soon become all but de rigueur in print. In part, this was in keeping with the official resolution of the artistic committee that oversaw its release, which read: *Muzykal'naia istoriia* "combines poetic atmosphere with realistic and truly comedic content, and in this sense is the first film in that genre."[8] But the film's commentators and its lay viewers (of which there were about eighteen million by the end of 1940, and more than a hundred million by the end of the 1940s) were also responding to the differences that they perceived between this film and the types of musical comedy that had effectively ruled the Soviet film industry to that point. What made *Muzykal'naia istoriia* more distinctively musical than all previous Soviet musicals? Which aspects of the film's musicality may have contributed to its designation as a new genre, and how? The following is the first attempt to address the generic turn that this film instigated in Soviet musical comedy on the brink of the 1940s.

Musical

Muzykal'naia istoriia begins, predictably, with music. The credits roll to the sounds of the opera *Carmen* by George Bizet, ever popular in the young Soviet state; and we quickly find ourselves at the theater, watching a performance of *Carmen* alongside a young man, the film's main protagonist, the taxi driver Petya Govorkov.[9] The music does not stop when the camera cuts to a tiny office where a young woman, Klava, is listening to the same opera on the radio. (Before long we learn that Klava is a dispatcher at Petya's garage). The sounds of *Carmen*, here (the theater)—live, there (the office)—canned (radio), bridge together these two seemingly disparate locations in the film's opening scene. There is a play here too with the nondiegetic and diegetic musical track, as the opera score is located both within and outside of the fictional space of the film. Transported from the theater to the office and back while continuing to hear the same musical piece, we are invited to perceive Petya and Klava, the film's future couple, as thoroughly linked before we ever see them together. What is more, brought back to the theater to hear Don José's final plea to Carmen, "Only please do not leave me!" in clear Russian, we understand that the love triangle in *Carmen* is meant to foreshadow, albeit ironically, the film's own structure of desire: while Petya is enthralled by the performance, another suitor is vying for Klava's affection.

This opening sequence reveals the film's modus operandi. Music and music-related pursuits—listening, singing, or theatergoing—come to bear directly on the film's proceedings, shaping its plot, surfacing in its heroes' musings, suggesting hidden relationships, and consequently producing an excess of meaning. This is, of course, how most musicals work, including cinematic ones, that is, through the interplay between their narratives (i.e., nonmusical segments) and their musical numbers. In the 1930s, the emergence in the United States of the so-called back-stage film musical, whose plot circled around various sorts of on-stage events, had brought forth "a natural" way to frame these kinds of narratives, according to Rick Altman, "for it permitted a maximum of singing with a minimum of justification."[10] Inspired by Hollywood, Grigori Alexandrov and Isaak Dunaevsky offered their own ways of naturalizing song within film narratives by progressively merging catchy tunes with stories of Soviet becoming. Their biggest hit, *Volga-Volga,* exemplified perhaps the most politically fecund marriage between the Soviet "master plot" and music.[11] Even if comically bumpy, the progress of the film's theme song—"Pesnia o Volge" (The Song of the Volga)—from an unassuming "natural" jingle dreamed up by a small-town mail carrier to a token of modern community, mirrored the utopian narrative of Soviet subjectivity. First timidly crooned by its author, but eventually written down in score, arranged for a variety of musical media, and finally ubiquitously played and sung, the song charted a course, through numerous hurdles, from raw matter to a disciplined, mindful new form.

Similarly to many stories of archetypal Soviet heroes, the story of the song offered a parable of transcendence. Propelling the plot of *Volga-Volga* was a musical tug-of-war between the two halves of the film's soon-to-be couple: Strelka, the folksy author of the Volga song, and Alyosha, a snobbish accountant who values classical music above all else. The trajectory of their eventual coming to terms with each other, by way of a new, shared acoustic identity, mirrored the model path toward social integration. Strelka and Alyosha could be together, the film showed, only after overcoming their opposing musical identities. Their little tune could exemplify the modern, Soviet community only by transcending any single style of composition or performance. This point is effectively made in the film's festive ending, the multi- and multiply-mediated apotheosis of the Volga song, in which the tune becomes an instant hit at a musical Olympiad held at the freshly built Moscow North River Station. Heard by turns as a solo line, in full orchestral rendition, sung a capella, played by a jazz band, dutifully read from notation, and freely improvised upon, the song emerges as supple enough to embrace as many different styles of delivery as there are groups to perform it—all while keeping its core, its original melody, fully intact.

The integration of multitudes within a single tune substantiated an important tenet of both Soviet ideology and socialist realist art: the belief in the capacity of essentially Soviet subject matter to assume myriad local forms. The collaborative melding of many modes of expression also served to encompass—in a sort of *mise-en-abîme*—the larger-than-life essence of the big and diverse Soviet family: multinational in form, solely socialist in content. *Volga-Volga*'s viewers are prompted to recognize themselves in one (or more) of the numerous musical styles written into its rich aural palette, and thus to join in the chorus multiplying before them on-screen. Their stylistic divergence, the film suggests, only makes their common identity stronger, as symbolized by the upbeat song. The film's visual apotheosis—comprising images of motor ships, lift cranes, airplanes, and a dirigible dominating the Moscow cityscape, capped with a panoramic view of the new state-of-the-art River Station—is accompanied by its aural apotheosis, which, in Peter Kupfer's words, "transcended the reality of the film world to become a symbol of the diversity of musical progress as well as the advancement of modernity in the Soviet Union."[12]

Another *Mise-en-abîme*

This larger-than-life quality has no place in *Muzykal'naia istoriia*. No one in the film composes, arranges, or miraculously sight-reads an unfamiliar piece of music. No single tune is presented multiple times or in different guises. Nearly all of the music we hear arrives already furnished with meaning and established habits of performance: it belongs to the classical canon ostensibly familiar both to the film's protagonists and its viewers. Bizet's *Carmen* serves as a prologue to the film's central action and as a meeting place for two kindred spirits, both of whom are opera aficionados: namely our hero Petya, a simple taxi driver who, living up to his name, likes to sing (*pet'*), and Vasily Fomich Makedonsky, "a former soloist of the Imperial theaters" who just happens to run an amateur opera company at the Club of Auto Transport Workers. After crooning one operatic aria after another into his new friend's expert ear, Petya finds himself cast in the role of Lensky in the club's upcoming production of Tchaikovsky's *Eugene Onegin*.

It is that well-known opera, which was staged in unprecedentedly large numbers all over the Soviet Union to mark Tchaikovsky's centenary during the filming of *Muzykal'naia istoriia,* that resounds in many of the film's subsequent scenes. Time and again we find ourselves watching auto transport workers learning to sing and act like nineteenth-century operatic aristocrats. So devotedly do these taxi drivers and mechanics spend their leisure time studying *Eugene Onegin* that lines from the opera enter into their everyday speech. After being reprimanded by Vasily Fomich for being late to rehearsal, the production's Onegin calls up a courteous ditty right from his part: "I ask you for forgiveness, I am a little late." The cheerful girl playing Olga seems to find a fitting expression of her own self in her character's famous line "I am incapable of gloomy yearning," a sentiment we find her reveling in offstage. The dilettante baritones and sopranos make no attempt to update the old-fashioned verses; on the contrary, they seem as thrilled to be reanimating the antiquated politesse as they are to reinhabit the old monocles, tuxedos, and gowns of the opera's wardrobe. With some practice and a little fine-tuning (courtesy of Vasily Fomich), they appear ready to enter the world of operatic make-believe.

Of all the characters, Petya seems to need the least coaching to act as Lensky: somewhat timid and easily stirred, he is a natural lyric hero. Like Lensky, he has no qualms about appropriating romantic clichés: without a moment's doubt he conscripts his protagonist's formal "I love you" in expressing his feelings to Klava for the first time. As if competing with the production of the Club of Auto Transport Workers, his own romantic relationship starts to follow the Pushkin-Tchaikovsky script soon after he joins the cast of *Eugene Onegin*. Late for his date with Klava at the workers' Polar Ball, Petya finds her talking and dancing with another driver. He waits, forlorn, near the ballroom's corner, only to be goaded by his co-star (and friend) "Onegin," who greets Petya with an iconic phrase from the opera: "Why aren't you dancing, Lensky?" Indeed, the whole episode replays a memorable scene from Tchaikovsky's *Eugene Onegin* (specifically act 2, scene 1), drawing the closest parallel so far between Petya's romance and Lensky's.

This sequence also offers a striking convergence of operatic and cinematic realities, and the key to the film's aesthetic economy. Classical (i.e., romantic) opera penetrates all narrative levels of *Muzykal'naia istoriia.* Petya is not the only character whose personal path is touched by the opera in one way or another. We may observe, with the delight of recognition, "Olga" and "Onegin" excitedly quoting from their parts. But if the charming "Olga" is a perfect fit with her character, the overly enthusiastic "Onegin" is a comically failed reflection of his self-possessed protagonist: he rushes his lines, his theatrical props get irrevocably damaged, and even with much noble striving he never succeeds in fully assuming his character's stately gait. His comic exertion to fit with his character is less of a stab at his notoriously arrogant hero than a botched attempt to handle such concrete forms of nineteenth-century behavior as carriage, pace, or intensity of expression. The operatic Onegin's purposely dignified conduct, filtered through "Onegin's" poorly coordinated body, becomes both highly desirable and hardly practicable. The amateur actor, trying in earnest to impersonate a fictional character, lends thereby much reality to the fiction itself. Through his maladroit gestures, operatic conventions emerge as antiquated shapes of living; his lack of thespian skill becomes almost indistinguishable from his inability to reanimate the habits of yore.

This discrepancy between the two Onegins makes manifest, by way of comic reversal, the conflation of opera and history that persists throughout *Muzykal'naia istoriia*. There is little doubt that our "Onegin" struggles to embody his character as Petya does his. The film, however, draws no distinction between the here and now of the opera's early nineteenth-century setting and that of its famed late-imperial productions, which Vasily Fomich and others constantly invoke. Each cast member's slipshod attempt to act brings about a lesson in proper performance, but whereas "Olga" assists "Onegin" in mastering the dignified walking and monocle handling typical of Pushkin's own time, Vasily Fomich expects "Lensky" to match the understated expressiveness of "a former soloist of the Imperial theaters." In trying to make their home in the operatic world, the film's characters simultaneously learn the ways in which the singers of their grandparents' generation made the imperial stages their homes. In so doing, they gloss over the differences between the era of Pushkin's *Eugene Onegin* (the 1820s and 1830s), the setting of Tchaikovsky's opera (1876–77), and the opera's heyday (circa 1900), thus melding the habits of Russia's golden age as memorialized by Tchaikovsky with the practices of his opera's silver-age legacy. In their eager attempts at performance, Tchaikovsky's heroes come through as having already passed through the able bodies of the heroes of the Bolshoi or Mariinsky.

Voice

One hero in particular is invoked in the film more than once: the lyric tenor Leonid Sobinov, imperial Russia's most celebrated Lensky by far. "Sobinov himself feared me!" declares Vasily Fomich, raising his finger high in the air, in the film's very first episode. This, rather than a list of his roles or the theaters at which he has performed, is his key credential. Having (allegedly) sung in Sobinov's company is sufficient to firmly establish Vasily Fomich as the film's mentor figure—no questions asked. He is the only one in the film who knows how to stage an opera or sustain a note, and so his expertise becomes the measure of his production's merit., As if to bolster Vasily Fomich's operatic authority, another old man with similar knowledge makes a backstage cameo appearance before the troupe's premiere of *Eugene Onegin* at the club. His role is to help "Onegin," who is impatiently trying to shove his arms through a fur coat's heavy sleeves for a forthcoming wintertime scene, to assume the proper operatic carriage. "Why are you pushing your arms through the sleeves? Onegin ought to just slip his coat on his shoulders [*Oneginu v nakidku polagaetsia*]!" the old man insists; to our "Onegin's" naive protestation ("But it's [supposed to be] freezing cold [in the scene]!"), he rejoins, "Don't you school me, young man: I served at the Mariinsky theater, I dressed Sobinov himself!" He thus reclaims, once again, the authority of the recent imperial past that is fast becoming a Soviet present. Our "Onegin," now clothed—thanks to the old man's assistance—in the (slipped-on) fur coat and a cylinder hat, looks as ready as ever to take the operatic stage.

But of course it is "Lensky" whose presence will ultimately take over the cinematic screen in *Muzykal'naia istoriia*, for it is Petya who is being primed to carry on the legacy of Pushkin, Tchaikovsky, and Sobinov. As we have already learned, his story has many affinities with that of his hero—even if his path ultimately diverges from Pushkin's ironic and Tchaikovsky's tragic emplotments. But as a matter of history, his path is also prefigured by that of Sobinov's Lensky, part and parcel of Russian opera's transition from the imperial to the Soviet stage.

In the aftermath of 1917, Sobinov was one of the few figures of international renown to remain in Russia; until his death in 1934, he remained a rare and genuine, in-the-flesh artifact of the silver age in the Soviet cultural landscape. His famously luminous voice (*luchezarnyi golos*) went through none of the discursive makeovers undergone by the operas he sang.[13] Celebrated in the 1900s as an acoustic token of Sobinov's personal virtue (the singer came to be known as much for his charity work as for his roles), his *tenore di grazia* continued to epitomize the moral equivalence of timbre and character throughout the 1920s and 1930s.[14] The lyric persona that he seemed to share with Lensky—which had become his calling card and a subject of much adoration since his first performance of the role in 1898—came to serve as a paragon of sincerity and self-discipline, the twin virtues of the ideal Soviet subject. ("The style of his art was so virtuous because he was virtuous himself," reconfirmed Kornei Chukovsky in his 1962 memoir *My Contemporaries*, still decreeing Sobinov's vocal mastery as a unique projector of both innate nobility [*blagorodstvo*] and the ethics of hard work [*truzhenichestvo*].)[15] Already having been bestowed with imperial Russia's highest artistic title, "The Soloist of His Imperial Highness," Sobinov was named "The People's Artist of the RSFSR" in 1923, and he was one of the first to officially exemplify excellence in the new republic.[16] By 1940, his posthumous legacy had begun to outgrow that which he had enjoyed during his life, with the number of items celebrating his artistry in print speedily rising. In 1936 a reputable higher education institution, the Saratov Conservatory, was named after him.[17] Now something of an institution himself, Sobinov joined Pushkin and Tchaikovsky in the pantheon of Russian culture's great artists, which was scrupulously assembled in the late 1930s to help inform Soviet notions of artistic value and to herald Soviet forms of creativity.[18]

It should come as no surprise, then, that Petya's rise from a plain-speaking taxi driver to, in his own words, "the soloist of an Academic, of the Order of Lenin, Opera Theater"—the version of social ascension that was specially reserved for Soviet subjects—involved taking on a handful of Sobinov's trademarks. Not only does the auto transport worker find himself cast as Lensky; the iconic role also brings with it Sobinov's signature locks (here supplemented by a Pushkin-era cylinder hat), capelet coat, and graceful posture, all of which had been multiply eternalized in print from 1900 on (see figure 11.1).[19]

That Petya is capable of carrying on the legend is evidenced by the ease with which he, unlike his buddy "Onegin," fits every one of his model's fixtures. On the day of the premiere, we see "Onegin" and "Lensky" readying themselves, together, for their first joint appearance in the opera's first act. In step with his previous behavior, "Onegin" keeps losing his props and his temper, proving it all but a miracle that he finally leaves for the stage. Petya, in contrast, is already dressed and appears as composed as his double, offering only a wistful smile at "Onegin's" continuing fits. He is, as it were, a natural successor to Sobinov, credibly making his model's signature characteristics his own.

A properly functioning wardrobe and effortless stride are, however, only peripheral steps on the path to the feted career of a soloist. To truly transform, Petya needs also to accede to some of Sobinov's personal traits, and first of all to his special voice, which is a key to his wholeness. That Petya's voice is of the proper variety is established at the film's outset, when he sings for the first time while driving Vasily Fomich home from the performance of *Carmen*. He is prompted by the critique to which his mentor-to-be subjects the tenor cast as Don José: "How could that silly Karabasov sing the flower song's high A-flat with an open sound!" Censuring and then mockingly imitating the unruly, coarse "open" sound usually produced by singers with no formal (i.e., classical) musical training, Vasily Fomich gives Petya—and us—a brief lesson in "proper" performance, reproducing the same musical phrase with a soft, delicate "closed" sound befitting the trained larynx of a bel canto singer. "Please forgive my lack of the knowledge which sound is open and which is closed," Petya artlessly says in response,

Figure 11.1. Sobinov as Lensky at Bolshoi (Leonid Vital'evich Sobinov. *Stat'i, rechi, vyskazyvaniia. Pis'ma k Sobinovu. Vospominaniia o L. V. Sobinove*, comp. K. N. Kirilenko (Moscow: Iskusstvo, 1970), photo insert after 5:192); and Petya as Lensky in *Muzykal'naia istoriia*; frame grab taken from *Muzykal'naia istoriia* (A Musical Story, dirs. Ivanovsky and Rappoport, 1940).

"but I would sing it in this way." As he goes on to croon one of the opera's main hits, we first observe Vasily Fomich keenly moving his lips, together with Petya's as if silently guiding the neophyte, and then humming along the instrumental countermelody to the main vocal line (as no fantasy orchestra accompanies Petya's solo); in the end, he completely shuts himself out of the song's aural space and turns into a swayed, if incredulous, listener. Petya may not know musical terminology, we are led to understand, but his singing—needless to say, with a perfectly closed sound—more than makes up for this trivial lack.

There is more to this sequence than directly meets either the ear or the eye. Vasily Fomich's gradual release of the song to Petya corresponds with the trajectory of the song's melody, as its surging phrases steadily open up to a musical climax stretched out by our singer. The camera angle also follows a similar course, moving from the *en face* position at the start of Petya's singing—maintaining the visual parity of the two faces in the frame—to the profile view that relegates the listening passenger to the rear of the frame while foregrounding, and even visibly lifting, the singing driver as his song approaches its radiant peak (see figure 11.2). These coalescing aural and visual routes shape the audience's perception of Petya's song and his singing. We may not know his vocal technique or recognize his music, but as the melodic curve of his song and the unfurling astonishment of his specialist listener sweep over the screen, they bid for and capture our attention.

Of course, the viewers would have most likely recognized Petya's lithe voice as that of the leading Soviet lyric tenor Sergei Lemeshev (1902–77), cast as Petya.

Figure 11.2. Petya sings for the first time (both frame captures from *Muzykal'naia istoriia*).

In the late 1930s, Lemeshev was a frequent guest at music radio programs; his Lensky had charmed Bolshoi audiences since 1931.[20] Moreover, the course of Lemeshev's life was so close to that of Petya's—humble roots, amateur singing, lucky break, preeminent mentors—that it could well have served as the screenplay's prototype.[21] Lemeshev's presence here, however, remains veiled just as effectively by the many allusions to the heroes mustered from Russia's past as by the film's focus on Petya's own radiant yet rocky path to operatic stardom. Even as a celebrity himself, and a real flesh-and-blood beneficiary of the Soviet regime, Lemeshev succeeds in the film insofar as he helps link history and the present as it progresses on the screen. It is Sobinov whose conduct and sound shine through Lemeshev's rendering of Petya's Lensky, and it is Petya whose talent prevails in the frame. *Muzykal'naia istoriia* invites us to follow this fictional hero as he little by little gains music-theatrical expertise, and through it, social expertise.

Listening

Petya's ability to grip his listeners' attention emerges as one of the film's most enduring subplots. Hearing Petya sing for the first time makes Vasily Fomich catch his breath, just as his singing similarly astonishes the numerous neighbors of Petya's communal apartment: we see their faces light up, one by one, as Petya commences his morning practice. His first outing with Klava that prompts him (rather expectedly) to break into a lyrical song, climaxes not with a kiss or an impassioned embrace but with a round of loud applause from the other couples at the picturesque lakeside. Even in a routine theatrical setting, such as a scheduled rehearsal of *Eugene Onegin* at the Club of Auto Transport Workers, brings about a surprising response to his voice: upon hearing Petya perform Lensky's aria, the orchestra's percussionist impulsively strikes his big drum, moved by Petya's singing. Shown to affect nearly everyone in just about any situation, Petya comes through as a subject as well as an object of the process that one of the film's minor characters proudly identifies as "making the classical heritage our own" (*osvaivaem klassicheskoe naslediie*).[22]

By 1940, mastering the classics had become a key component of the Soviet project of mass refinement. Being privy to the legacy of certain pedigreed writers, composers, painters, and other approved delegates of "world culture" was, in effect, a critical phase in the lengthy process of the formation of an ideal Soviet individual.[23] As Vadim Volkov and Catriona Kelly have shown, while *kul'turnost'* (culturedness) could come by way of refined everyday objects (such as lampshades or snow-white tablecloths) and one's commitment to social politesse at the beginning of the cultural revolution, in the second half of the 1930s "it would be increasingly sought in, and projected on to, the individual's inner world."[24] Among its other objectives, the concerted revival in the 1930s of a host of pre-revolutionary (and not necessarily Russian) authors and artworks—Stalinism's "Great Appropriation," in Katerina Clark's words—was to bear on the quality of every Soviet person's interior life. Mastering the classics meant not only gaining historical perspective (i.e., the (pre-scripted) consciousness of what had come before that was so crucial to Marxist teleology) but also developing special receptivity to the varied and complex forms of the human imaginary (i.e., honing one's aesthetic insight).[25] Apprenticing under Shakespeare or Schiller, Pushkin or Tchaikovsky, the new individual in training would rehearse and grow ever more skilled at the newly prioritized terms of social existence, predicated as they were on self-cultivation—for instance, the "love of the arts" (*liubov' k iskusstvu*), the "broad cultural horizon" (*shirokii kul'turnyi gorizont*), and the relentlessly reinforced refrain, "work on one's own self" (*rabota nad soboi*).[26] What is more, in claiming their right of entry into something previously accessible to only a few, this Soviet generation was expected to recognize their privilege by assuming and assimilating some of the already-established codes of aesthetic behavior.

Muzykal'naia istoriia stages and perpetuates this assimilation. The film, which foregrounds listening as its preferred mode of aesthetic engagement, shuttles between the comical and the didactic as it sketches the routes to exceptional receptivity that the newly nurtured Soviet population may (or may not) take. Petya's trajectory, from a dedicated operagoer and taxi driver to the star of a production being staged at a major opera house, demonstrates the potential outcome of successful assimilation. It is his willingness to assimilate, to let time-honored knowledge in, that paves his road to triumph. His often-comical naïveté, which makes him vulnerable to his rival's scheming and nearly costs him his romance, just as surely enables his progress toward his higher calling. With nothing to hold him back, Petya soaks up his repertory, duly abides by his mentor's decrees, and promptly accepts his co-workers' initiative to enroll in the conservatory.

As if to prove the new rule, the failure to assimilate the new aesthetic imperative receives its own satirical space in the film. Klava's ancillary wooer (the film's only villain, played by the veteran comedian Erast Garin) is Petya's nearly perfect opposite. "My behind-the-times parents gave me a vulgar [*poshloe*] name: Fyodor," he confesses to Klava during the dance he has just stolen from Petya at the Polar Ball, "but I've changed it, and now I go by the beautiful foreign name Alfreood."[27] It is the foreignness (i.e., the perceptual distance) of this ostensibly operatic identity that governs the whole of Alfred's behavior. Just like his name, his every utterance smacks of forgery. "I enjoy working on myself," Alfred boasts to Klava at the ball, pilfering the freshest Soviet maxim. "From five to six I dine, and from six to eight I work on myself," he goes on, turning the trendy tenet into a genuine counterfeit. His portrayal of self-cultivation—here likened to a dinner and safely circumscribed in time—already flouts the anticipated continuity and purposefulness of self-work. But what ultimately marks Alfred as an outsider is his inability to take pleasure in the incalculable, the sublime—in this case, the music. As much as he is attuned to fancy words, Alfred is deaf to musical sounds. The first time he appears on screen (in Klava's office), he immediately switches off the radio broadcast of *Carmen*. Halting the opera half note (a gesture amplified by Klava's startled "Why?"), Alfred is already revealed as the film's wrongdoer, whose later plotting against Petya comes as little surprise. (For example, he comes to the Club of Auto Transport Workers premiere not to listen to the music but to break up Petya and Klava.) His refusal to engage with the aesthetic renders him socially hopeless.[28] This verdict is sealed in the film's very last episode, when we see that all of the characters have progressed in their lives in one way or another—all, that is, but Alfred, who is still the same unmoved taxi driver chasing clients at the opera theater's doors.

Klava's evolution is paralleled by her engagement with music, but ironically, her relationship with Petya is threatened by Petya's growing dedication to the opera. As much as the music draws the two together, Petya's drastic and sudden increase in his appreciation for the art sets off a chain of misunderstandings needed to move the film's plot forward. The presence of Klava's other pursuer satisfies the structural requirements of a love triangle, yet here it is the opera, rather than the suitor, that represents the real threat—the third point in the triangle—to their relationship.

But of course (as was foreshadowed in the film's beginning), Klava ultimately passes the test. Her rise to purposeful listening is also, in effect, her own path to romantic contentment. She is repeatedly shown courting music: tuning in to a live opera radio broadcast, bathed in the sound of Petya's singing on their lakeside date, or duly attending the Club of Auto Transport Workers' premiere. However, it is not until we see Klava actively moved by what she hears—that is, until she emerges as a conspicuous and conscientious classical music consumer—that her story approaches its happy ending. The breakthrough happens after the main couple's breakup (during which Petya goes to train at the conservatory), when Klava, having not seen or heard Petya for an undefined period of time, suddenly hears his voice on the radio in a live opera broadcast.[29] She rushes from her faraway suburb to the theater in the city center, and her path is finally revealed as converging with Petya's as she waits backstage for him to finish his stellar performance. The complementariness of their allegiance to his now-mastered craft—the allegiance that needs to be openly, operatically, optimistically displayed—finally certifies Petya and Klava as a true couple.

The couple's felicitous coming together, the film's final climactic event, is a personal and concrete representation of the broader symbiosis running throughout *Muzykal'naia istoriia*, namely that between the makers and the recipients of classical music. Indeed, nearly every musical performance in the film is followed and paired with an act of listening; and each listener (save for Alfred) is, sooner or later, shown to have been transformed by the performance. We witness performers performing, yes, but so, too, do we see their listeners actively listening: whether enjoying or disliking, relating or rebuffing, all of them are interacting with what they are hearing. In the end, this double focus on reception as well as production, which underwrites the film's aesthetic regime, is what makes *Muzykal'naia istoriia* distinct, on some fundamental level, from the musicals of *Volga-Volga*'s vintage.

The musical comedies of Alexandrov and Dunaevsky showcased the fantastical productiveness of Soviet talent and so celebrated the Soviet nation as an essentially fertile, resilient, and vast social force. The theme songs in *Circus* ("How Broad Is My Country") and *Volga-Volga* ("The Song of the Volga") not only put certain tenets of Soviet ideology to music but also exemplified those tenets' conceptual import. Above any one particular musical style, variously extemporized upon in the course of their films, eminently paraphraseable—that is, always ready to be sung along to—these songs transmitted and reproduced something beyond their concrete musical mold: the numinous, transubstantiating awe of Soviet togetherness.

The canonical musical fare of *Muzykal'naia istoriia*, in contrast, hardly allowed for stylistic variation. What it offered instead was an established repository of mediated feeling—that is, an already-constituted form of togetherness. Growing into Tchaikovsky's Lensky, one of romantic opera's most cherished dreamers, revelers, and gentle sufferers, Petya inhabited and habituated what Richard Taruskin has described as the "finely calculated filter of musical genres and conventions" with which the composer set the scale and defined the scope of his protagonists' humanity.[30] By 1940, the year of Tchaikovsky's grandly and widely celebrated centenary, these finely filtered conventions, which spoke to (and for) the urbane sensibilities of the composer's social peers, had been publicly deemed to capture the "all-human emotional significance," rendering their generic associations with the aristocracy ostensibly beside the point.[31] Finding the root of its repertorial resilience in the "shared meaningfulness" (*obshcheznachimost'*) of *Eugene Onegin*'s "intonationally democratic" and hence still "emotionally effective" range of lyricism, the eminent Soviet musicologist Boris Asafiev ascertained the most fundamental level of the opera's contemporaneous appeal: the experiential resonance between its "finely tuned musical fabric" (*chutkaia muzykal'naia tkan'*) and its listeners' "susceptible" (*volnuemoe*) ear.[32] This alliance between particular musical substances and their hearers' perceptions of them, the proto-semiotic kernel of Asafiev's validation, was the very aesthetic imperative reproduced in the plotlines and actions of *Muzykal'naia istoriia*.[33] Propelled by, redoubling, and also thematizing the sympathetic economy of *Eugene Onegin*, this musical comedy celebrated emotional, rather than ideological, cohesion as a rightful communal unifier. The territory of affect mapped out in the romantic opera of Bizet or Tchaikovsky had been trodden with marked success in late-imperial productions and was resurfacing in the film as a new common social ground. The expression of Petya's personal drama demanded the same sort of reciprocity that had for years been accorded to his Lensky's operatic plight—both were shown, to use Richard Dyer's formulation, to be "related to ordinary and familiar, albeit generally unarticulated, aspects of sentient life, to the eddies of unprompted mood that constantly accompany us, to the differing intensities of our experience of the nameable emotions, and to the way we feel what we feel."[34] Unlike in earlier musical comedies, this film's spectators were invited not to sing along but rather to *feel* along with its characters as they feel along with the music: on either side of the screen, Petya's audiences were bound to be moved by his singing.[35]

That must have been the effect felt (and approved of) by the theater critic Efim Dobin, whose article in the journal *Iskusstvo i zhizn'* (Art and Life, 1940) later that year tackled the film's musicality in more depth than the earlier newspaper reviews. "This picture is very musical," Dobin wrote, echoing the already established position, "but do not take this as a tautology in relation to a musical film. This film's musicality is one of a higher order. The music does not enter the film as a mere raw material, but it merges harmoniously with the film's very essence. The penetrating lyricism of Tchaikovsky . . . is brought alive by the atmosphere of love that the film's youth feels for the music. . . . Sincere is their fondness for Petya, sincere is their love for his enchanting voice."[36] What made *Muzykal'naia istoriia* doubly musical for this critic was the concurrence he sensed between the film's musical sentiment and its characters' manifestations of affection—both perceived as essential and innate, as aspects of the same natural circuit of (or formulation of) feeling. While that circuit—Dobin's higher order—defined the scope of the film's togetherness, Petya, the source and the center of lyrical lines, lyrical singing, and lyrical listening, served as that togetherness's measuring stick. His was the scale that determined his friends' humanity, and his story cemented their communal bond.

A definitive test of this bond occurs near the film's turning point, when Petya's Orphic abilities temporarily go awry. We are in the thick of the *Eugene Onegin* premiere at the Club of Auto Transport Workers, about to witness what is possibly the opera's most stirring scene: the duel in the second act between Onegin and Lensky. As Petya prepares for his toughest challenge thus far, his life and his opera converge once again: before being fatally shot in *Onegin*, he is struck mute offstage by Alfred who (falsely) reveals to him that Klava never wants to see him again. Once on stage, the doubly heartbroken "Lensky" cannot start his most famous aria. We see the orchestra starting and halting and starting again; we hear the prompter repeating the aria's opening words—"Kuda, kuda . . ." (Whither, whither [whither have you fled, the golden days of my spring?])—but nothing seems to stir our hero, who is deeply frozen in his melancholy. Then something astonishing happens: the camera catches one spectator's worried face, his lips spewing out "Kuda, kuda," and then another's; quite a few more join in; even a stage technician is frantically tossing prompts from the wings at the flustered "Lensky." For a brief moment, the keen, involved, and unwavering audience hijacks the performance, their escalating desperation filling the void of Lensky's—or is it Petya's?—unsung melodrama (see figure 11.3).

However spectacular in and of itself, this takeover is qualified by the film's central lyrical drama that never stops unfolding. And in the absence of music, the cinematography takes over the lyrical thread. The hall's escalating anxiety comes into sight by way of a shot–reverse shot succession, initiated as a ballet of glances between Petya and Klava, the unsuspecting culprit of his immobilization. But the reverse shots of the film's central couple are interspersed with a medley of other reverse-shot liaisons, all in medium close-up. The same visual strategy—a cliché of an on-screen romance—links Petya not only with Klava but also with his distraught mother, with his worried conductor Vasily Fomich, with the panicking prompter, and with all those unspecified women and men from the audience whose despair at our hero's imminent failure, and whose love for a certain Tchaikovsky, appears just as deep as that of his closest kin.

Thus the film definitively articulated a renewed ideal of Soviet social attachment. The latest communal bond, rather than conveying the shared enthusiasm for the incredible future, dwelled in the present informed by the usable past. Circumscribed by romantic music, this social union approximated a romantic relationship: symbiotic, affectionate, at once turbulent and exhilarating. Feeling continued to star in Soviet musical comedy after *Muzykal'naia istoriia*. The title alone of Petrov and Ivanovsky's next film, which fused classical music and classical operetta, *Anton Ivanovich serditsia* (Anton Ivanovich Is Upset, 1941), communicated a permission to be vulnerable, even if on a strictly personal scale. In

Figure 11.3. Communal prompting (*from left to right*): Petya lost for words; Klava; a stage worker; the prompter; Petya's mother and sister; worried spectators. (All from *Muzykal'naia istoriia*).

a similar vein, Alexandrov and Dunaevsky moved from effect to affect in their postwar collaboration, *Vesna* (Spring, 1947), whose characters waxed lyrical on the joys of spring rather than the vastness of their motherland, elevating ostensibly human-size sentiments. Alexandrov's next—and last—musical film, *Kompositor Glinka* (The Composer Glinka, 1953), a lavish color biopic of the progenitor of nineteenth-century Russian romantic opera, integrated the lyrical strain of

Muzykal'naia istoriia with Alexandrov's trademark effervescence. But that integration already marked a different era, one in which romantic facade was a sign of the regime's imperviousness to alternative modes of sentience, musical or otherwise.

Notes

1. M. L'vov, "*Muzykal'naya istoriia,*" *Pravda,* October 18, 1940, 3.
2. A. Aleksandrov, "Muzykal'naia istoriia," *Izvestiia,* October 18, 1940, 2. Characteristically, neither review mentions the latest Soviet Cinderella movie, Grigori Alexandrov's *Svetlyi put'* (A Radiant Path, 1940), which was released mere weeks before *Muzykal'naia istoriia.* Also billed as a musical comedy, the film staged a yet different articulation of the storied plotline. See Anna Wexler Katsnelson, "The Tramp in a Skirt: Laboring the Radiant Path," *Slavic Review* 70, no. 2 (summer 2011): 256–78.
3. L'vov, "*Muzykal'naya istoriia,*" 3; Aleksandrov, "Muzykal'naia istoriia," 2.
4. On the proliferation and the role of Soviet musicals in the 1930s, see in particular David C. Gillespie, "The Sounds of Music: Soundtrack and Song in Soviet Film," *Slavic Review* 62, no. 3 (autumn 2003): 473–90; Richard Taylor, "Singing on the Steppes for Stalin: Ivan Pyr'ev and the Kolkhoz Musical in Soviet Cinema," *Slavic Review* 58, no. 1 (spring 1999): 143–59; Richard Taylor, "K topografii utopii v stalinskom miuzikle" (A Topography of Utopia in Stalinist Musical), and Katerina Clark, "'Chtoby tak pet', dvadtsat' let uchit'sia nuzhno: Sluchai *Volgi-Volgi*" (To Sing Like That You Have to Study for Twenty Years: A Case of *Volga-Volga*), both in *Sovetskoe bogatstvo. Stat'i o kul'ture, literatura i kino* (The Soviet Treasure: Articles on Culture, Literature, and Cinema), ed. Marina Balina, Evgeny Dobrenko, and Yury Murashov (St. Petersburg: Academic Project, 2002), 358–70 and 371–90, respectively; Rimgaila Salys, *The Musical Comedy Films of Grigorii Aleksandrov: Laughing Matters* (Bristol, UK: Intellect, 2009).
5. See Peter Kupfer, "Music, Ideology, and Entertainment in the Soviet Musical Comedies of Grigory Aleksandrov and Isaak Dunayevsky," PhD diss., University of Chicago, 2010.
6. The transcript of this discussion is housed at RGALI, d. 2450, op. 2, ed. khran. 939.
7. RGALI, d. 2450, op. 2, ed. khran. 939.
8. RGALI, d. 2450, op. 2, ed. khran. 939.
9. Bizet's *Carmen,* whose title character was a Gypsy tobacco-factory worker, was frequently staged in Moscow and Leningrad beginning in the early 1920s. Starting in the mid-1930s, the opera spread to more distant Soviet stages, including ones in Kharkov (1936), Kiev (1939), and Baku (1939).
10. Rick Altman, *The American Film Musical* (Bloomington: Indiana University Press, 1997), 210.
11. On Stalinist master narrative, see Katerina Clark, *The Soviet Novel: History as Ritual,* 3rd ed. (Bloomington: Indiana University Press, 2000).
12. Kupfer, "Music, Ideology, and Entertainment," 223.
13. On the newly made-over classical operas in the 1930s, see Marina Frolova-Walker, "The Soviet Opera Project: Ivan Dzerzhinsky vs. *Ivan Susanin,*" in *Cambridge Opera Journal* 18, no. 2 (July 2006): 181–216.
14. On the association between opera soloists and the notion of sincerity, see Anna Fishzon, "The Operatics of Everyday Life, or, How Authenticity Was Defined in Late Imperial Russia," in *Slavic Review* 70, no. 1 (winter 2011): 795–818.

15. Kornei Chukovskii, "Sobinov," in *Sovremenniki. Portrety i etiudy* (My Contemporaries: Portraits and Studies) (Moscow: Molodaia gvardiia, 1961), 377–82.

16. Sobinov received his "soloist" title in 1913, the year of the tercentenary of the house of Romanov, and the "People's Artist of RSFSR" only a decade later, in 1923. He also would have been decorated with the title "the People's Artist of the USSR" had he not died two years before the institution of the award.

17. Between 1934 and 1940 more than twenty brochures or articles in leading journals were dedicated to or included a discussion of Sobinov.

18. On the construction of the artistic and historical pantheon in the 1930s, see Kevin M. F. Platt and David Brandenberger, eds., *Epic Revisionism: Russian History and Literature as Stalinist Propaganda* (Madison: University of Wisconsin Press, 2006).

19. These had already become the signifying features of the character when lyric tenor Sergei Lemeshev, possibly the most celebrated of all Soviet Lenskys, was cast as Petya. Sobinov served as a model for the majority of Soviet tenors. There is, however, no mention of contemporaneous music-theater personalities in the film (save for the fictional characters who warrant nothing but criticism).

20. See S. Lemeshev *Put' k iskusstvu* (Road to Art) (Moscow: Iskusstvo, 1968).

21. Lemeshev's life was not, in fact, a prototype for the film's script. According to the film's director Alexander Ivanovsky, the lead scriptwriter Evgeny Petrov initially saw Petya as played and sung by Ivan Kozlovsky, another famous tenor of the time. See A. V. Ivanovskii, *Vospominaniia kinorezhissyora* (The Reminiscences of a Film Director) (Moscow: Iskusstvo, 1967), 235–42.

22. This minor character is the director of the club in which the amateur *Eugene Onegin* premieres, and he is brought into the picture specifically to utter his "programmatic" phrase during the performance's intermission.

23. The refreshed interest in and promulgation of the notion of world culture in the 1930s is detailed in Katerina Clark, *Moscow, the Fourth Rome: Stalinism, Cosmopolitanism, and the Evolution of Soviet Culture, 1931–1941* (Cambridge, MA: Harvard University Press, 2011), esp. chap. 5 ("'World Literature'/'World Culture' and the Era of the Popular Front (c. 1935–1936)."

24. Catriona Kelly and David Shepherd, eds., *Constructing Russian Culture in the Age of Revolution: 1881–1940* (Oxford: Oxford University Press, 1998), 300. See also Vadim Volkov, "The Concept of *Kul'turnost'*: Notes of the Stalinist Civilizing Process," in *Stalinism: New Directions*, ed. Sheila Fitzpatrick (London: Routledge, 2000), 210–30.

25. The return of the aesthetic as a socialist value is discussed in Clark's *Moscow, the Fourth Rome*, see esp. chap. 3 ("The Return of the Aesthetic").

26. In his "The Concept of *Kul'turnost'*," Volkov details the scope of the knowledge that certified Soviet individuals as cultured (see 223–25). A central practice on the way of becoming truly cultured was to "work on yourself," which mainly entailed studying and thereby assimilating a broad repertory of literary, musical, and fine-art works.

27. On the new fashion of changing names in the 1930s, see Sheila Fitzpatrick, *Everyday Stalinism: Ordinary Life in Extraordinary Times—Soviet Russian in the 1930s* (New York: Oxford University Press, 1999), esp. 83–84. In *Muzykal'naia istoriia*, however, this tendency is satirized precisely on the grounds of its "insincere" exoticism.

28. In a darker, more historically informed interpretation circa 1940, the split between the antagonist's politically correct outside and his scheming interior would render him not merely worthless but also blatantly harmful. However, as a comedy, the film reroutes this possibility.

29. The opera is Rimsky-Korsakov's *May Night*, and Petya performs the part of Levko. The film's original script by Evgenii Petrov had Lensky's last aria from Tchaikovsky's *Eugene Onegin* slotted for this scene. However, the film's directors decided to change the final musical number, maintaining that Lensky's swan song was hardly fit for a comedy's happy ending.

30. Richard Taruskin, *Defining Russia Musically* (Princeton, NJ: Princeton University Press, 1997), 54.

31. Akademik B. V. Asaf'ev, *"Evgenii Onegin," liricheskie stseny P. I. Chaikovskogo* (Moscow: Muzgiz, 1944), 12. See also Igor' Glebov (Asaf'ev's pen name), *Pamiati Petra Il'icha Chaikovskogo, 1840–1940* (Moscow: Muzgiz, 1940), in which the author likens Tchaikovsky to Shakespeare and Tolstoy precisely on the grounds of what he sees as their universal emotional appeal.

32. Asaf'ev, *"Evgenii Onegin,"* 2, 11. Asafiev describes the range of genres and conventions manipulated by Tchaikovsky as "интонационно-демократический комплекс городской песенно-романсной лирики" (intonationally democratic range of urban lyrical song and romance). *Eugene Onegin* is not the only constituent of the film's borrowed sound track. No matter their provenance, however, all other excerpts fall squarely within the same stylistic and generic range as Tchaikovsky's opera. The song Petya sings to Klava during their lakeside date is "Metelitsa," a romance in a folk style (music by Alexander Varlamov [1801–48] and lyrics by Dmitrii Glebov [1789–1843]). During his conservatory examination, Petya performs "Ah so fromm" ("Angel moi") from Friedrich von Flotow's opera *Martha* (1847). The aria "Spi, moia krasavitsa" (Sleep, My Beautiful One) from Rimsky-Korsakov's *May Night* that Petya performs at the film's end is another lyrical strophic piece in a quasi-folk style.

33. Speaking of the "substance" or "fabric" of music in his multiple historical studies, Asafiev generally blurs the distinction between musical score and musical performance, approaching a musical "work" as a process-driven phenomenon. That is why I likewise make no distinction here between Tchaikovsky's music as it "is" and as it "is performed," siding, for the sake of my argument, with Asafiev's abstract phenomenology.

34. Richard Dyer, "Side by Side: Nino Rota, Music, and Film," in *Beyond the Soundtrack: Representing Music in Cinema*, ed. Daniel Goldmark, Lawrence Kramer, and Richard Leppert (Berkeley: University of California Press, 2007), 249. For Dyer's now-classic take on the nonrepresentational level of feelings in musical, see his "Entertainment and Utopia," in *Only Entertainment*, 2nd ed. (London: Routledge, 2002), 19–35.

35. On socialist "feelings," see Emma Widdis's chapter 5, in this volume.

36. E. Dobin, *"Muzykal'naia istoriia," Iskusstvo i zhizn'* 10 (October 1940): 33.

12 The Music of Landscape

Eisenstein, Prokofiev, and the Uses of Music in Ivan the Terrible

Joan Neuberger

SERGEI EISENSTEIN WROTE repeatedly about sound and music in cinema, from his contribution to the collective "Statement on Sound," co-authored with Vsevolod Pudovkin and Grigori Alexandrov in 1928, through his discussion of audiovisual cinema and "vertical montage" in the montage essays of 1938 to 1940, to his late-1940s articles on Sergei Prokofiev, and color and sound.[1] Each of these built on the earlier work and confirmed his original commitment to sound as an active element in film art rather than a naturalistic underpinning for realism or affect. From his initial insistence on sound "as a new element of montage," Eisenstein developed increasingly complex multimedia, multisensory ideas about the ways sound contributed to producing meaning and experience for film viewers.

In this regard, it is surprising that more attention has not been paid to his eponymous chapter in *Nonindifferent Nature*, subtitled "The Music of Landscape and the Fate of Montage Counterpoint at a New Stage."[2] In that chapter, music is less a subject for analysis than it is the reigning metaphor for his current understanding of the structures of artistic composition. Written in 1944 and 1945, while editing part 1 of *Ivan Groznyi* (Ivan the Terrible, part 1, 1944; part 2, 1958] and finishing part 2, Eisenstein developed his earlier thoughts on montage and the "montage image," incorporating many of the insights he gained through work on the film.[3] The subject matter expanded far beyond the role of film sound and montage counterpoint, however, to explore the structures of artistic composition that make it possible to communicate thought and feeling in art and elicit responses from the audience. In short, Eisenstein argued that for a work of art to achieve universality and immortality, its composition must, first of all, correspond to our physical and psychological structures of feeling and cognition.[4] The artist must be able to break down a subject or idea into constitutive parts that are resonant with one another in multiple ways that then allow the viewer to reconstitute the parts into a new, higher, unified emotional and intellectual experience. That synthetic unity, which he called the "montage image," contained an abstract understanding of the subject at hand that derives from the process of joining disparate elements:

> Montage counterpoint as a form seems to correspond to that fascinating stage of the evolution of consciousness, when both preceding stages have been overcome, and the universe, dissected by analyses, is recreated once again into a single whole, revives by means of connections and interactions of separate parts, and appears as an excited perception of the fullness of the world perceived synthetically.[5]

Eisenstein found this "principle of unity in variety" in nature, in Chinese landscape painting, in select scenes from *Bronenosets Potemkin* (Battleship Potemkin, 1925), and in *Ivan the Terrible,* to name a few of the main examples he analyzes in this chapter. The processes of fragmentation and subsequent reconstruction into a higher unity grew out of Eisenstein's earlier ideas and practices, but he also found examples of such thinking about the abstract and the concrete in a typically diverse range of sources, from the painter Juan Gris to Edgar Allan Poe, Vladimir Mayakovsky, and Alfred Hitchcock.[6]

In *Nonindifferent Nature,* unity in variety is first of all discussed in emotional-cognitive terms. For example, *Ivan the Terrible* differs from previous films in that it represents a "knitting together into a more compact fabric" that does not revert to pre-montage cinema but rather develops montage from the mere juxtaposition of shots to what he calls "perceptible montage," or the accumulation of various kinds of sense responses into multifaceted, audiovisual images.[7] He sometimes calls this process of perception "synaesthesia," which he defines here as "the ability to gather *into one, all the variety of feeling brought from different areas by different organs of sensation.*"[8] What makes it possible to gather all this diverse material into one unified work is a structure of underlying emotional resonances:

> [M]ainly, it is necessary that everything, beginning from the actor's performance and ending with the play of the folds of his clothes, be equally immersed in the sound of that single, increasingly defined emotion that lies at the basis of the polyphony of a whole multifaceted composition.[9]

The key phrase here is the "sound of . . . emotion," a more traditional use of the concept of synesthesia understood as an involuntary neurological condition that activates multiple senses when only one sense is stimulated. Synesthetes might perceive numbers as associated with specific colors or colors associated with specific feelings. Throughout "The Music of Landscape," Eisenstein discusses the ways that artists have composed their works to simulate synesthetic responses in viewers. The text then also becomes an example of synesthesia, by using musical metaphors to talk about emotions, perception, responses to visual images, and unity in variety. Eisenstein's use of musical terminology is always more metaphorical than musicological; he uses the language of music to equate various structures of the visual arts and differentiate them from narrative and verbal arts. So, for example, in his discussion of unity in variety, Eisenstein writes that great works of art are structured like "a distinctive orchestra of [the] parts independently composing it."[10] He goes on to say that such unity is possible only when the diverse pieces are linked "tonally." Each shot has to be perfectly calibrated, in the same way that music "tonally expresses what is inexpressible in words." He never tells us specifically what he means by "tonal" expression in the non-audio parts of audiovisual montage, but he gives several hints and examples. "The changing figure of Ivan is expressed tonally throughout the film by the play of the actor's contour, the framing of the shot, and above all by the miracle of tonal photography of the cameraman Moskvin."[11] Here, "tone" represents Moskvin's subtle manipulation of the gradations of light as if they were notes on a scale, deployed to determine the register of emotional response. In fact, Eisenstein considers Moskvin's lighting itself to be musical. His "intonations of light" permeate the film, "echo[ing], from episode to episode, both the emotional mood of a scene and the emotional state of the tsar-protagonist."[12] In his article on Prokofiev, Eisenstein calls this form of synesthesia "the emotional-visual and semantic sensation of the event" (*emotsional'no-obraznoe i smyslovoe oshchushchenie*).[13]

Eisenstein had been writing about responses to the visual, and even the audiovisual, aspects of film in similar ways since at least the mid-1930s, so why does he suddenly choose to use musical language to write about such visual matters as the folds of cloth, lighting techniques, landscape painting, and color? There is no definitive way to answer this question, but the various possibilities are suggestive. Eisenstein had always been interested in those aspects of artistic production and reception associated with feelings or, in general, responses that are difficult to put in words. For the previous decade he was preoccupied with the ways that people seem to have continual access to their earliest, most intuitive ways of being, their earliest forms of perception. He imagined this state to be a wordless, formless, unified sense of ecstasy and freedom from form that he called the prelogical. Because visual images produce effects that are so much more amorphous than verbal images, and because they have effects that we register in our bodies or in our feelings, Eisenstein saw a direct connection between the visual arts and this prelogical state. In revisiting *Potemkin* while making *Ivan*, he was struck by the way that landscape was the element of film "least burdened with servile, narrative tasks," free therefore to convey pure feeling, and in this way share much with music, "with its hazily perceptible, flowing imagery."[14] Freed from character or storytelling, both music and landscape have the capacity of *"emotionally expressing what is inexpressible by other means."*[15]

When he was first writing about audiovisual or vertical montage, Eisenstein had not quite appreciated this degree of the "plasticity" of music or the very intricate ways that such plasticity allowed it to be blended with the visual, synesthetically, to create a rich, multisensory "montage image" that could be called polyphonic. This leads to the second point I want to make, which is that his profound satisfaction with Prokofiev's score for *Ivan the Terrible* seems to have enhanced his appreciation for the ways music contributed to the multisensory possibilities of cinema. Eisenstein had more control over the direction and uses of the score in *Ivan* than he'd had in *Alexander Nevsky* (1938), his first collaboration with Prokofiev. He was able to experiment with various strategies for using the music to enrich the polyphonic, synesthetic elements of montage. Although he referred more than once to *Ivan* as a project that brought him more pain than joy, his appreciation for Prokofiev's contribution to the film was genuine, deep, and productive.

Eisenstein wrote a great deal about his work with Prokofiev, which is both a blessing and a curse. It is a blessing to have, in his own words, a record of the role he wanted music to play, how music enriched his conception of polyphonic montage, and how he and Prokofiev together produced a score that could be so carefully synchronized with the visuals. It is a curse because Eisenstein's version of their collaboration is so compelling that one can all too easily believe that everyone involved viewed it the same way. New work by musicologists Simon Morrison and Kevin Bartig allows us to better see things from Prokofiev's point of view.[16] They show that, although the two artists remained good friends until Eisenstein's death in 1948, their collaboration was not always as easy as Eisenstein suggests. And while everyone agrees that Prokofiev was content to fulfill the director's vision of the film, Bartig shows that Prokofiev brought a great deal of independent musical knowledge to the project, with which he introduced additional layers of meaning through references to previous compositions.[17]

Eisenstein and Prokofiev's artistic collaboration succeeded against steep odds. The horrific conditions of wartime and transient exile interfered with production more than once, as did equipment failure and major illnesses suffered by both artists at the worst possible times. Yet the engaging, complex, and satisfying music that resulted makes *Ivan the Terrible* one of the greatest artistic collaborations of the twentieth century. As David Bordwell notes, music plays an especially prominent role in *Ivan the Terrible*.[18] It is miraculously well attuned, emotionally and structurally, to the scenes in which it appears and to Eisenstein's overall conception of cinematic polyphony. That attunement allows the music to enhance the emotional impact and thematic development of many scenes while providing emotional and thematic counterpoint to others. Musical cues offer continuity across the three hours of parts 1 and 2 by linking characters, scenes, and themes through the use of leitmotifs, sometimes in quite unexpected ways.

In every single scored scene, the music plays a significant role in producing the "swarm of lyric visions and representations" that makes up the montage image.[19] Eisenstein tells us how he thinks the composer succeeded in doing this:

> Prokofiev has the ability to "hear" in sounds the plastic visual depiction, [which] makes it possible for him to construct amazing aural equivalents of the visual depictions that fall in his field of vision. . . . In this particular sense, Prokofiev's music is surprisingly plastic, nowhere remaining mere illustration, but everywhere sparkling with jubilant figuration [*torzhestvuiushchei obraznost'iu*]; it reveals in amazing ways the internal movement of a phenomenon and its dynamic structure, which embody the emotion and meaning of the event.[20]

It is worth pausing here to note that Eisenstein uses a visual lexicon to identify the qualities of Prokofiev's music: plastic, depiction, illustration, and figuration. Reflecting here on the success of *Ivan*'s score, Eisenstein writes in the same synesthetic terms he finds so satisfying in the multisensory film. His specific examples are also wonderfully multisensory: the audio and the visual create something more than the sum of their parts. Eisenstein captures Prokofiev as he rehearses the orchestra in a piece that was to have accompanied the first scenes of Ivan's childhood, a lullaby called "*Okean-more, more-sinee*" (Ocean Sea, Deep Blue Sea). As Prokofiev walks "among the swaying bows of the musicians, he seems to be moving through waving feather grass."[21] More important, the individual musicians in the orchestra seem literally to perform the making of a montage image. Prokofiev tells Eisenstein, "This one is playing light gliding over the waves, that one—the swelling waves, this one, vastness and that one—the mysterious depth."[22] What's key here for Eisenstein is that the music does not attempt to copy nature but rather to

> re-create, call to life (but not copy from life) and collectively produce a wonderful image of the vast and boundless ocean, foaming like an impatient charger, heaving stormy breakers, or lying placidly, quietly sleeping, its blueness mottled with patches of sunlight, just as the builder of the Russian state sees it in his dream.[23]

In other words, Prokofiev was capable of composing music that conveyed "ocean blue," not only as a manifestation of nature but also as the color of Ivan's dream of extending the Russian empire to the Baltic Sea.

This is not analytical language. Eisenstein's passage helps us understand what it means for a visual artist to "think in images" and to translate that thinking into words. He found a near-perfect equivalent in Prokofiev's music for what he was trying to effect with synesthesia in moving pictures. His aim was never to tell a story that could be repeated word for word but rather to take advantage of what he thought were the unique and essential components of cinema: the nonverbal elements that absorb the viewer completely, that speak directly to feeling, and create complex experiences. He sought to understand the inner workings of a phenomenon so that he could break them down into components that could then be translated into episodes, images, and now sounds, which would produce in viewers the exact emotional and cognitive responses necessary to reconstruct the phenomenon in a way that created new emotional and intellectual experiences for them, new ways to understand the world. In this case, the montage image that Eisenstein described above was meant to be the "blueness of the ocean [that] is not merely the color of the sky reflected in its depth, but the color of the dream."[24] Note two things about this summary statement. First, Eisenstein might have been content to say that the blue of the ocean represented the color of the dream, but he can't resist making a little montage here: the dream equals sky *plus* ocean. Second, he does resist linking that dream with the overall narrative or even with Ivan's character or his situation at the time of the dream. This particular piece of music was to be played first when Ivan was a small child; it would only later come to represent his dream of a modern state. As a child, Ivan's future dreams were pure and simple—to reach the blue ocean—but nothing in Eisenstein's story remains pure or simple for long.

Neither Eisenstein nor Prokofiev wrote much about the larger political and moral issues raised in the film.[25] They were both politically cautious men, and there was obviously no advantage in making statements that could be misinterpreted. That said, it is difficult to see the music in *Ivan the Terrible* as glorifying Ivan or justifying mass murder in some simple or propagandistic way, as Richard Taruskin and many others have argued.[26] On the contrary, there is much to suggest that it serves the opposite purpose. That is not to say that Prokofiev intentionally composed a politically subversive score. He may have been ambivalent, he may have expected his music to be used differently, or he may have had a number of contradictory motives. Eisenstein himself was famous for hiding things in plain sight, which doesn't make it any easier to figure out exactly what he was trying to do. Whatever the explicit intentions of the two artists, the result is a score that challenges the official historiographical portrait of Ivan the Terrible that Eisenstein was expected to follow. That historiography depicted Ivan as the heroic founder of the modern centralized state and justified his use of mass violence for this larger political purpose. According to the official Stalinist interpretation, the establishment of the modern centralized state was worth the mass murder of its reactionary opponents.[27] Eisenstein and Prokofiev did not need to present a direct contradiction to the official historiography in order to challenge it. They only had to complicate the issues involved or suggest that individual motives in history can be contradictory, and that history itself takes unexpected paths, for the film to deviate from the narrative they were expected to follow.

The narrative uses of music are always tricky because, as Eisenstein noted, music is inherently nonnarrative; interpretation, then, depends on conventions.

Some chords are conventionally sad (in a given culture), and some combination of notes and rhythms usually connotes suspense or joy. In *Ivan the Terrible*, conventional sounds like thunderous brass and lyrical strings are often used in surprising ways to undermine the apparent narrative meaning of a scene. For example, the music associated with the poisoning of Ivan's mother is not, as might be expected, repeated during the poisoning of Ivan's wife, Anastasia, but instead returns at unexpected times, undermining conventional narrative expectations and challenging Ivan's justifications for revenge.[28] Bartig has found intertextual references to earlier compositions, by Nikolai Rimsky-Korsakov in particular, that are associated with representations of Ivan that complicate the way he is presented in the surface narrative of the film. Bartig's thorough analysis of the uses of leitmotifs suggests that the score undermines Ivan's specific justifications for his actions.[29] Simon Morrison's insightful analysis of specific uses of music in the film finds that the contradictions raised by the musical counterpoint show that historical and every other kind of logic is so disrupted as to leave human beings "helplessly" subject to the whims of fate.[30] That may be a reasonable interpretation of Prokofiev's *Ivan,* but it does not correspond to the film Eisenstein, a firm believer in patterns of human behavior, thought he was making. Kristin Thompson's careful taxonomy of sound-image relations in *Ivan* shows how the music at times fused closely with visual images and at other times contributed to patterns of temporal disruptions and discontinuities, but she claims that these had no political purpose.[31] Katherine Ossorgin, however, has found extensive narrative challenges in the original liturgical music and texts (not composed by Prokofiev) used in the film.[32] I agree with Bartig that it is exceptionally difficult to know how Prokofiev intended his music to be used or whether his supplements to Eisenstein's instructions were intended to challenge Ivan's legitimacy. In the end, it was Eisenstein, rather than Prokofiev, who was responsible for the way music and visuals combined in the film to create the montage image.

The examination of a single scene serves to demonstrate the ways Eisenstein used the score to effect a polyphonic and synesthetic montage image with subtle but discernible moral and political purpose. I also explore the ways Prokofiev's compositions are particularly well suited to this method of producing "emotional-visual and semantic meaning." In "P-R-K-F-V," Eisenstein wrote:

> What should not be lost sight of is the circumstance that the structure of the separate pieces shot for any scene is not accidental. . . . If a piece is a truly "montage" one, that is, not disconnected but meant to produce an image together with other pieces, it will, at the very moment it is shot, be infused with elements which characterize its inner essence and at the same time contain the seeds of the structure most suited for the fullest possible revelation of this essence in the finished compositional form.[33]

In addition to uncovering the source of its emotional and visual power, I would like to show what kind of "inner essence" is revealed in the nonverbal images and sounds, how they might move the story along, illuminate character, and create and complicate narrative meaning, all of which comment on the moral and political themes of the film.

There are two kinds of music in *Ivan the Terrible*: cues that occur only once, marking the character of specific scenes, and leitmotifs that are associated with themes or characters or events, the repetition of which links these various parts of the film in thematically revealing ways. The most impressive of these leitmotifs, and the one most often commented on, is the theme we hear first, during the credits, introducing Ivan and demonstrating his power. Another motif is associated with the poisoning of Ivan's mother, the single most important event in igniting Ivan's desire for revenge against the boyars. But there are several other leitmotifs that comment more slyly on the action through their combination and placement in the film. Especially interesting in this regard is the combination of motifs used in the short but pivotal scene in part 1 where Ivan's aunt and rival for power, Efrosinia Staritskaya, poisons Anastasia, Ivan's wife.[34]

At the end of the previous scene, we find Ivan sitting alone and reflecting. He has just finished a long day of tsarist business and seems to be feeling somewhat overwhelmed by the weight of power. He leans back, wrapping his ceremonial fur cloak around himself, as the camera cuts first to a close-up of a tapestry depicting the Holy Mother and Child and then to his wife, Anastasia, resting in bed, both of which seem to be images in Ivan's mind's eye. This juxtaposition suggests that he is meditating on an inner conflict between the public burden of ruling and the private comfort of his wife's company. Later he tells us he is divided over continuing his mission to centralize power in Russia in the face of growing opposition.

At the end of this scene, we hear the leitmotif that Thompson and Bartig identify as the "bright" version of the Ivan power theme, featuring high lyrical strings and woodwinds. This is one of the more obscure leitmotifs in that its associations (and interpretations) seem to vary considerably. Its meaning becomes clearer if we remember that Eisenstein and Prokofiev considered this the inverse of Ivan's power theme.[35] As I have argued elsewhere, one of the main structures underlying Eisenstein's conception of Ivan's persona and behavior is a public-private dialectic. His motives for acting against his enemies are always equal parts personal and political.[36] Ivan's conflicts between public and private, and indeed between wholeness and division, signaled by the inner monologue and the leitmotif, are further accentuated visually by the objects Eisenstein places around Ivan. The most prominent among these objects is a contraption of intersecting metal rings that casts huge shadows on the wall—an armillary sphere, used since ancient times to chart the movement of celestial bodies. The armillary sphere may have various associations in the film,[37] but on a purely visual level, circles are conventionally associated with wholes, a contrast with Ivan's own sense of inner division. Division is also conveyed by Ivan's dress. When he gets up from his desk to go to Anastasia, moving from his public to his private realm, Ivan

Figure 12.1. Screen capture from *Ivan the Terrible, Part 1* (Ivan Groznyi, dir. Eisenstein, 1945).

conspicuously slings his fur cloak, the symbol of tsarist power, half on and half off his body. In this context, the lyrical theme we hear in this scene isn't so much the soft, "bright" side of Ivan, in opposition to the hard, thunderous one, as it is the private in contrast to the public. Indeed, the theme recurs in moments when Ivan feels abandoned or alone, having sacrificed personal happiness for his historical mission, or when he is thinking about the burdens and responsibilities of power. It always functions to project Ivan's loneliness forward or backward in time.[38]

The murder scene begins as shots of Anastasia are ambiguously interspersed with shots of Ivan at work. Whether the scenes are in Ivan's mind, are happening unbeknownst to him in another part of the palace, or cleverly foreshadow events to come is unclear. A discordant transitional tone is struck by the appearance of Efrosinia Staritskaya, Ivan's most dangerous enemy. She has already threatened to do away with Anastasia, and the camera cuts to show her looming over the sleeping figure with an unmistakably sinister demeanor (figure 12.1).

At first, this scene seems to present us with a clearly defined good-versus-evil dialectic. But nothing in Eisenstein is ever what it seems. When Ivan finally leaves his office and arrives in the bedchamber, Anastasia is shifting uneasily in bed and Efrosinia is leaving. Ivan embraces his aunt with an inscrutable gesture, and Efrosinia hurries away downstairs but remains hidden in the shadows.

The lyrical "alone" theme has been playing during this whole transition. After Ivan rests his head on his wife, more like child to mother (echoing the tapestry) than husband to wife, the camera pulls back to show the softly lighted bedchamber above and the contrasting shadowed staircase where Efrosinia is hiding and eavesdropping below. The visual contrasts are as stark as the echoes. Anastasia rests amid soft bedclothes, surrounded by chests of overflowing jewels and candlelit tapestry icons: her space is dominated by curves and soft but bright light, suggesting holiness and innocence. In contrast, Efrosinia is a dark, scowling presence, lurking in the shadows, surrounded by hard stone walls and ledges, her face geometrically cut into angles by harsh rays of light, her body covered in black cloth from head to toe. During the course of the scene Ivan moves between the two women. Physically and emotionally volatile, he swings from sadness and affection to anger and fear.

When Ivan speaks, telling Anastasia that he can trust no one except her, the lyrical theme shifts for the first time, sinking into a lower register, and the camera cuts to Efrosinia looking melodramatically evil, more like a fairy tale witch than a high-ranking *boyarina*. When the camera cuts back to the saintly Anastasia and Ivan, the lyrical theme returns to its higher, sweeter register. Suddenly, a messenger dashes in with bad news from the battlefront; the strings increase in tempo, signaling another shift in mood and a note of suspense before stopping abruptly. Ivan is angry that his boyars lack the commitment to defend the motherland (his voice here is singsong, as if transitioning from music to speech and from his heavenly private sphere to the conflict-ridden public.). Anastasia tells him to be tough, and Ivan says he will; at that moment their image rhymes with the beginning of the scene (see figure 12.1), with Ivan now in Efrosinia's place (figure 12.2). For the moment, things are still organized along rather simple binary lines. Then Ivan rises and, leaning over the ledge but without seeing Efrosinia, threatens to take away the land of boyars who won't fight to defend Russia. This prompts several things to happen in quick succession: the messenger flees, flying down the stairs past Efrosinia, who responds to Ivan's threatening ambition with a warning of her own: "Watch your step, Tsar Ivan" (*Shiroko shagaesh' Tsar' Ivan*). From under a dark cloth, she produces a chalice with an embossed *sirin* (a sinister, female, birdlike siren spirit from Russian folklore) and pours poison into it. At this point a brand new piece of music begins (which only appears in one other scene): rhythmic, pulsating strings strike harsh, low, and slightly syncopated beats. The beats slash through the air aggressively, their division of time knifing through space. This is quickly interrupted by a low, almost parodic version of the lyrical "alone" theme, which sounds dark and brooding. That too stops when the tsar's "eye," Malyuta Skuratov, shows up with even worse news.

Malyuta plants himself in the middle of the space, more gargoyle than loyal watchdog (especially since his eyes fail him here). Malyuta announces that Andrei

Figure 12.2. Screen capture from *Ivan the Terrible, Part 1* (Ivan Groznyi, dir. Eisenstein, 1945).

Kurbsky, Ivan's close friend and highest-ranking officer, has been defeated in battle. At this news, Anastasia cries out and faints. The harsh, rhythmic strings pick
up again, just a few accentuating notes at a time, as Ivan rushes to his wife's aid,
blind to her feelings for Kurbsky, who not only tried to seduce the tsar's wife but
also may be guilty of treason. Ivan starts running around, looking for a drink
for his unconscious wife. As Anastasia's virtue slips and Kurbsky's is called into
question, we hear notes sliding down the scale, like someone's reputation slip-
ping into an abyss. It's actually a double slide, pausing partway down and picking
up again, as if marking both disloyalties. Ivan becomes increasingly frantic, and
the harsh strings resume: now sinister low and, at the same time, screechy high
(could that be the siren's call?). Efrosinia steps to the rescue, placing the poisoned
chalice on the ledge that separates her shadowy lair from the bright space above.
Even before Ivan finds it, the harsh strings give way to a brief moment in which
an oboe and strings play a variation of the original, lyrical "alone" theme, before
succumbing again to slow, descending, punctuating beats of those harsh, slashing strings. When Ivan grabs the chalice, he is diagonally aligned with Efrosinia,
joining them as co-murderers (figure 12.3), and the two musical themes alternate
again, more quickly now.

Figure 12.3. Screen capture from *Ivan the Terrible, Part 1* (Ivan Groznyi, dir. Eisenstein, 1945).

At this point, there is less than a minute of film time remaining before Anastasia's demise, but a lot is about to happen. Ivan rushes to Anastasia, and we hear a new little wavering, suspenseful cello phrase. In medium shot, Ivan hands Anastasia the chalice accompanied by a few more of those harsh notes. The camera cuts to Ivan looking up at his wife, with a familiarly worshipful gaze, typical of socialist realism, when ordinary people look at Stalin or gaze into the utopian future with blind devotion; and the harsh notes give way to that suspenseful little cello phrase. Then, in a stylistic device typical of this film, everything stops and runs briefly backward, before returning to the original forward motion. Eisenstein liked to use this kind of nonrealistic discontinuity and doubling to draw attention to important moments. Just as Anastasia is about to drink, she lowers the cup from her lips. Efrosinia pops up from behind the ledge—a seesaw movement, possibly suggesting the reversal to come. At that moment, for the first and only time, Efrosinia's move is accompanied by the original, lyrical "alone" theme, which accentuates her link with Ivan but also foreshadows her own parallel, inverse fate: she, too, will be left alone after her son's murder, for which she, like Ivan, is inadvertently responsible. The pause and reversal gives us a moment to gather our thoughts, register our impressions, consider everyone's fate, or simply to postpone the inevitable, but soon history inexorably moves on. Anastasia drinks from the cup. As she and Ivan lift it together, it blots out her image entirely, and a few more harsh string beats mark the last seconds of her life before giving way to another downward glide, linking her betrayal to her death. Fade to black.

Without knowing any more about the narrative before and after this scene, the music, lighting, chiaroscuro, setting, mise-en-scène, movement, and shot composition function here in accordance with Eisenstein's proposed polyphonic or multilayered dialectic. At the beginning of the scene the viewer is presented with a number of stark contrasts: Anastasia's and Efrosinia's qualities—light-dark, soft-stony, white-black, luxurious-austere—are associated with conventionally logical musical phrases: flowing lyrical or harshly syncopated. As the scene progresses and loyalties are called into question, moral uncertainties multiply, and at times the musical motifs underscore the reversals or suggest unspoken betrayals. In these narrative contexts, the visual and the musical cues add variations, increasing and decreasing in tempo and volume at the same time, moving up and down their scales both in conjunction with the narrative and against it, all of which has one desired effect of ratcheting up the emotional intensity. At the end of the scene, a number of musical and visual cues effect complete reversals, providing a momentary halt that makes the denouement all the more dramatic. One can easily view all this in purely aesthetic and emotional terms: every stylistic and sensory element contributes to the accelerating pace and emotional intensification of the scene; the dialectical conflict is sharpened with each shot of contrasting light and shadow, with each alteration of lyrical and warm musical phrases against the harsh, syncopated strings. But in his writing about the montage image, Eisenstein emphasized the ways that each element contributed to the generalizable abstraction of the episode, to something concrete (or at least something abstract and concrete at the same time). He wrote about an "emotional-visual *and semantic* sensation," and about the ways Prokofiev captured the "emotion and meaning [*smysl*] of the event." What is the point of complicating these dialectics if all this polyphonic business serves no meaning?[39]

As it happens, this scene raises some of the most profound issues dramatized in *Ivan the Terrible*, and the score contributes a sensory version of that narrative. What appears at the beginning as clear-cut conflict between good and evil is considerably murkier a short five minutes later. Throughout *Ivan the Terrible*, we are repeatedly asked to consider whether and in which circumstances killing is justified. Both Ivan and his enemies justify murder on the grounds that they are acting in the name of some greater good. These political murders are sandwiched between scenes of conventional warfare at the beginning and end of the film (in the battles of Kazan and Livonia, respectively), with conventional and widely accepted justifications of killing bracketing more debatable political and moral justifications. But even in warfare, we write rules to keep our instinct for violence and vengeance in check, and Eisenstein's Ivan reproaches Kurbsky at Kazan for unnecessary cruelty. Official Stalinist historiography claimed that Ivan's murder of his own people was justified because the boyars he attacked opposed the establishment of the Great Russian State, which was a historical necessity. Eisenstein was expected to conform to that argument, and on the surface, it appears as though he did. But in this scene, relatively early in what was to be a three-part epic, he already complicates the Stalinist political logic.

From the very first scene in which she appears, Efrosinia Staritskaya was Ivan's personal and political enemy. She opposes centralized rule and wishes to place her son, Vladimir, who is next in line for power, on the throne. At the beginning of the poisoning scene, she is portrayed as unequivocally evil, a dark *sirin* hungrily watching Anastasia, lurking in the shadows, hiding below ground, scowling, stony, and harsh. It is no surprise that she poisons the tsar's wife, because she has already threatened to do so. What is a surprise is that her victim's innocence is called into question, which leads directly to her death. That Ivan himself hands her the chalice that kills her further complicates the distribution of responsibility for Anastasia's death. In addition, when he threatens to take away the boyars' land, Ivan clearly gives Efrosinia justification for acting against him (by removing the one person he could trust). If this had occurred at the end of the film, it might be possible to argue that these were mild challenges to the film's moral regime. But they occur near the beginning and mark the first steps in complicating the political morality of a film that only multiplies such complications as it progresses.

The music in this scene does not just reiterate these narrative elements. Its emotional qualities and the ways each phrase is positioned create a nonverbal, sensory experience that carries the moral complexity. Each of the musical themes, for example, is briefly associated with its darker or lighter opposite, which has the effect of linking enemies, casting doubt on innocence, and muddying what should have been clear moral and political positions. Eisenstein expected us to register this, though perhaps unconsciously. Ivan's lyrical, private "alone" leitmotif is both darkened and briefly associated with Efrosinia. Her harsh slashing strings alternate with Ivan's lyrical theme most rapidly at the moment when the two characters are aligned visually as the chalice changes hands. Saintly Anastasia is scored with unambiguously descending notes. A tiny cello phrase of suspense or uncertainty is inserted when intention is becoming a deed and there's no turning back. At the only moment when it seems possible that the inevitable will be halted or reversed, Efrosinia gets a brief, against-type phrase of Ivan's sweet lyrical theme, but the harsh string beats resume to mark the inexorable moral descent. Musical repetition and differentiation make Ivan truly and not just accidentally responsible for Anastasia's death, and it differentiates this poisoning from that of Ivan's mother. The first poisoning produced pure and justifiable desire for revenge in Ivan, but this time Efrosinia is driven to act against Ivan at least partially because the policies he initiated genuinely threaten her. Kevin Platt has argued that because "blood flows around, and not through him," Ivan is neither perpetrator nor victim,[40] but not so here; in this scene Ivan is doubly morally culpable, both directly and indirectly responsible for Anastasia's death and yet unable to take responsibility for his actions.

The repetition of this scene's score reinforces the lines of complicated responsibility and justification. A unique leitmotif belonging to Efrosinia as murderer appears here and only once again—when Ivan revisits Anastasia's bedchamber in part 2, when another of his henchmen, Fyodor Basmanov, shows him the chalice that contained the poison that Ivan himself handed to his wife. When the chalice appears for the third time, it is accompanied by a different leitmotif, which is associated with another set of murders, similarly carried out by an unwitting murderer with unexpected consequences: Ivan's order to seize the boyar Andrei Shuisky, and Peter's murder of Efrosinia's son Vladimir, who Peter mistakes for Ivan. The three sets of murders are linked by a chain of events that ultimately question the wisdom of political murder and make us consider issues of responsibility. Ivan was reluctant to believe that a blood relative, his aunt Efrosinia, could have killed his wife, or that he himself could have had a hand in it. When he can no longer deny the truth, he takes his revenge by sacrificing another innocent victim and by sending him this very chalice as an invitation to the event at which the revenge will occur. Then Ivan manipulates the childlike Vladimir to take the knife meant for him. Ivan's rationale for murdering Vladimir is quite complex by the end of part 2: self-defense (Vladimir was party to the plot to kill Ivan), the good of Russia (the boyars' attempt to kill Ivan would have prevented the establishment of the Great Russian State), and righteous revenge against Efrosinia for killing Anastasia in the first place. But Vladimir was as innocent as Anastasia, and as guilty (which is to say, just a little). In the end it doesn't matter how evil Efrosinia is or how we calculate her motherly love for her son into our judgment of her. From a political perspective, what matters is that Ivan's justifications all ring hollow in multiple, polyphonic ways by the end of part 2. Our nonverbal viewing experience up to this point prepares us to understand that the end doesn't justify the means.

The doubled plot and the moral parallels and reversals are configured by the ways the music sounds and the ways it was juxtaposed to visual and narrative elements to exploit synesthesia and produce polyphony. Those dark, slashing strings; their alternation with lyrical passages (most of which disappear by part 2); the interplay of the music with the lighting, acting, and set design; and the linkage of the melodies as they rise and fall with our responses to ideas about movement all work together to create a multisensory montage image that translates sensory perception into ideas. That polyphonic sensory experience casts a shadow on every political and personal justification for killing, but it does so without drawing attention to the divergence from the official narrative. The synesthesia allows us to register subtle shifts in the film's moral economy, but the number of polyphonic elements alone makes each scene too complicated to consciously comprehend while watching the film. Eisenstein counted on us to take them in intuitively; to register them in our bodies; to apprehend them "prelogically" and to join that emotional, preverbal knowledge with our conscious intellectual perceptions at some later point. In this way, because music and visual image circumvent language, because of their very plasticity, they can "say" things that cannot be said directly.

In "The Music of Landscape" and "P-R-K-F-V," Eisenstein stresses the difference between mere coordination of sound and picture in conventional films and Prokofiev's ability to reproduce "the structural secret that emotionally expresses, above all, precisely that broad meaning of a phenomenon."[41] Applying his ideas about the montage image more broadly took Eisenstein beyond his earlier ideas about intellectual or vertical montage. In "The Music of Landscape," he sets out to explore the ways in which all the nonverbal aspects of film art can engage our senses and then come together to convey the underlying ideas of a film. Music provides his primary model for exploration and explanation because it is the least verbal and the most abstract of these elements and because he thought Prokofiev understood the ways that music and visual image were similarly structured. Eisenstein believed that Prokofiev's affinity with film made "it possible for the screen to reveal not only the appearance and substance of objects, but also, and notably, their peculiar inner structure. The logic of their existence. The dynamics of their development."[42] He was never able to explain precisely how Prokofiev composed film music so attuned to all the visual and sensory elements of his film, but the ways those compositions corresponded to the structures of his visual method pushed Eisenstein to more fully utilize the possibilities for all kinds of abstract and emotional expression. No longer the "clash of two inner harmonious collectives in an aggressive assault on each other," of his earlier montage thinking, but "separate operations merg[ing] into a single general production and taken all together, are combined in an amazing orchestra counterpoint experience of the process of collective work and creation."[43] Unlike simpler counterpoint, synesthetic polyphony produces the unity in variety that results from "not so much a struggle of equal powers, as an active conflict of contradictions within a single theme." When all the diverse elements that make up a film were properly synchronized, both among themselves and in conjunction with our own "inner melody," Eisenstein believed that viewers would be able to achieve one of those rare synthetic experiences of "mutual absorption" and "ecstatic merging." The individual and the collective, the human and the landscape, the prelogical and logical would "'sing' harmoniously" and produce the entirely new, transformative feelings, ideas, and understanding that make up a great work of art.[44]

Notes

1. Sergei Eisenstein, Vsevolod Pudovkin, and Grigorii Aleksandrov, "Statement on Sound," in *The Film Factory: Russian and Soviet Cinema in Documents, 1896–1939*, ed. Richard Taylor and Ian Christie (Cambridge, MA: Harvard University Press, 1988), 234–35; Sergei M. Eisenstein, *Selected Writings*, vol. 2 (of 4 vols.), *Towards a Theory of Montage*, ed. Richard Taylor and Michael Glenny (London: British Film Institute, 1988–96); Sergei M. Eisenstein "P-R-K-F-V," in *Notes of a Film Director* (New York: Dover, 1970), 149–67 (Russian version: Sergei Mikhailovich Eizenshtein, *Izbrannye proizvedeniia v shesti tomakh*, 6 vols. [Moscow: Iskusstvo, 1964–71, 5:457–73]); Sergei M. Eisenstein "From Lectures on Music and Color in *Ivan the Terrible*," *Selected Writings*, vol. 3, *Writings, 1934–47* (London: British Film Institute, 1996), 317–38.

2. Sergei Eisenstein, *Nonindifferent Nature*, trans. Herbert Marshall (Cambridge: Cambridge University Press, 1987), 216–383 (Russian version: Sergei Mikhailovich Eizenshtein, *Neravnodushnaia priroda*, 2 vols. [Moscow: Muzei kino, 2006], 2:310–507).

3. On the history of the manuscript, see Naum Kleiman's notes in Eizenshtein, *Neravnodushnaia priroda*, 2:537–39; on continuities with earlier montage essays, see Leonid Kozlov, notes in the first publication of *Neravnodushnaia priroda*, in Eizenshtein, *Izbrannye proizvedeniia*, 3:635–36. Many of the ideas that would form *Nonindifferent Nature* arose during Eisenstein's year in Mexico in 1931; see Masha Salazkina, *In Excess: Sergei Eisenstein's Mexico* (Chicago: University of Chicago Press, 2009); Robert Robertson, *Eisenstein on the Audiovisual: The Montage of Music, Image, and Sound in Cinema* (London: I. B. Tauris, 2009), 82–105.

4. Eisenstein, *Nonindifferent Nature*, 86 and passim.

5. Ibid., 286.

6. Sergei Eisenstein, "The Psychology of Composition," in *The Eisenstein Collection*, ed. Richard Taylor (London: Seagull Books, 2006), 249–85.

7. Eisenstein, *Nonindifferent Nature*, 292. A very useful taxonomy of Eisenstein's terms and concepts related to sound can be found in Robertson, *Eisenstein on the Audiovisual*, but missing there is the development of Eisenstein's ideas and practices around the time he was making, and writing about making, *Ivan the Terrible*, a historical dimension quite important to Eisenstein himself; see Eisenstein, *Nonindifferent Nature*, 283, 292–93, 296–97.

8. Ibid., 297 (italics in the original).

9. Ibid., 305.

10. Ibid., 302.

11. Ibid., 281.

12. Ibid.

13. Eisenstein, "P-R-K-F-V," 159; Eizenshtein, *Izbrannye proizvedeniia*, 5:468.

14. Eisenstein, *Nonindifferent Nature*, 217.

15. Ibid. (italics in the original).

16. Kevin Bartig, *Composing for the Red Screen: Prokofiev and Soviet Film* (Oxford: Oxford University Press, 2013); Simon Morrison, *The People's Artist: Prokofiev's Soviet Years* (Oxford: Oxford University Press, 2009); see also Tatiana Egorova, *Soviet Film Music: An Historical Survey* (Amsterdam: Harwood Academic Publishers, 1997).

17. Bartig, *Composing for the Red Screen*, 137–56.

18. David Bordwell, *The Cinema of Eisenstein* (Cambridge, MA: Harvard University Press, 1993), 248.

19. Eisenstein, *Nonindifferent Nature*, 256–57.

20. Eisenstein, "P-R-K-F-V," 163; Eizenshtein, *Izbrannye proizvedeniia*, 5:464, 470.

21. Eisenstein, "P-R-K-F-V," 162; Eizenshtein, *Izbrannye proizvedeniia*, 5:468.

22. Eisenstein, "P-R-K-F-V," 162; Eizenshtein, *Izbrannye proizvedeniia*, 5:468.

23. Eisenstein, "P-R-K-F-V," 162; Eizenshtein, *Izbrannye proizvedeniia*, 5:469.

24. Eisenstein, "P-R-K-F-V," 162; Eizenshtein, *Izbrannye proizvedeniia*, 5:469.

25. For the following discussion, I want to thank Kevin Bartig for the always illuminating and enjoyable conversations we have been carrying on sporadically about this subject.

26. Richard Taruskin, "Great Artists Serving Stalin Like a Dog," *New York Times*, May 28, 1995.

27. On Ivan the Terrible in Stalinist historiography, see Maureen Perrie, *The Cult of Ivan the Terrible in Stalin's Russia* (Basingstoke, UK: Palgrave, 2001); Kevin Platt and David Brandenberger, "Terribly Pragmatic: Rewriting the History of Ivan IV's Reign, 1937–1956," and "Internal Debate within the Party Hierarchy about the Rehabilitation of Ivan the Terrible," in *Epic Revisionism: Russian History and Literature as Stalinist Propaganda*, ed. Kevin Platt and David Brandenberger (Madison: University of Wisconsin Press, 2006), 157–89.

28. Joan Neuberger, *Ivan the Terrible: The Film Companion* (London: I. B. Tauris, 2003), 120–23.

29. Bartig, *Composing for the Red Screen*, 156, 159.

30. Morrison, *The People's Artist*, 246.

31. Kristin Thompson, *Eisenstein's Ivan the Terrible: A Neoformalist Analysis* (Princeton, NJ: Princeton University Press, 1981), 208–60 and passim.

32. Katherine Ermolaev Ossorgin, "Liturgical Borrowings as Film Music in Eisenstein's *Ivan the Terrible* (1944–46)" (paper presented at the annual meeting of the American Musicological Society, Quebec City, November 3, 2007).

33. Eisenstein, "P-R-K-F-V," 159.

34. For a detailed analysis that focuses on rhythm and treats additional aspects of Eisenstein's concept of polyphony in a different scene, see Lea Jacobs, "A Lesson with Eisenstein: Rhythm and Pacing in *Ivan the Terrible*, Part I," *Music and the Moving Image* 5, no. 1 (spring 2012): 24–46.

35. Bartig, *Composing for the Red Screen*, 149, citing Eisenstein's personal papers in RGALI: 1923/1/568/81.

36. Joan Neuberger, "Eisenstein's '*Ivan the Terrible*' as a Theory of History," *Journal of Modern History* (forthcoming).

37. Katerina Clark associates it with the wisdom and knowledge of the Renaissance, in "Sergei Eisenstein's *Ivan the Terrible* and the Renaissance: An Example of Stalinist Cosmopolitanism?" *Slavic Review* 71, no. 1 (2012): 53–54.

38. A list of the scenes accompanied by this leitmotif can be found in Thompson, *Eisenstein's Ivan the Terrible*, 220–21, though she leaves out a tiny piece of it in the scene where Fedor Basmanov and Ivan meet in Anastasia's bedchamber and Fedor reveals Efrosinia's role in the murder.

39. The main example Eisenstein uses to explain polyphony in *Nonindifferent Nature*, Ivan's mourning at his wife's coffin, is oriented toward showing how the structures of counterpoint and polyphony serve to bring out the basic idea of the scene: "The basic theme is Ivan's despair. . . . The *theme of despair* grows into the *theme of doubt*." Eisenstein, *Nonindifferent Nature*, 310 and 321.

40. Kevin M. F. Platt, *Terror and Greatness: Ivan and Peter as Russian Myths* (Ithaca, NY: Cornell University Press, 2011), 245.

41. Eisenstein, "P-R-K-F-V," 163; Eizenshtein, *Izbrannye proizvedeniia*, 470.

42. Eisenstein, "P-R-K-F-V," 162–63.

43. Eisenstein, *Nonindifferent Nature*, 285.

44. Ibid., 359, 333, 287, 358, 305.

13 The Full Illusion of Reality

Repentance, *Polystylism, and the Late Soviet Soundscape*

Peter Schmelz

"Both film and contemporary music are united by the idea of a super-polyphony [*superpolifoniia*] of space and meaning."

—Alfred Schnittke to Elena Petrushanskaya, "Iz besed o rabote v kino"[1]

"Which do you think is more important in film, noises or music? For me they play an equally important role. In film, noises and music know their place."

—Tengiz Abuladze in Margarita Kvasnetskaya, *Tengiz Abuladze: Put' k 'Pokaianiiu'*[2]

IN A PERESTROIKA-ERA manifesto from 1988 called "Cinema without Cinema," Russian cultural historian and critic Mikhail Yampolsky decried the focus on language in Soviet film, noting that the "Soviet film mentality" was "essentially *logocentric.*"[3] Yampolsky argued instead for greater recognition of the total film experience, drawing attention to both sight and sound. "No less important," he wrote, "is the sensual contact with the world on screen created by the richness of sight and sound, the rhythmic structures, and so on."[4] Yampolsky acknowledged that the technological backwardness of the Soviet film industry often led filmmakers to overlook these aspects, especially the synchronization of sight and sound, whose "inadequacy . . . also affects the plausibility of the screen world." After the breakthrough signaled by Dolby stereo at the end of the 1970s, the mono sound of Soviet films left much to be desired. Yampolsky further excoriated Soviet filmmakers:

> The ease, however, with which our directors approach the situation and march toward failure is amazing. As a result, they cannot achieve the full illusion of reality even on location. Why deny it: the barns in our films look less real than the spaceships in

Star Wars. In fact, this is caused by the replacement of the visual and audio dimension (that is, cinematic dimensions) by the verbal one. With tremendous artistic and
financial waste, verbosity is killing our films.[5]

What Yampolsky has in mind as "the full illusion of reality" is to a great extent
sonic. His next metaphor again focuses on speech, but also on sound: "The best
of our film makers tend to trust only the 'full-volume,' totally verbalized material." He somewhat ironically singles out Tarkovsky, that most silent—or nearly
silent—of filmmakers, as one who is "full volume"—that is, as someone who
"seemed often to distrust himself, overshadowing the magic of his imagination
with flowery literary phrases."

Yampolsky's conclusion is worth citing in full:

> And, finally, we must hammer home a few banal truths. It is important to understand
> that film is not only character, plot and conflict transferred onto celluloid, but that
> it is also a dance of light, space, sound, face and body on the screen. Only having
> adopted these simple truths and having understood the deeper workings of cinema
> can our directors finally create films that are interesting to watch.[6]

And, he might have added, interesting to hear. For many directors, enlivening
sound in late Soviet cinema meant enlivening their soundtracks with the noise
of the contemporary urban soundscape, most prominently with rock and roll or
other pop music—think of *Malen'kaia Vera* (Little Vera, dir. Pichul, 1988), among
others. Although perhaps not as logocentric as previous films, this (literally and
figuratively) monaural focus presents still another variant of the deafness Yampolsky critiques. In *Little Vera,* the opening vignette of Vera being rebuked by her
father, shouting to be heard above her blasting pop music, still remains vulnerable to Yampolsky's comment that "there must be less screaming in all the films
of the world than in a dozen Soviet 'industrial films'!"[7] Yet even if not wielded
as proficiently as Yampolsky might wish, sound—alongside the other sensual aspects of film he describes—mattered a great deal to some directors near the end
of the Soviet Union. One of the most successful, if not the most successful, films
of the glasnost era, Georgian director Tengiz Abuladze's *Monanieba/Pokaianie*
(Repentance, 1984), engages deeply with sound—or, to put it in Yampolsky's
terms, the "dance of light, space, sound, face and body on the screen."[8]

Although many late Soviet film critics remained beholden to the "despotism of the eye," some embraced aural metaphors or emphasized the return of
the senses, especially hearing, afforded by the recent sociopolitical transfor-
mations.[9] While writing of director Jauri Podniek's well-known documentary
on contemporary Soviet youth, *Vai viegli but jaunam?* (Is It Easy to Be Young?,
1986), Russian critic Alexander Kiselev spoke of the situation during glasnost as
a "deafening vacuum" into which society had emerged following the removal

of previous social restrictions. Audiences were newly liberated and now "ready to absorb whatever came [their] way."[10] Similarly, Sergei Mouratov referred to the new wave of documentary films, what he called "the unknown cinema," as "return[ing] us our sight, hearing, and voice—a social sight, a social hearing, and a social voice."[11] With both the blinkers and the earplugs of the previous era removed, Soviet citizens could now reexperience history—with eyes, and especially ears, wide open.

Repentance famously filled this deafening vacuum and quickly became emblematic of the new sight, hearing, voice—and memory—regained during perestroika. It "stunned a people into a state of awareness," David Remnick observed.[12] *Repentance* inspired hyperbolic reactions. As one Russian viewer reportedly declared after a screening, "how is it possible to live as before after such a film?"[13] In response, Soviet critics again grasped for sonic metaphors—in this case also invoking the classic Soviet (and Russian) idea of the "optimistic tragedy": "In *Repentance* the theme of the guilty without guilt, the sacrifice of the heroic and the beautiful in the name of 'the common good' takes on the sublime sound of a requiem, the optimistic meaning of high tragedy."[14] Another critic underscored *hearing* the truth that *Repentance* lays bare: "Art, great art has pronounced its heavy, much carried and much suffered word. Now it depends on us to hear it, to take it into our soul and heart. It's now up to us."[15] Still another noted the "warning bell" that *Repentance* sounded.[16]

Despite the immense attraction of the film, its disjunctions confounded Russian and Western viewers alike during perestroika. British film scholar Julian Graffy wrote: "*Repentance* is over-long and its stylistic confusion links it to the contradictory moods of the mid-1980s but it is a brilliantly acted and sometimes deeply moving evocation of the seductions of power."[17] Many agreed with Graffy. One young Soviet viewer responded: "I don't want to say anything bad about the director . . . but was it really impossible to shoot the film without those strange allegories?"[18] Georgian critic Tata Tvalchrelidze attempts to rescue the film by emphasizing the work's unity, writing of the "inclusion in a single work of various stylistic devices, outwardly mutually exclusive, yet supplementing one another in the general construction of the film itself, thereby creating the single organic poetic aesthetic of *Repentance*."[19] For Alexander Karaganov, *Repentance* conjures Eisenstein's "montage of attractions": "Abuladze in his own way, very distinctively applies the discoveries of the great director, creating 'collages' that combine the incompatible, and forces the action to emotional explosions. In the actual, easily narrated events, the imaginary also constantly creeps in."[20] Refusing to pin it down, Abuladze himself offered a perplexing assessment of the film's genre, calling it a "'sad phantasmagoria,' a 'grotesque tragicomedy,' or, perhaps, a 'lyrical tragicfarce.'"[21]

In the voluminous discussions surrounding *Repentance,* few have pointed to the role that its sound track contributes to its overall multifaceted affect and especially the manner in which it bolsters the effects that Tvalchrelidze and Karaganov describe: the combining of the incompatible, the actual shading into the imaginary. An exception was the composer Olga Tomas-Bosovskaya, who examined the film in a 1991 essay emphasizing (like Tvalchrelidze) both the "paradoxical contrasts" and the "internal unity" of both the film and its music.[22] The KINO File Film Companion to *Repentance* by Josephine Woll and Denise Youngblood also dissects the film in detail, including a "frame analysis" in which sound is one of the three components listed (alongside image and dialogue).[23] While providing a starting point, these analyses remain incomplete; this chapter tries to add another layer to the discussion they open.

In her survey of Soviet film music, Russian musicologist Tatiana Egorova also offers a description and analysis of the music in *Repentance,* and provides some important tools for considering the role of the entire range of the sound track (from noises to music) in Abuladze's film. Egorova places *Repentance* firmly among a group of Soviet films from the late 1970s and early 1980s that demonstrate a "passion for collage," borrowing from the "wave of collage" in contemporary "concert music" and film, and allied with "similar processes observed during that historical period in the development of poetry and painting."[24] She singles out Tarkovsky's *Zerkalo* (The Mirror, 1975), Vadim Abdrashitov's *Parad planet* (Parade of Planets, 1984), Elem Klimov's *Idi i smotri* (Go and See, 1985), and Nikita Mikhalkov's *Neokonchennaia p'esa dlia mekhanicheskogo pianino* (An Unfinished Piece for Player Piano, 1976), as well as films by American and European directors including Visconti, Bertolucci, Wajda, Coppola, and Bergman.[25] She might have added to the list Sergei Solov'ev's *ASSA* [1987], with its juxtapositions of popular and classical registers demarcating layers of time, past and present, or Valery Ogorodnikov's *Vzlomshchik* (The Burglar, 1987), a wide-ranging evocation of current Soviet sounds and musics.

Graffy's "stylistic confusion" might also be termed *polyphony,* or, as Egorova calls it, the "polystylistic principle."[26] Tomas-Bosovskaya also notes Abuladze's use of "polystylism, polyphony and the paradoxicality of mixing the outwardly incompatible."[27] And, as both Tomas-Bosovskaya and Egorova suggest, *Repentance*'s polystylism is deeply connected to the "contradictory moods of the mid-1980s" that Graffy describes, or, put another way, to the contemporary late Soviet soundscape. Polystylism circulated widely in the Soviet Union in the 1980s, and it traveled in circles beyond "concert music" and film. The avant-garde jazz composer and pianist Vyacheslav Ganelin often described his trio's music as "consciously polystylistic," and in 1984, the same year *Repentance* was shot, poet Nina Iskrenko penned a "Hymn to Polystylistics" ("Gimn polistilistike").[28]

But what exactly is polystylism? The term—and its near synonym *polyphony*—carry a great deal of theoretical baggage, both literary and musical. Polyphony is the more familiar of the two, largely from the writings of Mikhail Bakhtin.[29] Polystylism was first introduced by Soviet composer Alfred Schnittke (1934–98) in the early 1970s, and it proves a key term for understanding the multifaceted world of contemporary Soviet art music. Schnittke declared that "it is not possible in a short space to cover all the problems of such a vast and unfamiliar subject as the polystylistic method in modern music."[30] The term seems simple enough, suggesting some combination of divergent musical styles, but it also resists easy, capsule definitions. Its "many styles" act as a large umbrella, overshadowing quotation, allusion, collage, montage, and polyphony. Eclecticism often appeared as another equivalent, usually, but not always, in a pejorative sense. Like all theoretical terms the definition of polystylism (and its surrogates) constantly developed, stimulated by critical discussion and artistic practice. To dispel any potential confusion, therefore, the term's evolving use is carefully parsed here. We begin by considering Schnittke's own remarks about polystylism. These remarks lay the theoretical groundwork for the larger discussion of *Repentance* that follows. This discussion, in turn, focuses on several illustrative scenes, guided by Abuladze's own comments about film sound as well as by contemporary Soviet critical reactions to the film. This essay, in short, aims to apply Schnittke's (and contemporary Soviet commentator's) ideas about polystylism to an aurally attuned examination of *Repentance*.

Here I argue that it is exactly *Repentance*'s thoroughgoing polystylism, a polystylism permeating all of the sensual domains Yampolsky discusses—and especially its sound—that both realized Abuladze's multilayered aesthetic vision and helped ensure the film's success. Both form and content thrust *Repentance* to the forefront of the popular conversation. It is not just a matter of symbolism or semantics, as Egorova contends of films that employ quotations. *Repentance*'s polystylism is both more complicated and subtler than that, for it possesses meanings and elements of sound design and intention that work on multiple levels. Thus, not only does the intelligibility of each individual quotation matter; so do the totality of the quotations and their juxtapositions and interactions with one another over the entirety of the sound track. A more detailed, sonically sensitive account can begin to explain why even those Soviet viewers who otherwise disliked the film reacted positively to the sound track. And react positively they did. As one skeptical, anonymous filmgoer noted, the film seemed like a "mixture of comedy and tragedy. A real hodgepodge. Several corpses, but no sympathy. Some kind of explanation should precede the film. I did stay till the end, but mainly because of the acting, the music and the visual beauty."[31] The idea of polystylism suggests why this was the case.

The idea of applying polystylism to *Repentance*'s soundscape has repercussions beyond Schnittke or his work in film—as important and even indispensable as that topic is for understanding his creative output and his general aesthetic concerns. Although examining the polystylism in *Repentance* casts new light on those aesthetic concerns, it also acts as a case study for applying Schnittke's idea of polystylism to films other than those he himself scored. This application suggests the reciprocal relationships between Schnittke's polystylism, film sound, and the polystylistic Soviet soundscape. Polystylism informs our understanding of *Repentance* and its sound track, while also opening a new perspective on sound in late Soviet cinema. But *Repentance* further tells us about late Soviet sound and late Soviet hearing, as well as about the sense of self it engendered. In other words, it tells us about late Soviet orology, to borrow from ethnomusicologist Veit Erlmann's recent exploration of hearing, philosophy, and meaning.[32]

Polystylism in *Repentance* additionally proves an ideal opportunity for considering the role of music in sound studies. Focusing on sound achieves several disciplinary (and interdisciplinary) objectives. Perhaps most attractive is the way it eliminates exclusivity by circumventing intimidating musical nomenclature. Yet a careful balance must constantly be maintained: we cannot lose the music, for music remains an integral aspect of sound and sound tracks alike. Sound studies grew as much from specific strands of twentieth-century musical composition that rejected conventional compositional preconceptions—think Varèse, Cage, or electronic music—as it did from film studies (or any other discipline). Varèse called his music "organized sound," after all.[33] The discussion of *Repentance* that follows therefore attends to the entire spectrum of sounds—from ambient noises to music of all sorts. As Abuladze put it, "In film, noises [*shumy*] and music know their place."[34]

Schnittke's Polystylism

Egorova's notion of polystylism, while a good starting point, requires further critique, contextualization, and refinement. In general, she contends that quotations of preexisting music in film "help the spectator to decide correctly the film's system of moral, aesthetic and ethical ideals and values."[35] In the specific case of *Repentance*, Egorova suggests that "in order to solve this difficult problem [related to the film's unusual design], the directors [*sic*] of *Repentance* decided to use quotations from musical works, which were well known and therefore easily 'read' even by an inexperienced spectator and could carry important semantic information."[36] I want to press both of these basic points, further developing the implications of hearing *Repentance* as polystylistic by first turning to Schnittke's own comments about polystylism.

Tying Schnittke to *Repentance* in a general sense is not difficult, for his music and the film were both iconic glasnost artistic phenomena.[37] At the height of *Repentance*'s fame, Schnittke's celebrity and his status as the "heir of Shostakovich" had been established with a series of biting, bitter, and kaleidoscopic compositions, usually touted under the rubric of polystylism. Although his own engagement with the idea had faded by the mid-1980s, in the popular imagination Schnittke still remained the contemporary polystylist par excellence.[38]

By this time polystylism was everywhere in the Soviet Union. Svetlana Boym has noted the flourishing of eclecticism in the Soviet Union in the 1980s. She writes, "'Eclecticism' was a bad word until the 1980s. . . . In the 1980s, as an act of aesthetic revenge, eclecticism became a single concept that united many film directors, artists, and writers."[39] She might easily have added composers and musicians to the list, although doing so would somewhat disrupt her chronology. For in music, "eclecticism" had been flourishing since at least the 1960s, when numerous young Soviet composers, among them Arvo Pärt, Rodion Shchedrin, Boris Tchaikovsky, Valentin Silvestrov, and Edison Denisov, as well as Schnittke, penned compositions employing a variety of styles and techniques. The Estonian Pärt was first out of the gate with a piece titled *Collage on the Theme B-A-C-H* from 1964, apparently the first European or American art music composition to use the word *collage* in its title. This group of composers (along with other, even less familiar names) forms the "wave of collage" in concert music to which Egorova alludes, likely borrowing the phrase from Schnittke.

Therefore, when Schnittke began formulating the concept of polystylism over the course of the late 1960s and early 1970s, he was to some extent merely describing a practice that was already well in place and had even been positively received by official critics. The quotations and stylistic clashes in many of these works created dramatic narratives that could readily be reconciled to socialist realist demands for easy comprehensibility.[40] Pärt's *Pro et contra* (1966) begins with a blatant tonal chord (D major), held for a few moments (the "pro") followed immediately by a crashing dissonance, a noise really, comprised of every pitch in the chromatic scale sounded nearly simultaneously by the entire ensemble (the "contra"). Predictably, the pro vanquishes the (officially condemned) cacophony.

Schnittke first articulated the "polystylistic method" in a public lecture he presented at the UNESCO International Music Council Congress held in October 1971 in Moscow, a lecture that was published in at least two versions over the course of his lifetime.[41] "By the polystylistic method," Schnittke declared, "I mean not merely the 'collage wave' in contemporary music but also more subtle ways of using elements of another's style." Schnittke justified the necessity of his term, provided a detailed taxonomy (including the "principle of quotation" and the "principle of allusion"), and he also discussed the "preconditions" for its development. Most telling for our investigation of *Repentance* is the second of these preconditions, or what Schnittke called the "psychological":

the increase in international contacts and mutual influences, the change in our conception of time and space, the "polyphonization" of human consciousness [*polifonizatsiia soznaniia*] connected with the constantly growing stream of information and the polyphonization of art [*polifonizatsiia iskussva*]—we have only to remind ourselves of terms such as *stereophony, split-screen, multimedia,* etc.[42]

Polystylism and polyphony were related for Schnittke from an early stage, although the two terms were not exactly synonymous. *Polyphonic* appears to be more overarching than *polystylistic*: it is a more general trend related to human consciousness, technology, and art, and not tied specifically to music. This trend, moreover, relates to developments in film (e.g., split screen).

If the majority of his essay concentrates on the means of polystylism, Schnittke's peroration addresses the ends: the purposes and goals served by the approach. He states:

> In spite of all the complications and possible dangers of the polystylistic method, its merits are now obvious. It widens the range of expressive possibilities, it allows for the integration of "low" and "high" styles, of the "banal" and the "recherché"—that is, it creates a wider musical world and a general democratization of style.

The mixing of high and low was essential to Schnittke's conception of polystylism and plagued him throughout his career, eventually taking on stark moral characteristics. Yet here he advocates polystylism precisely because of its registral richness as well as the leveling function it performs: in other words, it attracts a wider audience. Schnittke also highlights polystylism's function as a chronicle: "In it we find the documentary objectivity of musical reality, presented not just as something reflected individually but as an actual quotation." And note how Schnittke employs familiar Soviet slogans—that is, "democratization" and "musical reality"—revealing polystylism's debts, like the general "collage wave" itself, to socialist realist theory and practice.

Schnittke further connects polystylism to film in his discussion of Italian composer Luciano Berio's *Sinfonia* (1968–69), a memorable collage built around the third movement of Gustav Mahler's Symphony No. 2. Schnittke remarked: "the richness of the collage polyphony [*kollazhnaia polifoniia*] in [Berio's] work is similar to the mixing of street sounds we hear on the soundtracks of Italian neorealistic films." Polystylism consistently conjured up references to film for Schnittke, and was consistently joined to polyphony. Schnittke also calls Berio's composition "an ominous apocalyptic reminder of our generation's responsibility for the fate of the world, expressed by means of a collage of quotations, of musical 'documents' from various ages—reminding one of cinema advertising in the 1970s [or documentary film] [*"kinopublitsistika 70-kh godov"* or *"dokumental'naia kinopublitsistika"*]."[43]

Film did not merely inform polystylism theoretically. Schnittke frequently attributed the concept to his practical experience composing music for a wide range of films, television shows, and cartoons, and especially to his work on Mikhail Romm's final film *Mir segodnia (i vse-taki ia veriu . . .)* (The World Today [And I Still Believe . . .], 1971–75).[44] Yet as he told East German musicologist Hannelore Gerlach in a 1977 interview, polystylism also emerged from the polyphonic soundscape of the time:

> My whole existence as a composer is a double life: I work six or seven months a year for films, then I have a few months left "for myself." The resulting divided musical consciousness, this opposition of musical planes, I feel as a disturbing, but perhaps also stimulating feature of my development. Because of the plenitude of continuous musical stimulus, mankind in general somehow lacks a unified musical consciousness. You can hear the radio, someone upstairs has the television turned up, next door there's rock music; somehow we've already got used to an Ives-atmosphere. So I think maybe it's my task to capture this whole stylistic kaleidoscope, just so as to reflect something of this reality.[45]

The descriptions Schnittke employs here—lacking a musically unified consciousness, stylistically kaleidoscopic reality—mesh neatly with the reception of *Repentance* that we have already sampled. In particular, Schnittke's assertions that quotations allow the "documentary objectivity of musical reality," and that polystylism "widens the range of expressive possibilities" while "[creating] . . . a general democratization of style" prove most useful for hearing *Repentance* polystylistically.

Abuladze's Polystylism

The film perhaps most suggestive of the polystylistic multiplicity of the late Soviet soundscape is also the film anchored least firmly in reality. Many critics recognized the tension between realism and allegorical phantasmagoria in *Repentance*. Karaganov underscored both the film's generic messiness and its realistic historical value:

> In *Repentance* there is living comedy, and the grotesque, and sketches of everyday life. But the philosophical-aesthetic layers created by Abuladze's screen tragedy influence the viewer above all through the enrichment of his historical thinking. You do not make a draft of history. The text of history is definitive. Addressing its dramatic lessons, the film helps its realistic understanding—for the sake of the confirmation of truth and justice in our life today.[46]

Another critic made a similar observation: "It is necessary to watch the film more than once in order to understand completely the complicated, metaphorical, and, somehow essentially, the crystal clear language of the images."[47] The central puzzle of the film thus lies in how it employs a relatively complicated dramatic, narrative, visual, and sonic structure to convey a "crystal clear" "realistic understanding"—the manner in which its images (aural and visual) are both complex and clear. As we shall see, the sound track's polystylism contributes crucially to this complicated balancing act. Notably, *Repentance*'s sound track consists entirely of quotations and appropriations both high and low. No composer is credited; instead, Abuladze's daughter, Nana Dzhanelidze, who also co-wrote the screenplay with Abuladze and Rezo Kveselava, is recognized for the "musical design" (*muzykal'noe oformlenie*).

Repentance became the best known of a set of three films directed by Abuladze that he viewed as an interconnected trilogy exploring seminal themes from Georgian history. The final film in the trilogy, *Repentance* concerns the interactions between the Aravidze and Barateli families over three generations. The central figures are Varlam Aravidze, a generic dictator whose mannerisms and appearance derive from Hitler, Stalin, Mussolini, and Beria and whose last name suggestively (if not pointedly) stems from the Georgian word for "no one" (*aravin*), Varlam's son, Avel, and his grandson, Tornike.[48] Varlam's vendetta against the upright, conscientious (and Christ-like) artist Sandro Barateli culminates in Sandro's arrest, imprisonment, torture, and eventual death, followed shortly thereafter by the arrest and death of his wife, Nino. Decades later, immediately following Varlam's death, Sandro and Nino's orphaned daughter Ketevan repeatedly exhumes Varlam's body, before being arrested and forced to defend herself. Her bizarre trial, the central framing event in the film, features knights in armor, Ketevan dressed in what one Russian critic dubbed "retro" attire, and a judge in a wig handling a Rubik's cube, that worldwide icon of 1980s popular culture.[49] (Soviet critics fixated on that cube.) The flashbacks initiated by Ketevan's testimony constitute the film's embedded narrative, the film within a film, and portray the deeply fraught interactions between her parents and Varlam. Inside and outside of the contemporary courtroom, the disputes among the survivors of these past wrongs, Avel, Ketevan—and, ultimately, the guilt-ridden, suicidal grandson Tornike—exemplify the themes of totalitarian oppression and its victims, and more important, the legacy such violence wreaks on individuals. Who, the film asks, is responsible, and, as its title suggests, who makes amends and how?

Ostensibly set in the 1980s, the fragmented, collage-like quality of the sound track in *Repentance* sounds more modern than that of the two previous films in Abuladze's trilogy, *Vedreba/Mol'ba* (The Plea, 1967) and *Natris khe/Drevo zhelaniia* (The Tree of Desire, aka The Wishing Tree, 1977). *The Plea,* based on an epic poem by Georgian writer Vazha-Pshavela (real name Luka Razikashvili, 1861–1915), is the most conventional—it has an alternately romantic and modernistic symphonic underscore, an old-fashioned soundscape to match its self-consciously archaic black-and-white images. *The Tree of Desire,* in contrast, while disappointing to a scholar of film music, is full of compelling details for one attuned to film sound. The sounds of nature overwhelm the film, especially those of water in many forms: the squelching of mud in the hands of the family digging in vain for a magic stone; the rushing of the fountain around which the town women gather to gossip; the climactic thunderstorm through which the two young, ill-fated lovers cavort; and finally the mud splattering the heroine, Marita, on her terrifying final ride through the town, paraded as an adulteress to be stoned to death. Close aural parallels exist between *The Tree of Desire* and *Repentance,* and, as we will see, the sound track of Marita's punishment reverberates in a climactic moment of *Repentance.*

Abuladze discusses in some detail the soundtrack at the harrowing climax of *The Tree of Desire*, a moment during which, in his source, the memoirs of Giorgi Leonidze (1899–1966), the action proceeds "wordlessly . . . and without a single sound." Abuladze continues:

> Music simply does not fit with those shots. Yet exactly those natural sounds and noises that accompany the episode of Marita's savage punishment created the mood of the boisterous yet mute procession of the crowd in the film. The cooing of 500 doves finding shelter under the dome of the abandoned cathedral, the clang of the heavy cathedral door which frightens off the doves, the clapping of their wings. And the normal sounds of morning in the village: dogs barking, cocks crowing, distant voices somewhere. . . . Such a sonic background, it seems to me, corresponded to the word of the author [i.e., "wordlessly" or "mutely"].[50]

Abuladze neglects to mention how heavily distorted and truly terrifying (and collage-like) these "natural sounds and noises" become in the actual sound track through various electronic means, including reverberation, amplification, and overdubbing. It becomes a piece of *musique concrète.*

As Abuladze's description of its climactic scene suggests, *The Tree of Desire* contains very little conventional music. In fact, what music there is can barely be categorized as such. Music appears three times, with each appearance acting as a "halo" that signals Marita as exceptional. She, after all, is explicitly identified by several villagers as the Virgin Mary. This "halo" consists of electronically altered xylophone or celesta fragments, above either cellos or a wordless mid-register chorus. (The distortion makes identifying the exact source or sources difficult.) The cue operates in a blurred region between music and sound, a region that Abuladze often exploited in his sound design. A slightly similar effect occurs twice in Abuladze's 1958 *Chuzhie deti* (Somebody Else's Children): when a picture of the dead mother of the children in the title first appears, a celesta briefly plays, echoed later in the film when her surrogate is found. Such examples complicate our understanding of Abuladze's declaration about the equivalent—yet apparently distinct—roles played in film by noises and music.[51]

One of the best-known moments in *Repentance,* "the scene with the logs," further illustrates this uneasy equivalency. While the auto-da-fé in *The Tree of Desire* found its ideal companion in noises, here Abuladze turned to music, but music of a particularly unusual hue. After Sandro's arrest, Nino and Ketevan search for information on his whereabouts. They wait in vain in a queue of similarly desperate women and children. And they hear of logs appearing at a depot on the outskirts of town bearing the inscriptions of prisoners' names and places of incarceration. The scene where they frantically search through piles of timber in an industrial wasteland for any sign of Sandro became one of the most commented upon in the film.[52] Abuladze remembered that while filming they "recorded natural sounds, the clatter of wheels, clanking, barking, voices, footsteps. But the composer Giya Kancheli (b. 1935), having watched the scene once it was shot, said 'I have some music that might be useful to you.' And he gave us the tape [of Arvo Pärt's music]."[53] Abuladze expressed his surprised response to Pärt's *Tabula rasa* (1977): "What is it—music? Musical noise? A moan?"[54] Thanks to its impact—its engagement with both noise and music—Abuladze decided to cut both the spoken dialogue and the ambient noises he had originally recorded. With Pärt's music, he declared, "everything was understood." This "musical noise" knew its place.

Abuladze called this scene the "emotional peak of the film."[55] In singling it out, some critics and viewers responded in language similar to Abuladze's evaluation of Pärt's somber music. In his 1987 review, Karaganov largely focuses on the film's visual elements. Even in this scene he describes only what he sees until he abruptly personifies it, conjuring phantom sounds that do not appear on the soundtrack: "The scene with the logs lasts for a long time. It is overfull with the sensation of human grief: it shouts, cries out, appealing to compassion."[56]

In her recent sensitive examination of the film, musicologist Maria Cizmic calls attention to the important ways in which Pärt's music helped Soviet viewers recover and process traumatic past events.[57] Yet isolating this scene and Pärt's music by removing it from the entirety of the film's soundtrack, as Cizmic does, does a disservice to the overall meaning and method of the film. Pärt's music is certainly an important aural component of *Repentance,* but not only for the reasons that Cizmic identifies. Rather, Pärt's music stands out because it does not stand out. It offers an unmarked blankness at the heart of the film that opposes the familiar elements comprising the remainder of the film's polystylistic soundscape. Its blankness allows viewers to project whatever sounds they wish upon the scene—to hear, like Karaganov (and Abuladze), the inaudible shouts and cries of Nino and Ketevan. (This observation applies as well to the music's later reappearance in another grief-filled scene involving Nino.[58])

Arguably, the most striking aspect of the "scene with the logs" is the way its soft conclusion is interrupted: with a bang. Cizmic convincingly proposes this as "perhaps the most jarring cut in the entire film."[59] The next scene clashes both visually and aurally. *Tabula rasa* is loudly trumped by Mendelssohn's "Wedding March" and ambient bird calls, while the darker, almost sepia hues of the previous scene give way to bright sunshine, lush greenery, and a large white piano that drew attention from a number of Soviet critics. This is an absurd, "fantastical" interrogation scene, one of the film's many skewed presentations of the familiar.[60] The interrogator—flanked by the goddess of justice Femida herself, eyes covered and scales in hand—accuses Sandro of being a member of an enemy organization. After the interrogator rings a small bell, the now-familiar knights lead in his friend Mikhail Korisheli, who has been arrested and who has denounced Sandro. Korisheli readily admits to the ridiculous accusation of attempting to dig a tunnel from Bombay to London, and to revealing as many enemies of the state as he could name. He attempts to persuade Sandro to do the same, thereby subverting the system by sheer overload. "They can't arrest them all," he insanely promises. The scene ends with Korisheli's scream, as he collapses onto the closed piano lid—the sounds of both the scream and piano crash are amplified, reverberated, distorted.

The jarring sonic crash of the familiar "Wedding March" into the tragic emptiness of Pärt's *Tabula rasa* in the preceding scene is just as vital to the overall aesthetic of the film as the abrupt visual shift between the scenes. The extreme figurative dissonance of the tune presents an ironic, if not spiteful, commentary on the sundering of the Baratelis' own marriage. Boris Vasiliev cites this as an example of farce, but farce fails to capture the agonizing collision here of the celebratory and the tragic, a collision that extends both throughout the interrogation scene as well as between the log and interrogation scenes.[61] There are multiple dissonances, multiple sonic (and visual) stylistic juxtapositions in this two-scene sequence, as throughout the entire film.

Another central sequence demonstrates Abuladze's careful balancing—and sometimes blending—of noises and music and its implications for the meaning and affect of *Repentance*. This sequence, Nino's nightmare, follows Varlam's visit to the Barateli household. Sonically, it recalls the auto-da-fé in *The Tree of Desire,* albeit at a more frantic clip.[62] In the Baratelis' darkened apartment, Sandro sits behind the piano, playing softly as Nino sleeps reclined in an armchair. Sandro's playing begins nearly inaudibly but slowly creeps to attention. He is playing Claude Debussy's prelude "Des pas sur la neige" ("Footprints in the snow," 1909–10), a melancholy rocking in the left hand accompanied by intermittent melodic arcs in the right. Slowly we move into a nightmarish realm. The volume of the Debussy piece gradually increases but is now overlaid by dripping water.[63] Aqueous sounds accompany Nino and Sandro, in nightgowns, hurrying down a dark tunnel pursued by unknown figures; the sounds of stomping, splashing water are synchronized inexactly with their movements. Debussy continues sounding as a shaky, handheld camera follows the two; the colliding soundscapes—music and water—mark the merging of reality and nightmare.

The panicked running through water cuts off with the next visual cut. Now we see Sandro and Nino fleeing through the empty streets of an empty city, pursued by armored knights on horseback and Varlam in a convertible. The two desperately try to escape, running this way and that as the sound track reverberates with distorted, unidentifiable sounds reminiscent of the sound track during the auto-da-fé sequence: shrieking, industrial sounds—the roar of an airplane? These, in turn, continue over the next jump cut as we see Sandro and Nino running over a plowed field, trying to seek refuge with a farmer. They then appear buried up to their necks in the soil, hidden until the farmer points out their location to the still-advancing Varlam and his henchmen. The hallucinatory sounds collide with the incongruous and strange visual shifts. Sound track (noises and music) and image do not match here. Debussy fades in and out, reappearing on a clear frontal shot of Varlam in the car in the field.

The film cuts to the two heads buried in the field and gradually zooms in on Nino's face as Varlam sings the final two lines from Manrico's aria "Di quella pira" from act 3, scene 2 of Verdi's opera *Il trovatore*: "Unhappy mother, I am flying to save you; or at least to die with you" ("Madre infelice, corro a salvarti").[64] These are familiar, for they were heard not long before in the film, during Varlam's impromptu salon with the Baratelis. Then, the aria was pretentious; now it becomes a mocking commentary, especially in Varlam's rapid, excessively repetitive rendition of the final line. As Tvalchrelidze notes, Varlam sings here like a "dilettante, slightly false, like earlier. . . . But this time the singing is reminiscent of a true call of victory, unbridled, eccentrically grotesque."[65] The lines are grotesque because Varlam sings of rescuing a mother to a mother who is trapped, literally buried alive. In Abuladze's filmmaking, sounds and images reappear, transformed and transforming.

The final sonic moments in *Repentance* warrant special mention. Of the several classics from the Western art-music canon quoted in the film, Beethoven predictably predominates (including the Ninth Symphony's "Ode to Joy"). His *Moonlight Sonata* appears near the end of the film, as Avel plays it moodily for his wife, Guliko, and a few passive guests following the successful prosecution of Ketevan in the just concluded trial. (The preceding scene ends with Ketevan announcing to Tornike, Varlam's grandson, that she is to be committed to an insane asylum.) The camera focuses first on Avel's hands at the piano keys, followed by a long shot of the gathered guests, drinking, around the piano, followed by a shot of Avel's head and torso; he closes his eyes, not needing the sheet music—he knows his Beethoven. Next we focus on Guliko's stony face as she slowly smokes, exhaling languidly. Yet again Beethoven symbolizes a world whose moral compass has foundered (as in Stanley Kubrick's 1971 film *A Clockwork Orange*). Abuladze suggests that even the classics cannot redeem those stained by sin, a conclusion emphasized by the next events, and particularly the next musical cue. The register abruptly shifts from high to low, and the popular intrudes, signaling the film's final tragedy.

Popular music plays an integral role in the polystylism of *Repentance,* as it did in Schnittke's theory and practice.[66] There are several occasions when popular music saturates the film's sound track, but the one that carries the most weight comes last. Tornike furiously interrupts the Beethoven recital to excoriate his father: "What have you done?! . . . This is not a house but a grave! . . . After this you are not a man." His enraged father slaps him. Just as Tornike retreats to his room to shoot himself (with a gun given to him by his grandfather), more guests barge in. The mood before was bleak, nocturnal; now they celebrate, toting in a radio playing the disco hit "Sunny" (1976) by the West German band Boney M.

Egorova mishears this scene. She links the pop music in the film, and especially its ending, to Varlam's egomania:

> Here, suddenly, the aggressive rhythms of rock and lively disco tunes show a distinct resemblance to the equally pushy, self-assured and energetic music of Varlam. A shot which sounds out to the music of the group Boney M is the closing link in the vicious circle of the evil father's and son's corruption: this shot ends the life of Varlam's grand-son Tornike, who has decided to pay in this awful way for the monstrous doings of his grandfather.[67]

But the popular music here does not mark generational identity as much as comment ironically on generational difference—thereby pointing to the ethical center of the film. By the mid 1980s, popular music had become a contentious symbol in Soviet culture and politics (and film).[68] Pop music (predictably) represented liberation for some (mainly the young), even as it (predictably) heralded new dangers for others (mainly the old). Schnittke is representative. Despite his enthusiastic appropriation of popular music in his early polystylistic scores, especially the Symphony No. 1, later in life he thought of popular culture—including popular music—as the "most direct manifestation of evil in art."[69] Schnittke was not alone. For many listeners pop music encapsulated anxieties about the new youth culture and its own blankness, its own illegibility.

Repentance flips the values of that equation. Rather than Tornike, his parents are the disco fans. This musical characterization had been broached a few scenes earlier, during Tornike's "nightmarish vision," when he sees his mother dancing seductively to modish new wave music before his grandfather's waking corpse.[70] Tornike is an exception: he escapes from the stereotypical role of pop-music-loving youth. Rather than withdrawing from history, he engages with its full weight: he is the moral center of the story. The music signals his parents' immaturity, their inability to accept adult responsibilities. The shot signals

Tornike's difference from the generation of his parents and grandparents, as well as from his own.

In the sequence that follows, his grief following his son's suicide knowing no limits, Avel finally accepts responsibility. He repents. In a frenzy, he descends into his father's bunker, into the depths—to hell on earth—to curse Varlam's existence and its genetic wrath. In a jump cut, Avel returns to the surface; now he unearths his father's grave, completing the task that Ketevan had started, and for which she was found guilty and sentenced. From the sound of the shovel crunching the earth, the clacking of a train emerges. (We hear but do not see the train cars that we saw but did not hear at the beginning of the scene with the logs.) The train sounds clatter over the next cut, which presents Avel and the corpse atop the hills ringing the city. As Avel heaves the corpse over the precipice, a distorted, sonic scream erupts, another instance of Abuladze's *musique concrète* sound design. The scream—heavily distorted, unclear in origin—is followed a beat later by another sampling of birds, recalling the climax of *The Tree of Desire*. But rather than doves, here we encounter "a murder of crows flying off, noisily cawing."[71] (The scream itself might be a crow.) Unlike the sound track from the scene with the logs, now the sounds unambiguously burst from Avel's throat. But they are also inhuman, channeling the expiation of his moral inheritance—an exorcism of devilish guilt. (They also allude to Korisheli's earlier distorted scream in the "Wedding March" interrogation scene.)

The very conclusion of the film returns to more familiar markers: a return to the "tender sounds of a guitar [playing] an old waltz" (as the screenplay reads) first heard at the very outset of the film. We again join Ketevan in her bakery, where she crafts cakes and desultorily debates Varlam's legacy with an apologist. "They say that his sins gave him no peace," she says.[72] The entire preceding action apparently proves a warped daydream.

The soundtrack soon shifts, pivoting upon a much-cited exchange. An old woman approaches the bakery window and asks, "Tell me, does this street lead to a church?" "No," Ketevan replies. "This is Varlam Street, and this street does not lead to a church." The old woman's answer became a clarion call for the newly awakened spiritual consciousness of glasnost: "But then why is it necessary? What is the point of a street if it does not lead to a church?"[73] Her oracular pronouncement concluded, the old woman (played by the venerated Georgian actress Veriko Anjaparidze) turns and heads away from the bakery "along a long street leading who knows where," accompanied by the reverent choral strains of the "Ingemisco Tanquam Reus" of the "Dies Irae" movement from Charles Gounod's oratorio *Mors et vita* (1885). (Abuladze uses measures 59–93.[74]) The liturgical text from the requiem mass appropriately deals with absolution and redemption, its overt religiosity signaling a clear break from the spiritual prohibitions of the old Soviet Union. Although not as familiar as the other classical chestnuts in the film—the

Moonlight Sonata before Tornike's suicide, or the "Ode to Joy" during Sandro's sentencing and execution—the Gounod quotation offered a decisive contrast to the stylistic jumble of the film.

Conclusion

The noises and music help to unravel many of the vexing narrative enigmas in *Repentance*. Egorova argues that the familiarity of its musical quotations render the difficulties of the film comprehensible to viewers. Recall her comments that because they are "easily read," such references can "help the spectator to decide correctly the film's system of moral, aesthetic and ethical ideals and values."[75] But the quotations are unreliable guideposts; they are false friends. Rather than solving puzzles, often they are meant to be puzzling themselves. They emphasize, rather than "decide correctly," the film's "muddling of epochs." The Russian critic Lakshin declared about *Repentance*:

> I'll speak openly: I am not a great fan of the cinematographic "avant-garde," of surrealism, significant symbols. But here it evokes the muddle of epochs without distracting from the idea, but enlarging the idea. When is the action taking place? Never and always. Where is it taking place? Nowhere and everywhere. Everywhere, where laws are flouted, the human personality, and terror, denunciations, and fear become the accustomed condition of society.[76]

As Abuladze himself noted: "All of those images are not simply a grotesque style or surrealism, but an element of the film's contents. Otherwise, I could not convey in the film the absurd reality of the 'epoch of Varlam.'" Of the images he refers to, several are sonic:

> Tell me, without the white piano, without Mendelssohn's wedding march, without the goddess justice Femida in the guise of a pretty girl with scales in her hands and blindfolded eyes, how would I shoot the fantastic, almost implausible scene of the interrogation of the artist Sandro in the "department" of Varlam? How to comprehend and convey to the contemporary viewer that absurd "Varlamism," under which the formerly courageous and honest citizen Mikhail Korisheli levels against himself a monstrous slander . . . ? An absurd, fantastical reality demands appropriate means of expression.[77]

The disparate sound track—its range of noises and music—buttressed the disjointed style of *Repentance,* of reality shading into nightmare. The familiarity of the sonic images often only amplified their nightmarish character, as the "Wedding March" and Manrico's aria both illustrate. At other moments, however, the film's familiar styles intentionally make obvious gestures. They are meant to be read straight. "The whole system of images in the film provides for a range of varied readings," Abuladze explained. "Yet," he added, "there are episodes in the film that just do not tolerate varied readings. Their ideas should be unequivocal to viewers."[78] But the unambiguity at these moments, and particularly at the film's close, serves only to further emphasize the ambiguity of the whole.

At the film's most potent points, the styles rub uncomfortably against one another, providing friction and unease while conveying subtle secondary meanings. This is what Tvalchrelidze and Tomas-Bosovskaya miss when they stress the film's "single organic poetic aesthetic" or its "internal unity," claims meant to parry the predicted Soviet criticisms of formlessness and incoherence. *Repentance*'s aesthetic is absurd reality, fantastical multiplicity. Any unity it possesses results from a thoroughgoing disunity.

Repentance spoke as much about the present as the past. Its polystylistic soundscape helped fill the deafening vacuum of perestroika. Although the film takes place in a grotesque past and a fantastical present, it is also strangely familiar. Its soundscape reflects the polystylism of the age: fractured yet recognizable. Maya Turovskaya once remarked that in Alexander Sokurov's *Dni zatmeniia* (Days of the Eclipse, 1988), "the space stretches and warps the time."[79] In *Repentance*, sound, space, and time are all stretched and warped by one another, or more specifically, made multiple, made polystylistic. Or, to return to Schnittke, *Repentance* marked a super-polyphony of space and content, both aural and visual. The film's super-polyphony captured the full illusion of reality—even its deceptions, its unreality.

Tatyana Tolstaya has described the polyphony of glasnost, but her polyphony, like the contemporary films Yampolsky so passionately condemned, is "essentially logocentric." "And the word flooded the land," she declares.[80] But it is clear that during glasnost more than just words flooded the land; so did sounds: multifarious, multifaceted sounds. But they had been washing over the land for some time. The polyphonic soundscape of the late Soviet Union encapsulated in Schnittke's polystylism reflected a welling over of history that began during the Thaw; by the 1980s many had become saturated, satiated with a twinned sense of nostalgia and of an encroaching ending. Past, present, and future became malleable. *Repentance*'s disparate aural quotations and their collisions—in short, its polystylism—made this phantasmagoria paradoxically, if not impossibly, simultaneously more and less real. The film spoke to the unreal reality of the present and became the breakout hit of perestroika, the embodiment of a new artistic and social epoch.

Notes

1. Elena Petrushanskaia, "Iz besed o rabote v kino," *Muzykal'naia akademiia* 2 (1999): 96; published earlier in German as Alfred Schnittke and J. [Jelena] Petruschanskaja, "Ein Gespräch mit Alfred Schnittke: Die Möglichkeiten des Dialogs zwischen Bild und Musik im Film," *Sowjetwissenschaft. Kunst und Literatur* 36, no. 2 (1988): 280.

2. Margarita Kvasnetskaia, *Tengiz Abuladze: Put' k 'Pokaianiiu'* (Moscow: Kul'turnaia revoliutsiia, 2009), 113.

3. Mikhail Yampolsky, "Cinema without cinema," in *Russian Critics on the Cinema of Glasnost,* ed. Michael Brashinsky and Andrew Horton (Cambridge: Cambridge University Press, 1994), 12.

4. Ibid., 13.

5. Ibid.

6. Ibid., 17.

7. Ibid., 15.

8. Yampolsky seems ambivalent about *Repentance,* discussing its "extraordinary timeliness" that "can attract great numbers," but cautioning that "today's director cannot depend on the perpetual discovery of formerly forbidden subjects." Ibid., 15.

9. Tom Paulin, "The Despotism of the Eye," in *Soundscape: The School of Sound Lectures, 1998–2001,* ed. Larry Sider, Diane Freeman, and Jerry Sider (London: Wallflower Press, 2003), 35–48.

10. Alexander Kiselev, "Deafening Voids," in *Russian Critics on the Cinema of Glasnost,* ed. Michael Brashinsky and Andrew Horton (Cambridge: Cambridge University Press, 1994), 67.

11. Sergei Mouratov, "The Unknown Cinema: Documentary Screen, Glasnost Era," *Journal of Film and Video* 44, nos. 1–2 (1992): 13.

12. David Remnick, *Lenin's Tomb: The Last Days of the Soviet Empire* (New York: Vintage, 1993), 42.

13. Quoted in T. Mamaladze, "Pritcha i pravda," in *Pokaianie,* ed. Viktor Bozhovich (Moscow: Kinotsentr, 1988), 133.

14. Neia Zorkaia, "Dorogoi, kotoraia vedet k Khramu," *Iskusstvo kino* 5 (1987): 51; quoted in Julie Christensen, "Tengiz Abuladze's Repentance and the Georgian Nationalist Cause," *Slavic Review* 50, no. 1 (1991): 165.

15. Viktor Bozhovich, "Ispytanie: O kinotrilogii T. Abuladze," *Druzhba narodov* 3 (1988): 213; quoted in Christensen, "Tengiz Abuladze's *Repentance,*" 165.

16. Tat'iana Khlopliankina, "Pod zvuki nabatnogo kolokola," in *Pokaianie,* ed. Viktor Bozhovich (Moscow: Kinotsentr, 1988), 162.

17. Julian Graffy, "Abuladze, Tengiz E.," in *The BFI Companion to Eastern European and Russian Cinema* (London: British Film Institute, 2000), 11.

18. Quoted in Khlopliankina, "Pod zvuki nabatnogo kolokola," 159.

19. T. Tvalchrelidze, "Prozrenie cherez pokaianie," in *Pokaianie,* ed. Viktor Bozhovich (Moscow: Kinotsentr, 1988), 123.

20. A. Karaganov, "Sud sovesti," in *Pokaianie,* ed. Viktor Bozhovich (Moscow: Kinotsentr, 1988), 136.

21. Bozhovich, *Pokaianie,* 7.

22. Ol'ga Tomas-Bosovskaia, "Paradoksy Pokaianiia," in *Iz proshlogo i nastoiashchego sovremennoi otechestvennoi muzyki,* ed. E. B. Dolinskaia (Moscow: Moskovskaia gos. konservatoriia Im. P.I. Chaikovskogo, 1991), 61 ("paradoxical contrasts"), 64 ("internal unity"), and 66 ("dialectical unity"). I am indebted to Svetlana Nadler for tracking this article down for me.

23. Josephine Woll and Denise Youngblood, *Repentance: The Film Companion* (London: I. B. Tauris, 2000).

24. Tatiana Egorova, *Soviet Film Music: An Historical Survey,* trans. Tatiana A. Ganf and Natalia A. Egunova (Amsterdam: Harwood, 1997), 238.

25. Ibid., 238–47.

26. See Andrew Horton and Michael Brashinsky, *The Zero Hour: Glasnost and Soviet Cinema in Transition* (Princeton, NJ: Princeton University Press, 1992), 41; Christensen, "Tengiz

Abuladze's Repentance and the Georgian Nationalist Cause," 163 and 175; and Egorova, *Soviet Film Music*, 238.

27. Tomas-Bosovskaia, "Paradoksy Pokaianiia," 60.

28. Virgil Mihaiu, "Ganelin Trio: Prophetic Visions," *Jazz Forum* 91 (1984): 34; Nina Iskrenko, *Neskol'ko slov* ([Paris?]: AMGA, 1991), 6–7.

29. See, e.g., Mikhail Bakhtin, *Problems of Dostoevsky's Poetics*, edited and translated by Caryl Emerson, *Theory and History of Literature*, vol. 8 (Minneapolis: University of Minnesota Press, 1984); and the helpful overview of the term in Gary Saul Morson and Caryl Emerson, *Mikhail Bakhtin: Creation of a Prosaics* (Stanford, CA: Stanford University Press, 1990), 231–68.

30. Alfred Schnittke, "Polystylistic Tendencies in Modern Music," in *A Schnittke Reader*, ed. Alexander Ivashkin, trans. John Goodliffe (Bloomington: Indiana University Press, 2002), 87 (unless otherwise noted, all references and quotations that follow are to this text, with slight emendations by the author). The paper has a lengthy publication history. For a detailed enumeration, see Peter J. Schmelz, *Such Freedom, If Only Musical: Unofficial Soviet Music during the Thaw* (New York: Oxford University Press, 2009), 366–67.

31. A. Bogdanov and V. Vil'chek, " 'Pokaianie' i 1000 ispovedei: zametki sotsiologov," in *Pokaianie*, ed. Viktor Bozhovich (Moscow: Kinotsentr, 1988), 153; quoted in Woll and Youngblood, *Repentance*, 97–98.

32. Veit Erlmann, *Reason and Resonance: A History of Modern Aurality* (New York: Zone, 2010), esp. introduction.

33. Edgard Varèse, "The Liberation of Sound," in *Perspectives on American Composers*, ed. Benjamin Boretz and Edward T. Cone (New York: W. W. Norton, 1971), 32.

34. Kvasnetskaia, *Tengiz Abuladze*, 113.

35. Egorova, *Soviet Film Music*, 238.

36. Ibid., 239.

37. Schnittke himself expressed doubts about the excessive topicality of *Repentance*, declaring: "it bears the mark of a not very deeply relevant awareness of the present moment." Al'fred Shnitke and Alexander Ivashkin, *Besedy s Al'fredom Shnitke* (Moscow: Kul'tura, 1994), 185.

38. See, e.g., Grigorii Pantielev, "Piat' simfonii Al'freda Shnitke," *Sovetskaia Muzyka* 10 (1990): 81.

39. Svetlana Boym, *Common Places: Mythologies of Everyday Life in Russia* (Cambridge, MA: Harvard University Press, 1994), 250.

40. See Schmelz, *Such Freedom, If Only Musical*, 245–57; as well as Peter Schmelz, "A Genealogy of Polystylism: Alfred Schnittke and the Late Soviet Culture of Collage," *Abstracts Read at the 75th Annual Meeting of the American Musicological Society*, Philadelphia, November 12–15, 2009, 49, http://www.ams-net.org/abstracts/2009-Philadelphia.pdf; also part of my book in progress, "Sonic Overload: Polystylism as Cultural Practice in the Late USSR."

41. Alfred Schnittke, "Polystylistic Tendencies in Modern Music," 87–90.

42. Note that at this point the version of the text he delivered in October 1971 includes the phrase "pluralization of art" (*pliuralizatsiia iskusstva*) rather than *polyphonization*. See *Muzykal'nye kul'tury narodov: traditsii i sovremennost'* (Moscow: Sovetskii kompozitor, 1973), 290; and Schnittke, "Polistilisticheskie tendentsii sovremennoi muzyki," in V. Kholopova and E. Chigareva, *Al'fred Shnitke: Ocherk zhizni i tvorchestva* (Moscow: Sovetskii kompozitor, 1990), 329. Compare to the Russian text in Alfred Schnittke, *Stat'i o muzyke*, ed. Aleksandr Ivashkin (Moscow: Kompozitor, 2004), 99.

43. The original version of this clause was "documentary film" (*dokumental'naia kinopublitsistika*). See V. Kholopova and E. Chigareva, *Al'fred Shnitke: ocherk zhizni i tvorchestva* (Moscow: Sovetskii kompozitor, 1990), 330; see also Schmelz, *Such Freedom, If Only Musical*, 303n.

44. For more on Schnittke's work on this documentary, see Schmelz, *Such Freedom, If Only Musical*, 306–7.

45. Hannelore Gerlach, *Fünfzig sowjetische Komponisten* (Leipzig: Peters, 1984), 363–64; quoted in David Fanning, liner notes to Alfred Schnittke, *Concerto Grosso No. 1, u.a.*, Deutsche Grammophon CD 429 413-2 (1990), 5.

46. Karaganov, "Sud sovesti," 137.

47. V. Lakshin, "Neproshchaiushchaia pamiat'," in *Pokaianie*, ed. Viktor Bozhovich (Moscow: Kinotsentr, 1988), 131.

48. Bozhovich, *Pokaianie*, 5.

49. Ibid. See also Tvalchrelidze, "Prozrenie cherez pokaianie," 124.

50. Kvasnetskaia, *Tengiz Abuladze*, 114.

51. Ibid., 113.

52. See Tatyana Khloplyankina, "On the Road That Leads to Truth," in *Russian Critics on the Cinema of Glasnost*, ed. Michael Brashinsky and Andrew Horton (Cambridge: Cambridge University Press, 1994), 52; see also "Letter from a Viewer," in *Pokaianie*, ed. Viktor Bozhovich (Moscow: Kinotsentr, 1988), 167. Youngblood finds this "the movie's most powerful and heart-rending scene." See Denise Youngblood, review of *Repentance*, *American Historical Review* 95, no. 4 (1990): 1134. Woll and Youngblood label this only as "mournful music." See Woll and Youngblood, *Repentance*, 45.

53. Bozhovich, *Pokaianie*, 11–12.

54. Ibid., 12 ("Chto eto—muzyka? Muzykal'nyi shum? Ston?") and 80 ("strannaia, dalekaia, skorbnaia melodiia sterla vse zvuki zhizni").

55. Kvasnetskaia, *Tengiz Abuladze*, 171.

56. Karaganov, "Sud sovesti," 136.

57. Maria Cizmic, *Performing Pain: Music and Trauma in Eastern Europe* (New York: Oxford University Press, 2012), 97–132.

58. Ibid., 128–30.

59. Ibid., 120.

60. Bozhovich, *Pokaianie*, 80–84.

61. Boris Vasil'ev, "Prozrenie," in *Pokaianie*, ed. Viktor Bozhovich (Moscow: Kinotsentr, 1988), 145.

62. Bozhovich, *Pokaianie*, 8.

63. This composition is not identified in the screenplay; see ibid., 65.

64. Translation from Giuseppe Verdi, *Il trovatore*, James Levine, Metropolitan Opera Orchestra and Chorus, Sony CD, S2K 48 070 (1994).

65. Tvalchrelidze,"Prozrenie cherez pokaianie," 123.

66. Pace Woll and Youngblood, Beethoven's *Moonlight Sonata* was not Lenin's favorite piece of music. See Woll and Youngblood, *Repentance*, 81. According to Gorky, his favorite was the *Appassionata*. See William Kinderman, *Beethoven* (Berkeley: University of California Press, 1997), 113.

67. Egorova, *Soviet Film Music*, 241.

68. See Sergei Zhuk, *Rock and Roll in the Rocket City: The West, Identity, and Ideology in Soviet Dniepropetrovsk, 1960–1985* (Baltimore: John Hopkins University Press, 2010), and Alexei Yurchak, *Everything Was Forever, Until It Was No More: The Last Soviet Generation* (Princeton, NJ: Princeton University Press, 2005).

69. Alfred Schnittke, *A Schnittke Reader*, ed. Alexander Ivashkin, trans. John Goodliffe (Bloomington: Indiana University Press, 2002), 22–23.

70. Bozhovich, *Pokaianie*, 97.

71. Ibid., 113.

72. Ibid., 27.

73. Ibid., 114.

74. This excerpt appears on pages 61–64 (rehearsal letters C to 3 before E) in the score: Charles Gounod, *Mors et vita: A Sacred Trilogy,* piano-vocal score by O. B. Brown (London: Novello, Ewer and Co., 1885). The recording in the film is taken from: Sh. Guno [Charles Gounod], *Smert' i zhizn': Fragmenty iz oratorii,* Melodiia LP SM 02779-80(e) (1971?).

75. Egorova, *Soviet Film Music,* 238.

76. Lakshin, "Neproshchaiushchaia pamiat'," 128.

77. Bozhovich, *Pokaianie,* 12.

78. Ibid., 16.

79. Maya Turovskaya, "The Days of Eclipse," in *Russian Critics on the Cinema of Glanost,* ed. Michael Brashinsky and Andrew Horton (Cambridge: Cambridge University Press, 1994), 112.

80. Tatyana Tolstaya, *Pushkin's Children: Writings on Russia and Russians* (New York: Houghton Mifflin, 2003), 93.

14 Russian Rock on Soviet Bones

Lilya Kaganovsky

VALERY TODOROVSKY's 2008 film *Stilyagi* (The Hipsters) opens with a scene at a local Soviet clinic. A patient has come for a chest X-ray, complaining of a severe cough. We hear the nurse scolding him for excessive smoking, we see the X-rays produced and examined, but it is only when we see the same X-ray plate being cut into the shape of a circle, and a hole being burned in the exact middle with a cigarette, that we understand the relationship of this opening sequence to the rest of film: the X-ray can be used to make a homemade gramophone record, a phenomenon that was referred to in the 1950s and 1960s as "rock on bones" (*rok na kostiakh*): Western rock recorded onto "Soviet" bones.

Set in 1955 and 1956, just after the death of Stalin but before the Twentieth Party Congress and Khrushchev's "Secret Speech," *Stilyagi* is a musical (or a musical comedy, or a musical tragicomedy) about a brief, but very vibrant, Soviet counterculture moment when a generation of postwar Soviet youth, exposed for the first time to movies, music, and styles from the West, attempted to reproduce through their clothes, music, dance, and overall attitude a certain kind of international style. The basic plot centers on the romance of Mels and Pol'za, beginning with his conversion from a straight-laced Komsomol member to full-fledged *stilyaga,* his expulsion from the Komsomol, her pregnancy, and the group's eventual dispersal. Despite Todorovsky's disclaimers, the film is a true musical in the Hollywood sense of the genre, where the emotional and narrative weight is given to the song and dance numbers, loosely connected by a minimal plot.

The film is highly stylized: the Soviet masses are shown in uniform gray, whereas the *stilyagi* wear loud, colorful clothing (figures 14.1 and 14.2). (Todorovsky noted that in terms of costuming, they greatly exaggerated both the outrageous fashions and the uniformity of the Soviet masses to make the difference clearer; the original costumes that replicated the actual clothes worn by *stilyagi* looked too "innocent" and failed to communicate the effect they had had on regular Soviet citizens.[1]) This same tendency toward hypertrophy is carried over into the formal aspects of the film, which employs cartoon captions to remind us that we are watching a fictive, two-dimensional world. Handwritten notes, with arrows pointing out "Broadway" or "Fred's digs," appear over shots of Gorky

Figure 14.1. The gray masses; frame grab from *Stilyagi* (The Hipsters, dir. Todorovsky, 2008).

Figure 14.2. Mels transformed; frame grab from *Stilyagi*.

Street and the Stalinist high-rise apartment building on Kotelnicheskaya Naberezhnaya in which one of the characters lives (figure 14.3).[2]

Overall, there is an insistence on a *lack* of a certain kind of historical mimeticism. The film doesn't strive for historical accuracy (unlike, for example, the American television show *Mad Men,* which is obsessed with re-creating the 1960s exactly), but instead tries to give the contemporary viewer the "impression" of the 1950s.[3] Echoes of socialist realism—and Stalin-era musical comedies in particular[4]—easily mix with references to *West Side Story* (dir. Wise and Robbins, 1961), *Grease* (dir. Kleiser, 1978), Pink Floyd's *The Wall* (dir. Parker, 1982), and Baz Luhrmann's *Moulin Rouge!* (2001). With its garish "Technicolor" palate, its reworking of serious rock songs into campy musical numbers, its cartoon

Figure 14.3. Cartoon captions; frame grab from *Stilyagi*.

captions, and the overall insistence on visual ahistoricism, *Stilyagi* reads at first glance as simply a postmodern pastiche, devoid of critical weight. The film took nearly ten years from conception to execution, and it was officially released on December 25, 2008, with the help of TV Channel 1 (Pervyi kanal) and the television channel Rossiia. The television release was timed to coincide with the New Year holiday, with a shortened and censored version premiering on January 1, 2010, on RTR, which helped cement its status as a "film-celebration" (*fil'm-prazdnik*) meant as light entertainment for a mass audience. (Interestingly enough, the television release cut the opening sequence of the film in which we watch Bob making a homemade record from the X-ray plate, among other changes.[5]) In this chapter, I trace some of the history of the musical as it unfolded in American and Soviet cinemas and the ways in which those legacies (sometimes similar, sometimes diverse) manifest themselves in *Stilyagi*, Todorovsky's postmodern, post-Soviet extravaganza.

From *Jolly Fellows* to *Stilyagi*

Like many Soviet film directors before him, Todorovsky does not use the term *musical* when referring to his film. He argued that Russian audiences would not understand the genre (and therefore would not see the movie), since Soviet and Russian cinema has never produced any real musicals in the Hollywood sense. Konstantin Meladze, a rock musician and the film's musical director, claimed to be "unfamiliar" with musicals and argued that they were "unnatural" for Russian cinema. Instead, he described *Stilyagi* as a "musical comedy, in the style of *Veselye rebiata* and *Volga-Volga* (Jolly Fellows and Volga-Volga, dir. Alexandrov, 1934 and 1938). Film critics and reviewers have referred to the film alternatively as a musical comedy, a musical, and a musical tragicomedy, often coming back specifically to the Stalinist musical comedies exemplified by Alexandrov (who directed) and Isaak Dunaevsky (who wrote the music). Thus, it may be worth pausing here to consider the notion of the musical film as it emerges both from its Soviet and its Hollywood traditions, before considering the ways in which Todorovsky's *Stilyagi* fuses the two genres.

One of the debates surrounding the coming of sound to cinema focused on the question of how music would work in sound film. The purpose of music as an accompaniment to film in the silent period, as Julie Hubbert has pointed out in her article on Sergei Eisenstein's theory of film music, was primarily to reinforce mood, characters, or geographic locations—and in most cases little thought was given to how music might structure the visual image.[6] We can see some of this discussion about the "cinefication of music" (*kinofikatsiia muzyki*) in the pages of *Zhizn' iskusstva* (The Life of Art, one of the prominent arts journals of the period) in 1929.[7] The discussion was started by the head of the Leningrad film studio's (Lenfil'm) script department, Adrian Piotrovsky, in an attempt to articulate the relationship of music to the new "sound" film (*tonfil'ma*). Piotrovsky suggests that for music to become a truly contemporary art (which is to say, for Piotrovsky, "revolutionary art" as opposed to bourgeois art), it needs to transform itself along the lines of avant-garde cinema. Cinema, according to Piotrovsky, is an industrial art based on two principles: "on industrial technology, as a method of registration of raw material, and on montage, as a method of its organization." Similarly, music must become the "capturing of the world's sounds, regardless of their material source." "The reconstruction of music along the principles of cinema—that is to say, the principles of *montage* and the registration on tape of disorganized naturalized fragments of the world's sounds" would lead to a new form of art: the sound film as "pure music."[8]

For Piotrovsky, contemporary music was in crisis: its standard form was nonindustrialized and therefore backward (Piotrovsky refers to this as *kustarnoe proizvodstvo,* meaning something "hand-made," rustic, primitive), and this crisis could not be resolved in the long term by turning to a kind of "global" music—that is to say, by incorporating the music of "native peoples," including, of course, "Negros."[9] Instead, he proposes that music becomes "industrialized"—that is to say, a photographic recording of the sounds of the world, organized by means of montage.

In a follow-up article, S. Gres, who dismisses Piotrovsky's argument regarding the "cinefication of music" and the need to move music toward "natural sounds" arranged by means of montage, nevertheless agrees that part of the problem with nonindustrialized music is its unique and singular performance. Even on the radio, which, according to Gres, is "a fully industrialized apparatus," each performance of a musical piece happens only once; what is lacking are the means of mechanical reproduction (*mekhanizirovannoe povtorenie*). Arguing against the gramophone as a petty-bourgeois invention intended for the drawing room and, as such, of little value to Soviet mass culture or society, Gres underscores its limit also in terms of volume and duration—by the record on which the music is recorded. The gramophone needle has done its duty, Gres suggests, and the next step is sound photography (*zvukovaia fotografiia*).[10]

Anticipating Walter Benjamin, Gres notes that mechanical reproduction will bring music—in its recorded form—to the masses: the same recording will be placed in a box and sent to *everyone (vsem-vsem-vsem),* to cities and villages, where it will sound a countless number of times without any loss to the quality of the recording, and in all possible gradations of volume—from the living room to the concert hall, to the open air—anywhere where you might set up the basic attributes of the radio: the amplifier and the loudspeaker (*gromkogovoritel'*). For Gres, sound film represents precisely this moment of the industrialization (mechanical reproduction) of music, which relies of the simultaneous recording and reproduction of the sound and image tracks. He notes silent film's dedication to the acquisition of speech, as well as the general need for an apparatus that will allow for the synchronic (simultaneous) recording and the simultaneous reproduction of the elements of "movement and sound." Here the goal is both talking and sound cinema.

The issue of film and music is also picked up in the same issues of *Zhizn' iskusstva* by V. Bogdanov-Berezovsky as part of the discussion of the release of *Novyi Vavilon* (The New Babylon, dir. Kozintsev and Trauberg, 1929).[11] Bogdanov-Berezovsky notes that this is the first time that music has been composed specifically for film: Dmitry Shostakovich has written an original musical score to accompany this latest FEKS (Factory of the Eccentric Actor) film. However, lacking the necessary technology to produce synchronized sound, either in recording or in reproduction, means that the music, though composed for the film, remains separate from it. "Can we really call this film music?" asks the critic. If, he suggests, "the demonstration of the film is mechanized, then the accompanying music should also be subjected to mechanization. Only this would ensure the non-separation [*nerazryv*] of the film from its musical illustration."

A similar question haunts another of Piotrovsky's editorials for *Zhizn' iskusstva*, called "Sound Film" (*Tonfil'ma*).[12] Here Piotrovsky begins by describing Alexander Shorin's development of sync-sound technology in Leningrad (and, briefly, Pavel Tager's in Moscow) and the proximity of Soviet cinema to producing sound films, asking, what roads should Soviet sound cinema take? He is specifically interested in the ways in which Soviet cinema must be different from American and European sound film, whose direction in 1929 was toward dialogue and the reproduction of naturalistic sound effects. Specifically, Piotrovsky mentions the unheard of and unprecedented sensation created by *The Jazz Singer* and Al Jolson's "cabaret" songs.[13]

For Piotrovsky, this focus on "sensation" (singing and dancing) meant that sound cinema had abandoned the editing and optical techniques of its earlier, silent years. For the Soviet film industry, argues Piotrovsky, this kind of cinema would signal a return to its prerevolutionary bourgeois roots; instead, we must think of sound in film as independent expressive material rather than naturalistic effects. Like Sergei Eisenstein, Vsevolod Pudovkin, and Grigori Alexandrov's earlier "Statement on Sound" (1928), Piotrovsky is arguing specifically for contrast: nonparallel construction, confrontation, and disjuncture. Instead of having the sound track "passively" following the course set by the image track, Piotrovsky advocates for the dialectical possibilities of conflict, struggle, and disagreement. This would provide the new sound film with political and social value (as opposed to the merely aesthetic, naturalistic, reactionary forms of American and European sound cinema); it would give Soviet cinema "immunity" from the "reactionary disease of the naturalized sound film."

But by 1929, the pages of *Zhizn' ikusstva* (as well as other journals and newspapers) were filled with talk of the "crisis in Soviet cinema" and Soviet films' apparent inability to be "intelligible to the masses." "We call our cinema Soviet," writes Leningrad director Pavel Petrov-Bytov, in another editorial in *Zhizn' iskusstva*, "Do we have the right to call it that at present? In my view, we do not." We have no workers' and peasants' cinema, he stresses. There is no cinema that speaks to the everyday *byt* of the masses, and the masses answer by leaving the theater:

> What do we have to offer the peasant woman, thinking with her ponderous and sluggish brain about her husband who has gone to make a living in the town, about the cow that is sick in the dirty cowshed with tuberculosis of the lungs, about the starving horse that has broken its leg, about the child that is stirring in her womb? What are we providing for her? What are we proposing to provide? *New Babylon? The Happy Canary?* What Babylonian barbarism on our part! What stupid parasitic self-satisfaction at the summits of culture!
>
> "What have you done for me?" the worker asks. "For goodness sake: *October, New Babylon, The Happy Canary,*" we answer familiarly. He does not say a word but swings his hand and slugs us.[14]

These masses—the workers and the peasants—are the real audience of Soviet cinema, and the audience missed almost entirely by radical avant-garde filmmakers. "For peasants we have to make straightforward realistic films with a simple story and plot," writes Petrov-Bytov, "We must talk in his own sincere language about the cow that is sick with tuberculosis, about the dirty cowshed that must be transformed into one that is clean and bright, about the child that is stirring in the peasant woman's womb, about crèches for the child, about rural hooligans, the kolkhoz, and so on." Every film must be useful, intelligible and familiar to the millions, Petrov-Bytov stresses. "We are surrounded by such obscenity, such dirt, poverty, coarseness, and thickheadedness."[15] Soviet cinema must sift through this "vile filth" on the "dung hill of everyday life" to uncover the "beautiful life" hidden deep within.

As Richard Taylor and Ian Christie point out, we can "detect the kernel of the later doctrine of Socialist Realism," that informs this way of thinking.[16] Indeed, for the Soviet film industry, the first shift in ideology can be traced back to the 1928 All-Union Party Conference on Cinema, which decreed that Soviet cinema "must furnish a 'form that is intelligible to the millions.'"[17] From this point forward, Soviet films had to be entertaining first and foremost: unlike their avant-garde predecessors, they were obliged to have plot and to be organized around a story line. In his 1933 "Tvorcheskie zadachi templana," Boris Shumyatsky wrote: "We need genres that are infused with optimism, with the mobilizing emotions, with cheerfulness, *joie-de-vivre* and laughter. Genres that provide us with the maximum opportunity to demonstrate the best Bolshevik traditions: an implacable attitude to opportunism, with tenacity, initiative, skill and a Bolshevik scale of work."[18] "The victorious class wants to laugh with joy. That is its right and Soviet cinema must provide its audiences with this joyful Soviet laughter."[19] He urged a concentration on three genres: drama, comedy, and fairy tales. Of the 308 films produced in the 1930s, 54 were made for children, and of the musical comedies, 12 were set in factories and 17 took place on collective farms: one strongly got the impression, as Richard Taylor wrote, "that the countryside was a round of never-ending dancing and singing."[20]

In his notes from Kremlin screenings a year later, Boris Shumyatsky reported that Stalin was particularly interested in "light" films, noting specifically, "The audience needs joy, cheerfulness, and laughter. They want to see themselves on the screen." Shumyatsky spends a long time accounting for the lack of humor in current Soviet cinema, before assuring Stalin that the next films coming up— *Jolly Fellows, Entuziasty* (The Enthusiasts, dir. Simonov, 1934[21]), and *Garmon'* (The Accordion, dir. Savchenko, 1934]—would be refreshingly comical, cheerful, and joyful *(bodrye i radostnye)*.[22]

The Stalinist musical comedy was born precisely out of this need for light, joyous movies, in which the audience would be able to recognize themselves on the screen.[23] But it was also born from the very introduction of sound to cinema: as Richard Barrios has argued, "As the one genre not possible in silent film, musicals were inevitable." For Barrios, *The Broadway Melody* (dir. Beaumont, 1929) marked the true beginning of the musical sound film. It established that genre as a potent, even irresistible, form of entertainment, giving "stature" to talking film at a crucial time in its evolution.[24] It was "[neither] theater nor cinema, but something altogether new," as René Clair commented after seeing *The Broadway Melody*.[25]

The Hollywood musical gets its reputation as an "escapist" genre from the musicals produced in the early 1930s—the image of tuxedoed Fred Astaire and high-heeled Ginger Rogers dancing their way through the Great Depression.[26] But the 1930s musical was also a tool for the reaffirmation of the American dream that seemed to have been lost or sacrificed after the stock market crash of 1929. In his article "Some Warners' Musicals and the Spirit of the New Deal," Mark Roth has suggested that the musical is not so much an opiate or drug that puts the spectators to sleep inducing them to ignore the problems of the real world, but rather that it disarms the spectator, lowering his or her resistance, allowing ideologically laden messages to sneak through. For Roth, the spirit of the New Deal, for example, found its expression in the Warner musicals of the period. Films like *42nd Street* and *Footlight Parade* (both directed by Bacon, 1933) demonstrated a spirit of unity, optimism, and pride that was being fostered by the rhetoric of the Roosevelt administration that hoped to repair the shattered American dream.[27]

In a Warners' musical each person was shown to be part of an interdependent group. The musicals focused on the production of a show within the film (a standard musical gimmick) and involved, among other things, famously elaborate chorus-line-style musical numbers, choreographed by Busby Berkeley, in which scantily clad rows of girls kicked together or formed pyramids on enormously spectacular sets. (We see a similar conceit in Alexandrov's 1936 *Tsirk* [Circus], which borrows from these earlier American musicals.) The dance numbers in particular symbolized the importance of social cohesion and harmony while reaffirming the American dream of unity and social cohesion at a time of strife and social unrest.

For Soviet cinema and its new search for a "cinema for the millions," Igor Savchenko's *The Accordion* and Alexandrov's *Jolly Fellows* similarly represented the birth of the new genre of musical comedy while rejecting the designation "musical" because of its association with bourgeois culture (both Savchenko and Shumyatsky, for example, called *The Accordion* the "first attempt at musical operetta"). Coming on the heels of the adoption of socialist realism as the official "method" of all Soviet art, Stalinist musical comedies became a way to link the notion of "reality in its revolutionary development" to the "feeling of utopia" generated by the musical.[28] Or, as Richard Taylor has put it, "What better genre to help create [the dream of mass utopia], once sound cinema had arrived, than the musical?"[29]

The musical negotiates between realistic narrative and fantastical musical numbers, and the transition from the one to the other (often quite forced) is part of what makes the musical recognizable as such, at least in its Hollywood form. In classic Hollywood cinema, musical numbers interrupt, or provide a break from, the narrative flow.[30] The three broad tendencies of musicals, as Richard Dyer has noted, are those that keep narrative and number clearly separated (most typically, the backstage musical); those that retain the division between narrative as problems and numbers as escape, but try to "integrate" the numbers by a whole set of papering-over-the-cracks devices (e.g., the well-known cue for a song); and those that try to dissolve the distinction between narrative and numbers, "thus implying that the world of the narrative is also (already) utopian."[31]

For Soviet cinema, the two leading figures in the production of Soviet musicals were of course Alexandrov and Ivan Pyriev. When Eisenstein and Alexandrov returned from Mexico in May 1932, Shumyatsky asked Eisenstein to make a musical comedy (as part of Shumyatsky's dream of "Sovetskii Golivud")—Eisenstein refused, but Alexandrov accepted and the new genre of the Stalinist musical comedy was born. Most notably, Alexandrov produced (in close collaboration with Dunaevsky) *Jolly Fellows, Circus, Volga-Volga,* and *Svetlyi put'* (The Radiant Path, 1941), films that are considered the epitome of the genre to this day. They specifically reflected the cultural mandate to "turn fairy tales into reality," ideology plus entertainment, and the creation of an ideal Soviet space filled with singing and dancing.

Todorovsky's reluctance to qualify *Stilyagi* as a "musical" echoes the earlier sentiments (and ideology) of Soviet directors, pointing us back to the history of Soviet musical film production. Bypassing the years in between—in which Soviet cinema turned away from the mass utopia of the *kolkhoz* musical and toward the lyrical,[32] the *avtorskaia pesnia* (auteur song), and the "bard song" and "guitar poetry" of singers such as Bulat Okudzhava and Vladimir Vysotsky—*Stilyagi* insists on a cinematic history that appears to tie it squarely back not to Hollywood but to Stalinism. Meladze's qualification of *Stilyagi* as a "musical comedy, in the style of *Jolly Fellows* and *Volga-Volga*," is meant to emphasize its historical link to Soviet cinematic production, and specifically, its continuation of a generic tradition that comes not from the United States but from the Soviet Union.

From New York to Stalino

The relationship of the Soviet Union to the West is at the very heart of this film. In a sequence where Mels learns to play the saxophone by listening to Charlie Parker, we see a close up of the shortwave radio dial, marking the names of various cities, including New York and Stalino. The image suggests that these disparate locations in the West and the East are linked by the power of music. *Stilyagi* gives us a glimpse at a subculture that first emerged in the 1940s, influenced by the American films shown in Soviet cinemas. Real *stilyagi* sported pompadours à la Elvis Presley, assembled wardrobes out of American land-lease clothes available through state-run secondhand shops (in addition to sewing their own or buying items on the black market), and danced the twist and the boogie-woogie, not only in their homes but also in state-run cultural centers. Indeed, by the early 1960s, twist contests were organized by public parks in Sochi, on the Black Sea coast, where hundreds of thousands of young people from all corners of the

Soviet Union spend their summers. As Alexei Yurchak notes, these dances were not only more openly tolerated but also explicitly taught.[33] *Stilyagi* were part of a general cultural rebirth of the 1950s that included creative experiments with literature, poetry, Western music, and foreign clothes—but they represented its extreme edge. They were much made fun of in the press, and newly established "Komsomol patrols" on the streets targeted those young people who had a "provocative look" (*vyzyvaiushchii vid*). They were also always under the threat of being arrested for "rootless cosmopolitanism" (Stalin's campaign that lasted from 1948 to his death in 1953) and "blind worship of the West," which remained a criminal offense punishable by law.

The term *stilyagi* became popular after the 1949 publication of a satirical article called "Stilyagi"[34] in the humor magazine *Krokodil*, and it was used disparagingly throughout the 1950s and 1960s to make fun of this new generation of nonconformists (figure 14.4). *Stilyagi* was the term used by Soviet propaganda; the actual *stilyagi* called one other *chuvak* and *chuvikha*, and *shtatniki*—in reference to the United States and American culture. The meaning of the word *stiliaga*, however, has two possible English language origins: the less likely (but more interesting) source might be the verb *to steal*, though the more likely, generally accepted etymology is the noun *style* (*stil'*). What unites both of these, however, is the musical context: in the language of jazz performers, *dut' stiliagu* means to "steal" a composition, that is to say, to play it in someone else's style. This is of course applicable to *stilyagi* as a whole: not only was their entire style—clothing and hairstyles, musical tastes, moral values—"borrowed" from the West, but by the time the latest fashions made it to the Soviet Union (dropped as care packages by the Americans or brought back in suitcases from defeated Germany), by the time trophy films, new jazz records, and fashion magazines showed up in the Soviet Union, they were already out of date. The *stilyagi* copied, in other words, a style that was already passé.

Todorovsky's film takes up precisely this problem of originality and imitation. The opening sequence of the film that shows us the production of a homemade record—before we meet the actual *stilyagi*—underscores the importance of music for both the film and the counterculture. The homemade record, known as "rock on bones" or "rock on ribs" (*rok na rebrakh*), was a true Soviet invention: a combination of a lack of raw materials and pure ingenuity. As Yurchak puts it, in the 1950s, the demand for Western jazz and rock and roll, boosted by the popularity of shortwave radio and films, as well as by the virtual absence of these kinds of music on Soviet state-produced records, led to the invention of "an independent technology" for copying music. Original Western records with jazz and rock and roll (as well as samba, tango, and spirituals) were copied on used plastic X-ray plates, which gave them their slang name. Writing about these in *Back in the USSR: The True Story of Rock in Russia*, music critic Artemy Troitsky

Figure 14.4. The monkeys among us; frame grab from *Stilyagi*.

stressed that "these were actual X-ray plates—chest cavities, spinal cords, broken bones—rounded at the edges with scissors, with a small hole in the center and grooves that were barely visible on the surface."[35]

The technology involved two connected turntables, an amplified electrical signal, and a heated sapphire needle cutting grooves into the surface of the plastic plate. In Leningrad, these were sold clandestinely in front of the central music store Melodiya (as well as at city markets and near radio shops) and would sell out immediately. Yurchak notes that the particular materiality of the "rock on bones" and the obvious metaphors these X-rays invited were not lost on Soviet fans. Made by means of Soviet technology, yet copying Western music, these homemade records produced a kind of "uncanny intimacy": intimate space that the bones and arteries of the Soviet body provided a space for the sounds coming from "elsewhere." This was a great representation of the mix of the two kinds of cultures—Soviet and Western—as both internal and external to the "body" of the Soviet state.[36]

Indeed, the original title of Todorovsky's film was *Boogie on Bones* (*Bugi na kostiakh*), seemingly speaking to the East-West connections pointed to by the homemade records. But the musical subtext here is actually much subtler than this. Once the notion of writing an original score for the film was abandoned (Todorovsky argues that because of a lack of a musical tradition in Russian cinema, there were no composers who could single-handedly write all the musical numbers for the film the way that Dunaevsky had for Alexandrov), Todorovsky turned to archival recordings of the music of the 1930s to 1950s but quickly realized that those wouldn't work either. To begin with, the actual (that is to say, historical) *stilyagi* had little relation to rock and roll; they listened to fairly old-fashioned jazz. Their musical idols were Louis Armstrong, Duke Ellington, and above all Glenn Miller, whose "Chattanooga Choo Choo" was considered something of an anthem.[37] But more important for Todorovsky, the real *stilyagi* listened to *American* music, and the notion of making a contemporary Russian (*rossiiskii*) film with old American rock seemed "absurd."[38] Working closely with Margulis, he turned instead to Soviet rock music of the 1980s and 1990s, which was made, as Todorovsky claimed, by the "children of *stilyagi*," who had inherited their parents' countercultural tendencies:

> In the first place, the people who created Russian rock were very similar to the stilyagi in their world-view. Second, they too wanted to be different, this too was counter-culture. And third: they were the children of stilyagi. The generation of Tsoi and [Viacheslav] Butusov was born from the people who in listened to boogie-woogie in the fifties. So everything fell into place.[39]

Thus, while all of the musical numbers in the film are covers, they are covers of late-Soviet or post-Soviet rock songs rearranged in the style of 1950s jazz and rock and roll and are given new lyrical content.[40] Specifically, the film uses hits from such well-known Soviet rock groups as Machina Vremeni (Time Machine), Kino, Zoopark (Zoo), Nautilus Pompilius, Nol' (Zero), Bravo, Calibri, Chaif, and Brigada S (Brigade S). In fact, to better understand the musical sound track of this film, we need to go back not to the Soviet 1950s (or the American 1930s or 1940s) but to the Soviet 1980s and the first Soviet films to use rock and roll as their sound track.

The period of "late socialism" that began on or around 1968 and lasted until about 1986 was marked by a change from the optimism of the Thaw to the pessimism of Stagnation. But while cinema may have been experiencing a kind of political and aesthetic stagnation (though, of course, it too was not monolithic), in other ways, the period of late socialism, as Yurchak and others have shown, was incredibly vibrant in terms of different kinds of underground movements: non-conformist art, conceptualism in poetry, and the birth of Soviet rock music were some of the most prominent and recognizable antiestablishment discourses that began to emerge from beneath the cracks of a worn-out and crumbling ideology.

By the early 1980s, rock music in particular began to play a significant role in youth counterculture, and the film that captured that spirit of rebellion was Sergei Soloviev's 1987 cult film *ASSA*, which starred Tatiana Drubich and Sergei "Afrika" Bugaev, and ended with a performance by Viktor Tsoi, the lead singer of the group Kino, of their hit song, "My zhdem peremen" ("We Are Waiting for Change"). In the final sequence, we watch Tsoi take the stage, and as the camera cuts away from him, there's a background shift—instead of the restaurant in a provincial town where the film is set, we see Tsoi performing at a rock concert at the Zelenyi Theater to millions of Kino fans holding up lit matches. And in fact, the final sequence was filmed as a live concert, with millions of fans in attendance. The year was 1987; and the place was Moscow, Soviet Union. When audiences first watched this sequence in the late 1980s, its power lay in part with the cult status of the performer, but also in part with a new attention to youth culture, and the possibility of radical political change. Though many of the film's characters do not survive to the end, the film nevertheless offered the viewer a glimmer of hope and a kind of renewal for a nation poised on the edge of an abyss.[41]

Todorovsky's film returns precisely to this moment. Indeed, many of the bands we see listed in the final credits for *ASSA* are also credited with songs in *Stilyagi*. While seemingly commenting on the Soviet 1950s, musically it is referencing the late 1980s and the history of a late-Soviet counterculture. The choice of using Soviet rock in a new "retro" form (and the consequent absence of American or Western rock and roll or jazz) speaks to something vital at the heart of this picture: the film is actually not an exploration of the Soviet Union's relationship to the West but rather of the Soviet Union's (and now, Russia's) relationship to itself.

The key scene for this is the Komsomol meeting that takes places about two-thirds through the film, when we are told the origin of our protagonist's name. As part of the transformation from Komsomol member to *chuvak*, Mels drops the last letter of his name, becoming "Mel" (just as Fedor becomes "Fred," Polina becomes "Polly,"[42] and Boris becomes "Bob"). But the real significance of this is made clear only when Katya, the Komsomol leader, points out the original meaning of Mels: an abbreviation of Marx, Engels, Lenin, Stalin. What happens, she asks, if we drop the last letter? The seemingly insignificant letter *s*?

I would suggest that we can actually read the missing *s* in two ways: it points, on the one hand, to the missing Stalin (physically dead but not yet "buried" in 1955), but it also points, on the other hand, to the missing Soviet period as a whole, for which, under Putin's first terms as president, Russian cinema (and television) had been exhibiting a fair amount of nostalgia. While on the surface the film presents a group of imitators (Soviet youth dressed in Western fashion) and delivers its message by means of rather conventional and derivative aesthetic techniques, it is nevertheless trying to speak about originality and nonconformity.

This is quite different from another recent nostalgic production—AMC's television show *Mad Men* (premiered on July 19, 2007). Set in 1960s in New York, *Mad Men* shows us a world of uniformity, of men in gray flannel suits coming home to their Stepford wives. As the 1960s advance, that uniformity begins to break down, but what the show is ultimately interested in is not counterculture but the mainstream: it wants to document the era of American cultural dominance and the cracks that begin to appear beneath its well-polished surface. *Mad Men* is of course a show famously obsessed with period accuracy, a certain kind of "realism," and a coherent visual style. Although Matthew Weiner, the show's creator, claimed that "style" was not the star of the show, *Mad Men* gets most noticed for its period look: midcentury modern furniture, international architectural style, Brooks Brothers suits, and dresses modeled on Dior's "new look."

Compared to *Mad Men*'s highly polished visuals, *Stilyagi* appears almost as a kind of farce, and this is also true if we compare it to the very stylish look of Soviet cinema in the 1960s, with its crisp black and white photography, long takes, and use of the fish-eye lens. Compared to the mod clothes and cinema verité camerawork, *Stilyagi* appears as an outrageous, garish, melodramatic, Technicolor caricature of the new wave films of the 1960s. One is tempted, as Diane Koenker has suggested, to take the film's look as a metaphor for the transformed Moscow of today, which rebuilds both cathedrals and hotels as Las Vegas parodies of the former real things.[43]

Yet despite its visual garishness and conventional cinematic language, *Stilyagi* wants to give us a glimpse of a genuine countercultural moment, of what it meant to be a nonconformist in a country where such things were not simply unwelcomed but also were routinely criminalized.[44] While it makes many references to the States (Mels learns to play saxophone by listening to Charlie Parker; Pol'za has an off-screen romance with a black man and gives birth to a mixed-race baby; Fred gives up his outrageous clothes and his girlfriend Betsy for a career as a diplomat in New York), the film is not concerned with America per se, or even with the "Imaginary West."[45] Instead, its gaze is insistently turned inward: this is suggested by its anachronistic choice of music and is spelled out perhaps most clearly in the film's conclusion.

After a brief period of living the highlife, the group of *stilyagi* falls apart: Bob is arrested for trying to buy American records; Dryn gets drafted to spend five years on a submarine; Betsy has a nervous breakdown and is shipped out of town; Polly loses her sense of fun as soon as she has the baby. And when Fred returns from the United States, sporting a look that pretty closely resembles that of Don Draper on *Mad Men*, he reveals to Mels the uncomfortable truth: "Mel, understand me," he says, "they don't have stilyagi over there" *(tam net stiliag).* Mels is heartbroken, but the most important realization comes at this point: "But we are here!" he says.

Like Fred's arrival from America, the real "death blow" to the historical *stilyagi* came from the West with the Seventh International Festival of Youth and Students, which took place in Moscow in 1957. As Troitsky notes, thousands of real, live young foreigners flooded into virginal Moscow. Among them were jazz musicians, beatnik poets, and modern artists, and all of them were fashionably dressed and knew how to dance to rock and roll. As the "real stilyaga" Alexei Kozlov put it, "I had suspected as much earlier, but during the Festival we all became convinced that our style and our music and our idols all belonged to the distant past. Some stilyagi remained after the Festival, but these were the backward elements, pure imitators who were hopelessly behind the times."[46]

The closing musical number of the film, "Shaliai-valiai," underscores the notion of the "end of history." As Mels and Polly perform their final number

Figure 14.5. March of the nonconformists; frame grab from *Stilyagi*.

walking down "Broadway" (Moscow's Gorky Street), they are joined not only by all the *stilyagi* of the film but also by punks, rockers, goths, and many other conspicuous "nonconformists" (*neformaly*). As Todorovsky notes, in this final sequence Mels and Polly cross not only space (Gorky Street, now Tverskaya) but also time: leaving 1956 to arrive in contemporary Moscow. The director mentions that, for example, the ads on the buildings were left in to underscore the difference between 1950s Moscow and now (figure 14.5).

"Shaliai-valiai" is played as a kind of anthem—the closing number prefigures the recent marches of the noncompliant (*marsh nesoglasnykh*) and was referred to as the march of the nonconformists (*marsh neformalov*). But the song also borrows something of the sentiment of Nautilus Pompilius's "Goodbye, America" (Poslednee pis'mo), which bids farewell to the United States, the one we will never see.[47] The lyrics of "Shaliai-valiai" are purely nostalgic: "Good-bye, dear friend / You are leaving all of a sudden / You are going without saying farewell, you are going for no reason . . . I thought we still had another five years / I thought we still had time to drink beer and to talk."

Given the context, it is clear that we are saying good-bye to the decade, but also perhaps—again, coming back to the choice of music—to the Soviet period as a whole. The choice of late-Soviet rock for *Stilyagi* unites what we might think of as two endings: the end of Stalinism and the end of the Soviet Union. As Yurchak has suggested, in the 1990s "the Imaginary West was no longer to be found anywhere and was lost forever . . . [but] the greatest discovery of all was that one could now turn back to the Soviet past with an equally astonished glance."[48]

Todorovsky's film stages its historical moment as a unique, unrepeatable event. Despite being shown on Russian television, *Stilyagi* is of course not a television series, and its non-seriality and non-repeatability is precisely at stake in its representation of the period as a closed and finished event.

There is no realism here, no attempt at historical accuracy. The film favors the overhead crane shot, and its use is particularly apt for the closing musical number, ensuring distance by giving us a bird's-eye view of the events below. But on the other hand, the film ties together the 1950s and the 1990s, the Hollywood musical and the Stalinist musical comedy, the United States and the Soviet Union, and the Soviet Union and Russia. American culture is subsumed by Soviet culture (the way that Mels, by listening to Charlie Parker, manages to give Polly a black baby[49]), and it is Soviet culture that appears unique, original, and greatly to be missed.

From Tverskaya to Bolotnaya

When I first began writing about this film, *Stilyagi* seemed to me to be participating in precisely the kinds of cultural nostalgia and forgetting that was so prevalent under the first decade of Putin's presidency: "post-Soviet nostalgia" (or *ostalgie*, as it is called in Germany) reimagines the crash of communism as "the crash of something very personal, innocent, and full of hope, of the 'passionate sincerity and genuineness' that marked childhood and youth."[50] "That time had a completely different color than ours," film director and now head of Mosfil'm Studio Karen Shakhnazarov said in a 2008 interview with *Izvestiia*. "I am convinced that empires crumble at the level of the personal. . . . It wasn't the deployment of soldiers to Afghanistan in December that was responsible for the Soviet empire falling apart, but Beatles and Rolling Stones records."[51]

Since its release in 2008, the film's reception has split into three radically different (but related) positions: the journalist Vladimir Soloviev, the rock critic Artemy Troitsky, the film reviewer for the newspaper *Kommersant,* Arina Borodina, and many other liberal cultural observers all found that *Stilyagi* made an important statement about individuality, about the right to be different, about the possibility of independent thought. This film, as Troitsky put it, is absolutely "anti-government" (*antigosudarstvennyi*). The reverse sentiment was articulated by arch-conservative critics, who found that the film was an attack on our glorious Soviet past, claiming that the *stilyagi* really were enemies of the people seduced by American mass culture and an affront to "normal" Soviet postwar youth. The film distorted Soviet history with typical anti-Soviet stereotypes, they wrote, focusing on the threat of arrest (such as the reference to the packed suitcase in the hall, readied in case of midnight raid), mentions of the Gulag, and the like.[52] But perhaps the most interesting response came from the writer Alexander

Kabakov, who found that the film was a lighthearted comedy about something that should have actually been taken quite seriously: the fate of anti-Soviet youth (Kabakov refers to them as the first dissidents) who tried to live expressly outside the Soviet norm and were persecuted and arrested. The word *stilyaga*, he stresses, was coined not by the members of the counterculture group themselves but by those who made fun of them.

In light of the "stolen" Duma election of 2011 and Putin's third presidential campaign, however, the film can be read in yet another way. It is simply a coincidence, but nonetheless a telling one, that the film was made with support from Mikhail Prokhorov, who in 2008 was still merely an oligarch but who in 2011 emerged as a critic and opponent of Putin's renewed bid for the presidency. And it is significant, I think, that in its choice of music, Todorovsky's film goes back precisely to the late 1980s or early 1990s, a period (as opposed to the 2000s) that can still be understood as precisely countercultural. What *Stilyagi* celebrates is nonconformity and non-consensus. Despite its visual (and even to some degree, musical) conventionality, this film is precisely about not doing as you are told, about radical free thought, about the possibility of difference and noncompliance.

This possibility of an alternative way of thinking and being has been recently brought to the fore by the arrest and trial of the Russian feminist punk-rock collective Pussy Riot (figure 14.6).[53] Arrested a few weeks after their performance of their punk prayer "Mother of God, Chase Putin Away!" (*Bogoroditsa, Putina progoni*) at the Cathedral of Christ the Savoir in Moscow and sentenced to two years in a women's labor colony for "hooliganism," the Pussy Riot trial revealed once again the way Russian power protects itself from the possibility of dissention. As Slavoj Žižek wrote in his response to the trial: "What is a modest Pussy Riot obscene provocation in a church compared to the accusation against Pussy Riot, this gigantic obscene provocation of the state apparatus which mocks any notion of decent law and order?"[54] "By and large, the three members of Pussy Riot are not the ones on trial here," wrote Nadezhda Tolokonnikova in her closing statement at the trial, "If we were, this event would hardly be so significant. This is a trial of the entire political system of the Russian Federation." [55]

Since late 2011, Russia is once again experiencing something like revolution. "Today's educational institutions teach people, from childhood, to live as automatons," wrote Maria Alyokhina in her closing statement, "Not to pose the crucial questions consistent with their age. They inculcate cruelty and intolerance of nonconformity. Beginning in childhood, we forget our freedom."[56] As Todorovsky suggests, *Stilyagi* is not about a particular era or group but about the very possibility of dissent, of not going along with the "gray masses."[57] The demonstrations and protests in Moscow and St. Petersburg were only the first signs of the possibility of such transformation. But for a brief moment, they looked not

Figure 14.6. Pussy Riot (© 2011 Феномен; http://fenomen.ws/uchastnicy-gruppy-pussy-riot
-zaderzhany-za-penie-o-straxe-putina/).

unlike the utopian vision of unity in nonconformity imagined by Todorovsky's
film: from the march of nonconformists (*neformalov*) to the march of the noncompliant (*nesoglasnykh*), with rock and roll once again trying to speak truth to
power.

Notes

1. Sergei Nekrasov, "Istoriia o stiliagakh—ideal'nyi siuzhet dlia muzykal'nogo fil'ma.
Interv'iu s Valeriem Todorovskim," *Kinobiznes segodnia*, no. 170 (December 15, 2008), http://
www.kinobusiness.com/content/view/1510/31/.

2. The *Vysotki* or *Stalinskie vysotki* ("Stalin's high-rises") are a group of skyscrapers in
Moscow designed in the high Stalinist style. They were built from 1947 to 1953 (some work
extended years past official completion dates) in an elaborate combination of Russian baroque
and gothic styles, with the same technology used in the building of American skyscrapers.

3. In an interview, screenwriter Yury Korotkov argued that while the film does not represent the reality of the 1950s, it nevertheless appears quite realistic to the contemporary viewer.
G. Litvinov, *Stiliagi. Kak eto bylo* (Moscow: Amfora, 2009), 304.

4. Cinematic references to Soviet and post-Soviet films include not only Grigori Alexandrov's *Tsirk* (Circus, 1936) and specifically, the famous lullaby scene of the unconditional
acceptance of a mixed-race baby, but also Pavel Lungin's *Taksi-Bliuz* (Taxi Blues, 1990),
which casts punk singer Petr Mamonov as an alcoholic jazz-saxophone player whose career is

rescued when he meets a visiting African American saxophonist who invites him to perform in the United States. As Helena Goscilo suggests, the theme of blackness is central not only to jazz but also to creativity and music as a mode of resisting oppression, that is, expressing the non-mainstream self. In *ASSA*, for example, the singer Vitya (musician Dmitry Shumilov, in heavy brown makeup) is repeatedly introduced as "our Soviet Negro," the offspring of an Angolan freedom-fighting father and a Russian mother. Vitya is also, allegedly, a saxophone player, but although he wears a saxophone around his neck as he dances and lip-synchs to Yury Chernavsky's tune, he is never shown playing the instrument. As Susan Larsen notes, Vitya's unpersuasive chocolate makeup, like his saxophone, is a marker of the extent to which this particular rhythm reads as "black" in the Soviet context. The combination of "black" skin and saxophone is a persistent sign, a cliché in fact, as she suggests, of late Soviet and post-Soviet cinema with musically themed plots. I am grateful to Helena Goscilo and Susan Larsen for these observations, which I am happy to reproduce here.

5. The following scenes were cut from the television release: Bob making the homemade gramophone record, Bob's arrest, the sex scene between Mels and Pol'za, and Pol'za's mother threatening to send Mels and his family to the gulag.

6. Julie Hubbert, "Eisenstein's Theory of Film Music Revisited: Silent and Early Sound Antecedents," in *Composing for the Screen in Germany and the USSR*, ed. Robynn J. Stilwell and Phil Powrie (Bloomington: Indiana University Press, 2008), 127.

7. Adrian Piotrovskii, "Kinofikatsiia muzyki," *Zhizn' iskusstva*, no. 9 (1929): 4—part of a series of articles in *Zhizn' iskusstva* starting with Piotrovskii, followed by P. Vul'fius, V. Beliaev, and S. Gres.

8. Piotrovskii, "Kinofikatsiia muzyki," 4.

9. Ibid.

10. "Industrializatsiia muziki," *Zhizn' iskusstva*, no. 13 (1929): 2.

11. V. Bogdanov-Berezovskii, "Novyi Vavilon," *Zhizn' iskusstva*, no. 11 (1929): 13. For more on Dmitry Shostakovich's music for *New Babylon*, see Joan Titus's chapter on in this volume.

12. Adrian Piotrovskii, "Tonfil'ma," *Zhizn' iskusstva* 30 (1929): 4–5.

13. As Douglas Gomery and others have noted, *The Jazz Singer* (dir. Crosland, 1927) premiered on October 6, 1927, to lukewarm reviews, but the four Vitaphone segments of Jolson's songs proved very popular, and by April 1928 "it had become clear that *The Jazz Singer* show had become the most popular entertainment offering of the 1927–1928 season." See Douglas Gomery, "Coming of Sound," in *Film Sound: Theory and Practice*, ed. Elisabeth Weis and John Belton (New York: Columbia University Press, 1985), 14, 15.

14. Pavel Petrov-Bytov, "U nas net sovetskoi kinomatografii," *Zhizn' iskusstva*, April 21, 1929, 8; translated as "We Have No Soviet Cinema," in *The Film Factory: Russian and Soviet Cinema in Documents 1896–1939*, ed. Richard Taylor and Ian Christie (New York: Routledge, 1994), 259–62 (261).

15. "We Have No Soviet Cinema," 261–62.

16. Richard Taylor and Ian Christie, "1929: Introduction," in *The Film Factory: Russian and Soviet Cinema in Documents 1896–1939*, ed. Richard Taylor and Ian Christie (New York: Routledge, 1994),247.

17. Ol'khovyi, ed., *Puti kino. Pervoe Vsesoyuznoe partiinoe soveshchanie po kinematografii* (Moscow: Tea-kino-pechat', 1929), 429–44.

18. Boris Shumiatskii, "Tvorcheskie zadachi templana," *Sovetskoe kino* 12 (December 1933): 1–15 (1).

19. Boris Shumiatskii, *Kinematografiya millionov. Opyt analiza* (Moscow: Kinofotoizdat, 1935), 249.

20. For a full account, see Richard Taylor, "Boris Shumyatsky and the Soviet Cinema in the 1930s: Ideology as Mass Entertainment," *Historical Journal of Film, Radio and Television* 6, no. 1 (1986): 43–64.

21. This film was released under the title *Vesennie dni* (Spring Days).

22. "A driani podobno *Garmon'* bol'she ne stavite?" Zapisi besed B. Z. Shumiatskogo s I.V. Stalinym posle kinoprosmotrov. 1934 g. (Publikatsiia i kommentarii A. S. Troshina), *Kinovedcheskie zapiski* 61 (2002): 281–346.

23. On Soviet musicals in the 1930s, see in particular Richard Taylor, "Singing on the Steppes for Stalin: Ivan Pyr'ev and the Kolkhoz Musical in Soviet Cinema," in *Slavic Review* 58, no. 1 (spring 1999): 143–59; Taylor, "K topografii utopii v stalinskom miuzikle" and Katerina Clark, "'Chtoby tak pet', dvadtsat' let uchit'sia nuzhno: Sluchai *Volgi-Volgi,* both in *Sovetskoe bogatstvo. Stat'i o kul'ture, literature i kino,* ed. Marina Balina, Evgeny Dobrenko and Yury Murashov (St. Petersburg: Akademicheskii proekt, 2002), 358–70 and 371–90, respectively; David C. Gillespie, "The Sounds of Music: Soundtrack and Song in Soviet Film," in *Slavic Review* 62, no. 3 (autumn 2003): 473–90; Rimgaila Salys, *The Musical Comedy Films of Grigorii Aleksandrov: Laughing Matters* (Chicago: University of Chicago Press, 2009).

24. Richard Barrios, *A Song in the Dark: the Birth of the Musical Film,* 2nd ed. (Oxford: Oxford University Press, 2010), 59.

25. René Clair, quoted in ibid., 67.

26. For literature on the musical (that goes well beyond 1930s Hollywood), see Jane Feur, *The Hollywood Musical* (Bloomington: Indiana University Press, 1982); Rick Altman, *The American Film Musical* (Bloomington: Indiana University Press, 1988); *Hollywood Musical: The Film Reader,* ed. Steven Cohan (New York: Routledge, 2001); *Movie Music, the Film Reader,* ed. Kay Dickinson (New York: Routledge, 2003); Steven Cohan, *Incongruous Entertainment: Camp, Cultural Value, and the MGM Musical* (Durham, NC: Duke University Press, 2005); *The Hollywood Film Musical Reader,* ed. Mervyn Cooke (Oxford: Oxford University Press, 2010).

27. Mark Roth, "Some Warners' Musicals and the Spirit of the New Deal," *Velvet Light Trap,* no. 77 (winter 1977): 1–7.

28. The First All-Union Congress of Soviet Writers (August 1934) marked the official implementation of the term *socialist realism* for all Soviet art. See *Pervyi vsesoiuznyi s"ezd sovetskikh pisatelei: Stenograficheskii otchet* (Moscow: Khudozhestvennaia literatura, 1934).

29. Taylor, "Singing on the Steppes for Stalin," 145.

30. Despite the director's disclaimers, Todorovsky's *Stilyagi* is a true musical in that sense, since it is built on preexisting numbers that interrupt the narrative. A counterexample would be a film like Jacques Demy's *The Umbrellas of Cherbourg* (Les parapluies de Cherbourg, 1964), which is not considered a musical because the film's dialogue is all sung as recitative. Formally, *Umbrellas of Cherbourg* is an operetta in that both songs and dialogue advance the action.

31. Richard Dyer, "Entertainment and Utopia," in *Only Entertainment,* 2nd ed. (London: Routledge, 2002), 28.

32. On the lyrical turn in Soviet musicals after 1940, see Anna Nisnevich in this volume; on breaking Stalinist cinematic conventions of body and voice, see Oksana Bulgakowa, in this volume.

33. Alexei Yurchak, *Everything Was Forever, Until It Was No More: The Last Soviet Generation* (Princeton, NJ: Princeton University Press, 2005), 175.

34. D. G. Beliaev, "Stiliaga," *Krokodil,* no. 7 (March 1949).

35. Artemy Troitsky, *Back in the USSR: The True Story of Rock in Russia* (London: Faber and Faber, 1988), 19.

36. Yurchak, *Everything Was Forever,* 183.

37. Troitsky, *Back in the USSR*, 15.

38. Lelia Smolina and Vladimir Zakharov, "Seks, Komsomol, Rok-n-roll. Valerii Todorovskii o 'Stiliagakh', den'gakh, sekse i kinokritike," *Empire*, November 2008, http://www.web citation.org/5w9gGbq6R.

39. Ibid.

40. There are similarities here to *Grease* (dir. Kleiser, 1978), for which new original music was written in the style of 1950s pop, and Baz Luhrmann's *Moulin Rouge!* (2001), which, while set in 1899, uses songs from the mid- to late twentieth century, all of them covers rather than original recordings.

41. *ASSA* and Rashid Nugmanov's *Igla* (The Needle, 1988) were two landmark films of the perestroika era. The films acquired cult status almost immediately upon their release, in large part because they were the first feature films in which the sounds of the unofficial, quasi-underground Russian rock scene were heard in Soviet movie theaters. The final scene of *ASSA*, in which Viktor Tsoi sings "We are waiting for change," is invoked, for example, in the concluding scenes of films as diverse as Sergei Loban's *Pyl'* (Dust, 2005), Alexei Balabanov's *Gruz 200* (Cargo 200, 2007), and Soloviev's *2-ASSA-2* (2009). For detailed readings of *ASSA*, *Rok* [Rock, dir. Uchitel',1988], and *Stilyagi*, see Ekaterina Vasil'eva and Nikita Braginskii, *Noev kovcheg russkogo kino: ot "Sten'ki Razina" do "Stiliag"* (n.p.: Globus Press, 2012), 403–7, 418–22, 528–33.

42. Like Mel's, Pol'za's name is an acronym for *Pomnim Lenina zavety* (We remember Lenin's commandments).

43. Diane Koenker, "Behind the Curtain: Sex and Style in the Soviet 1960s," unpublished ms.

44. As they are again: see St. Petersburg's new laws recriminalizing homosexuality, transgender, and other queer identities.

45. See Yurchak, *Everything Was Forever*.

46. Quoted in Troitsky, *Back in the USSR*, 18.

47. "Goodbye, America" (Poslednee pis'mo, Nevidimka, 1985). An earlier number, "Skovany odnoi tsep'iu" (Bound by One Chain), was written by Nautilus Pompilius for their 1986 album *Razluka* (Separation); it was reworked for the film with new lyrics by Konstantin Meladze.

48. Yurchak, *Everything Was Forever*, 206.

49. "Listen, Mel, I think you listened to a little too much Charlie Parker!" Fred tells him when he is first shown Mels and Polly's mixed-race baby.

50. Yurchak, *Everything Was Forever*, 206.

51. Vita Ramm, "Kinorezhisser Karen Shakhnazarov: 'V raspade sovetskoi imperii kliuchevuiu rol' sygrali 'bitly' i 'rollingi'," *Izvestiia*, February 11, 2008.

52. This review was published on the website for the St. Petersburg Communist Party and is therefore a little hard to take seriously. However, it does precisely invert the "liberal" sentiment.

53. Pussy Riot is a Russian feminist punk-rock collective based in Moscow. Founded in August 2011, it consists of approximately twelve members who wear brightly colored balaclavas and use only nicknames during interviews. They stage unannounced provocative performances about Russian political life in unusual and unauthorized locations, such as the Elokhovo Cathedral, Lobnoe Mesto in Red Square, on top of a trolley, or on scaffolding in in the Moscow metro. These performances are edited into videos and posted on the Internet. For articles, interviews, and performances of Pussy Riot, see http://pussy-riot.livejournal.com.

54. Slavoj Žižek, "The True Blasphemy: Slavoj Žižek on Pussy Riot," *Dangerous Minds*, August 10, 2012, http://dangerousminds.net/comments/the_true_blasphemy_slavoj_zhizhek _on_pussy_riot.

55. "Pussy Riot Closing Statements," *n+1*, August 13, 2012, http://nplusonemag.com/pussy -riot-closing-statements.

56. Ibid.

57. Smolina and Zakharov, "Seks, Komsomol, Rok-n-roll."

Bibliography

Adorno, Theodor W. "The Essay as Form." Translated by Robert Hullot-Kentor and Frederic Will. *New German Critique* 32 (1984): 151–71.

Agamben, Giorgio. *Language and Death: The Place of Negativity.* Translated by Karen E. Pinkus with Michael Hardt. Minneapolis: University of Minnesota Press, 1991.

Alyokhina, Maria, Nadezhda Tolokonnikova, and Yekaterina Samutsevich. "Pussy Riot Closing Statements." August 13, 2012. http://nplusonemag.com/pussy-riot-closing -statements.

Allilueva, Svetlana I. *Tol'ko odin god.* Moscow: Kniga, 1990.

Alter, Nora M., and Lutz Koepnick, eds. *Sound Matters: Essays on the Acoustics of Modern German Culture.* New York: Berghan Books, 2004.

Altman, Rick. *The American Film Musical.* Bloomington: Indiana University Press, 1997.

———, ed. "Cinema/Sound." Special issue, *Yale French Studies* 60 (1980).

———. *Silent Film Sound.* New York: Columbia University Press, 2004.

———. "Sound Studies: A Field Whose Time Has Come." *Iris* 27 (spring 1999): 3–4.

———, ed. *Sound Theory, Sound Practice.* New York: Routledge, 1992.

Améry, Jea. *Geburt der Gegenwart. Gestalten und Gestaltung der westlichen Zivilisation seit Kriegsende.* Open und Freiburg im Breisgau: Walter-Verlag, 1961.

Anderson, Trudy. "Why Stalinist Musicals?" *Discourse* 17, no. 3 (spring 1995): 38–48.

Andrievskii, Aleksandr. *Postroenie tonfil'ma.* Moscow: Gosudarstvennoe izdatel'stvo khudozhestvennoi literatury, 1931.

Anikst, Aleksandr. "*Gamlet* Grigoriia Kozintseva." *Iskusstvo kino* 6 (1964): 5–15.

Anoshchenko, Nikolai. "Nasha zvukovaia fil'ma." *Kino i zhizn'* 4 (1929): 14–15.

"ARRK. Stenogramma lektsii tov. Avraamova v gruppe zvukovogo kino ARRKa." *Kinovedcheskie zapiski,* no. 53 (2001): 300–313.

Asaf'ev, B.V. *Izbrannye trudy.* Vol. 5. Moscow: Izd. Akademii Nauk SSSR, 1957.

———. *Muzykal'naia forma kak protsess.* Moscow: Gosudarstvennoe izdatel'stvo muzykal'nyi sektor, 1930.

———. *Muzykal'naia forma kak protsess. Kniga 2, Intonatsiia.* Moscow: Gosudarstven- noe muzykal'noe izd.-vo, 1947.

———[Igor' Glebov]. *Pamiati Petra Il'icha Chaikovskogo, 1840–1940.* Moscow: Muzgiz, 1940.

———. "Evgenii Onegin," *liricheskie stseny P. I. Chaikovskogo.* Moscow: Muzgiz, 1944.

Averbakh, E., ed. *Rozhdenie zvukovogo obraza: Khudozhestvennye problemy zvukozapisi v ekrannykh iskusstvakh i na radio.* Moscow: Iskusstvo, 1985.

Avraamov, Arsenii. "Sinteticheskaia muzyka." *Sovetskaia muzyka* 8 (1939); reprinted as "Sinteticheskaia muzyka." *Kinovedcheskie zapiski* 53 (2001): 313–33.

———. "Sintonfil'ma." *Proletarskoe kino* 9–10 (1933): 47–51.

Azarin, A. "Muzykal'nye siurprizy." *Kino* (December 11, 1935): 3.

Bakhtin, Mikhail. *Problems of Dostoevsky's Poetics.* Edited and translated by Caryl Emerson. Minneapolis: University of Minnesota Press, 1984.

Balázs, Béla. *Early Film Theory: Visible Man and The Spirit of Film*. Translated by Rodney Carter. Edited by Erica Carter. London: Berghan Books, 2010.

———. *Iskusstvo kino*. Moscow: Goskinoizdat, 1945.

———. *Theory of the Film: Character and Growth of a New Art*. London: Dennis Dobson, 1952.

Barrios, Richard. *A Song in the Dark: The Birth of the Musical Film*. Oxford: Oxford University Press, 2010.

Barskova, Polina. "Sergei Loznitsa, *The Siege*." Review. *Kino Kultura* 24 (2009). http://www.kinokultura.com/2009/24r-blokada.shtml.

———. "The Spectacle of the Besieged City: Repurposing Cultural Memory in Leningrad, 1941–1944." *Slavic Review* 69, no. 2 (2010): 327–55.

Barthes, Roland. *Image-Music-Text*. New York: Hill and Wang, 1978.

Bartig, Kevin. *Composing for the Red Screen: Prokofiev and Soviet Film*. Oxford: Oxford University Press, 2013.

———. "Lieutenant Kizhe: New Media, New Means." In *Prokofiev and His World*, edited by Simon Morrison, 376–400. Princeton, NJ: Princeton University Press, 2008.

Beilenhoff, Wolfgang, and Sabine Hänsgen. "Speaking about Images: The Voice of the Author in Ordinary Fascism." *Studies in Russian and Soviet Cinema* 2, no. 2 (2008): 141–54.

Beliaev, D. G. "Stiliaga." *Krokodil*, no. 7 (March 1949).

Belton, John. "1950s. Magnetic Sound: The Frozen Revolution." In *Sound Theory/Sound Practice*, edited by Rick Altman, 153–70. New York: Routledge, 1992.

Belton, John, and Elisabeth Weis, eds. *Film Sound: Theory and Practice*. New York: Columbia University Press, 1985.

Berdy, Michele, Dmitrii Buzadzhi, Dmitrii Ermolovich, Mikhail Zagot, Viktor Lanchikov, and Pavel Palazhchenko. "Kinoperevod: Malo chto ot Boga, mnogo chto ot Goblina." *Mosty* 8, no. 4 (2005): 52–62.

Berggol'ts, Ol'ga. *Stikhi, Proza*. Moscow: Khudozhestvennaia literatura, 1961.

Bernatchez, Hélène. *Schostakowitsch und die Fabrik des Exzentrischen Schauspielers*. Munich: Martin Meidenbauer Verlagbuchhandlung, 2006.

Bertellini, Giorgio. "Dubbing *L'arte muta*: Poetic Layerings around Italian Cinema's Transition to Sound." In *Re-Viewing Fascism*, edited by Jacqueline Reich and Piero Garofalo, 30–82. Bloomington: Indiana University Press, 2002.

Beumers, Birgit, ed. *The Directory of World Cinema: Russia*. Bristol, UK: Intellect, 2011.

———. *Pop Culture Russia!* (Santa Barbara, CA: ABC-CLIO, 2005).

Bidlack, Richard. "Lifting the Blockade on the Blockade." *Kritika: Explorations in Russian and Eurasian History* 10, no. 2 (spring 2009): 333–51.

Bleiman, Mikhail. "Chelovek v sovetskoi fil'me 1: istoriia odnoi oshibki." *Sovetskoe kino* 5–6 (1933): 48–57.

———. "Chelovek v sovetskoi fil'me 2: fil'ma obozrenie." *Sovetskoe kino* 8 (1933): 51–60.

———. "Chelovek v sovetskoi fil'me 3: v poiskakh novogo stila." *Sovetskoe kino* 9 (1933): 27–42.

———. *O kino—svidetel'skie pokazaniia*. Moscow: Iskusstvo, 1973.

Bliumbaum, Arkadii. "Ozhivaiushchaia statuia i voploshchennaia muzyka: konteksty 'Strogogo iunoshi.'" *Novoe literaturnoe obozrenie* 1 (2008): 138–89.

Blok, D. "Muzyka v kino." *Kino*. January 22, 1935: 3.

Blok, D., and S. Bugoslavskii. *Muzykal'noe soprovozhdenie v kino*. Moscow: Teakinopechat', 1929.

Bogdanov-Berezovskii, V. "Novyi Vavilon." *Zhizn' iskusstva* 11 (1929): 13.

Bogorov, Ansel'm. "Nachalo: iz vospominanii Ansel'ma Bogorova." In *Tsena kadra. Kazhdyi vtoroi-ranen, kazhdyi chetvertyi ubit. Sovetskaia frontovaia kinokhronika 1941–1945 gg. Dokumenty i svidetel'stva*, edited by Valerii Fomin, 167–71. Moscow: Kanon, 2010.

Boltianskii, Grigorii, ed. *Kino-spravochnik*. Moscow: Teakinopechat', 1929.

Bordwell, David. *The Cinema of Eisenstein*. Cambridge, MA: Harvard University Press, 1993.

———. *Narration in the Fiction Film*. Madison: University of Wisconsin Press, 1985.

Born, Georgia, and David Hesmondhalgh, eds. *Western Music and Its Others: Difference, Representation and Appropriation in Music*. Berkeley: University of California Press, 2000.

Boym, Svetlana. *Common Places: Mythologies of Everyday Life in Russia*. Cambridge, MA: Harvard University Press, 1994.

Bozhovich, Viktor, ed. *Pokaianie*. Moscow: Kinotsentr, 1988.

Braithwaite, Rodric. *Moscow 1941: A City and Its People at War*. London: Profile, 2007.

Brandenberger, David, and Kevin M. F. Platt. "Internal Debate within the Party Hierarchy about the Rehabilitation of Ivan the Terrible." In *Epic Revisionism*, edited by Kevin M. F. Platt and David Brandenberger, 179–93. Madison: University of Wisconsin Press, 2006.

Brashinsky, Michael, and Andrew Horton, eds. *Russian Critics on the Cinema of Glasnost*. Cambridge: Cambridge University Press, 1994.

Brodsky, Joseph. "Spoils of War," in *On Grief and Reason*, 8–9. New York: Farrar, Straus & Giroux, 1995. Also printed in *Threepenny Review*, no. 64 (winter 1996): 6–9.

Brown, Malcolm H. "The Soviet Russian Concepts of 'Intonazia' and 'Musical Imagery.'" *Musical Quarterly* 60 (1974): 557–67.

Brown, Royal S. *Overtones and Undertones: Reading Film Music*. Berkeley: University of California Press, 1994.

Bugoslavskii, Sergei. "Formalizm v kinomuzyke." *Kino*. February 16, 1936: 3.

———. *Mul'tiplikatsionnyi fil'm*. Moscow: Kinoizdat, 1936.

———. "Muzyka v fone." *Kino*. May 28, 1936, 4.

———. "Za prostotu v muzyke." *Kino*. February 21, 1935. 3.

———. "Zhivoi svidetel' nashikh dnei." *Kino*. February 4, 1935. 4.

Bugoslavskii, Sergei, and Vladimir Messman. *Muzyka i kino*. Moscow: Kinopechat', 1926.

Bulgakowa, Oksana. *Sovetskii slukhoglaz: kino i ego organy chuvstv*. Moscow: Novoe literaturnoe obozrenie, 2010.

Bull, Michael, and Les Back, eds. *The Auditory Culture Reader*. Oxford, UK: Berg, 2003.

Burke, Marina. "Eisenstein and the Challenge of Sound." *Kinema: A Journal for Film and Audiovisual Media* (2008). http://www.kinema.uwaterloo.ca.

Butovskii, Iakov. "Monologi prozoi," *Kinovedcheskie zapiski* 94–95 (2010): 307–27.

Carey, Gary. *Marlon Brando: The Only Contender*. London: Houder and Stoghton, 1986.

Cheremukhin, M. *Muzyka zvukovogo fil'ma*. Moscow: Goskinoizdat, 1939.

———. "Na podstupakh k muzykal'noi kinodramaturgii." *Iskusstvo kino* 11 (1936): 51–53.

———. "O realisticheskom stile v muzyke kino." *Iskusstvo kino* 6 (1936): 52–54.
———. "Rol' kompozitora v kino." *Iskusstvo kino* 11 (1935): 50–58.
Chion, Michel. *Audio-vision: Sound on Screen.* Edited and translated by Claudia Gorb-
man. New York: Columbia University Press, 1994.
———. *Film: A Sound Art.* Translated by Claudia Gorbman. New York: Columbia
University Press, 2009.
———. *The Voice in Cinema.* Translated by Claudia Gorbman. New York: Columbia
University Press, 1999.
Christensen, Julie. "Tengiz Abuladze's *Repentance* and the Georgian Nationalist Cause."
Slavic Review 50, no. 1 (1991): 163–75.
Christie, Ian. "Soviet Cinema: Making Sense of Sound." *Screen* 23, no. 2 (July–August
1982): 34–49.
Christie, Ian, and John Gillet, eds. *Futurism/Formalism/FEKS: Eccentrism and Soviet
Cinema 1918–1936.* London: British Film Institute, 1978.
Christie, Ian, and Richard Taylor, eds. *Inside the Film Factory: New Approaches to
Russian and Soviet Cinema.* London: Routledge, 1991.
Chukovskii, Kornei. "Sobinov." In *Sovremenniki. Portrety i etiudy,* 377–82. Moscow:
Molodaia gvardiia, 1961.
Cizmic, Maria. *Performing Pain: Music and Trauma in Eastern Europe.* New York:
Oxford University Press, 2012.
Clapperton, James. "The Siege of Leningrad as Sacred Narrative: Conversations with
Survivors." *Oral History* 35, no. 1 (2007): 49–60.
Clark, Katerina. "Aural Hieroglyphics? Some Reflections on the Role of Sound in Recent
Russian Films and Its Historical Context." In *Soviet Hieroglyphics: Visual Culture
in Late Twentieth-Century Russia,* edited by Nancy Condee, 1–22. Bloomington:
British Film Institute and Indiana University Press, 1995.
———. "'Chtoby tak pet', dvadtsat' let uchit'sia nuzhno: Sluchai *Volgi-Volgi.*" In *Sovets-
koe bogatstvo. Stat'i o kul'ture, literature i kino,* edited by Marina Balina, Evgeny
Dobrenko, and Yury Murashov, 371–90. St. Petersburg: Academic Project, 2002.
———. *Moscow, the Fourth Rome: Stalinism, Cosmopolitanism, and the Evolution of
Soviet Culture, 1931–1941.* Cambridge, MA: Harvard University Press, 2011.
———. "Sergei Eisenstein's *Ivan the Terrible* and the Renaissance: An Example of Stalin-
ist Cosmopolitanism?" *Slavic Review* 71, no. 1 (2012): 49–69.
———. *The Soviet Novel: History as Ritual.* 3rd ed. Bloomington: Indiana University
Press, 2000.
Cohan, Steven, ed. *Hollywood Musical: The Film Reader.* New York: Routledge, 2001.
———. *Incongruous Entertainment: Camp, Cultural Value, and the MGM Musical.*
Durham, NC: Duke University Press, 2005.
Condee, Nancy. *Imperial Trace: Recent Russian Cinema.* New York: Oxford University
Press, 2009.
Cooke, Mervyn, ed. *The Hollywood Film Musical Reader.* Oxford: Oxford University
Press, 2010.
Crary, Jonathan. "Response to Visual Culture Questionnaire," *October* 77 (summer
1996): 33.
Davis, R. W. *The Soviet Economy in Turmoil, 1929–1930.* Cambridge: Cambridge Univer-
sity Press, 1989.

Dickinson, Kay, ed. *Movie Music, the Film Reader*. New York: Routledge, 2003.
———. *Off Key: When Film and Music Won't Work Together*. Oxford: Oxford University Press, 2008.
Dobin, Efim. "Muzykal'naia istoriia." *Iskusstvo i zhizn'*. October 1940, 33.
Dos Passos, John. *Midcentury*. Cambridge, MA: Riverside Press, 1961.
Durikin, Vladimir. "Illiuzion stal dlia menia vtorym domom." In *Kinoteatr Gosfil'mofonda Rossii Illiuzion: vchera, segodnia, zavtra*, edited by Vladimir Solov'ev, 190–91. Moscow: RID Interreklama, 2008.
Ďurovičová, Nataša. "The Hollywood Multilinguals: 1929–1933." In *Sound Theory/Sound Practice*, edited by Rick Altman, 138–53. New York: Routledge, 1992.
———. "Vector, Flow, Zone: Towards a History of Cinematic Translation." In *World Cinemas, Transnational Perspectives*, edited by Nataša Ďurovičová and Kathleen E. Newman, 90–120. New York: Routledge, 2010.
Dyer, Richard. "Entertainment and Utopia." In *Only Entertainment*, 2nd ed., 19–35. London: Routledge, 2002.
———. "Side by Side: Nino Rota, Music, and Film." In *Beyond the Soundtrack: Representing Music in Cinema*, edited by Daniel Goldmark, Lawrence Kramer, and Richard Leppert, 246–59. Berkeley: University of California Press, 2007.
Egorova, Tatiana. *Soviet Film Music: A Historical Survey*. Translated by Tatiana A. Ganf and Natalia A. Egunova. Amsterdam: Harwood Academic Publishers, 1997.
Egoyan, Atom, and Ian Balfour, eds. *Subtitles: On the Foreignness of Film*. Cambridge, MA: MIT Press, 2004.
Eisenstein, Sergei. *Eisenstein: Selected Writings*. Vol. 2, *Towards a Theory of Montage*. Edited by Richard Taylor and Michael Glenny. London: British Film Institute, 1991.
———. *Eisenstein: Selected Writings*. Vol. 3, *Writings, 1934–47*. Edited by Richard Taylor and Michael Glenny. London: British Film Institute, 1996.
———. *Nonindifferent Nature*. Translated by Herbert Marshall. Cambridge: Cambridge University Press, 1987. Russian version published as Sergei Mikhailovich Eizenshtein. *Neravnodushnaia priroda*. 2 vols. Moscow: Muzei kino, 2006.
———. "P-R-K-F-V." In *Notes of a Film Director*, 149–67. New York: Dover, 1970. Russian version published as Sergei Mikhailovich Eizenshtein. *Izbrannye proizvedeniia v shesti tomakh*. Vol. 5 of 6 vols. Moscow: Iskusstvo, 1964–71.
———. "The Psychology of Composition." In *The Eisenstein Collection*, edited by Richard Taylor, 249–85. London: Seagull Books, 2006.
Eisenstein, Sergei, Vsevolod Pudovkin, and Grigorii Aleksandrov. "Budushchee zvukovoi fil'my. Zaiavka." *Zhizn' iskusstva*. August 5, 1928, 4–5. Translated as "Statement on Sound." In *The Film Factory: Russian and Soviet Cinema in Documents 1896–1939*, edited by Richard Taylor and Ian Christie, 234–35. London: Routledge, 1988.
Englert, Brigit, and Nginjai Paul Moreto. "Inserting Voice: Foreign Language Film Translation as a Local Phenomenon in Tanzania." *Journal of African Media Studies* 2, no. 2 (April 2010): 225–39.
Erlmann, Veit. *Music, Modernity and the Global Imagination*. Oxford: Oxford University Press, 1999.
———. *Reason and Resonance: A History of Modern Aurality*. New York: Zone, 2010.

Eshun, Kodwo. *More Brilliant Than the Sun: Adventures in Sonic Fiction*. London: Quartet Books, 1998.

Fawcett, Peter. "Translating Film." In *On Translating French Literature and Film*, edited by Geoffrey T. Harris, 65–88. Amsterdam: Rodopi, 1996.

Fay, Laurel. *Shostakovich: A Life*. Oxford: Oxford University Press, 2000.

Feur, Jane. *The Hollywood Musical*. Bloomington: Indiana University Press, 1982.

Fishzon, Anna. "The Operatics of Everyday Life; or, How Authenticity Was Defined in Late Imperial Russia." *Slavic Review* 70, no. 1 (2011): 795–818.

Fitzpatrick, Sheila. *Everyday Stalinism. Ordinary Life in Extraordinary Times: Soviet Russian in the 1930s*. New York: Oxford University Press, 1999.

———, ed. *Stalinism: New Directions*. London: Routledge, 2000.

Fomin, Valerii, ed. *Kino na voine. Dokumenty i svidetel'stva*. Moscow: Materik, 2005.

———, ed. *Tsena kadra. Kazhdyi vtoroi—ranen, kazhdyi chetvertyi ubit. Sovetskaia frontovaia kinokhronika 1941–1945 gg. Dokumenty i svidetel'stva*. Moscow: Kanon, 2010.

Fomin, Valerii, and Aleksandr Deriabin, eds. *Letopis' rossiiskogo kino: 1863–1929*. Moscow: Materik, 2004.

———, eds. *Letopis' rossiiskogo kino: 1930–1945*. Moscow: Materik, 2007.

Frolova-Walker, Marina. "The Soviet Opera Project: Ivan Dzerzhinsky vs. Ivan Susanin." *Cambridge Opera Journal* 18 (2006): 181–216.

Gabrilovich, Evgenii. "Problema geroia." *Kino*. May 22, 1935: 3.

Gachev, D. *Esteticheskie vzgliady Didro*. 2nd ed. Moscow: Gosudarstvennoe izdatel'stvo khudozhestvennoi literatury, 1961.

———. "Muzyka v zvukovom kino." *Iskusstvo kino* 4 (1934): 34–42.

Gaiba, Francesca. *The Origins of Simultaneous Interpretation: The Nuremberg Trial*. Ottawa: University of Ottawa Press, 1998.

Gaiduk, V. P. "'Tikhii' perevod v kino." *Tetradi perevodchika* 15 (1978): 93–100.

Gambier, Yves. "Screen Transadaptation: Perception and Reception." *Translator* 9, no. 2 (2003): 171–89.

Gan, Aleksei. *Konstruktivizm*, Tver': Tverskoe izdatel'stvo, 1922, 62–64.

Gartsman, M. "Ne plokho, no i ne sovsem eshche khorosho." *Sovetskii ekran* 15 (April 9, 1929).

Genika, Iurii. "Uchebno-eksperimental'naia gruppa pri ARRK." *Kino* (August 20, 1929): 5.

Genis, V. L. "Nevozvrashchentsy 1920-kh - nachala 1930-kh godov." *Voprosy istorii* 1 (2000): 46–63.

Gerlach, Hannelore. *Fünfzig sowjetische Komponisten*. Leipzig: Peters, 1984.

Gillespie, David C. "The Sounds of Music: Soundtrack and Song in Soviet Film." *Slavic Review* 62, no. 3 (2003): 473–90.

Gilroy, Paul. "Sounds Authentic: Black Music, Ethnicity, and the Challenge of a 'Changing Same.'" *Black Music Research Journal* 11, no. 2 (autumn 1991): 111–36.

Gofman, E. "K istorii sinkhronnogo perevoda." *Tetradi perevodchika* 1 (1963): 20–26.

Golubev, Vladimir. "Zapiski kinomana." *Kinovedcheskie zapiski* 64 (2003): 303–29.

Gomery, Douglas. "Coming of Sound." In *Film Sound: Theory and Practice*, edited by Elisabeth Weis and John Belton, 5–36. New York: Columbia University Press, 1985.

———. *The Coming of Sound: A History*. New York: Routledge, 2005.

Gorbman, Claudia. *Unheard Melodies: Narrative Film Music*. Bloomington: Indiana University Press, 1987.

Gorfunkel', Elena. *Smoktunovskii*. Moscow: Iskusstvo, 1990.

Gorham, Michael S. *Speaking in Soviet Tongues: Language Culture and the Politics of Voice in Revolutionary Russia*. DeKalb: Northern Illinois University Press, 2003.

Gornitskaia, Nina, ed. *Iz istorii Lenfil'ma, Stat'i, vospominaniia, dokumenty, 1920-e gody*. Leningrad: Iskusstvo, 1968.

Gounod, Charles. *Mors et vita: A Sacred Trilogy*. Piano-vocal score by O. B. Brown. London: Novello, Ewer and Co., 1885.

Graffy, Julian. "Abuladze, Tengiz E." In *The BFI Companion to Eastern European and Russian Cinema*, 10–11. London: British Film Institute, 2000.

Gres, S. "Industrializatsiia muzyki." *Zhizn' iskusstva* 13 (1929): 2.

Grigor'ev, V. "Pionery leningradskoi mul'tiplikatsii." In *Iz istorii Lenfil'ma*. 207. 2nd ed. Leningrad: Iskusstvo, 1970.

Gusev, Aleksei. "Nekomu soperezhivat'." *Imperiia dramy* (January 2010). http://www.alexandrinsky.ru/magazine/rubrics/rubrics_376.html.

Hanon, Charles Louis. *The Virtuoso Pianist, in Sixty Exercises*. Translated by Theodore Baker. New York: G. Schirmer, 1928.

Hänsgen, Sabine. "'Audio-vision.' O teorii i praktike rannego sovetskogo zvukovogo kino na grani 1930-kh godov." In *Sovetskaia vlast' i media*, edited by Hans Günther and Sabine Hänsgen, 350–64. St. Petersburg: Akademicheskii proekt, 2006.

Hanslick, Eduard. *On the Musically Beautiful: A Contribution towards the Revision of the Aesthetics of Music*. Translated by Geoffrey Payzant. Indianapolis, IN: Hackett, 1986.

Haynes, John. *New Soviet Man: Gender and Masculinity in Stalinist Soviet Cinema*. Manchester, UK: Manchester University Press, 2003.

Heil, Jerry T. *No List of Political Assets: The Collaboration of Iurii Olesha and Abram Room on "Strogii Iunosha" [A Strict Youth (1936)]*. Munich: Verlag Otto Sagner, 1989.

Hirsch, Francine. *Empire of Nations: Ethnographic Knowledge and the Making of the Soviet Union*. Ithaca, NY: Cornell University Press, 2005.

Hitchens, Gordon. "Mind-Bending, Discomforts at USSR's Fest for Asia, Africa." *Variety* (June 12, 1974): 22.

Horton, Andrew, and Michael Brashinsky. *The Zero Hour: Glasnost and Soviet Cinema in Transition*. Princeton, NJ: Princeton University Press, 1992.

Hubbert, Julie. "Eisenstein's Theory of Film Music Revisited: Silent and Early Sound Antecedents." In *Composing for the Screen in Germany and the USSR*, edited by Robynn J. Stilwell and Phil Powrie, 127–47. Bloomington: Indiana University Press, 2008.

Iezuitov, Nikolai. "Dela i liudi sovetskoi kinematografii." *Proletarskoe kino* 15–16 (1932): 11–19.

———. "O stiliakh sovetskogo kino 1: (Kontseptsiia razvitiia sovetskogo kinoiskusstva)." *Sovetskoe kino* 3–4 (1933): 35–55.

———. "O stiliakh sovetskogo kino 2." *Sovetskoe kino* 5–6 (1933): 31–47.

Ioffe, Ieremiia. *Muzyka sovetskogo kino: osnovy muzykal'noi dramaturgii*. Leningrad: GMNII, 1938.

———. *Sinteticheskaia istoriia iskusstv: vvedenie v istoriiu khudozhestvennogo myshle-niia*. Leningrad: Lenizogiz, 1933.

———. *Sinteticheskoe izuchenie iskusstva i zvukovoe kino*. Leningrad: G.M.N.I.I., 1937. Republished in I. I. Ioffe, *Izbrannoe: 1920-30-e gg*. St. Petersburg: Petropolis, 2006.

Iskrenko, Nina. *Neskol'ko slov*. Paris: AMGA, 1991.

"Itogi raboty sovetskoi khudozhestvennoi kinematografii za 1944 g." In *Kino na voine: Dokumenty i svidetel'stva*, edited by V. Fomin, 715–18. Moscow: Materik, 2005.

Iutkevich, Sergei, ed. *Kino: Entsiklopedicheskii slovar'*. Moscow: Sovetskaia entsiklope-diia, 1987.

Ivanovskii, Aleksandr Viktorovich. *Vospominaniia kinorezhissera*. Moscow: Iskusstvo, 1967.

Ivanov-Vano, Ivan. *Kadr za kadrom*. Moscow: Iskusstvo, 1980.

Izvolov, Nikolai. "Moment ozhivleniia spiashchei idei." *Kinovedcheskie zapiski*, no. 15 (1992): 290–96.

Jacobs, Lea. "A Lesson with Eisenstein: Rhythm and Pacing in Ivan the Terrible, Part I." *Music and the Moving Image* 5, no. 1 (spring 2012): 24–46.

Jakobson, Roman. "Noveishaia russkaia poeziia." In *Raboty po poetike*. Moscow: Prog-ress, 1987. Originally published as *Noveishaia russkaia poeziia. Nabrosok pervyi: podstupy k Khlebnikovu*. Prague: Politika, 1921.

———. "Shifters, Verbal Categories and the Russian Verb." In *Selected Writings*. Vol. 2, *Word and Language*, 130–47. The Hague: Mouton, 1971.

Kabalevskii, D. "Muzyka glubokogo chuvstva." *Kino*. November 6, 1935. 4.

Kagan, M. S. "O kul'turologicheskoi i esteticheskoi kontseptsii I. I. Ioffe." In *I. Ioffe: Izbrannoe: 1920-30-e gg*, 642. St. Petersburg: Petropolis, 2006.

Kaganovsky, Lilya. "The Materiality of Sound: Esfir Shub's Haptic Cinema." Unpub-lished manuscript.

———. "The Voice of Technology and the End of Soviet Silent Film: Grigorii Kozint-sev and Leonid Trauberg's *Alone*." *Studies in Russian and Soviet Cinema* 1, no. 3 (2007): 265–81.

Karaganov, A. "Sud sovesti." In *Pokaianie*, edited by Viktor Bozhovich, 134–37. Moscow: Kinotsentr, 1988.

Karmen, Roman. *No pasaran!* Moscow: Sovetskaia Rossiia, 1972.

Katsnelson, Anna Wexler. "The Tramp in a Skirt: Laboring the Radiant Path." *Slavic Review* 70, no. 2 (2011): 256–78.

Kavaleridze, Ivan. "My raznoshchiki novoi very." *Iskusstvo kino* 12 (1966): 33–34.

———. *Sbornik statei, vosponinanii*. Kiev: Mistetsvo, 1988.

Kelly, Catriona, and David Shepherd, eds. *Constructing Russian Culture in the Age of Revolution: 1881–1940*. Oxford: Oxford University Press, 1998.

Kenez, Peter. "The Cultural Revolution in Cinema." *Slavic Review* 47, no. 3 (1988): 414–33.

Kepley, Vance, Jr., "The First *Perestroika*: Cinema under the First Five-Year Plan." *Cin-ema Journal* 35, no. 4 (1996): 31–53.

Kerouac, Jack. *On the Road*. Edited by Scott Donaldson. New York: Viking Press, 1979.

Kessler, Michael, and Thomas Y. Levin, eds. *Siegfried Kracauer. Neue Interpretationen*. Tübingen: Stauffenburg-Verlag, 1990.

Khersonskii, Khrisanf. *Stranitsy iunosti kino*. Moscow: Iskusstvo, 1965.

Khlebnikov, Velimir. *Tvoreniia*. Moscow: Sovetskii pisatel', 1987. Translated as Velimir Khlebnikov. *Collected Works*. Translated by Ronald Vroon. Cambridge, MA: Harvard University Press, 1987–97.

Khlopliankina, Tat'iana. "Po doroge, vedushchei k pravde." In *Pokaianie*, edited by Viktor Bozhovich, 137–41. Moscow: Kinotsentr, 1988. Translated as Tatyana Khloplyankina, "On the Road That Leads to Truth." In *Russian Critics on the Cinema of Glasnost*, edited by Michael Brashinsky and Andrew Horton, 51–53. Cambridge: Cambridge University Press, 1994.

———. "Pod zvuki nabatnogo kolokola." In *Pokaianie*, edited by Viktor Bozhovich, 156–62. Moscow: Kinotsentr, 1988.

Kholopova, V., and E. Chigareva. *Al'fred Shnitke: ocherk zhizni i tvorchestva*. Moscow: Sovetskii kompozitor, 1990.

Kinderman, William. *Beethoven*. Berkeley: University of California Press, 1997.

Kino (Leningrad), no. 40, October 6, 1929.

Kiselev, Alexander. "Deafening Voids." In *Russian Critics on the Cinema of Glasnost*, edited by Michael Brashinsky and Andrew Horton, 65–67. Cambridge: Cambridge University Press, 1994.

Knipper, L. "Kino i muzyka." *Iskusstvo kino* 4 (1936): 39–42.

Koenker, Diane. "Behind the Curtain: Sex and Style in the Soviet 1960s." Unpublished manuscript.

Korganov, Tomas, and Ivan Frolov. *Kino i muzyka*. Moscow: Iskusstvo, 1964.

Kozintsev, Grigorii. "Deriuga i dudochka." In *D. Shostakovich, Stat'i i materialy*, edited by G. M. Shneerson, 120–31. Moscow: Sovetskii kompozitor, 1976.

———. *Glubokii ekran*. Moscow: Iskusstvo, 1971.

Kracauer, Siegfried. *Theory of Film: The Redemption of Physical Reality*. New York: Oxford University Press, 1960.

Kramer, Paul A. "Power and Connection: Imperial Histories of the United States in the World." *American Historical Review* 116, no. 5 (December 2011): 1348–91.

Kriukov, N. "Opyt kompozitora." *Kino* (April 6, 1936): 3.

Krukones, James. "Peacefully Coexisting on a Wide Screen: Kinopanorama vs. Cinerama, 1952–66." *Studies in Russian and Soviet Cinema* 4, no. 3 (2010): 283–305.

Krumrey, Horst-Volker. *Entwicklungsstrukturen von Verhaltensstandarden: eine soziologische Prozessanalyse auf der Grundlage deutscher Anstands- und Manierenbücher von 1870 bis 1970*. Frankfurt am Main: Suhrkamp, 1984.

Kupfer, Peter. "Music, Ideology, and Entertainment in the Soviet Musical Comedies of Grigory Aleksandrov and Isaak Dunayevsky." PhD diss., University of Chicago, 2010.

Kvasnetskaia, Margarita. *Tengiz Abuladze: Put' k Pokaianiiu*. Moscow: Kul'turnaia revoliutsiia, 2009.

Lacasse, Germain. *Le bonimenteur de vues animées: Le cinéma muet entre tradition et modernité*. Quebec City, QB: Nota Bene, 2000.

La Guardia, Robert. *Montgomery Clift: A Biography*. London: W. H. Allen, 1977.

Lahusen, Thomas. "From Laughter 'Out of Sync' to Post-Synchronized Comedy: How the Stalinist Film Musical Caught Up with Hollywood and Overtook It." In *Socialist Cultures East and West: A Post–Cold War Reassessment*, edited by Dubravka Juraga and M. Keith Booker, 31–42. New York: Praeger, 2002.

Lakshin, V. "Neproshchaiushchaia pamiat'." In *Pokaianie,* edited by Viktor Bozhovich, 127–32. Moscow: Kinotsentr, 1988.

Lannin, Steve, and Matthew Caley, eds. *Pop-fiction: The Song in Cinema.* Bristol, UK: Intellect, 2005.

Lanzmann, Claude. *Au sujet de Shoah: Le film de Claude Lanzmann.* Paris: Belin, 1990.

Lastra, James. *Sound Technology and the American Cinema.* New York: Columbia University Press, 2000.

Lebedev, Nikolai. *Ocherk istorii kino SSSR.* 2nd ed. Moscow: Iskusstvo, 1965.

Legoshin, V. "Zvuk kak smysl." *Kino i zhizn'* (April 1, 1930): 14.

Lemeshev, S. *Put' k iskusstvu.* Moscow: Iskusstvo, 1968.

Leyda, Jay. *Kino: A History of the Russian and Soviet Film.* Princeton, NJ: Princeton University Press, 1983.

Liber, George O. *Alexander Dovzhenko: A Life in Soviet Film.* London: British Film Institute, 2002.

Likhacheva, Tat'iana. "Iz vospominanii proshlykh let." *Zhizn' v kino.* 4th ed. Moscow: Iskusstvo, 1994.

Lissa, Zofia. *Estetika kinomuzyki.* Moscow: Muzyka, 1970.

Listov, Viktor. "Kino: iskusstvo ili promyshlennost'? (Iz opyta kommentariev k gosudarstvennym aktam 20-30-kh godov)." In *Teoreticheskie chteniia pamiati S. I. Iutkevicha.* Moscow: VNIIK, 1992.

Litvinov, G. *Stiliagi. Kak eto bylo.* Moscow: Amfora, 2009.

Lotman, Iurii, and Iurii Tsivian. *Dialog s ekranom.* Tallin: Aleksandra, 1994.

MacFadyen, David. "Cinematic *Abuse* as Self-Affirmation: Russian Video Mash-ups, Illegal Social Networking, and the Rise of Bekmambetov's 'Office Plankton.'" *Kinokultura* 27 (2010). http://www.kinokultura.com/2010/27-macfadyen.shtml.

———. *Èstrada?! Grand Narratives and the Philosophy of the Russian Popular Song 1982–2000.* Montreal: McGill-Queen's University Press, 2001.

———. *Red Stars: Personality and the Soviet Popular Song after 1955.* Montreal: McGill-Queen's University Press, 2001.

———. *The Sad Comedy of El'dar Riazanov: An Introduction to Russia's Most Popular Filmmaker.* Montreal: McGill-Queen's University Press, 2003.

———. *Songs for Fat People: Affect, Emotion and Celebrity in the Soviet Popular Song, 1900 to 1955.* Montreal: McGill-Queen's University Press, 2002.

Macheret, Aleksandr. "Dela i liudi." *Proletarskoe kino* 13–14 (1932): 11–13.

———. *Khudozhestvennye techeniia v sovetskom kino.* Moscow: Iskusstvo, 1963.

———. "Realizovannyi optimizm." *Sovetskoe kino* 1–2 (1934): 55–64.

MacKay, John. "*Disorganized Noise:* Enthusiasm and the Ear of the Collective." *Kinokultura* 7 (2005). http://www.kinokultura.com.

Mamaladze, T. "Pritcha i pravda." In *Pokaianie,* edited by Viktor Bozhovich, 132–34. Moscow: Kinotsentr, 1988.

Margolit, Evgenii. "Problema mnogoiazychiia v rannem sovetskom zvukovom kino (1930–1935)," in *Sovetskaia vlast' i media,* ed. Hans Günther and Sabine Hänsgen, 378–86. St. Petersburg: Akademicheskii proekt, 2006.

Matthews, P. H. *Oxford Concise Dictionary of Linguistics.* Oxford: Oxford University Press, 2005.

McQuere, Gordon D. "Boris Asafiev and Musical Form as a Process." In *Russian Theoretical Thought in Music,* edited by Gordon D. McQuere, 217–52. Ann Arbor: University of Michigan Research Press, 1983.

Meyer-Kalkus, Reinhart. *Stimme und Sprechkünste im 20. Jahrhundert*. Berlin: Akademie-Verlag, 2001.

Michalski, Milena. "Promises Broken, Promise Fulfilled: The Critical Failings and Creative Success of Abram Room's *Strogii iunosha*." *Slavonic and East European Review* 82, no. 4 (October 2004): 820–46.

Mihaiu, Virgil. "Ganelin Trio: Prophetic Visions." *Jazz Forum* 91 (1984): 34.

Mikosha, Vladislav. "'Ia ostanavlivaiu vremia.' Vospominaniia frontovogo operatora." *Iskusstvo kino* 5 (2005): 91–115.

Miller, Jamie. *Soviet Cinema: Politics and Persuasion under Stalin*. London: I. B. Tauris, 2010.

Monson, Ingrid. "Hearing, Seeing, and Perceptual Agency." *Critical Inquiry* 34, no. 2 (2008): S36–S58.

Morrison, Simon. *The People's Artist: Prokofiev's Soviet Years*. Oxford: Oxford University Press, 2008.

Morson, Gary Saul, and Caryl Emerson. *Mikhail Bakhtin: Creation of a Prosaics*. Stanford, CA: Stanford University Press, 1990.

Mouratov, Sergei. "The Unknown Cinema: Documentary Screen, Glasnost Era." *Journal of Film and Video* 44, nos. 1–2 (1992): 9–18.

Mur, Leo. "Zvukovaia konferentsiia ARRK." *Kino i zhizn'*, no. 24 (1930): 20.

Muratova, Kira. "Iskusstvo rodilos' iz zapretov, styda i strakha." *Iskusstvo Kino* 2 (1995). Reprinted in *Iskusstvo Kino* (2001): 138–49.

"Nachali uchit'sia." *Kino* (October 29, 1929): 1.

Naremore, James. *Acting in the Cinema*. Berkeley: University of California Press, 1988.

Nedobrovo, Vladimir. *FEKS, Grigorii Kozintsev, Leonid Trauberg*. Moscow: Kinopechat', 1928.

Nekrasov, Sergei. "Istoriia o stiliagakh—ideal'nyi siuzhet dlia muzykal'nogo fil'ma. Interv'iu s Valeriem Todorovskim." *Kinobiznes segodnia*, no. 170 (December 15, 2008). http://www.kinobusiness.com/content/view/1510/31/.

Nelson, Amy. *Music for the Revolution: Musicians and Power in Early Soviet Russia*. University Park: Pennsylvania State University Press, 2004.

Neuberger, Joan. *Ivan the Terrible: The Film Companion*. London: I. B. Tauris, 2003.

———. "Eisenstein's 'Ivan the Terrible' as a Theory of History." *Journal of Modern History* (forthcoming).

Nichols, Bill. *Introduction to Documentary*. Indianapolis: Indiana University Press, 2001.

———. *Representing Reality: Issues and Concepts in Documentary*. Bloomington: Indiana University Press, 1991.

Nornes, Abé Mark. *Cinema Babel: Translating Global Cinema*. Minneapolis: University of Minnesota Press, 2007.

Olesha, Iurii. "Vystuplenie." *Pervyi vsesoiuznyi s"ezd sovetskikh pisatelei: Stenograficheskii otchet*. Moscow: Khudozhestvennaia literatura, 1934.

———. "Zavist'." In *Zavist', Tri tolstiaka, Ni dnia bez strochki*, 12–112. Moscow: Khudozhestvennaia literatura, 1989.

Ol'hovoi, B. S. *Puti kino. Pervoe vsesoiuznoe partiinoe soveshchanie po kinematografii*. Moscow: Teakinopechat', 1929.

Ordzhonikidze, G. Sh. "O dinamike natsional'nogo stilia." In *Muzykal'nye kul'tury narodov. Traditsii i sovremennost'*. Moscow: Sov. kompozitor, 1973.

Orlova, E. M. *B. V. Asaf'ev, put' issledovatelia i publitsista*. Leningrad: Muzyka, 1964.

Ossorgin, Katherine Ermolaev. "Liturgical Borrowings as Film Music in Eisenstein's *Ivan the Terrible* (1944–46)." Paper presented at the annual meeting of the American Musicological Society, Quebec City, Canada, November 2007.

"Otkrytoe pis'mo." *Iskusstvo kino* 3 (1962): 63.

Pantielev, Grigorii. "Piat' simfonii Al'freda Shnitke." *Sovetskaia muzyka* 10 (1990): 81–87.

Pasternak, Boris. *Perepiska s Ol'goi Freidenberg.* Edited by Elliot Mossman. New York: Harcourt and Brace, 1981.

Paulin, Tom. "The Despotism of the Eye." In *Soundscape: The School of Sound Lectures, 1998–2001,* edited by Larry Sider, Diane Freeman, and Jerry Sider, 35–48. London: Wallflower Press, 2003.

Perrie, Maureen. *The Cult of Ivan the Terrible in Stalin's Russia.* Basingstoke, UK: Palgrave, 2001.

Petrov, Andrei, and Natalia Koles'nikova. *Dialog o kinomuzyke.* Moscow: Iskusstvo, 1982.

Petrov-Bytov, Pavel. "U nas net sovetskoi kinomatografii." *Zhizn' iskusstva* (April 21, 1929): 8. Translated as "We Have No Soviet Cinema." In *The Film Factory: Russian and Soviet Cinema in Documents 1896–1939,* edited by Richard Taylor and Ian Christie, 259–62. New York: Routledge, 1994.

Piataev, A. S. "Chto takoe individual'nost'? V diskussionnom poriadke." *Kino* 40 (1933): 3.

Piotrovskii, Adrian. "Kinofikatsiia muzyki." *Zhizn' iskusstva* 9 (1929): 4.

———. "Tonfil'ma." *Zhizn' iskusstva* 30 (1929): 4–5.

———. "Tonfil'ma v poriadke dnia." In *Teatr. Kino. Zhizn'.* Leningrad: Iskusstvo, 1969.

Platt, Kevin M. F. *Terror & Greatness: Ivan and Peter as Russian Myths.* Ithaca, NY: Cornell University Press, 2011.

Platt, Kevin M. F., and David Brandenberger, eds. *Epic Revisionism: Russian History and Literature as Stalinist Propaganda.* Madison: University of Wisconsin Press, 2006.

Popov, F. "Obraz kommunista na ekrane." *Sovetskoe kino* 1–2 (1934): 6–14.

"Postanovlenie tresta Ukrainfil'm o zapreshchenii fil'ma *Strogii iunosha.*" *Kino* (July 28, 1936): 2.

Pozner, Valérie. "Le bonimenteur 'rouge': Retour sur la question de l'oralité à propos du cas soviétique." *Cinémas* 14, nos. 2–3 (2004): 143–78.

Prendergast, Roy M. *Film Music: A Neglected Art.* 2nd ed. New York: Norton, 1992.

Prim, N. "Neobkhodim perelom." *Kino* (October 29, 1929): 1.

"Privet Vserabisu!" *Kino,* June 3, 1924.

Prokhorov, Alexander. "Cinema of Attractions versus Narrative Cinema: Leonid Gaidai's Comedies and El'dar Riazanov's Satires of the 1960s." *Slavic Review* 62, no. 3 (fall 2003): 455–72.

Pytel, Marek. *New Babylon: Trauberg, Kozintsev, Shostakovich.* London: Eccentric Press, 1999.

Rajagopalan, Sudha. *Indian Films in Soviet Cinemas: The Culture of Movie-going after Stalin.* Bloomington: Indiana University Press, 2009.

Rapée, Erno. *Encyclopedia of Music for Motion Pictures.* New York: Belwin, 1925.

Razlogov, Kirill. "Moi festivali." Unpublished manuscript, 2011.

———. "Stanovlenie." *Iskusstvo kino* 2 (1969): 135–38.

Razumnyi, Aleksandr. *U istokov . . . : vospominaniia kinorezhissera.* Moscow: Iskusstvo, 1975.

———. "Usilim tempy." *Kino i zhizn'*, no. 1 (1930): 7, 28–51.

Redaktsiia (editorial). *Kino: dvukhnedel'nik obshchestva kinodeiatelei* (October 20, 1922): 1.

Reich, Jacqueline. "Mussolini at the Movies: Fascism, Film, and Culture." In *Re-Viewing Fascism: Italian Cinema 1922–1943*, edited by Jacqueline Reich and Piero Garofalo, 3–29. Bloomington: Indiana University Press, 2002.

Remnick, David. *Lenin's Tomb: The Last Days of the Soviet Empire*. New York: Vintage, 1993.

Renov, Michael. *The Subject of Documentary*. Minneapolis: University of Minnesota Press, 2004.

Riabchikova, Natalia. "Sorokhuki i desiataia muza." *Menedzher kino*, no. 49 (2008): 34–41.

Riley, John. *Dmitri Shostakovich: A Life in Film*. London: I. B. Tauris, 2005.

———. "Myth, Parisity, and Found Music in *New Babylon*." *DSCH Journal* 4 (winter 1995): 34–40.

Robertson, Robert. *Eisenstein on the Audiovisual: The Montage of Music, Image and Sound in Cinema*. London: I. B. Tauris, 2010.

"Roscherkom pera unichtozhaetsia trud mnogikh dnei." *Kino* (February 11, 1931): 2.

Roth, Mark. "Some Warners' Musicals and the Spirit of the New Deal." *Velvet Light Trap* 77 (winter 1977): 1–7.

Russo, Mariachiara. "Simultaneous Film Interpreting and Users' Feedback." *Interpreting* 7, no. 1 (January 2005): 1–26.

Sadkovskii, Ivan. *O kul'ture povedeniia sovetskoi molodezhi; stenogramma publichnoi lektsii*. Moscow: N.p., 1958.

Salazkina, Masha. *In Excess: Sergei Eisenstein's Mexico*. Chicago: University of Chicago Press, 2009.

Salys, Rimgaila. *The Musical Comedy Films of Grigorii Aleksandrov: Laughing Matters*. Bristol, UK: Intellect, 2010.

Sandomirskaia, Irina. "A glossolalic glasnost and the re-tuning of the Soviet subject: sound performance in Kira Muratova's *Asthenic Syndrome*." *Studies in Russian and Soviet Cinema* 2, no.1 (2008): 63–83.

Saricheva, Elizaveta. *Stsenicheskaia rech'. Uchebnk dlia teatralnykh vuzov*. Moscow: Iskusstvo, 1956.

Sarkisova, Oksana. "Folk Songs in Soviet Orchestration: Vostokfil'm's Song of Happiness and the Forging of the New Soviet Musician." *Studies in Russian and Soviet Cinema* 4, no. 3 (2010): 261–81.

Saxton, Libby. *Haunted Images: Film, Ethics, Testimony and the Holocaust*. London: Wallflower, 2008.

Schmelz, Peter. "A Genealogy of Polystylism: Alfred Schnittke and the Late Soviet Culture of Collage." *Abstracts Read at the 75th Annual Meeting of the American Musicological Society*, 49. Philadelphia: American Musicological Society, 2009. http://www.ams-net.org/abstracts/2009-Philadelphia.pdf.

———. *Such Freedom, If Only Musical: Unofficial Soviet Music during the Thaw*. New York: Oxford University Press, 2009.

Schmölders, Claudia, "Die Stimme des Bösen. Zur Klanggestalt des Dritten Reiches." *Merkur* 581 (1997): 681–93.

——. "Stimmen von Führern. Auditorische Szenen 1900–1945." In *Zwischen Rauschen und Offenbarung. Zur Kultur- und Mediengeschichte der Stimme*, edited by Friedrich Kittler, Thomas Macho, and Sigrid Weigel, 175–95. Berlin: Akademie-Verlag, 2002.

Schneerson, G. M, ed. *D. Shostakovich, Stat'i i materialy*. Moscow: Sovetskii kompozitor, 1976.

Schnittke, Alfred. *A Schnittke Reader*. Edited by Alexander Ivashkin. Translated by John Goodliffe. Bloomington: Indiana University Press, 2002.

——. *Stat'i o muzyke*. Edited by Aleksandr Ivashkin. Moscow: Kompozitor, 2004.

Schnittke, Alfred, and J. [Jelena] Petruschanskaja. "Ein Gespräch mit Alfred Schnittke: Die Möglichkeiten des Dialogs zwischen Bild und Musik im Film." *Sowjetwissenschaft. Kunst und Literatur* 36, no. 2 (1988): 272–80.

Schnitzer, Luca, Jean Schnitzer, and Martin Marcel, eds. *Cinema in Revolution*. New York: Da Capo Press, 1973.

Schöne, Albrecht. *Literatur im audiovisuellen Medium. Sieben Fernsehdrehbücher*. Munich: Beck, 1974.

Schönherr, Beatrix. "So kann man heute nicht mehr spielen. Über den Wandel der sprecherischen Stilideale auf der Bühne seit den 60er Jahren." In *Sprache Kultur Geschichte sprachhistorische Studien zum Deutschen*, edited by Maria Pümpel-Madder and Beatrix Schönherr, 145–69. Innsbruck: Institut für Germanistik, 1999.

Schwitalla, Johannes. "Vom Sektenprediger zum Plauderton. Beobachtungen zur Prosodie von Politikerreden vor und nach 1945." In *Texttyp, Sprechergruppe, Kommunikationsbereich. Studien zur deutschen Sprache in Geschichte und Gegenwart. Festschrift für Hugo Steger zum 65. Geburtstag*, edited by Heinrich Löffler and Karlheinz Jakob u.a., 208–24. Berlin: de Gruyter, 1994.

Shatina, Zinaida. "Kinoteatr Illiuzion v moei zhizni." In *Kinoteatr Gosfil'mofonda Rossii Illiuzion: vchera, segodnia, zavtra*, edited by Vladimir Solov'ev, 47–93. Moscow: RID Interreklama, 2008.

Shcherbachev, V. "Muzyka v kino." *Iskusstvo kino* 3 (1936): 22–23.

Sheinberg, Esti. *Irony, Satire, Parody, and the Grotesque in the Music of Shostakovich: A Theory of Musical Incongruities*. Aldershot, UK: Ashgate, 2000.

Shkliarovich, A. "Chto takoe 'predvaritel'nyi period'." *Iskusstvo kino* 7 (1933): 27–30.

Shohat, Ella, and Robert Stam. "The Cinema after Babel: Language, Difference, Power." *Screen* 26, nos. 3–4 (May 1985): 35–58.

Sholpo, Evgenii. "Iskusstvennaia fonogramma na kinoplenke kak tekhnicheskoe sredstvo muzyki." Edited by N. A. Izvolov, with A. S. Deriabin. *Kinovedcheskie zapiski* 53 (2001): 334–35, 340.

Shostakovich, Dmitrii. *Muzyka k dramaticheskim spektakliam*. Edited by Lev Solin. Moscow: Sovetskii kompozitor, 1977.

——. "O muzyke k 'Novomu Vavilonu'." *Sovetskii ekran* 11 (1929): 5.

Shtaier, B. "O mekhanizme sinkhronnogo perevoda." *Tetradi perevodchika* 12 (1975): 101–11.

Shub, Esfir'. *Zhizn' moia—kinematograf*. Moscow: Iskusstvo, 1972.

Shumiatskii, Boris. "A driani podobno *Garmon'* bol'she ne stavite? . . ." Zapisi besed B. Z. Shumiatskogo s I.V. Stalinym posle kinoprosmotrov. 1934 g. (Publikatsiia i kommentarii A. S. Troshina), *Kinovedcheskie zapiski* 61 (2002): 281–346.

———. *Kinematografiia millionov. Opyt analiza.* Moscow: Kinofotoizdat, 1935.

———. "Tvorcheskie zadachi templana." *Sovetskoe kino* 12 (December 1933): 1–15.

Silverman, Kaja. *The Acoustic Mirror: The Female Voice in Psychoanalysis and Cinema.* Bloomington: Indiana University Press, 1988.

Smolina, Lelia, and Vladimir Zakharov. "Seks, Komsomol, Rok-n-roll. Valerii Todorovskii o 'Stiliagakh', den'gakh, sekse i kinokritike." *Empire.* November 2008. http://www.webcitation.org/5w9gGbq6R.

Snelling, David. "Upon the Simultaneous Translation of Films." *Interpreters' Newsletter* 3 (1990): 14.

Sokolov, I. "Plan velikikh rabot." *Kino i zhizn'* 10 (April 1, 1930): 5–6.

Solev, V. "Absolute Music by Designed Sound." *American Cinematographer* (April 1936): 146–48, 154–55.

Solov'ev, Vladimir, ed. *Kinoteatr Gosfil'mofonda Rossii Illiuzion: vchera, segodnia, zavtra.* Moscow: RID Interreklama, 2008.

Sol'skii, V. *Zvuchashchee kino.* Moscow: Teakinopechat', 1929.

Sovetskii ekran 47 (1927): 14.

Srinivas, S. V. "Is There a Public in the Cinema Hall?" *Framework* 42 (2000). http://www.sarai.net/research/media-city/resouces/film-city-essays/sv_srinivas.pdf.

Stern, Jonathan. *The Audible Past: Cultural Origins of Sound Reproduction.* Durham, NC: Duke University Press, 2003.

Stilwell, Robyn, and Phil Powrie, eds. *Composing for the Screen in Germany and the USSR: Cultural Politics and Propaganda.* Bloomington: Indiana University Press, 2008.

Stoler, Ann Laura. "Tense and Tender Ties: The Politics of Comparison in North American History and (Post) Colonial Studies." *Journal of American History* 88, no. 3 (December 2001): 829–65.

Stroeva, Vera. "O druge." In *Pisatel'-boets. Vospominaniia o Vsevolode Vishnevskom,* 142–62. Moscow: Sovetskaia Rossiia. 1963.

Taruskin, Richard. *Defining Russia Musically.* Princeton, NJ: Princeton University Press, 1997.

Taylor, Richard. "Boris Shumyatsky and the Soviet Cinema in the 1930s: Ideology as Mass Entertainment." *Historical Journal of Film, Radio and Television* 6, no. 1 (1986): 43–64.

———. "But Eastward, Look, the Land Is Brighter: Towards a Topography of Utopia in the Stalinist Musical." In *100 Years of European Cinema: Entertainment or Ideology?,* edited by Diana Holmes and Alison Smith, 11–26. Manchester, UK: Manchester University Press, 2000.

———. "K topografii utopii v stalinskom miuzikle." In *Sovetskoe bogatstvo. Stat'i o kul'ture, literature i kino,* edited by Marina Balina, Evgeny Dobrenko, and Yury Murashov, 358–70. St. Petersburg: Academic Project, 2002.

———. "Singing on the Steppes for Stalin: Ivan Pyr'ev and the Kolkhoz Musical in Soviet Cinema." *Slavic Review* 58, no. 1 (1999): 143–59.

———. "Soviet Socialist Realism and the Cinema Avant-Garde." *Studies in Comparative Communism* 17, nos. 3–4 (1984): 185–202.

Taylor, Richard, and Ian Christie, eds. *The Film Factory: Russian and Soviet Cinema in Documents 1896–1939.* London: Routledge and Kegan Paul, 1988.

Thompson, Emily. *The Soundscape of Modernity: Architectural Acoustics and the Culture of Listening in America, 1900–1933.* Cambridge, MA: MIT Press, 2002.

Thompson, Kristin. "Early Sound Counterpoint." *Yale French Studies* 60 (1980): 115–40.

———. *Eisenstein's Ivan the Terrible: A Neoformalist Analysis.* Princeton, NJ: Princeton University Press, 1981.

Tikhanova, V. ed. *Rasstrel'nye spiski, vypusk 2: Vagan'kovskoe kladbishche, 1926–1936.* Moscow: Memorial, 1995.

Titus, Joan. *Hearing Shostakovich: Music for Early Soviet Cinema.* Oxford: Oxford University Press, forthcoming.

———. "Modernism, Socialist Realism, and Identity in the Early Film Music of Dmitry Shostakovich, 1929–1932." PhD diss., Ohio State University, 2006.

Tolstaya, Tatyana. *Pushkin's Children: Writings on Russia and Russians.* New York: Houghton Mifflin, 2003.

Tomas-Bosovskaia, Ol'ga. "Paradoksy *Pokaianiia.*" In *Iz proshlogo i nastoiashchego sovremennoi otechestvennoi muzyki,* edited by E. B. Dolinskaia, 59–69. Moscow: Moskovskaia gosudarstvennaia konservatoriia imeni P. I. Chaikovskogo, 1991.

Trauberg, Leonid. "Comment est né 'La Nouvelle Babylone,' (1978)." *L'avant-scene du cinema* 217 (December 1978): 8.

Troitsky, Artemy. *Back in the USSR: The True Story of Rock in Russia.* London: Faber and Faber, 1988.

———. *Tusovka: Who's Who in the New Soviet Rock Culture.* London: Omnibus, 1990.

Tsekhanovskii, Mikhail. "Dela i liudi kak professional'nyi urok." *Proletarskoe kino* 19–20 (1932): 14–16.

———. "O zvukovoi risovannoi fil'me." *Kino i zhizn'* 34–35 (1930): 14–15.

Tseitlin, Boris. "Zvukovaia bestolkovshchina." *Proletarskoe kino,* nos. 2–3 (1931): 57–60.

Tsivian, Yuri. "Russia 1913: Cinema in the Cultural Landscape," in *Silent Film,* 209. Edited by Richard Abel. New Brunswick, NJ: Rutgers University Press, 1996.

Tull, James Robert. "B. V. Asaf'ev's Musical Form as a Process: Translation and Commentary." PhD diss., Ohio State University, 1977.

Turovskaya, Maya. "The Days of Eclipse." In *Russian Critics on the Cinema of Glanost,* edited by Michael Brashinsky and Andrew Horton, 112–13. Cambridge: Cambridge University Press, 1994.

Turovskaia, Maia. "Gollivud v Moskve, ili sovetskoe i amerikanskoe kino." *Kinovedcheskie zapiski* 97 (2011): 51–63.

———. "Trofeinye fil'my poslevoennoi Rossii." Paper presented at the Hybridität in Literatur, Kunst und Medien der russischen Moderne und Postmoderne, Universität Konstanz, Switzerland, June 2006.

———. "Zritel'skie predpochteniia 70-kh." *Kinovedcheskie zapiski* 11 (1991): 92–96.

Tvalchrelidze, T. "Prozrenie cherez pokaianie." In *Pokaianie,* edited by Viktor Bozhovich, 119–27. Moscow: Kinotsentr, 1988.

Urban, Michael, and Andrei Evdokimov. *Russia Gets the Blues: Music, Culture and Community in Unsettled Times.* Ithaca, NY: Cornell University Press, 2004.

Vainkop, Iulii. "Muzyka k 'Novomu Vavilonu." *Rabochii i teatr* (April 1, 1929): 9.

Van Houten, Theodore. *Dmitri Sjostakovitsj, een leven in angst.* Van Gruting: Westervoort, 2006.

———. *Leonid Trauberg and His Films: Always the Unexpected.* 'S-Hertogenbosch: Art and Research, 1989.

Varèse, Edgard. "The Liberation of Sound." In *Perspectives on American Composers,* edited by Benjamin Boretz and Edward T. Cone, 25–33. New York: W. W. Norton, 1971.

"V ARRKe." *Kino* (September 24, 1929): 3.

Vasil'ev, Boris. "Prozrenie." In *Pokaianie,* edited by Viktor Bozhovich, 144–50. Moscow: Kinotsentr, 1988.

Vasil'eva, Ekaterina, and Nikita Braginskii, eds. *Noev kovcheg russkogo kino: ot "Sten'ki Razina" do "Stiliag."* Vinnytsia, Ukraine: Globus Press, 2012.

"V chem zhe delo?" *Proletarskoe kino,* nos. 5–6 (1931): 1–4.

Venuti, Lawrence. *The Translator's Invisibility.* London: Routledge, 1994.

Vertov, Dziga. *Tri pesni o Lenine.* Edited by Elizaveta Svilova-Vertova and Vitalii Furtichev. Moscow: Iskusstvo 1972.

Vetrov, V. "Gans Eisler o muzyke v zvukovom kino." *Kino* (July 17, 1935): 3.

Vishnevetskaia, S. "Dokumental'naia trilogiia Vs. Vishnevskogo." *Iskusstvo kino* 4 (1958): 108–12.

Vishnevskii, Veniamin. *25 let sovetskogo kino.* Moscow: Goskinozdat, 1945.

———. "Istoriia Gosudarstvennogo Instituta Kinematografii v khronologicheskikh datakh." In *Istoriia VGIKa. Kniga 1 (1919–1934),* edited by Marat Vlasov, 8–20. Moscow: VGIK, 2000.

Vishnevskii, Vsevolod. *Leningrad: dnevniki voennykh let: 2 noiabria 1941 goda-31 dekabria 1942.* Vol. 1. Moscow: Voenizdat, 2002.

———. "Leningrad v bor'be. Literaturnyi variant stsenariia khudozhestvenno-dokumental'nogo fil'ma otcheta ob oborone Leningrada v 1941–1942 gg." *Iskusstvo kino* 4 (1958): 113–28.

———. *Stat'i, dnevniki, pis'ma o literature i iskusstve,* Moscow: Sovetskii pisatel', 1961.

———. "Uporno k novomu iskusstvu." In *Sobranie sochinenii, v 5 tomakh,* 5:340–46. Moscow: Khudozhestvennaia literatura, 1954–61.

Vol'man, Nina. *Efim Uchitel'.* Leningrad: Iskusstvo: Leningradskoe otdelenie, 1976.

Volkov, N. "Na zvukovye temy: nekotorye osobennosti zvukovoi khudozhestvennoi kinematografii." *Iskusstvo kino* 8 (1933): 61–70.

Volkov, Vadim. "The Concept of *Kul'turnost':* Notes of the Stalinist Civilizing Process." In *Stalinism: New Directions,* edited by Sheila Fitzpatrick, 210–30. London: Routledge, 2000.

Vysotskii, Mikhail. *Sistemy kino i stereozvuk.* Moscow: Iskusstvo, 1972.

"Vyvody komissii po chistke ARRK." *Kino* (February 11, 1931): 3.

Weithases, Irmgard. *Geschichte der deutschen Vortragskunst im 19. Jahrhundert.* Weimar: Böhlau, 1940.

———. *Zur Geschichte der gesprochenen deutschen Sprache.* 2 vols. Tübingen: Max Niemeyer Verlag, 1961.

Westad, Odd Arne. *The Global Cold War: Third World Interventions and the Making of Our Times.* Cambridge: Cambridge University Press, 2005.

Widdis, Emma. "Faktura: Depth and Surface in Early Soviet Set Design." *Studies in Russian and Soviet Cinema* 3, no. 2 (2009): 5–32.

———. "Socialist Senses: Film and the Creation of Soviet Subjectivity." *Slavic Review* (fall 2012): 590–618.

Wierzbicki, James, James Nathan Platte, and Colin Roust, eds. *The Routledge Film Music Sourcebook.* New York: Routledge, 2011.

Wilson, Elizabeth. *Shostakovich: A Life Remembered*. Princeton, NJ: Princeton University Press, 2006.

Woll, Josephine, and Denise Youngblood. Repentance: *The Film Companion*. London: I. B.Tauris, 2000.

Yakubov, Manashir, ed. "Dmitry Shostakovich's Music to the Silent Film *The New Babylon*." In *Dmitry Shostakovich: New Collected Works*. Vol. 122, "The New Babylon." Moscow: DSCH, 2004.

Yampolsky, Mikhail. "Chekhov/Sokurov: Repetition and Recollection." *New Formations* 22 (May 1994): 48–58.

———. "Cinema without Cinema." In *Russian Critics on the Cinema of Glasnost*, edited by Michael Brashinsky and Andrew Horton, 11–17. Cambridge: Cambridge University Press, 1994.

Yangirov, Rashit M. "Talking Movie or Silent Theater? Creative Experiments by Vasily Goncharov." In *The Sounds of Early Cinema*, edited by Richard Abel and Rick Altman, 110–20. Bloomington: Indiana University Press, 2001.

Yankovskii, B. "Akusticheskii sintez muzykal'nykh krasok"(excerpted from *Teoriia i praktika graficheskogo zvuka*). *Kinovedcheskie zapiski* 53 (2001): 353–68.

Youngblood, Denise. Review of *Repentance*. *American Historical Review* 95, no. 4 (1990): 1133–36.

———. *Soviet Cinema in the Silent Era, 1919–1935*. Ann Arbor: University of Michigan Research Press, 1985.

Yurchak, Alexei. *Everything Was Forever, Until It Was No More: The Last Soviet Generation*. Princeton, NJ: Princeton University Press, 2005.

Zagot, M. A. "Kinofestival'." *Mosty* 10, no. 2 (2006): 70–75.

Zhuk, Sergei. *Rock and Roll in the Rocket City: The West, Identity, and Ideology in Soviet Dniepropetrovsk, 1960–1985*. Baltimore: John Hopkins University Press, 2010.

Contributors

Kevin Bartig is Assistant Professor of Musicology at Michigan State University. He is author of *Composing for the Red Screen: Prokofiev and Soviet Film* (Oxford University Press, 2013), as well as articles and reviews in *Journal of Musicology, Kritika, Notes,* and several essay collections. Current projects include a study of Soviet-American musical exchange, for which he was awarded a fellowship from the John W. Kluge Center at the Library of Congress.

Oksana Bulgakowa, Professor of Film Studies at the Gutenberg University in Mayans, is a Moscow-born scholar who lives in Berlin. She has published extensively on Russian and German cinema. Her two most recent books are *Fabrika zhestov* (The Factory of Gestures; Novoe literaturnoe obozrenie, 2005, and companion DVD, *Factory of Gestures: On Body Language in Film,* 2008), and *Sovetskii slukhoglaz: Kino i ego organy chuvstv* (The Soviet Hearing Eye: Cinema and Its Sense Organs; Novoe literaturnoe obozrenie, 2010). She has also directed a number of films (*Stalin—A Mosfilmproduction,* 1993; *The Different Faces of Sergei Eisenstein,* 1998); curated exhibits; and developed multimedia projects, including "The Visual Universe of Sergei Eisenstein," Daniel Langlois-Foundation, Montreal, 2005.

Jeremy Hicks is Senior Lecturer in Russian at Queen Mary University of London, where he has taught courses on Russian film and literature since 1998. He is author of *Dziga Vertov: Defining Documentary Film* (I. B. Tauris, 2007) and *First Films of the Holocaust: Soviet Cinema and the Genocide of the Jews, 1938–46* (University of Pittsburgh Press, 2012). He has also published various articles on Russian and Soviet film, literature, and journalism in *Russian Review, Studies in Russian and Soviet Cinema, Kinovedcheskie zapiski, Revolutionary Russia,* and *Historical Journal of Film, Radio and Television.*

Nikolai Izvolov is a film historian and cinema researcher. Combining meticulous scientific research with a creative assembly, Izvolov led a large number of reconstructions of the first Russian masterpieces that had been considered lost forever. He is author of *Fenomen kino: Istoriia i teoriia* (The Phenomenon of Film: History and Theory; Materik, 2005), he has also cooperated on several film and documentary projects, including the biography of Alexander Medvedkin by Chris Marker (*The Last Bolshevik; Le tombeau d'Alexandre,* 1992). He is head of the Department of the History of Russian Cinema at the Moscow Cinema Art Institute, where he is developing a film digital commentary method called Hyperkino.

Lilya Kaganovsky is Associate Professor of Slavic, Comparative Literature, and Media and Cinema Studies, and Director of the Program in Comparative Literature at the University of Illinois, Urbana-Champaign. Her publications include *How the Soviet Man Was Unmade* (University of Pittsburgh Press, 2008); articles on Soviet and post-Soviet cinema; and the co-edited multidisciplinary volume of essays *Mad Men, Mad World: Sex, Politics, Style and the 1960s* (Duke University Press, 2013). She is a member of the editorial board of the journal *Studies in Russian and Soviet Cinema* and regularly contributes film reviews to the online cinema journal *KinoKultura*. Her current project looks at the Soviet film industry's transition to sound (1928–1935).

Evgeny Margolit is a film critic and film historian. His essays have appeared in the journals *Iskusstvo kino, Kinovedcheskie zapiski,* and *Seans.* He is author of *Sovetskoe kinoiskusstvo: Osnovnye etapy rossiiskogo kino* (Soviet Cinema: The Main Stages of Formation and Development; Moscow, VZNUI, 1988), *Iz"iatoe kino, 1924–1953* (Withdrawn Film, 1995, with B. Shmyrov), and, most recently, *Zhivye i mertvoe. Zametki k istorii sovetskogo kino 1920-1960kh godov* (The Living and the Dead: Notes on Soviet Cinema, 1920–1960s; Seans, 2012). Currently, he teaches courses on Russian and Soviet cinema at the Professional School for Screenwriting and Directing (VKSR).

Joan Neuberger is Professor of History at the University of Texas at Austin. She is author of an eclectic range of publications, including *Hooliganism: Crime and Culture in St. Petersburg, 1900–1914* (University of California Press, 1993) and *Ivan the Terrible: The Film Companion* (I. B. Tauris, 2003); co-author of *Europe and the Making of Modernity, 1815–1914* (Oxford University Press, 2005); and co-editor of *Imitations of Life: Melodrama in Russia* (Duke University Press, 2001) and *Picturing Russia: Explorations in Visual Culture* (Yale University Press, 2008). She has published numerous articles on Sergei Eisenstein and is currently completing *This Thing of Darkness: Eisenstein's "Ivan the Terrible" in Stalinist Russia.*

Anna Nisnevich is Assistant Professor of Musicology at the University of Pittsburgh. She has published on opera and film sound in *Cambridge Opera Journal, Opera Quarterly,* and *Studies in Russian and Soviet Cinema,* and she has lectured for the San Francisco Opera and the Pittsburgh Symphony. Among her research interests are reception history and broader intersections of musical and social experience. She is currently completing a book titled *How Tchaikovsky Became Soviet.*

Valérie Pozner is a researcher at the CNRS (French National Center for Scientific Research) in the Atelier de Recherche sur l'Intermédialité et les Arts du Spectacle (Research Workshop on Intermedia and the Performing Arts) and currently President of the French Association of Research in Film History (AFRHC). She is author of numerous works on the 1920s, including essays on issues in film theory and historical films, literary adaptations, works on oral accompaniment for projections of silent films from the 1910s until the 1930s, and the relation between image and written text (title cards), among other topics. Her most recent publications include an edition of Shklovsky's texts about cinema (1918–1932), with translation and notes: *Viktor Chklovski, Textes sur le cinéma* (Édition L'Âge d'Homme, 2011); and the edited volume *Kinojudaica: Les représentations des juifs dans le cinéma de Russie et d'Union soviétique des années 1910 aux années 1980* (Nouveau Monde Éditions, 2012). Currently, she is completing a project on Soviet cinema's transition to sound from 1927 to 1933. Her new collective project is devoted to the history of cinema in Soviet Union between 1939 and 1949, and it will include an exhibition at Mémorial de la Shoah in Paris (opening in fall 2014) about film documents of the Holocaust filmed by Soviet cameramen and a collective monography.

Elena Razlogova is Associate Professor of History and Co-Director of the Centre for Oral History and Digital Storytelling at Concordia University, Montreal. She has published articles on U.S. radio history and on contemporary public opinion about detentions at Guantánamo Bay. She also served as an executive producer on a historical digital exhibit project *Gulag: Many Days, Many Lives*. She is author of *The Listener's Voice: Early Radio and the American Public* (University of Pennsylvania Press, 2011). She is currently working on a correlative history of the "morality of snitching" in the United States and the Soviet Union during the Cold War.

Natalie Ryabchikova is a PhD student in the Film Studies Program at the University of Pittsburgh (with a concentration in Slavic). She has contributed to *Directory of World Cinema: Russia* (Intellect, 2010) and has written HYPERKINO commentary for Sergei Eisenstein's *Strike* released as part of Ruscico DVD series Kino Academia. Her articles on early Russian and Soviet film history have appeared in *Kinovedcheskie zapiski, Menedzher kino,* and *Studies in Russian and Soviet Cinema.*

Masha Salazkina is Research Chair in Transnational Media Arts and Culture at Concordia University, Montreal. She is author of *In Excess: Sergei Eisenstein's Mexico* (University of Chicago Press, 2009) and has published in *Cinema Journal, Screen, October, KinoKultura,* and several edited collections on film theory and history. She is currently at work on a book project that traces a trajectory of materialist film theory through the discourses of early Soviet cinema, institutional film cultures of Italy from the 1930s to the 1950s, and critical debates surrounding the emergence of third cinema in Latin America.

Peter J. Schmelz is Associate Professor of Musicology and Chair of the Department of Music at Washington University in St. Louis. He is currently completing a book on polystylism as cultural practice in the late Soviet Union, focusing on the music of Alfred Schnittke and Valentin Silvestrov. He received a National Endowment for the Humanities Fellowship in 2011, and his first book, *Such Freedom, If Only Musical: Unofficial Soviet Music during the Thaw* (Oxford University Press, 2009), was awarded the ASCAP Deems Taylor Award in 2010.

Joan Titus is Associate Professor in Musicology at the University of North Carolina, Greensboro. Her research focuses on cultural politics and policy and their relationship to the musical arts, particularly in Soviet Russia, the American Southwest, and most currently, North Africa. Her publications address music for Russian cinema, as well as Native American music festivals. Her book, *Hearing Shostakovich: Music for Early Soviet Cinema* (Oxford University Press, forthcoming) examines narrative and reception in Dmitry Shostakovich's early film scores. Her current projects engage women and music for Russian and Soviet cinema, as well as women's music in Morocco.

Emma Widdis is Reader in Russian studies at the University of Cambridge and Fellow of Trinity College. Her publications include *Visions of a New Land: Soviet Film from the Revolution to the Second World War* (Yale University Press, 2003), and *Alexander Medvedkin* (I. B. Tauris, 2004). Her recent work addresses different dimensions of a cultural history of the senses in Soviet Russia, with a particular focus on the status of touch. With film at its center, but also exploring broader debates on home decoration, clothing, and manufacture, the project directs attention to the importance of touch, of sensory pleasure, across diverse aspects of the Soviet discursive field, to trace the evolution of competing models of Soviet feeling and sensation.

Index

CPSIA information can be obtained
at www.ICGtesting.com
Printed in the USA
BVOW06s1847081116
467262BV00019B/131/P